T0153075

THE QUOTABLE
JEWISH
WOMAN

OTHER WORKS BY ELAINE BERNSTEIN PARTNOW

Books
The Quotable Woman: The First 5,000 Years
Everyday Speaking for All Occasions, *with Susan Partnow*
The Female Dramatist, *with Lesley Hyatt*
The New Quotable Woman
The Quotable Woman: Eve–1799
Photographic Artists and Innovators, *with Turner Browne*
Breaking the Age Barrier
The Quotable Woman: 1800–1981

Performance Works
Movers & Shakers: Living History Portrayals of Notable Women
Hear Us Roar: A Woman's Connection
Hispanic Women Speak
A Visit with Emily Dickinson

THE QUOTABLE
JEWISH
WOMAN

Wisdom, Inspiration & Humor
from the Mind and Heart

EDITED AND COMPILED BY

ELAINE BERNSTEIN PARTNOW

For People of All Faiths, All Backgrounds

JEWISH LIGHTS Publishing

Woodstock, Vermont

The Quotable Jewish Woman:
Wisdom, Inspiration & Humor from the Mind and Heart

2004 First Printing
© 2004 by Elaine Bernstein Partnow

All rights reserved. No part of this book may be reproduced or transmitted in any form or by any means, electronic or mechanical, including photocopying, recording, or by any information storage and retrieval system, without permission in writing from the publisher.

For information regarding permission to reprint material from this book, please mail or fax your request in writing to Jewish Lights Publishing, Permissions Department, at the address / fax number listed below, or e-mail your request to permissions@jewishlights.com.

Library of Congress Cataloging-in-Publication Data
The quotable Jewish woman : wisdom, inspiration & humor from the mind and heart / [compiled by] Elaine Bernstein Partnow.
p. cm.
Includes bibliographical references and index.
ISBN 1-58023-193-4 (hardcover)
1. Jewish women—Quotations. I. Partnow, Elaine.
PN6081.5.Q58 2004
808.8'99287'089924—dc22

2004006431

Manufactured in Canada

For People of All Faiths, All Backgrounds
Published by Jewish Lights Publishing
A Division of LongHill Partners, Inc.
Sunset Farm Offices, Route 4, P.O. Box 237
Woodstock, VT 05091
Tel: (802) 457-4000   Fax: (802) 457-4004
http://www.jewishlights.com

As I learned of the careers of some of the great women of Israel—of the Mendelssohn daughters, of Sarah Copia Sullam, Deborah Ascarelli, high in the councils of the Italian Court, of Rebecca Gratz, most beloved and honored woman of her time, who served as the model for Rebecca in Scott's *Ivanhoe*, of Emma Lazarus, equally beloved a century later, of Grace Aguilar and a host of others—a new pride possessed me. More cause for worship, more examples of nobility, richer race consciousness.

—REBEKAH BETTELHEIM KOHUT, *My Portion: An Autobiography*, 1927

I close my eyes and think of Grandma tasting a bit of her childhood each Chanukah when she prepared the latkes as her mother had made them before her.

My mother, my aunts, my own grandmothers float back to me, young and vibrant once more, making days holy in the sanctuaries of their kitchens, feeding me, cradling me, connecting me to the intricately plaited braid of their past, and even at this moment, looking down the corridor of what's to come, I see myself join them as they open their arms wide to enfold my children and grandchildren in their embrace.

—FAYE MOSKOWITZ, *And the Bridge Is Love*, 1991

To my wonderful and amazing sisters,

Susan Partnow

and Judith Partnow Hyman

The sparkle and warmth I see in their eyes

when they welcome the Shabbat queen

has kept Judaism alive for me

CONTENTS

INTRODUCTION

Few who are reading these words are not familiar with the prayer uttered by Orthodox men in shul, "Lord, I thank thee that I was not born a woman."* Some may also have knowledge of the Apostle Paul's admonition that women be silent in church. To both statements, I say, "Why?" Women have been silenced for centuries, from the immolation of an estimated five million women during the Inquisition to the prohibition against owning property, having a bank account, and voting—the latter in place in our own country up until less than a hundred years ago and still in place in much of the world.

It has become my life's work to search for the voices of women and place them before the public, in books and in performance. This journey naturally leads to history books, where I have found very little mention of women in general; the same has held true in books about Jewish history. Of course, the Four Matriarchs and the Prophetesses are *de rigueur*, as are Golda Meir; Anne Frank; usually Henrietta Szold, the founder of Hadassah; and Emma Lazarus, whose poetry is so famously enshrined on the base of the Statue of Liberty. But beyond that—*bubkes*, or close to it. For example, in *The Haunted Smile: The Story of Jewish Comedians in America* by Lawrence J. Epstein (2001), of the 356 people cited, 68 were women, 43 of whom were Jewish (even though, on the cover, it pictures two—Roseanne Barr and Gertrude Berg—along with seven men). Rabbi Benjamin Blech, who authored two books for *The Complete Idiot's Guide* series—*Jewish History and Culture* and *Understanding Judaism*, both 1999 publications—barely mentions any women. *The Big Book of Jewish Humor* by William Novak and Moshe Waldoks came out in 1981. Okay, a long time ago—but, what?—there weren't plenty of women humorists and comics back

---

* Not to be flippant, this part of the morning prayer of the Orthodox Jew is often taken out of context and used as an antiwomen statement. Its actual context concerns the keeping of the commandments: because there are many more commandments for men than for women, the Jewish man's thankfulness derives from the idea that he has been given the opportunity to fulfill that many more commandments for the Lord.

then? Yet of the 60 or so cited, only one—Judith Viorst—is included. Even the old classic *Pride of Our People*, a 1979 biographical dictionary of 100 "outstanding Jewish men and women," by David C. Gross, did better than that, profiling 14 women. Thank heaven for the likes of *Lilith* magazine; Ma'yan, The Jewish Women's Project (http://www.mayan.org/mayan.asp); the Jewish Women's Archive (http://www.jwa.org); and all the wonderful books that have been published in the last fifteen years or so about Jewish women, many of which are cited in these pages, else we might be truly invisible to the greater public eye.

CRITERIA

I have become a real maven of women's quotations, this being my sixth collection (the first five were subsequent editions of *The Quotable Woman*). The work has always inspired me but perhaps never so much as with this collection. If *tikkun olam* is the true mission of the Jews, our raison d'etre, then the women in this book are messengers of that mission. In biblical times they may have been called prophetesses, as were Deborah, Huldah, and Miriam, whose words appear here. All of the women whose works contributed to these pages, be they scholarly or social, literary or theatrical, political or spiritual, have helped heal the world with their ideas, their activism, their service, their talent, and their labor, bringing tears and laughter, thought and reason to a world sorely in need of all these.

My upbringing was not an especially observant one: we attended the synagogue on high holidays and lit the menorah at Chanukah. I went to Sunday school and was confirmed. The year of my confirmation, I attended special classes where I had arguments with my rabbi, who defined a "good Jew" as one who went to shul. In these pages I make no judgments as to whether or not some of the sources of the quotes were "good" Jews, "bad" Jews, or "apathetic Jews." Wherever their personal faith has led them, they are Jewish women who have been notable in their lifetimes. You will find women born and raised Jewish who have become secular; women born and raised Jewish who are observant in some fashion—whether Orthodox, Reform, Conservative, or Reconstructionist; a few women who converted to Judaism, like Aviel Barclay, the *sofer stam* (Jewish ritual scribe), Marilyn Monroe, and Elizabeth Taylor; some, like newspaper columnist Susan Jacoby, who did not discover their Jewish roots until adulthood; and many half-Jews, like Gloria Steinem,

Dorothy Parker, Lillian Hellman, Frida Kahlo, and Muriel Spark, some of whom have chosen to identify as Jews or at least acknowledge their Jewishness, others of whom have paid it no heed whatsoever. There were a few women I came across who were, I felt sure from a variety of indications, Jewish, but as I had no real evidence to support my belief, and as these particular women had clearly chosen not to identify as Jews, they have not been included.

I was often astonished to discover that someone I was quite familiar with from my previous probings into women's history, or my exposure to the world at large, was Jewish, when I had had no idea before: Nobel Prize–winning biochemist Gerty Cori, financial adviser Sylvia Porter, actor Simone Signoret, writer-editor Robin Morgan, philosopher-writer Ayn Rand, singer Laura Nyro, actor Winona Ryder. And then there were the women whom I'd never heard of before: the *New Yorker* columnist Emily "Mickey" Hahn, the "lady rabbi" Ray Frank, athlete Bobbie Rosenfield, suffragist Ernestine Rose, dancer-choreographer Anna Sokolow, and lots more. That's part of the fun of this book— these discoveries. In fact, I discovered so many, I could not include them all; I'm sure I could create a second book! There are a plethora of Jewish women who have been or are movers and shakers in the world, whose words are inspiring. But at last I had to say, "*Dayenu!*—It is enough."

For a quotation to be included, the only criteria were my own sensibilities: if it made me *kvell*, if I laughed or was moved to tears, if I found myself nodding in agreement or my brow furrowing in thought, if I was moved in some way, and not *farblondjet* by what I'd read, if the language was admirable, the ideas crisp, the purpose laudable, it was included. I generally avoided foul language, but did not exclude it as long as it was part of a passage that embodied a greater purpose than merely to inflame or be salacious. I generally avoided esoteric language, but did not exclude it as long as the meaning of the passage was clear even without knowing the specifics of some of the terminology. I did not avoid ideas that were not in sync with my own but tried to be eclectic and to represent many sides of controversial issues. I did avoid jargon. I did avoid quotations that were dull, flat, mean-spirited (unless I *plotzed* with laughter, which Joan Rivers often made me do), cliquish, or obtuse, even if it meant a certain woman of note would not be represented in these pages. And I did try to include as much humor as I could: laughter heals. If I overlooked some favorite pearls of wisdom of yours, send 'em on—there could be another edition!

OVERVIEW

There are more than 2,400 quotations in these pages from 317 women: some are represented with only one quote, others with fifteen or more. To offer you as many quotations as possible while keeping the book to a modest size, I truncated certain oft used titles, for example:

> Four Centuries of Jewish Women's Spirituality, Umansky, Ellen M., and Ashton, Dianne (eds.), 1992, has been shortened to Four Centuries, 1992.

A List of Full & Abbreviated Titles is included near the end of the book. When it did not interfere with the flow of a quotation, I included translations in the quotations section; otherwise, you will find them in the Glossary, also located near the end of the book. There is also an Index of Women Quoted, indicating page numbers where quotes from each author appear, a tool that allows you to locate quotations by author rather than subject.

It took only a little chutzpah to include several quotations from my own previous works throughout the text, but I do feel quite chagrined that three of the eleven quotations that appear in the tiny section on Pets & Animals are from my own poems: but pets and animals are among my favorite things to write about and that, apparently, is a rarity among Jewish women.

QUOTATIONS SECTION

I have tried to include just enough information in the citation of each quotation to help you find the original source for more in-depth exploration, if you are so inclined. Citations indicate whether a quotation is direct, or by a second or third party. The following examples should clarify:

> Hannah Arendt, Men in Dark Times, 1968
> Nikki Stiller, "A State of Emergency," Shaking Eve's Tree, 1990
> Edith Mendel Stern, "Women Are Household Slaves," American Mercury, January 1949

The above are direct citations, meaning the woman wrote either the book itself or the story or article in the book or magazine or newspaper cited.

Fanny Brice in *Funny Women*, Unterbrink, 1987
Bonnie Friedman in *New York Times*, 14 March 1999
Gwyneth Paltrow in "It Was a Real Awakening for Me" by Dotson
    Rader, *Parade* magazine, 17 January 1999
Grace Paley in *Women Writing in America* by Blanche H. Gelfant,
    1984

In the above instances, the women were quoted in books or articles written by someone else; these are second-party citations.

Gertrude Stein, Quoted by Thornton Wilder in *Writers at Work*
    (1st), 1958

In this last example, a third-party citation, there was a piece about Thornton Wilder in the book written or edited by someone else, and in that piece Wilder quoted Gertrude Stein.

All biblical passages are from the King James version, with the exception of those passages that do not appear in it: Judith and Esther (lettered verses only); these, when cited, are from the Jerusalem version.

When you see a passage in its entirety within quotation marks, it indicates a character's voice from the story, rather than the voice of the narrative.

SUBJECTS

Because I did not want to have quotations repeated under more than one subject (forgive any oversights, please), readers may disagree with some of the categories in which they're placed. I was often presented with conundrums impossible to resolve, to wit: "In the United States we have a society pervaded from top to bottom by contempt for the law."—Barbara Tuchman. "United States of America" or "Law & Order"—which would you choose? Or, try this one: "The professed purpose of the United States military is to maintain the peace, but its methods towards this goal are destructive and have resulted in the promotion of suffering and death of foreign peoples, as well as of its own."—Susan Schnall. "United States of America" or "War, Weapons & the Military"? Here's another challenge: "Jake wants the children to have everything money can buy, and I want them to have everything money can't buy."—Gertrude Berg. "Money" or "Children"? You can see what I was faced with! To help you find just the quotation you're looking for, each subject is cross-referenced under other possibilities, so if you don't find it in one section, move on to the other.

BIOGRAPHIES

I was most *ferklempt* when struggling to whittle down the stories of some of the most incredible women I've ever encountered to one little paragraph for the biographical section. Women like scholar-journalist Ruth Gruber, Hadassah founder Henrietta Szold, nurse-activist Lillian Wald, Golda Meir, and oh so many others, who had accomplished so much in their lifetimes. What to include? What to leave out? How to condense? Again, when to say, *"Dayenu!"* By the same token, try as I might, there were some women on whom very little information was available; that, too, was frustrating.

Names appearing in brackets after a new entry indicate that the contributor does not use those names but they are part and parcel of her legal name; for example, Allred, Gloria [Rachel Bloom Bray], is known to the public simply as Gloria Allred.

Whenever possible, I included birth names as well as information on husbands and children. Unfortunately, despite thoroughgoing forays into various "Who's Who" reference books as well as the Internet, that information was not always available. But I corresponded with many of the contributors via e-mail, and almost all of them were very clear that their families were an important part of their lives and mention of them was important to them. It's important to me, too: I like to know that someone is a grandmother, or has been divorced or widowed; it humanizes them for me. I thought readers would feel the same way, so, rather than forsake substance for form, I chose the former.

It has become the practice to use the terms *actor* and *comedian* rather than *actress* and *comedienne*, a move to a less sexist language which follows the same path as that of the use of *poet* rather than *poetess* and *author* rather than *authoress*: these diminutives came about as a labeling of *lesser* and *other*, unlike such words of ancient origin like *princess* and *goddess*.

For biblical women, I referred to Funk and Wagnall's *New Standard Bible Dictionary* as well as considerable research on the web.

A Personal Note

With this book, I changed my name. My birth certificate bears the name Elaine Thelma Partnow (actually Paratnow, a misspelling). As soon as I hit fourth grade and the teasing started, Thelma was truncated to T. By high school, tired of the inquisitiveness about the initial, I dropped all references to a middle name. So throughout my college years, my professional years as an actor, and later as an author, as well as in the course of my thirty-year marriage, I was simply Elaine Partnow. About five years ago I got an itch to take back my middle name or replace it with my mother's birth name—Bernstein. Not quite ready for so big a change, my last book, *The Quotable Woman: The First 5,000 Years*, bore my girlhood moniker—Elaine T. Partnow.

Last year, my father died. Already certain, at the age of four, that it was my destiny to be an actor, I promised Dad, who adored his three daughters but longed for a son, that I would carry on the family name. At the cemetery, watching his coffin ensconced alongside my mother's, who died in 1973, a battle began in the innermost reaches of my identity: yes, I bore my father's name, but what about my mother's?

The Bernsteins are a large clan. Our family circle, the first incorporated in the state of New York, boasts around four hundred members. This year we are having a seventieth reunion in the Catskills. I will be there, as will my sisters and many dear cousins. This book will be there, and I will be performing some living history portraits for my extended family, portraying Golda Meir, Bella Abzug, Sophie Tucker, and others. I am proud of the Bernstein name, proud of its Jewish identity, and of my own. Why don't I add my mother's name to my father's? I asked myself.

Issues of identity are immense. Partnow is not a particularly ethnic name (probably Partnov or Partnovsky when my grandfather emigrated from Russia around the turn of the century); however, Bernstein is. In these times of rising anti-Semitism, my identity as a Jew resonates with my ideals of justice and egalitarianism; choosing to make my ethnicity obvious is one way of making an ongoing statement that defends those ideals. Also, as a new implant in the densely Baptist regions of northern Florida, I didn't want to feel like I was "passing." The good people I encounter in my new area are often devout—and presumptive: my new name clarifies my religious identity in the simplest of ways. From the time I write these words to the time I see them in print, I will have become accustomed, I assume, to this new outspokenness wrought by my "new" name—Elaine Bernstein Partnow.

ACKNOWLEDGMENTS

As with any creative endeavor, one cannot complete a work without the input, support, and aid of many people. I would like to thank those who helped me translate certain terms and passages: my sister, Susan Partnow (who also sent me gobs of material via e-mail, leading me to some great discoveries) and my friend Sue Witkovsky, both represented in these pages as the notable women they are, and Sue's mom, Annie, who is fluent in Yiddish, as is my cousin Jerry Bernstein, who also racked his memory to help; my nephew David Hyatt, who lives in Israel, and his sister, my adored Lesley Hyatt, who both helped me with many Hebrew and religious terms; friends Michele Kort and Janice Price. Dozens of contributors were good enough to send me biographical information about themselves; I enjoyed corresponding with them and appreciate their goodwill. Several organizations and publications really went all out to support my efforts: the Authors Registry of New York; staff members at Lilith magazine and Ma'yan, The Jewish Women's Project (http://www.mayan.org/mayan.asp); and the organizers and maintainers of the Jewish Women's Archive (http://www.jwa.org). My neighbor, April Rivers, worked for me part time during her senior year in high school doing data entry, and I could not have completed the manuscript in a timely way without her efforts. The editorial staff at Jewish Lights Publishing, especially Emily Wichland; Amanda Dupuis, whose careful editing genuinely improved the manuscript; and Stuart M. Matlins: seldom have I worked with publishers who were so supportive, so inclusive, and so Johnny-on-the-spot with responses to one's questions. Editor Sandee Brawarsky, whose keen eye and diligence made a considerable difference in the consistency and lack of repetition throughout the work. My agent, Sheree Bykofsky, and especially her associate, Janet Rosen, without whom I could not have written such a winning proposal.

Always last but never least, my dear husband, Turner Browne: his steadfast and delicious mastery in the kitchen, his insistence that I stop for meals, take a break to go kayaking or fishing, his unending support and affection and his fabulous shoulder rubs, keep me balanced and healthy and energetic when I'm headed for a deadline. With Turner I never say dayenu—I always want more!

A last two quotations, the first, anonymously written, represents, in no uncertain terms, my own feelings about having made this book and my responsibility for any flaws you may find, as well as joy:

> The Tao has no expectations.
> The Tao demands nothing of others.
> The Tao does not speak.
> The Tao does not blame.
> The Tao does not take sides.
> The Tao is not Jewish.

But I am.

Anne Frank wrote to her diary: "I hope that you will be a great support and comfort to me." I hope this book will bring great support, comfort—and *naches* —to you!

In sisterhood,
Elaine Bernstein Partnow
Live Oak Island, Florida

ACTORS, COMEDIANS & PERFORMERS

(*also see* Humor & Comedy *and* Show Biz, Sports & Entertainment)

With all the Jewish comics in the world, how come Israel doesn't have a "Laughing Wall"?

—LOTUS WEINSTOCK, *The Lotus Position*, 1982

❧

Fame for a comedian is like a degree to a doctor. You can't practice without it.

—LOTUS WEINSTOCK, Stand-up routine

❧

Actors may know how to act, but a lot of them don't know how to behave.

—CARRIE FISHER, *Postcards from the Edge*, 1987

❧

In the theater I was always at ease, but in pictures there was the camera following me around like a cop.

—FANNY BRICE in *The Fabulous Fanny* by Norman Katkov, 1953

❧

I want to be known as an actress. I'm not royalty.

—ELIZABETH TAYLOR in *Elizabeth* by Dick Sheppard, 1974

❧

Unfortunately, I am involved in a freedom ride protesting the loss of the minority rights belonging to the few remaining earthbound stars. All we demanded was our right to twinkle.

—MARILYN MONROE, Telegram to Mr. and Mrs. Robert Kennedy, 13 June 1962

You can never count anybody out in this business. I've seen actors with careers deader than my mother's brisket come back to life and win Academy Awards.
—RITA RUDNER, *Tickled Pink*, 2001

~

I don't think an actor should be afraid to be unlovable—particularly in comedy; you have to be willing to look like a fool.
—MADELINE KAHN in *Drama-Logue*, 1984

~

[The Divine Miss M is] an exaggeration of all the things I never thought I wanted to be. Though I tell you, since I've started doing her I've become much more like her than I ever thought was possible.
—BETTE MIDLER in *Women in Comedy*, Martin, 1986

~

Women come in here and sit at the tables up front, and I can hear them whispering, "Oh, she's so dirty! She's so dirty!" Well, if they're so pure, how the hell do they know what I'm talking about? People want to know where I learn all these words. I went to a grammar school one day and went up to the bathroom. There they were, right on the wall.
—PEARL WILLIAMS in *Funny Women*, Unterbrink, 1987

~

I started off as a moron in *Kiss Them for Me*, worked my way up to imbecile in *Adam's Rib*, and have carved my current niche as a noble nitwit [in *Born Yesterday*].
—JUDY HOLLIDAY in *Women in Comedy*, Martin, 1986

~

I love Baby Snooks, and when I play her I do it as seriously as if she were real.... I am Snooks. For twenty minutes or so, Fanny Brice ceases to exist.
—FANNY BRICE, *Women in Comedy*, Martin, 1986

~

Being a funny person does an awful lot of things to you. You feel that you mustn't get serious with people. They don't expect it from you, and they don't want to see it. You're not entitled to be serious, you're a clown, and they only want you to make them laugh.

—FANNY BRICE in *The Fabulous Fanny* by Norman Katkov, 1953

There is not one female comic who was beautiful as a little girl.

—JOAN RIVERS in *Los Angeles Times*, 10 May 1974

I'm a woman who's a comic, not a woman's comic.

—ELAYNE BOOSLER in *Women in Comedy*, Martin, 1986

He often said I was the greatest no-talent star in the business.

—GYPSY ROSE LEE, *Gypsy*, 1957

I'm the last of the truly tacky women. I do trash with flash and sleaze with ease.

—BETTE MIDLER in *Funny Women*, Unterbrink, 1987

A career is born in public—talent in privacy.

—MARILYN MONROE, Quoted by Gloria Steinem in *The First Ms. Reader*, 1972

Listen, my name's Barbra Streisand. With only two *a*'s. In the first name, I mean. I figure that third *a* in the middle, who needs it.

—BARBRA STREISAND in *Streisand: Her Life* by James Spada, 1995

When I'm performing I'm not afraid of anything or anybody. But when I'm just me I have this fright of being a disappointment to people.

—BARBRA STREISAND in *Streisand: Her Life* by James Spada, 1995

My singing is very therapeutic. For three hours I have no troubles—I know how it's all going to come out.

—BEVERLY SILLS, Interview, CBS-TV, 1975

As more of us [actresses] are moving into producing and directing, the level of creativity among women has become very high, and therefore our relationships have changed—have themselves become more creative.

—LEE GRANT in *Ms.*, November 1975

Every now and then, when you're on stage, you hear the best sound a player can hear. It's a sound you can't get in movies or in television. It is the sound of a wonderful, deep silence that means you've hit them where they live.

—SHELLEY WINTERS in *Theatre Arts*, June 1956

The thing that I find fun about performing is telling stories and creating characters.

—JUDY KAYE in "Broadway's Favorite Diva" by Sheryl Flatow, *Playbill* magazine, n.d.

I take a breath when I have to.

—ETHEL MERMAN in *Time*, 27 February 1984

ADVERTISING, IMAGE & THE MEDIA
(*also see* Books, Writers & Poetry *and* Money, Business & Economics)

Packaging is all heaven is.

—EVE BABITZ, *Eve's Hollywood*, 1974

When we look at the Empire State Building or the Washington Monument, nobody yells "Penis!" We are used to seeing the world through male images, not our own likenesses.

—JUDY CHICAGO in *Exposures*, Brown, 1989

I do have this quality that is very childlike. But how long can it last? How long can you be cute?

—GOLDIE HAWN in *Women in Comedy*, Martin, 1986

—

All I have to do is remember to be dumb when I'm out, and smart when I'm home.

—JUDY HOLLIDAY in *Women in Comedy*, Martin, 1986

—

All the cosmetics names seemed obscenely obvious to me in their promises of sexual bliss. They were all firming or uplifting or invigorating. They made you *tingle*. Or *glow*. Or feel *young*. They were all prepared with hormones or placentas or royal jelly. All the juice and joy missing in the lives of these women were to be supplied by the contents of jars and bottles.

—ERICA JONG, *How to Save Your Own Life*, 1977

—

We're a public that is brought up on deception, through advertising.... We're accustomed to being deceived. We allow ourselves to be deceived. Advertising is really responsible for a lot in the deterioration of American public perceptions.

—BARBARA TUCHMAN in *A World of Ideas* by Bill Moyers, 1989

—

Don't we realize we're a business, we single girls are? There are magazines for us, special departments in stores for us. Every building that goes up in Manhattan has more than fifty percent efficiency apartments...for the one million girls who have very little use for them.

—GAIL PARENT, *Sheila Levine Is Dead and Living in New York*, 1972

—

Is it my imagination, or is everything becoming too hard to open? These days, even to get inside a box of cookies you have to be a safecracker. I have music CDs I've been trying to open for years. I use them as coasters.

—RITA RUDNER, http://www.ritafunny.com, 2003

I would like to become president of a major TV network, and then I would ban all commercials that make women look like imbeciles—that would mean 24 hours of uninterrupted programming.

—ROBIN TYLER, Stand-up routine

Television has proved that people will look at anything rather than at each other.

—ANN LANDERS, Advice Column

Women's magazines are precisely the formula for unsatisfying male-female relations. Men can never meet the exaggerated expectation that they will provide all meaning, content, and purpose in women's lives. Women can never meet the exaggerated expectation (their own and those of men) that they will be eternally beautiful, young, pliable and pleasing.

—RIANE EISLER, *Sacred Pleasure*, 1995

The media is still dominated by men, many of whom think of women in a very sexist way. They cover them in a sexist way, and they do *not* cover them because of sexism.

—GLORIA ALLRED in *Perspectives*, Fall 1996

Spin, incidentally, was a relatively new term for what Leonard used to call bullshit.

—RITA RUDNER, *Tickled Pink*, 2001

Everyone wants edge these days. You tell them it's edgy, they love it.

—JUDY BLUME, *Summer Sisters*, 1998

Industrial societies turn their citizens into image-junkies; it is the most irresistible form of mental pollution. Poignant longings for beauty, for an end to probing below the surface, for a redemption and celebration of the body of the world. Ultimately, having an experience becomes identical with taking a photograph of it.

—SUSAN SONTAG, *On Photography*, 1977

—

Growing up female in America. What a liability! You grew up with your ears full of cosmetic ads, love songs, advice columns, whoreoscopes, Hollywood gossip, and moral dilemmas on the level of TV soap operas. What litanies the advertisers of the good life chanted at you! What curious catechisms!

—ERICA JONG, *Fear of Flying*, 1973

—

One set of messages of the society we live in is: Consume. Grow. Do what you want. Amuse yourselves. The very working of this economic system, which has bestowed these unprecedented liberties, most cherished in the form of physical mobility and material prosperity, depends on encouraging people to defy limits.

—SUSAN SONTAG, *AIDS and Its Metaphors*, 1989

—

The mail grew me up in a hurry.

—ANN LANDERS in *Time*, 21 August 1989

—

With publicity comes humiliation.

—TAMA JANOWITZ in *International Herald Tribune*, 8 September 1992

AGE & AGING

From birth to age eighteen, a girl needs good parents. From eighteen to thirty-five, she needs good looks. From thirty-five to fifty-five, she needs a good personality. From fifty-five on, she needs good cash.

—SOPHIE TUCKER, Remark, 1953

I'm forty-nine but I could be twenty-five except for my face and my legs.
—NADINE GORDIMER, "Good Climate, Friendly Inhabitants,"
Not for Publication and Other Stories, 1965

—

Say "no" to the fountain of youth and turn on the fountain of age.
—BETTY FRIEDAN, Speech, Quoted in *Seattle Post-Intelligencer*, 30 January 1993

—

Language is a boxing match in which we must spar daily, warding off the negative suggestions that age is our worst enemy. Indeed, it is our best friend.
—ELAINE BERNSTEIN PARTNOW, *Breaking the Age Barrier*, 1981

—

Thank God for the head. Inside the head is the only place you got to be young when the usual place gets used up.
—GRACE PALEY, *Later the Same Day*, 1985

—

You know you're getting old, when your back starts going out more than you do.
—PHYLLIS DILLER in Earl Wilson's "Broadway" column, 8 September 1978

—

One does not get better but different and older and that is always a pleasure.
—GERTRUDE STEIN, *The Crack-Up*, Edmund Wilson, ed., 1945

—

I have always felt that a woman had the right to treat the subject of her age with ambiguity until, perhaps, she passed into the realm of over ninety. Then it is better she be candid with herself and with the world.
—HELENA RUBINSTEIN, *My Life for Beauty*, 1966

—

The two women gazed out of the slumped and sagging bodies that had accumulated around them.
—NADINE GORDIMER, "Vital Statistics," *Not for Publication and Other Stories*, 1965

But it's hard to be hip over thirty
When everyone else is nineteen
> —JUDITH VIORST, *It's Hard to Be Hip Over Thirty…*, 1968

That's what I want to be when I grow up, just a peaceful wreck holding hands with other peaceful wrecks.
> —TILLIE OLSEN, "Hey Sailor, What Ship?," *Tell Me a Riddle*, 1960

Being seventy is not a sin.
> —GOLDA MEIR in *Reader's Digest*, July 1971

We need to break through the age mystique by continuing to grow, solving problems, making social changes. We need to see our age as an uncharted adventure.
> —BETTY FRIEDAN, Speech, Quoted in *Seattle Post-Intelligencer*, 30 January 1993

"Oh, my God. I've just told you how old I am. Nobody knows how old I am. I'm going to have to kill you now."
> —RITA RUDNER, *Tickled Pink*, 2001

With my mother age is a disguise; she puts it on with a wink. (Some wink.) But with my father it is another matter altogether. Age is revealing him; the essential in him; completing the job.
> —BETTE HOWLAND, *Things to Come and Go*, 1983

The older we get, the more extraordinary life becomes—and the more amazing our capacity to experience its fullness.
> —RABBI SHIRA MILGROM, *Four Centuries*, 1992

The older I get the funnier I get…. Think what I'll save in not having my face lifted.
> —PHYLLIS DILLER in *Women in Comedy*, Martin, 1986

Age is a subjective experience, as is time.... A moment of ecstasy may seem to last beyond its objective measurement on the clock, so may days or weeks of idleness appear to vanish without a trace. It is the same with age—for what is age but time?

—ELAINE BERNSTEIN PARTNOW, *Breaking the Age Barrier*, 1981

A lemon tree, like everything else, has a chronological age. But what are the ages of the lemons it bears? Each has its own age. So it is with us. The fruits we bear during infancy are quite different from those of adolescence. The varying seasons of early, middle, and late adulthood all blossom anew, bearing fresh fruit, green fruit that needs ripening.

—ELAINE BERNSTEIN PARTNOW, *Breaking the Age Barrier*, 1981

Growing up means letting go of the dearest megalomaniacal dreams of our childhood. Growing up means knowing they can't be fulfilled. Growing up means gaining the wisdom and the skills to get what we want within the limitations imposed by reality—a reality which consists of diminished powers, restricted freedoms and, with the people we love, imperfect connections.

—JUDITH VIORST, *Necessary Losses*, 1986

"...So yeah, anyway—I'm thirty-four and my mother is desperate for me to get married. She thinks settling down is what you should be doing at thirty-four. How would she like it if I turned to her the day she hits eighty and said: 'Hey, Mum—when are you going to break your hip? All your friends are breaking theirs'?"

—SUE MARGOLIS, *Spin Cycle*, 2001

Most old people are disheartened to be living in the ailing house of their bodies, to be limited physically and economically, to feel an encumbrance to others—guests who didn't have the good manners to leave when the party was over.

—BARBARA WALTERS, *How to Talk with Practically Anybody about Practically Anything*, 1970

Before I lost my mother, she told me her greatest fear was being a burden to her children. Nothing, nothing I could say could ease her concern. Her dignity was at stake. So for the sakes of all our moms and dads who have reached the golden years, let's get them a benefit that means something, that's straightforward and not confusing, a benefit that they can trust—a true Medicare benefit.

—BARBARA BOXER, Radio Address, 21 June 2003

All of us, ultimately, will join one of the most despised, neglected and abused groups in [American] society.

—GERDA LERNER, *Why History Matters*, 1997

I have no patience with anyone born after World War II. You have to explain everything to these people.

—SELMA DIAMOND in *Funny Women*, Unterbrink, 1987

Old people can be fun if they're not yours.

—EMILY LEVINE, Stand-up routine

The hatred of the youth culture for adult society is not a disinterested judgment but a terror-ridden refusal to be hooked into the, if you will, ecological chain of breathing, growing, and dying. It is the demand, in other words, to remain children.

—MIDGE DECTER, *The New Chastity*, 1972

It's hard for a young girl to have patience for old age sitting and chewing all day over the past.

—FANNIE HURST, *Cosmopolitan*, 1917

At age 11, girls are sure of what they know. But at 12 or 13, when they take on the feminine role, they become uncertain. They begin to say, "I don't know."

Their true selves go underground.... We women become ourselves again after 50. When the feminine role is over, we re-emerge.

—GLORIA STEINEM in *Parade* magazine, 17 May 1992

—

Old age is like a plane flying through a storm. Once you're aboard, there's nothing you can do. You can't stop the plane, you can't stop the storm, you can't stop time. So one might as well accept it calmly, wisely.

—GOLDA MEIR, Quoted by Oriana Fallaci in *L'Eurepeo*, 1973

—

If anything is a surprise then there is not much difference between older or younger because the only thing that does make anybody older is that they cannot be surprised.

—GERTRUDE STEIN, *Everybody's Autobiography*, 1937

—

Time, thou all kindly, confer upon me, at the ripeness of old age, mildness.

—BERTHA PAPPENHEIM, "Prayers, I," Stephanie Forchheimer, tr., 1946

—

Asked if she worshiped regularly: Honey, at my age, I don't do anything regularly.

—SELMA DIAMOND in *Funny Women*, Unterbrink, 1987

—

All of you young people who served in the war. You are a lost generation.... You have no respect for anything.

—GERTRUDE STEIN, *A Moveable Feast*, 1964

—

What really distinguishes this generation in all countries from earlier generations...is its determination to act, its joy in action, the assurance of being able to change things by one's own efforts.

—HANNAH ARENDT, *Crises of the Republic*, 1972

—

Aging is a man's destiny, something that must happen because he is a human being. For a woman, aging is not only her destiny...it is also her vulnerability.

—SUSAN SONTAG in *Saturday Review*, October 1971

Being over seventy is like being engaged in a war. All our friends are going or gone and survive amongst the dead and the dying as on a battlefield.
—MURIEL SPARK, *Memento Mori*, 1959

—

Why can't we build orphanages next to homes for the elderly? If someone's sitting in a rocker, it won't be long before a kid will be in his lap.
—CLORIS LEACHMAN in *Good Housekeeping*, October 1973

—

One's prime is elusive. You little girls, when you grow up, must be on the alert to recognize your prime at whatever time of your life it may occur. You must then live it to the full.
—MURIEL SPARK, *The Prime of Miss Jean Brodie*, 1961

—

Asked for the key to her longevity at 80: Keep breathing.
—SOPHIE TUCKER, Speech, 13 January 1964

ANTI-SEMITISM

(*also see* Jews & Judaism *and* Racism, Sexism & Other Prejudices)

The word "Jew" is in constant use, even among so-called refined Christians, as a term of opprobrium, and is employed as a verb, to denote the meanest tricks.
—EMMA LAZARUS in *Century*, February 1883

—

Ever since I was a little girl I remember my father telling me that I had a passion for justice. But I think it was really a passion against injustice which originated from my feelings of the injustice of anti-Semitism.
—BETTY FRIEDAN in *Lilith* 1, No. 1, 1976

How many great Jewish ideas and ideals died behind the walls of ghettoes during the Middle Ages even before seeing the light of day, or behind the invisible ghetto walls of modern Jewry?

—HANNAH SENESH, *Hannah Senesh*, 1966

Anti-Semitism is a criminal weapon used against society by the unsuccessful,
the bigoted, the depraved, the ignorant, the neurotic, the failures. It thrives on
terror, hunger, unemployment, hate, resentment. It is mob psychology dis-
played at its lowest and most unreasoning.

—EDNA FERBER, *A Peculiar Treasure*, 1939

I shall not be bitter if others fail to grasp what is happening to us Jews. I work
and continue to live with the same conviction and I find life meaningful—yes,
meaningful....

—ETTY HILLESUM, *An Interrupted Life*, 1983

The nature of the Jew is governed by the same laws as human nature in general. In England, France, Germany and the rest of Europe (except, Spain), in
spite of the barbarous treatment and deadly persecution they have suffered,
they have lived and spread and outlived much of the poisonous rancor and
prejudice against them, and Europe has been none the worse on their account.

—ERNESTINE LOUISE ROSE, (c. 1860), American Jewish
Historical Society, http://www.ajhs.org, 2003

Every time I hear Poland described reductively as an anti-Semitic country, I
bridle in revolt, for I know that the reality is far more tangled than that.

—EVA HOFFMAN, *Exit Into History*, 1993

Jews are the specter haunting Eastern Europe these days...an absence that is
itself felt as a presence, a wrongness.... Perhaps, if we don't always have a conscious conscience, we have a subliminal one, from which the memory of past
wrongs is not so easily erased.

—EVA HOFFMAN, *Exit Into History*, 1993

"It's enough the gentiles have stopped trying to tear down Judaism and left the job to Jews, who do it better."

—JOANNE GREENBERG, "Children of Joy" (1966), *Shaking Eve's Tree*, 1990

That every Jew in the world was alive through a miracle. That since Egypt's Pharaoh, persecutors had tried to do to Jews what Hitler was now trying to do in Europe. Before Hitler, I was an innocent, convinced that some day there would be no more nationalism, no more racism, no more anti-Semitism. Hitler had taught me I was wrong. I became a "Hitler Jew" with three thousand years of history.

—RUTH GRUBER, *Haven*, 1983

One of the fundamentals of Zionism is the realization that anti-Semitism is an illness which can neither be fought against with words, nor cured with superficial treatment. On the contrary, it must be treated and healed at its very roots.

—HANNAH SENESH, *Hannah Senesh*, 1966

ARTISTS, THE ARTS & CREATIVITY

(*also see* Celebrities, Heroes & Sheroes *and* Show Biz, Sports & Entertainment)

After some years in the art world trying to pretend I wasn't a woman, I decided for better or worse I had to be who I was.

—JUDY CHICAGO in *Exposures*, Brown, 1989

I never painted dreams. I painted my own reality.

—FRIDA KAHLO in *Frida*, Herrera, 1983

A photograph is a secret about a secret. The more it tells you the less you know.
—DIANE ARBUS in *Diane Arbus*, Patricia Bosworth, 1985

I really believe there are things nobody would see if I didn't photograph them.
—DIANE ARBUS, *Diane Arbus*, 1972

The camera is a kind of license.
—DIANE ARBUS, *Diane Arbus*, 1972

One's art adjusts to economic necessity if your metabolism does.
—LEE GRANT in *New York Times*, 12 August 1973

Art destroys silence.
—ALICIA SUSKIN OSTRIKER, "The Eighth and Thirteenth," *The Little Space*, 1998

Art always seems to be catching up to life.
—LEE GRANT in *Ms.*, November 1975

I think art, literature, fiction, poetry, whatever it is, makes justice in the world.
That's why it almost always has to be on the side of the underdog.
—GRACE PALEY in *Ms.*, March 1974

I don't end [my dances], because I don't feel there's any ending.... That's the
Jew in me. Ask the world a question, and there's no answer. All I do is present
what I feel, and you, you answer. You answer.
—ANNA SOKOLOW in Jewish Women's Archive (http://www.jwa.org), 20 August 2003

He visited the Museum of Modern Art, and was standing near the pool looking at his dark reflection when a curator of the museum noticed him. "My, my,

what a fine work of art that is!" the curator said to himself. "I must have it installed immediately."

—ROSALYN DREXLER, *The Cosmopolitan Girl*, 1975

I'd rather sit on the floor in the market of Toluca and sell tortillas, than to have anything to do with these "artistic" bitches of Paris. They sit for hours on the "cafés" warming their precious behinds, and talk without stopping about "culture" "art" "revolution" and so forth thinking themselves the gods of the world.... Gee whiz!

—FRIDA KAHLO in *Frida*, Herrera, 1983

The great thing about the AIDS NAMES quilt is that everybody and their brother and sister made those pieces without any thought of whether they had talent. You have art giving you a healing process. You have art giving you redemption.

—MIRIAM SCHAPIRO in *Parade* magazine, 1998

Every work of art is an "act of faith" in the vernacular sense of being a venture into the unknown. The artist must dive into waters whose depths are unplumbed, and trust that he or she will neither be swallowed up nor come crashing against a cement surface four feet down, but will rise and be buoyed upon them.

—DENISE LEVERTOV, "Work That Enfaiths," *New and Selected Essays*, 1992

Art...means nothing if it simply decorates the dinner-table of power which holds it hostage.

—ADRIENNE RICH in *Ms.*, November/December 1997

There is the falsely mystical view of art that assumes a kind of supernatural inspiration, a possession by universal forces unrelated to questions of power and privilege or the artist's relation to bread and blood.... The song is higher than the struggle.

—ADRIENNE RICH, *Blood, Bread, and Poetry*, 1986

I want you to know, dear children, that there does not exist in the whole world a single teacher who is capable of teaching art. To do that is truly impossible.

—FRIDA KAHLO in *Frida*, Herrera, 1983

Authors and actors and artists and such
Never know nothing, and never know much.

—DOROTHY PARKER, "Bohemia," *Sunset Gun*, 1928

There is nothing fiercer than a failed artist. The energy remains, but, having no outlet, it implodes in a great black fart of rage which smokes up all the inner windows of the soul.

—ERICA JONG, *Fear of Flying*, 1973

Perhaps all artists were, in a sense, housewives: tenders of the earth household.

—ERICA JONG, "The Artist as Housewife: The Housewife as Artist,"
The First Ms. Reader, 1972

A woman can make the choice to be an artist and decide to go all the way, but there is still tremendous guilt. You feel as though you're stealing power.

—MIRIAM SCHAPIRO in *Exposures*, Brown, 1989

The artist should belong to his society, yet without feeling that he has to conform to it…. Then, although he belongs to his society, he can change it, presenting it with fresh feelings, fresh ideas.

—ANNA SOKOLOW in Jewish Women's Archive (http://www.jwa.org), 20 August 2003

We have made a space to house our spirit, to give form to our dreams.

—JUDY CHICAGO in *Womanspace*, February/March 1973

If I can't give birth to a live human being, I can give birth to the ideas and struggles within me.

—PENINA V. ADELMAN, *Miriam's Well*, 1986

The painting is never what is *there*,
It throbs with the mystery
Of your own sick-to-death soul
Which demands, like everything alive,
Love.

—ALICIA SUSKIN OSTRIKER, "From the Prado Rotunda: The Family
of Charles IV and Others," *The Little Space*, 1998

—

I never knew I was a Surrealist till André Breton came to Mexico and told me
I was.

—FRIDA KAHLO in *Frida*, Herrera, 1983

—

I paint myself because I am so often alone, because I am the subject I know best.

—FRIDA KAHLO in *Frida*, Herrera, 1983

—

Obviously the good lady [melody] has a tough constitution. The more attempts
made against her, the more she blooms with health and rotundity. It is interesting to note that all those accused of being her murderers are becoming, in
turn, her benefactors and saviors.

—WANDA LANDOWSKA, "Why Does Modern Music Lack Melody?"
(9 February 1913), *Landowska on Music*, 1964

—

Music of the past has become a distant and vague country where everything is
totally different from our surroundings, our life, our art, our impressions, and
our concepts.

—WANDA LANDOWSKA, "Music of the Past" (1905), *Landowska on Music*, 1964

—

I don't want to be an exhibitionistic coloratura who merely sings notes. I'm
interested in the *character*.

—BEVERLY SILLS in *Divas*, Sargeant, 1959

The fate of a song that had become part of folklore is inscrutable.

—RAISA DAVYDOVNA ORLOVA, *Memoirs*, 1983

It hurts me not to love music, because I feel my spirit is hurt by not loving it. But there's nothing to be done about it; I shall never understand music, and never love it. If I occasionally hear music I like, I can't remember it; so how could I love a thing I can't remember.

—NATALIA GINZBURG, "He and I," *Italian Writing Today*, 1967

Drumming is a celebration of numbers—dividing time with sounds to reveal the wonderful cycles and numerical relationships that exist in the universe.

—RAQUY DANZIGER, Note to author, December 2003

That's the advantage of playing in a band with girls. As soon as a bloke gets a guitar in his hands he's unbearable.

—JUSTINE FRISCHMANN, "Elastica limits" by Andrew Smith,
Observer, 10 March 2002

But I cannot help it if, having never stopped working, I have learned a great deal, especially about this divine freedom that is to music the air without which it would die. What would you say of a scientist or of a painter who, like stagnant water, would stop his experimentation and remain still?

—WANDA LANDOWSKA, "Letter to a Former Pupil" (1950),
Landowska on Music, 1964

In the final analysis, "style" is art. And art is nothing more or less than various modes of stylized, dehumanized representation.

—SUSAN SONTAG, *Against Interpretation*, 1966

Real art has the capacity to make us nervous.

—SUSAN SONTAG, *Against Interpretation*, 1966

Much of modern art is devoted to lowering the threshold of what is terrible. By getting us used to what, formerly, we could not bear to see or hear, because it was too shocking, painful, or embarrassing, art changes morals.

—SUSAN SONTAG, *On Photography*, 1977

Surrealism is the magical surprise of finding a lion in a wardrobe, where you were "sure" of finding shirts.

—FRIDA KAHLO in *Frida*, Herrera, 1983

But, in the end, I believe that to be a creative person and not to be able to express it in your own terms is difficult, and eventually intolerable, for any human being anywhere.

—FAY KANIN in *American Women Playwrights*, Shafer, 1995

It's my feeling that the highest aspiration of the [screen] writer is to be a writer-executive in the sense that he goes on to control his material in one further aspect by producing or directing it. I believe every writer who can should try to accomplish that. Because it's the best way he can get his work done well.

—FAY KANIN in *American Women Playwrights*, Shafer, 1995

While other [film] crafts have to sit around chewing their fingernails waiting for a movie to be put together, writers have one great strength. They can sit down and generate their own employment and determine their own fate to a great extent by the degree of their disciplines, their guts, and their talents.

—FAY KANIN in *The Screenwriter Looks at the Screenwriter* by William Froug, 1972

BEAUTY & APPEARANCE

(*also see* Fashion & Shopping *and* Food, Drink & Diet)

"You're not pretty, Miriam-mine, so you better be smart. But not too smart."
—MARGE PIERCY, *Small Changes*, 1973

—

Brainy women had a special obligation to look particularly chic and sexy, she believed, and she prided herself on never looking like a teacher or a librarian.
—SHARON NIEDERMAN, "A Gift for Languages," *Shaking Eve's Tree*, 1990

—

They just elected me Miss Phonograph Record of 1966. They discovered my measurements were 33⅓, 45, 78!
—PHYLLIS DILLER, Stand-up routine

—

There's nothing moral about beauty.
—NADINE GORDIMER, *The Late Bourgeois World*, 1966

—

Beauty is here to stay. Beauty doesn't vanish. We do.
—BETTE HOWLAND, *Things to Come and Go*, 1983

—

Re her visit to the beauty parlor: I was there five hours—and that was just for the estimate.

—PHYLLIS DILLER, Stand-up routine

—

Re beauty tips: Why do you listen to her [Arlene Dahl]? Chances are you'll never look like her. Better you should listen to me because the chances are you will look like me.

—TOTIE FIELDS, Stand-up routine

There are some implausible standards out there. It's really sad when I spend time with girls who are 11 years old and think they're fat.
—JENNIFER CONNELLY in "A Mind of Her Own" by Jane Gardner,
NW magazine, March 2002

There should be more diversity. There are all different kinds of beauty in the world. I mean, why aren't mothers glorified? Instead, sex goddesses are glorified!
—JENNIFER CONNELLY in "A Mind of Her Own" by Jane Gardner,
NW magazine, March 2002

I break all the rules and wear everything. Ruffles, ostrich feathers, fox coats. You look fat in fox anyway, so if you start fat, you only look a little fatter.
—TOTIE FIELDS in Funny Women, Unterbrink, 1987

She has more chins than a Chinese phone book.
—JOAN RIVERS, Stand-up routine

With a heavy French accent: Why do I have no wrinkles at 40? Because I never move a muscle in my face.
—LOTUS WEINSTOCK, Stand-up routine

It's very important to emphasize what is good or beautiful so as not to have a gloomy face when you meet some youngster who has begun to guess.
—GRACE PALEY, Just As I Thought, 1998

Sometimes this face looks so funny
That I hide it behind a book
Sometimes this face has so much class
That I have to sneak a second look.
—PHOEBE SNOW, "Either or Both," Phoebe Snow, 1973

Plastic surgery must be like childbirth without the child, Eva reasoned. After a while, if you're satisfied with the results, you forget the pain and want to do it again.

—RITA RUDNER, *Tickled Pink*, 2001

If I'da known you [the audience] were going to be on both sides of me I'd have gotten my nose fixed.

—BARBRA STREISAND in *Streisand: Her Life* by James Spada, 1995

On having plastic surgery: No woman on the stage today can afford to have a nose that is likely to keep on growing until she can swallow it.

—FANNY BRICE in *Funny Woman* by Barbara W. Grossman, 1991

I've always been proud of the Jews, but never so proud as tonight because tonight I wish I had my old nose back.

—JEAN CARROLL, Stand-up routine

The psychic scars caused by believing you are ugly have a permanent mark on your personality.

—JOAN RIVERS in *Los Angeles Times*, 10 May 1974

At this time of my life, age thirty-seven, the only thing I had to do about gray hair was extract one strand at a time, but I already had plans to eradicate one irritating vertical crease between my eyebrows. I'd read in *Elle* about this magical remedy, Botox. A little shot of botulism. No beau of mine would ever boast, Lily doesn't wear a lick of makeup.

—DELIA EPHRON, *Big City Eyes*, 2000

The beauty myth moves for men as a mirage; its power lies in its ever-receding nature. When the gap is closed, the lover embraces only his own disillusion.

—NAOMI WOLF, *The Beauty Myth*, 1990

Women have face-lifts in a society in which women without them appear to vanish from sight.

—NAOMI WOLF, *The Beauty Myth*, 1990

There are no ugly women, just lazy ones.

—HELENA RUBINSTEIN, *My Life for Beauty*, 1966

Someday, when I'm awfully low,
When the world is cold,
I will feel a glow just thinking of you
And the way you look tonight.

—DOROTHY FIELDS, "The Way You Look Tonight," *Swing Time* (film), 1936

BOOKS, WRITERS & POETRY
(*also see* Advertising, Image & the Media; Communication; *and* Stories & Myths)

Books go out into the world, travel mysteriously from hand to hand, and somehow find their way to the people who need them at the *times* when they need them…. Cosmic forces guide such passings-along.

—ERICA JONG, *How to Save Your Own Life*, 1977

Throughout all history, books were written with sperm, not menstrual blood.

—ERICA JONG, *Fear of Flying*, 1973

First they make something, then they murder it. Then they write a book about how interesting it is.

—GRACE PALEY, "The Long-Distance Runner," *The Collected Stories*, 1994

Sometimes I try my hand at turning out small profundities and uncertain short stories, but I always end up with just one single word: God.

—ETTY HILLESUM, *An Interrupted Life*, 1983

A real writer tells the truth, and that's how he changes the world.

—LILIAN NATTEL, *The River Midnight*, 1999

The word is my fourth dimension.

—CLARICE LISPECTOR, Profile by Rachel Gutierrez, Carla Sherman, tr., http://www.vidaslusofonas.pt (Lives of the Portuguese-Speaking World), 2000

One way or another the book had entered upon a new phase in its existence.... The total alienation of the product from its author had been accomplished. The book had become a grown-up daughter off on her continental tour, without so much as a look over her shoulder or a thought to spare for her old mother left to fend for herself at home.

—EUGENIA GINZBURG, *Within the Whirlwind*, 1979

I hear the books in all the rooms
breathing calmly

—DENISE LEVERTOV, "August Daybreak," *Breathing the Water*, 1989

The novel...depended on the pretense of objectivity to lend it the status of truth: a little world seen full and clear.

—HARRIET ROSENSTEIN, "Reconsidering Sylvia Plath" *The First Ms. Reader*, 1972

Routine, disposable novels, able to provide relief or distraction but not in themselves valuable—like the smoked cigarette, the used whore, the quick drink—are exactly suited to the conventions of their consumers.

—CAROLYN G. HEILBRUN, *Toward a Recognition of Androgyny*, 1973

This is not a novel to be tossed aside lightly. It should be thrown with great force.

—DOROTHY PARKER in *Algonquin Wits*, Robert E. Drennan, ed., 1968

—

A novel is like the physicist's premise of an expanding universe…. A play is just the reverse.

—CYNTHIA OZICK, "Old Hand as Novice," *Fame and Folly*, 1996

—

I did not choose this subject; it had long ago chosen me…. I only knew that I had lived through something which was considered central to the lives of women…a key to the meaning of life; and that I could remember little except anxiety, physical weariness, anger, self-blame, boredom, and divisions within myself.

—ADRIENNE RICH, *Of Woman Born*, 1976

—

The writer has a grudge against society, which he documents with accounts of unsatisfying sex, unrealized ambition, unmitigated loneliness, and a sense of local and global distress. The square, overpopulation, the bourgeois, the bomb and the cocktail party are variously identified as sources of the grudge. There follows a little obscenity here, a dash of philosophy there, considerable whining overall, and a modern satirical novel is born.

—RENATA ADLER, *Toward a Radical Middle*, 1969

—

A poem does invite, it does require. What does it invite? A poem invites you to feel. More than that: it invites you to respond. And better than that: a poem invites a total response.

—MURIEL RUKEYSER, *The Life of Poetry*, 1949

—

The universe of poetry is the universe of emotional truth. Our material is in the way we feel and the way we remember.

—MURIEL RUKEYSER, *The Life of Poetry*, 1949

poetry can be quite dangerous propaganda,
especially since all worthwhile propaganda
ought to move its readers like a poem.
Graffiti do that; so do some songs,
and rarely, poems on a page.

—ROBIN MORGAN, Introduction, *Sisterhood Is Powerful*, 1970

the true nature of poetry. The drive
to connect. The dream of a common language.

—ADRIENNE RICH, "Origins and History of Consciousness,"
The Dream of a Common Language, 1978

I see the life of North American poetry at the end of the century as a pulsing,
racing convergence of tributaries—regional, ethnic, racial, social, sexual—
that, rising from lost or long-blocked springs, intersect and infuse each other
while reaching back to the strengths of their origins.

—ADRIENNE RICH, *What Is Found There*, 1993

Poetry can break open locked chambers of possibility, restore numbed zones to
feeling, recharge desire.

—ADRIENNE RICH, *What Is Found There*, 1993

It is the Saturday before the Day of Atonement. I should have gone to synagogue, but instead I wrote a poem....

—HANNAH SENESH, *Hannah Senesh*, 1966

Poets...are the only people to whom love is not only a crucial, but an indispensable experience, which entitles them to mistake it for a universal one.

—HANNAH ARENDT, *The Human Condition*, 1958

I tell my students that they must write what they are afraid to write; and I attempt to do so myself.

—ALICIA SUSKIN OSTRIKER, "The Eighth and Thirteenth," *The Little Space*, 1998

—

Women and poets see the truth arrive,
Then it is acted out,
then lives are lost, and all the newsboys shout.

—MURIEL RUKEYSER, "Letter to the Front," *Beast in View*, 1944

—

It is the responsibility of the poet to say many times: there is no freedom without justice and this means economic justice and love justice.

—GRACE PALEY, "Responsibility," *Begin Again: Collected Poems*, 2000

—

I am a writer, and burning bridges behind me is part of the cost of the work.

—ANNE ROIPHE, *1185 Park Avenue: A Memoir*, 1999

—

It is a sad paradox that when male authors impersonate women, they are said to be dealing with "cosmic, major concerns"—but when we impersonate *ourselves* we are said to be writing "women's fiction" or "women's poetry."

—ERICA JONG in Ms., April 1974

—

The question of for whom do we write nevertheless plagues the writer, a tin can attached to the tail of every work published.

—NADINE GORDIMER, *Nobel Lectures*, 1991

—

Any writer of any worth at all hopes to play only a pocket-torch of light—and rarely, through genius, a sudden flambeau—into the bloody yet beautiful labyrinth of human experience, of being.

—NADINE GORDIMER, *Nobel Lectures*, 1991

Writers themselves don't analyze what they do; to analyze would be to look down while crossing a canyon on a tightrope.

—NADINE GORDIMER, *Nobel Lectures*, 1991

A writer must always try to have a philosophy and he should also have a psychology and a philology and many other things. Without a philosophy and a psychology and all these various other things he is not really worthy of being called a writer. I agree with Kant and Schopenhauer and Plato and Spinoza and that is quite enough to be called a philosophy. But then of course a philosophy is not the same thing as a style.

—GERTRUDE STEIN in *Voices: A Memoir* by Frederic Prokosch, 1983

[The writer is like a] beast howling inside a coal-furnace, heaping the coals on itself to increase the fire.

—CYNTHIA OZICK in *Writers at Work* (8th), 1988

Coiled in the bottommost pit of every driven writer is an impersonator—protean, volatile, restless, and relentless.

—CYNTHIA OZICK, *Fame and Folly*, 1996

He knows nothing about literature—most great writers don't; all they know is life.

—CYNTHIA OZICK, *Trust*, 1966

Always roused by the writing, always denied.
...My work died.

—TILLIE OLSEN, *Silences*, 1965

Finding language that will allow people to act together while cherishing each other's individuality is probably the most feminist and therefore truly revolutionary function of writers.

—GLORIA STEINEM, *Outrageous Acts and Everyday Rebellions*, 1983

They're fancy talkers about themselves, writers. If I had to give young writers advice, I would say don't listen to writers talking about writing or themselves.
—LILLIAN HELLMAN in *New York Times*, 21 February 1960

—

It seems like every time I want to write
I can't
I'm always holding a baby
one of my own
or one for a friend
—MERLE FELD, "We All Stood Together," *Four Centuries*, 1992

—

Re working with a team of all male writers: It's like being Red China. I'm there, they just don't recognize me.
—SELMA DIAMOND in *Funny Women*, Unterbrink, 1987

—

I use everything I find in my brain—experiences, impressions, memories, reading matter by other writers—everything, including the people who surround me and impinge on my awareness. It isn't a question in my mind of being nice or not nice. I can't help it any more than I can help breathing. I am not apologizing or defending myself: there it is. I do it and I will always do it as long as I write.... People who mind should stay away from writers.
—EMILY "MICKEY" HAHN, *Nobody Said Not to Go*, Ken Cuthbertson, 1998

—

It's difficult to become a writer, a woman writer. To arrange one's life for writing, often at sacrifice; to believe in one's work when there may be little or no support; to commit to one's own imaginative processes when real life pushes women toward committing far more strongly toward other people's endeavors—these acts essential to becoming serious about one's work require a strength that few writers believe they possess and that they must improvise, like their stories, as they go along.
—SHARON NIEDERMAN, Introduction, *Shaking Eve's Tree*, 1990

These sentences are born of a concentration in the writer that runs so deep, is turned so far inward, it achieves the lucidity of the poet.... The material is at one with the voice speaking.

—VIVIAN GORNICK, *The End of the Novel of Love*, 1997

Particularly in our age, when we are trying to create a peaceful society, it is instructive to know that the pen can be as mighty as the sword. For in the end it was this seemingly tiny tool that was to literally stand reality on its head.

—RIANE EISLER, *The Chalice and the Blade*, 1987

As Hemingway once said, or was thought to have said, [to write well] one must have a built-in shit detector. But to have that, one must have smelled shit at least a few times.

—ROSALYN DREXLER in *Contemporary Women Playwrights*, Betsko, 1987

I am writing for myself and strangers. This is the only way that I can do it.

—GERTRUDE STEIN, *The Making of Americans*, 1906–1908

Only amateurs say that they write for their own amusement. Writing is not an amusing occupation. It is a combination of ditch-digging, mountain-climbing, treadmill and childbirth. Writing may be interesting, absorbing, exhilarating, racking, relieving. But amusing? Never!

—EDNA FERBER, *A Peculiar Treasure*, 1939

Re collaborating with her husband, Joe Bologna: We wrote together in a synagogue...in a public school cafeteria.... Near a pool in Arizona...in our bedroom...in the double whirlpool. I wake him up in the middle of the night and say, "How about this?"

—RENEE TAYLOR in *Funny Women*, Unterbrink, 1987

The ink flows, the pen chases
Its shadow across the page

Seldom does the phone ring
Interrupting thought
>—BLU GREENBERG, "Resisting Yom Hashoah 1985," *Four Centuries*, 1992

One would always like to write about eternal verities in a letter destined to travel across seas. One can be reasonably sure of holding the same opinion on them two weeks after writing. But a flippant, or a trivial, or even a humorous mood cannot be expected to last until a letter takes a long ocean trip, and then the reader has a wrong conception of the writer as he actually is.
>—HENRIETTA SZOLD, *Lost Love*, Shargel, 1997

Joyce's Molly rejoicing. Bellow fanning fire, Updike fingering apertures, Oates wildly sowing, Roth wroth. And so on.
>—CYNTHIA OZICK, *The Puttermesser Papers*, 1997

The writer is either a practicing recluse or a delinquent, guilt-ridden one; or both. Usually both.
>—SUSAN SONTAG in *New York Times*, 5 January 1986

CELEBRATIONS & HOLIDAYS
(*also see* Faith, Religion, the Bible & Spirituality *and* Jews & Judaism)

I close my eyes and think of Grandma tasting a bit of her childhood each Chanukah when she prepared the latkes as her mother had made them before her. My mother, my aunts, my own grandmothers float back to me, young and vibrant once more, making days holy in the sanctuaries of their kitchens, feeding me, cradling me, connecting me to the intricately plaited braid of their past, and even at this moment, looking down the corridor of what's to come, I see myself join them as they open their arms wide to enfold my children and grandchildren in their embrace.
>—FAYE MOSKOWITZ, *And the Bridge Is Love*, 1991

The freedom of Shabbat comes from the potential it holds to control time, per-haps the most far-reaching form of freedom anyone can experience.... It offers a day when instead of fighting time we luxuriate in it. Instead of feeling chained to a routine, we may break loose and breathe freely.

—FRANCINE KLAGSBRUN, *The Fourth Commandment*, 2002

Even the most harried workdays become tolerable when you know a day of holy peace is shortly arriving. The days succeeding the day of rest become days of light too. They shimmer with the afterglow of a revived spirit.

—RABBI NAOMI LEVY, *To Begin Again*, 1998

Celebrating a Sabbath day is a way to take one day out of each week and live it differently. In peace. It is not only a time to stop work, it is also a time to stop thinking about work. It is not a restriction, it is a freedom.

—RABBI NAOMI LEVY, *To Begin Again*, 1998

Sabbath! That is the word which we, as Mothers in Israel, must brave again. Ours it is to be the saviors of our people. Ours it is to arouse courage and hope in the leaders of the nation's destiny.

—REBEKAH BETTELHEIM KOHUT, "Welcoming Address" NCJW Proceedings, 1896

Year after year, the Haggadah, the retelling of Israel's liberation from bondage, came to us in my father's authoritative bass voice, annotated by the symbols, songs, and rituals that he brought upstage like some great maestro conducting the solo parts of the seder symphony. It took me years to see that my father's virtuosity depended on my mother's labor and that the seders I remember with such heartwarming intensity were sanctified by her creation even more than his.

—LETTY COTTIN POGREBIN, *Deborah, Golda, and Me*, 1991

All rituals are paradoxical and dangerous enterprises, the traditional and the improvised, the sacred and the secular. Paradoxical because rituals are conspic-uously artificial and theatrical, yet designed to suggest the inevitability and absolute truth of their messages. Dangerous because when we are not convinced by a ritual we may become aware of ourselves as having made them up, thence on the paralyzing realization that we have made up all our truths; our ceremonies, our most precious conceptions and convictions—all are mere inventions.

—BARBARA MYERHOFF, *Number Our Days*, 1979

Ritual places personal experience in the public realm where it may be witnessed, dealt with, and shared.

—PENINA V. ADELMAN, "The Womb and the World," *Four Centuries*, 1992

Growing up, it just wasn't Thanksgiving unless my mother got nervous and yelled, my sister got high-strung and slammed a few doors, and dad overate to the point of indigestion and acute gastritis. Ah, the good ol' days.

—FRAN DRESCHER, *Cancer, Schmancer*, 2002

For Thanksgiving last year I made a seventeen-pound turkey...(*pot pie*).

—WENDY LIEBMAN, Stand-up routine

It is Thanksgiving
I am thankful for the joy and the task
The soft burp of cranberries popping in
    the boiling pot
The smoothing whir of electric beaters
    ironing out yams
The surprise of Everest peaks looming up
    out of soft white foam
    for the stirring

—ELAINE BERNSTEIN PARTNOW, "A Woman Cooking," 1978

Did you know there's a new Jewish holiday? It's October 21, the day the new Cadillacs go on sale.

—PEARL WILLIAMS, Stand-up routine

With the loss of tradition we have lost the thread which safely guided us through the vast realms of the past, but this thread was also the chain fettering each successive generation to a predetermined aspect of the past. It could be that only now will the past open up to us with unexpected freshness and tell us things that no one as yet has ears to hear.

—HANNAH ARENDT in *Nomos I: Authority*, Carl J. Frederich, ed., 1958

Tradition implies process and change, the movement of the past into the future, the continual forging of links on an unending chain.

—FANCHON SHUR, *The Book of Blessings*, 1992

CELEBRITIES, HEROES & SHEROES

(*also see* Actors, Comedians & Performers *and* Show Biz, Sports & Entertainment)

Great men can't be ruled.

—AYN RAND, *The Fountainhead*, 1943

The great can also contain the little, but by the laws of nature there is no way that the little can contain the great.

—NATALIA GINZBURG, *Little Virtues*, 1985

To reach those shining pebbles,
that soil where uncommon men
have labored in their virtue
and left a store of seeds for planting!

—DENISE LEVERTOV, "A Common Ground," *The Jacob's Ladder*, 1961

Fame will go by and, so long, I've had you, fame. If it goes by, I've always known it was fickle. So at least it's something I experienced, but that's not where I live.

—MARILYN MONROE in *Look*, 3 August 1962

I do feel slightly like I'm having sex with the world at the moment, and I'm not sure if it's going to like me in the morning.

—JUSTINE FRISCHMANN in "Elastica Limits" by Andrew Smith,
Observer, 10 March 2002

She [Marie Curie] died a famous woman denying
her sounds
denying
her wounds came from the same
source as her power

—ADRIENNE RICH, "Power," *The Dream of a Common Language*, 1978

"I never wanted to be a hero, but on the other hand I am not anxious to culti-vate cowardice."

—GERTRUDE STEIN, "Adele," *Q.E.D.*, 1903

As I learned of the careers of some of the great women of Israel—of the Mendelssohn daughters, of Sarah Copia Sullam, Deborah Ascarelli, high in the councils of the Italian Court, of Rebecca Gratz, most beloved and honored woman of her time, who served as the model for Rebecca in Scott's *Ivanhoe*, of Emma Lazarus, equally beloved a century later, of Grace Aguilar and a host of others—a new pride possessed me. More cause for worship, more examples of nobility, richer race consciousness.

—REBEKAH BETTELHEIM KOHUT, *My Portion: An Autobiography*, 1927

"Hero" is the surprising word that men employ when they speak of Jack the Ripper.

—SUSAN BROWNMILLER, *Against Our Will*, 1975

President Reagan is a lot like E.T. He's cute, he's lovable, and he knows noth-ing about how Americans live.

—ELAYNE BOOSLER, Stand-up routine

He [William J. Clinton] reminded me of my mom because like her, he was an ostrich, putting his head in the sand because he didn't like confrontation.

—MONICA LEWINSKY in *Monica's Story* by Andrew Morton, 1999

Celebrities used to be found in clusters, like oysters—and with much the same defensive mechanisms.

—BARBARA WALTERS, *How to Talk with Practically Anybody about Practically Anything,* 1970

Those who know the joys and miseries of celebrity…know…it is a sort of octo-pus with innumerable tentacles. It throws out its clammy arms on the right and on the left, in front and behind, and gathers into its thousand little inhaling organs all the gossip and slander and praise afloat to spit out again at the pub-lic when it is vomiting its black gall.

—SARAH BERNHARDT, *The Memoirs of Sarah Bernhardt,* 1977

"Do you think he is a brave man?" "Either too much of a coward to face it—or the bravest, facing it in solitude, not sharing the fear. Perhaps we'll never find out."

—YAËL DAYAN, *Death Had Two Sons,* 1967

CHANGE

Well, people change and forget to tell each other. Too bad—causes so many mistakes.

—LILLIAN HELLMAN, *Toys in the Attic,* 1959

What will never change is the will to change and the fear of change.
—HARRIET GOLDHOR LERNER, *The Dance of Intimacy*, 1989

How wonderful it is that nobody need wait a single moment before starting to improve the world.
—ANNE FRANK, *The Diary of a Young Girl*, 1947

Nothing changes. The bones of the mammoths are still in the earth.
—ADRIENNE RICH, "End of an Era," *Snapshots of a Daughter-in-Law*, 1963

Changes in consciousness are a very strange thing. Suddenly we see what was there all the time. And we wonder how it could for so long have been invisible to us.
—RIANE EISLER, *Sacred Pleasure*, 1995

Slowly we adjust, but only if we have to.
—ELLEN GOODMAN, Syndicated column

Every daring attempt to make a great change in existing conditions, every lofty vision of new possibilities for the human race, has been labeled Utopian.
—EMMA GOLDMAN, "Socialism: Caught in the Political Trap,"
Red Emma Speaks, 1972

The appeal of the New Right is simply that it seems to promise that nothing will change in the domestic realm. People are terrified of change there, because it's the last humanizing force left in society, and they think, correctly, that it must be retained.
—GERDA LERNER in *Ms.*, September 1981

Meanwhile, for now, this must suffice:
that murder and resurrection are the levers of change,

that creation and complexity are one,
that miracle is contradiction.

> —ROBIN MORGAN, "Easter Island, II: Arrival," *Monster*, 1972

The moment of change is the only poem.

> —ADRIENNE RICH, "Images for Godard," *The Will to Change*, 1971

That man is a creature who needs order yet yearns for change is the creative contradiction at the heart of the laws which structure his conformity and define his deviancy.

> —FREDA ADLER, *Sisters in Crime*, 1975

Butterflies fluttering
soon feel at home in the sea—
This stone
inscribed with the 'fly
has placed itself in my hand—

In place of a homeland
I hold out for the world to transform—

> —NELLY SACHS, Acceptance speech poem, Janice Price with Elaine Bernstein Partnow, trs., Nobel Prize Awards (Stockholm), 1966

So often I heard people paying blind obeisance to change—as though it had some virtue of its own. Change or we will die. Change or we will stagnate. Evergreens don't stagnate.

> —JUDITH ROSSNER, *Nine Months in the Life of an Old Maid*, 1969

What was she to say now to her father, who thought change was the only serious mistake that could be made in a life?

> —JUDITH ROSSNER, *Any Minute I Can Split*, 1969

Anything in history or nature that can be described as changing steadily can be seen as heading toward catastrophe.

—SUSAN SONTAG, *AIDS and Its Metaphors*, 1989

CHILDREN

(*also see* Family & Relatives; Fathers & Fatherhood; *and* Mothers & Motherhood)

Give me children, or else I die.

—RACHEL, Genesis 30:1, Bible

The birth of a mother and a father is initiated by the Promethean event of the birth of the first child.

—JUDITH PARTNOW HYMAN, *Becoming a Father*, 1995

All God's children are not beautiful. Most of God's children are, in fact, barely presentable.

—FRAN LEBOWITZ, *Metropolitan Life*, 1978

Parents of young children should realize that few people, and maybe no one, will find their children as enchanting as they do.

—BARBARA WALTERS, *How to Talk with Practically Anybody about Practically Anything*, 1970

I want to have children, but my friends scare me. One of my friends told me she was in labor for 36 hours. I don't even want to do anything that feels good for 36 hours.

—RITA RUDNER, Stand-up routine

I was such an ugly baby a furrier tried to club me.

—JOAN RIVERS, Stand-up routine

...you will find
your own way
hard and true
And I'll find mine
cause I'm growing with you

—LAURA NYRO, "To a Child," *Mother's Spiritual*, 1984

"The joy, the reason to believe," my mother said, "the hope for the world, the baby, holy with possibility, that is all of us at birth." And she began to cry, out of the dream and its telling now. "Still I feel the baby in my arms, the human baby," crying now so I could scarcely make out the word, "the human baby, before we are misshapen; crucified into a sex, a color, a walk of life, a nationality...and the world yet warring and winter."

—TILLIE OLSEN, *Mother to Daughter, Daughter to Mother*, 1984

There are few places outside his own play where a child can contribute to the world in which he finds himself. His world: dominated by adults who tell him what to do and when to do it—benevolent tyrants who dispense gifts to their "good" subjects and punishment to their "bad" ones, who are amused at the "cleverness" of children and annoyed by their "stupidities."

—VIOLA SPOLIN, *Improvisation for the Theater*, 1963

Many years' familiarity with the children's attempts to play in the streets has not made me indifferent to its pathos, which is not the less real because the children are unconscious of it. In the midst of the pushcart market, with its noise, confusion, and jostling, the checker or crokinole board is precariously perched on top of a hydrant, constantly knocked over by the crowd and patiently replaced by the little children.

—LILLIAN D. WALD, *The House on Henry Street*, 1915

Raising a child in the city is a great thing and a horrid thing.

—JENNIFER CONNELLY, Article by Rick Leider in *Black Cat,* January 1999

—

It's clear that most American children suffer too much mother and too little father.

—GLORIA STEINEM in *New York Times,* 26 August 1971

—

Love, by reason of its passion, destroys the in-between which relates us to and separates us from others. As long as its spell lasts, the only in-between which can insert itself between two lovers is the child, love's own product…. Through the child, it is as though the lovers return to the world from which their love had expelled them.

—HANNAH ARENDT, *The Human Condition,* 1958

—

Strange new problems are being reported in the growing generations of children whose mothers were always there, driving them around, helping them with their homework—an inability to endure pain or discipline or pursue any self-sustained goal of any sort, a devastating boredom with life.

—BETTY FRIEDAN, *The Feminine Mystique,* 1963

—

What the vast majority of American children need is to stop being pampered, stop being indulged, stop being chauffeured, stop being catered to. In the final analysis it is not what you do for your children but what you have taught them to do for themselves that will make them successful human beings.

—ANN LANDERS, *Ann Landers Says "Truth Is Stranger,"* 1968

—

Have we now come to the point where it is the children who are being asked to change or improve the world?

—HANNAH ARENDT, "Reflections on Little Rock," 1959

—

All children are musicians; all children are artists.

—SUSAN WITKOVSKY in *San Francisco Chronicle,* 19 December 1971

The merits of good child care for all who need it or want it are many. The health and well-being of our society depend on it. Those unconvinced are people who have no need of high-quality public programs, and who choose not to see the children and parents who suffer from lack of them.

—SUSAN WITKOVSKY, "The Impediments to Public Day Care Programs in San Francisco," Master's Thesis, San Francisco State University (now California State University), 1974

It is destroying, dissolving him utterly, this helpless warmth against him, this feel of a child.

—TILLIE OLSEN, "Hey Sailor, What Ship?," *Tell Me a Riddle*, 1960

It might sound a paradoxical thing to say—for surely never has a generation of children occupied more sheer hours of parental time—but the truth is that we neglected you. We allowed you a charade of trivial freedoms in order to avoid making those impositions on you that are in the end both the training ground and proving ground for true independence. We pronounced you strong when you were still weak in order to avoid the struggles with you that would have fed your true strength. We proclaimed you sound when you were foolish in order to avoid taking part in the long, slow, slogging effort that is the only route to genuine maturity of mind and feeling.

—MIDGE DECTER, *Liberal Parents/Radical Children*, 1975

The only thing I know for sure is that I would rather have a child than a book.

—ANNE ROIPHE, *Fruitful*, 1996

"What are my daughters worth? They're only good to sit in the house, a burden on their parents' neck, until they're married off. A son, at least, prays for the souls of his parents when they're dead; it's a deed of piety to raise sons."

—MARY ANTIN, "Malinke's Atonement," *America and I*, 1990

I love my parents and they're wonderful people, but they were strict, and I still look for ways to get even. When I got my own apartment for the very first time and they came to stay with me for the weekend, I made them stay in separate bedrooms.

—ELAYNE BOOSLER, Stand-up routine

My mother said I drove her crazy. I did not drive my mother crazy. I flew her there. It was faster.

—ROBIN TYLER, Stand-up routine

"When you deny your parents, you deny the ground under your feet, the sky over your head. You become an outlaw, a pariah"

—ANZIA YEZIERSKA, *Red Ribbon on a White Horse*, 1950

My mom says I'm her sugarplum.
My mom says I'm her lamb.
My mom says I'm completely perfect
Just the way I am.
My mom says I'm a super-special wonderful terrific little guy.
My mom just had another baby.
Why?

—JUDITH VIORST, "Some Things Don't Make Any Sense at All,"
If I Were in Charge of the World and Other Worries…, 1981

At the core of every child is an intact human.

—RIANE EISLER, *Tomorrow's Children*, 2000

Children are being given a false picture of what it means to be human. We tell them to be good and kind, nonviolent and giving. But on all sides they see media images and hear and read stories that portray us as bad, cruel, violent, and selfish.

—RIANE EISLER, *Tomorrow's Children*, 2000

Well, you have children so you know: little children little troubles, big children big troubles—it's a saying in Yiddish. Maybe the Chinese said it too.

—GRACE PALEY, "Zagrowsky Tells," *Later the Same Day*, 1985

—

Children are the true connoisseurs. What's precious to them has no price—only value.

—BEL KAUFMAN, *Up the Down Staircase*, 1964

—

I was very overprotected as a child. My tricycle had seven wheels. And a driver....

—RITA RUDNER, Stand-up routine

—

It seems to me that during my childhood, the fact that I was hearing was kindly overlooked.

—LEAH HAGER COHEN [who was raised at the Lexington School for the Deaf in New York where her parents worked and lived], *Train Go Sorry: Inside a Deaf World*, 1994

—

Do you remember when you were little, before the boys came, before your father became the world's most Jewish person, when you were the only child and the apple of everyone's eye, we called you Zisa Punim, Sweet Face. Remember? And one day you got separated from your mother in a big department store—oy, she was frantic, hysterical, searching everywhere for you, when over the loudspeaker comes a voice: "Will Zisa Punim's mother please report to Customer Service?" You thought it was your name.

—CAROL K. HOWELL, "The Make-up Lesson," *The William and Mary Review*, Spring 2001

—

I am opposed to the custodial idea of day care. That is a mistake. Enrichment is what we are after.

—SUSAN WITKOVSKY in *San Francisco Chronicle*, 19 December 1971

Give me a girl at an impressionable age, and she is mine for life.
—MURIEL SPARK, *The Prime of Miss Jean Brodie*, 1961

—

A girl's voice yowling can carry high as heaven.
—MIRIAM ULINOVER, "The Old Prayer Book," *Der bobes oyster*
(The Grandmother's Treasure), 1922

—

I wish I dared shout it out to every young girl not to run away for a moment
from her natural destination.... I mean exclusive love and loving.
—HENRIETTA SZOLD in *Woman of Valor* by Irving Fineman, 1961

—

For months for years each one of us
    had felt her own yes growing in her
    slowly forming as she stood at windows waited
    For trains mended her rucksack combed her hair
—ADRIENNE RICH, "Phantasia for Elvira Shatayev [leader of a
women's climbing team, all of whom died in a storm on Lenin Peak
in August 1974]," *The Dream of a Common Language*, 1978

—

Posterity trembles like a leaf
and we go on making heirs and heirlooms.
—ADRIENNE RICH, "The Demon Lover," *Leaflets*, 1969

—

When I got pregnant, my mother got nauseous.
—ELAYNE BOOSLER in *Women in Comedy*, Martin, 1986

—

"What's the matter?"

"I'm gay," Mindy said.

"You're kidding?"

"Yes, but I am pregnant."

"You're gay and you're pregnant?" asked her confused parent.

"No. I'm only pregnant."

"So why did you say you were gay?"

"To make it easier to take that I'm pregnant."

—RITA RUDNER, *Tickled Pink*, 2001

Although she still had three months to go, Mindy already felt the hefty, protective tug of maternal obligation. Indeed, the bond was so strong she was considering not having the umbilical cord cut right away, but leaving it intact so she could keep track of her child's whereabouts until he or she was at least twenty-one.

—RITA RUDNER, *Tickled Pink*, 2001

"I think that when kids are born, they should be implanted with subdermal locators. The nurse could put it in right when he or she does the silver nitrate drops."

—FAYE KELLERMAN, *Stalker*, 2000

This idea of the child's right to her own body is a radical one. In the traditional patriarchal family, there is no such concept. The child is the legal property of the father. Only in the last century have reforms of law and custom recognized the *mother's* custodial rights to her child. The concept that the child, too, might have some individual rights or interests not represented by either parent is even more recent.

—JUDITH LEWIS HERMAN, *Father-Daughter Incest*, 1981

Her parents had searched through the past, consulted psychiatrists, took every moment to bits. In no way should she [their daughter] be explained.

—MURIEL SPARK, *Reality and Dreams*, 1997

CITIES & STATES

(*also see* Nations & the World *and* United States of America)

This city [San Francisco] typifies the American dream of a sense of tolerance and openness, with different people living closely together, carefully, with respect for the law, not impinging their will on others but living with a growing mutual respect.

—DIANNE FEINSTEIN in *San Francisco Examiner*, 4 March 1979

—

Texas air is so rich you can nourish off it like it was food.

—EDNA FERBER, *Giant*, 1952

—

It was part of the Texas ritual. We're rich as son-of-a-bitch stew but look how homely we are, just as plain-folksy as Grandpappy back in 1836. We know about champagne and caviar but we talk hog and hominy.

—EDNA FERBER, *Giant*, 1952

—

The serpent's name was Hollywood.

—ELAINE BERNSTEIN PARTNOW, *Hear Us Roar*, 1988

—

Hollywood expediently ignored reality.

—MARJORIE ROSEN, *Popcorn Venus*, 1973

—

This is a period of great *angst*. The impermanence and flimsiness of houses built on faults, subject to landslides, add to a former apartment dweller's sense of insecurity. The stage-set quality of the streets, the green and blue spotlights illuminating every sallow palm in front of Hollywood court apartments, the 40-foot neon cross overlooking the freeway.

—LEE GRANT in *New York Times*, 12 August 1973

Where is Hollywood located? Chiefly between the ears. In that part of the American brain lately vacated by God.

—ERICA JONG, *How to Save Your Own Life*, 1977

Hollywood's a place where they'll pay you a thousand dollars for a kiss, and fifty cents for your soul. I know, because I turned down the first offer often enough and held out for the fifty cents.

—MARILYN MONROE, *Marilyn Monroe In Her Own Words*, 1990

I knew my friend Patti was a big-time Hollywood agent the first time I saw her dial a telephone with a pencil.

—WENDY WASSERSTEIN, *Bachelor Girls*, 1990

[Hollywood] is like a small town. It has its own set of values, narrow and small…. I wouldn't want to raise my son here, in a town where people are judged by the size of their swimming pools.

—BARBRA STREISAND in *Streisand: Her Life* by James Spada, 1995

Hollywood is where, as my husband says, people who were somebody someplace else come to be a nobody.

—ROSEANNE BARR, *My Life as a Woman*, 1989

You cannot live in Los Angeles for any period of time without eventually trying to write a screenplay. It's like a flu bug that you catch…. Even the plumber has a screenplay in his truck.

—GILDA RADNER, *It's Always Something*, 1989

Culturally, Los Angeles has always been a humid jungle alive with seething L.A. projects that I guess people from other places can't see. It takes a certain kind of innocence to like L.A., anyway.

—EVE BABITZ, *Eve's Hollywood*, 1974

L.A. is a really easy city to feel lost in, like you have no control of your life, because in fact, you don't. So much of it is waiting around for people to allow you to do what you do best.

—DEBRA MESSING, "Grace Under Pressure" by Ian Williams,
P.O.V. magazine, November 1999

There are two modes of transport in Los Angeles: car and ambulance. Visitors who wish to remain inconspicuous are advised to choose the latter.

—FRAN LEBOWITZ, *Social Studies*, 1981

Southern California has been so overdeveloped that they might as well just build the entire coastline into one huge strip mall. At this point, we should just be able to walk from one strip mall to the other without interruption. There's no point to space—why should we have empty spaces? We don't want it. Empty space just scares us.

—SANDRA BERNHARD, *May I Kiss You on the Lips, Miss Sandra?*, 1998

If the word for London is decency and the word for New York is violence, then, beyond doubt, the word for Cairo is tenderness. Tenderness is what pervades the air here.

—VIVIAN GORNICK, *In Search of Ali-Mahmoud*, 1973

Every French town has an Avenue Victor Hugo. We never have a Mark Twain Street.

—BARBARA TUCHMAN in *New York Times*, 28 February 1979

I can tell by your eye shadow, you're from Brooklyn, right?... Me too. My mother has plastic covers on all the furniture. Even the poodle. Looked like a barking hassock walking down the street.

—ELAYNE BOOSLER, Stand-up routine

Because I am a New Yorker, my experience is the more truly, the more typically, American one. It is my America that is moving in on them [Middle America]. God is about to bless them with an opportunity, and may He also save them from it, but there is no turning back now.

—MIDGE DECTER, *The Liberated Woman and Other Americans*, 1971

...diehard Manhattanites. To leave the city, unless it was to go someplace thrilling like Paris, they would have to be towed.

—DELIA EPHRON, *Big City Eyes*, 2000

They [New Yorkers] live as if in an enormous chicken coop that is dirty and uncomfortable. The houses look like bread ovens and all the comfort that they talk about is a myth. I don't know if I am mistaken but I'm only telling you what I feel.

—FRIDA KAHLO in *Frida*, Herrera, 1983

Re the Bon Soir club in Greenwich Village: A nine-year-old boy came in here the other night, and when he left he was thirty-eight.

—PHYLLIS DILLER, Stand-up routine

"That's the New York thing, isn't it. People who seem absolutely crazy going around telling you how crazy they used to be before they had therapy."

—JUDITH ROSSNER, *Any Minute I Can Split*, 1969

This city [New York] is neither a jungle nor the moon.... In long shot: a cosmic smudge, a conglomerate of bleeding energies. Close up, it is a fairly legible printed circuit, a transistorized labyrinth of beastly tracks, a data bank for asthmatic voice-prints.

—SUSAN SONTAG, *I, Etcetera*, 1979

New York, home to the vivisectors of the mind, and of the mentally vivisected still to be reassembled, of those who live intact, habitually wondering about their states of sanity, and home of those whose minds have been dead, bearing the scars of resurrection....

—MURIEL SPARK, *The Hothouse by the East River*, 1973

Builders in South Florida are like God in the universe. Their handiwork is everywhere, but they are nowhere to be seen. They move on, leaving Gardens of Eden all over the place, and nothing quite finished.

—BETTE HOWLAND, *Things to Come and Go*, 1983

In Florida, plants carry their roots with them; whole forests crawling on their bellies, recumbent trunks with roots that noose and lasso. They have claws, tusks, fangs, beaks. They can take anchor anywhere—the shallowest places; an inch or two of soil; on water; on other plants; on nothing at all—on air.

—BETTE HOWLAND, *Things to Come and Go*, 1983

The disappearance of the physical walls of the Ghetto has, however, not meant for all Jewish communities religious tolerance and freedom of conscience, nor the recognition of equality for other religious communities.

—BERTHA PAPPENHEIM in *Jewish Review*, January 1913

...the Law and the Wall: only so far shall you go and no further, uptown forbidden, not your language, not your people, not your country.

—TILLIE OLSEN, "Hey Sailor, What Ship?," *Tell Me a Riddle*, 1960

CIVIL RIGHTS, SOCIAL MOVEMENTS & ACTIVISM

(*also see* Community & Citizenship; Feminism & Women's Liberation; Politics, Politicians & Leadership; *and* Racism, Sexism & Other Prejudices)

Let us go forth with fear and courage and rage to save the world.

—GRACE PALEY, *Just As I Thought*, 1998

We will be victorious if we have not forgotten how to learn.

—ROSA LUXEMBURG, *The Crisis in the German Social Democracy*, 1919

The uneasy sense of battles won, only to be fought over again, of battles that should have been won, according to all the rules, and yet are not, of battles that suddenly one does not really want to win, and the weariness of battle altogether—how many women feel it?

—BETTY FRIEDAN, *The Second Stage*, 1981

The defiance of established authority, religious and secular, social and political, as a world-wide phenomenon may well one day be accounted the outstanding event of the last decade.

—HANNAH ARENDT, *Crises of the Republic*, 1972

There is all the difference in the world between the criminal's avoiding the public eye and the civil disobedient's taking the law into his own hands in open defiance. This distinction between an open violation of the law, performed in public, and a clandestine one is so glaringly obvious that it can be neglected only by prejudice or ill will.

—HANNAH ARENDT, *Crises of the Republic*, 1972

Two years' imprisonment for having made an uncompromising stand for one's Ideal. Why that is a small price.
—EMMA GOLDMAN in *Emma Goldman in America* by Alice Wexler, 1984

—

I am merely honoring the law by breaking it.
—ROSE PASTOR STOKES in *Fire and Grace*, Zipser, 1989

—

To go to prison for big principles will be truly a privilege.
—ROSE PASTOR STOKES in *Fire and Grace*, Zipser, 1989

—

I used to want to change the world. Now, I just want to leave the room with dignity.
—LOTUS WEINSTOCK, *The Lotus Position*, 1982

—

It is my contention that civil disobedients are nothing but the latest form of voluntary association, and that they are thus quite in tune with the oldest traditions of the country.
—HANNAH ARENDT, *Crises of the Republic*, 1972

—

She filled her house with blacks, and white parsons who went around preaching Jesus was a revolutionary, and then when the police walked in she was surprised.
—NADINE GORDIMER, *The Conservationist*, 1975

—

Children's liberation is the next item on our civil rights shopping list.
—LETTY COTTIN POGREBIN, "Down with Sexist Upbringing," *The First Ms. Reader*, 1972

—

Civil rights groups hold no monopoly position among those discontented with legislative or executive action who seek the aid of the courts.
—RUTH BADER GINSBURG in *Georgia Law Review 539*, 1981

Action without a name, a "who" attached to it, is meaningless.
—HANNAH ARENDT, *The Human Condition*, 1958

If thou save not thy life tonight, tomorrow thou shalt be slain.
—MICHAL, Book of 1 Samuel, c. 550 B.C.E., Bible

I did not understand that wanting doesn't always lead to action.
—JUDY CHICAGO, *Through the Flower*, 1975

In the civil rights and feminist movements, we identified as universalists. We were afraid of seeing ourselves as too driven by our particularities; it wouldn't have been proper to call ourselves radical Jews. But that is exactly what we were.
—PAULA DORESS-WORTERS in *The Journey Home* by Joyce Antler, 1997

Fighting back. On a multiplicity of levels, that is the activity we must engage in.
—SUSAN BROWNMILLER, *Against Our Will*, 1975

It's always time for a change for the better, and for a good fight for the full human rights of every individual.
—BESS MYERSON in *AFTRA* magazine, Summer 1974

One of the most important developments in modern politics has been the unprecedented phenomenon of masses of people organizing, not just against those who violently oppress them, but against the oppression of others—and even against the use of violence itself.
—RIANE EISLER, *Sacred Pleasure*, 1995

American social movements: they rise fast, they wane fast, and they seem to disappear. History tells us that this is not really true.
—GERDA LERNER in *Ms.*, September 1981

Ten years from now, as I see it, either the movements for change will be totally annihilated, dispirited or ground down—or they will really have entered the mainstream and created major changes. It has come to the point of maximum push.

—GLORIA STEINEM in *Redbook*, April 1974

If anything has characterized the [peace] movement, from its beginning and in all its parts, it has been a spirit of decentralization, local autonomy, personal choice, and freedom from dogma.

—RENATA ADLER, *Toward a Radical Middle*, 1969

It seemed cowardly to me not to protest whenever I considered an act of injustice was being done to me or to others. Many a time when I was considered fearless, my actions were due rather to a sense of fear—fear lest I be weak and cowardly; fear lest I be weighed and found wanting.

—MAUD NATHAN, *Once Upon a Time and Today*, 1974

The modern mystics of muscle who offer you the fraudulent alternative of "human rights" versus "property rights," as if one could exist without the other, are making a last, grotesque attempt to revive the doctrine of soul versus body. Only a ghost can exist without material property; only a slave can work with no right to the product of his effort.

—AYN RAND, *Atlas Shrugged*, 1957

We have gained a lot in social freedom and individual rights, which is the thing that I personally believe in more intensely than anything else—the right of the individual to guide his own life, to think for himself, to live where he wants. We have created a society in which the individual is self-managing and insofar as he can economically manage, he can determine his own fate.

—BARBARA TUCHMAN in *A World of Ideas* by Bill Moyers, 1989

It isn't until you begin to fight in your own cause that you (a) become really committed to winning, and (b) become a genuine ally of other people struggling for their freedom.

—ROBIN MORGAN, *Sisterhood Is Powerful*, 1970

The most vital right is the right to love and be loved.
—EMMA GOLDMAN, *Anarchism and Other Essays*, 1911

Centuries of slavery do not provide a fertile soil for intellectual development or expression.
—MIRIAM SCHNEIR, *Feminism: The Essential Historical Writings*, 1972

Escape the birthplace; walk into the world
Refusing to be either slave or slaveholder.
—MURIEL RUKEYSER, "Secrets of American Civilization,"
The Speed of Darkness, 1968

The genius of any slave system is found in the dynamics which isolate slaves from each other, obscure the reality of a common condition, and make united rebellion against the oppressor inconceivable.
—ANDREA DWORKIN, *Our Blood*, 1976

Every human being merits respectful consideration of his rights and his personality.
—LILLIAN D. WALD, *The House on Henry Street*, 1915

Today, we can be defeated in regards to laws, to appropriations, to representation, but if we are truly transforming consciousness, we cannot be defeated.
—GERDA LERNER in *Ms.*, September 1981

CIVILIZATION & PROGRESS

(*also see* Individuals, Self-Realization & Human Nature *and* Society & Social Classes)

Civilization is the progress toward a society of privacy. The savage's whole existence is public, ruled by the laws of his tribe. Civilization is the process of setting man free from men.

—AYN RAND, *The Fountainhead*, 1943

I believe that the conquest of nature, control of the environment, the rise of patriarchal religion, Vetruvian man as a measure, the development of the scientific and medical minds, the industrial revolution, the burning of witches, are all part of the institutionalization of patriarchal culture. The systematic burning of Jews in the Holocaust is part of the outcome of this historical situation. You can't understand the Holocaust except from a feminist perspective. Without a feminist perspective, the consequences of patriarchy will mystify you.

—JUDY CHICAGO in *Exposures*, Brown, 1989

I don't believe civilization can do a lot more than educate a person's senses. If it's truth and honor you want to refine, I think the Jews have some insight. Make no images, imitate no God. After all, in His field, the graphic arts, He is pre-eminent. Then let that One who made the tan deserts and blue Van Allen belt and the green mountains of New England be in charge of Beauty, which He obviously understands, and let man, who was full of forgiveness at Jerusalem, and full of survival at Troy, let man be in charge of good.

—GRACE PALEY, "Just As I Thought," *Enormous Changes at the Last Minute*, 1960

Humans lived here once; it became sacred only when they went away.

—ADRIENNE RICH, "Shooting Script Part I," *The Will to Change*, 1971

The collective unconscious is the living history brought to the present in consciousness.

—MURIEL RUKEYSER in Ms., April 1974

The old love for life and nature and the old ways of sharing rather than taking away, of caring for rather than oppressing, and the view of power as responsibility rather than domination did not die out.

—RIANE EISLER, The Chalice and the Blade, 1987

The status quo protects itself by punishing all challengers.

—GLORIA STEINEM, "Sisterhood," The First Ms. Reader, 1972

Man's unique reward, however, is that while animals survive by adjusting themselves to their background, man survives by adjusting his background to himself.

—AYN RAND, For the New Intellectual, 1961

Surviving meant being born over and over.

—ERICA JONG, Fear of Flying, 1973

Simplicity is the peak of civilization.

—JESSIE SAMPTER, The Speaking Heart (unpub. autobio.)

The many images of the Goddess [in Neolithic and Minoan art] in her dual aspect of life and death seem to express a view of the world in which the primary purpose of art, and of life, was not to conquer, pillage, and loot but to cultivate the earth and provide the material and spiritual wherewithal for a satisfying life.

—RIANE EISLER, The Chalice and the Blade, 1987

COMMUNICATION

(*also see* Books, Writers & Poetry *and* Language, Languages & Words)

What is the answer? (I was silent.) In that case, what is the question?
—GERTRUDE STEIN, *What Is Remembered*, Alice B. Toklas, 1963

Not talking and not listening get us nowhere.
—LETTY COTTIN POGREBIN, *Deborah, Golda, and Me*, 1991

The only thing that anybody can understand is mechanics and that is what makes everybody feel that they are something when they talk about it. About every other thing nobody is of the same opinion nobody means the same thing by what they say as the other one means and only the one who is talking thinks he means what he is saying even though he knows very well that that is not what he is saying.
—GERTRUDE STEIN, *Everybody's Autobiography*, 1937

And I will speak less and less to you
And more and more in crazy gibberish you cannot understand:
witches' incantations, poetry, old women's mutterings....
—ROBIN MORGAN, "Monster," *Monster*, 1972

It's an indulgence to sit in a room and discuss your beliefs as if they were a juicy piece of gossip.
—LILLIAN HELLMAN, *Watch on the Rhine*, 1941

The impulse to enter, with other humans, through language, into the order and disorder of the world, is poetic at its root as surely as it is political at its root.
—ADRIENNE RICH, *What Is Found There*, 1993

Can we talk?

—JOAN RIVERS, Catchphrase

In our house, the direct statement was seldom used as a vehicle for communication. Innuendo was the order of the day.

—GLORIA DEVIDAS KIRCHHEIMER, Preface, *Goodbye, Evil Eye*, 2000

"My mother gave away my dolls when I was twelve, did I ever tell you? It took me years to get over that. I never told her how I felt, because I was afraid of her scorn. I waited all my life for her to ask me about myself, but she never did. That's what 'too late' is. Talk to me."

—CAROL K. HOWELL, "Tornado Watch Cookbook," *Shaking Eve's Tree*, 1990

He had had a habit throughout the twenty-seven years of making a narrow remark which, like a plumber's snake, could work its way through the ear down the throat, halfway to my heart. He would then disappear, leaving me choking with equipment.

—GRACE PALEY, *Enormous Changes at the Last Minute*, 1960

Consciousness-raising groups…begin with the term "rapping"—which is a process in which people in groups pretend that they are not simply self-absorbed because they are talking to each other.

—MIDGE DECTER, *Crazy Salad* by Nora Ephron, 1973

Consciousness-raising is at the very least supposed to bring about an intimacy, but what it seems instead to bring about are the trappings of intimacy, the illusion of intimacy, a semblance of intimacy.

—NORA EPHRON, *Crazy Salad*, 1975

my lifetime
    listens to yours.

—MURIEL RUKEYSER, "Käthe Kollwitz," *The Speed of Darkness*, 1968

In these days, when a dialogue between parents and their children has become possible...it is necessary that in this dialogue we show ourselves for what we are, imperfect, in the hope that our children will not resemble us but be stronger and better than us.

—NATALIA GINZBURG, *Little Virtues*, 1985

Gossip is the opiate of the oppressed.

—ERICA JONG, *Fear of Flying*, 1973

While gossip among women is universally ridiculed as low and trivial, gossip among men, especially if it is about women, is called theory, or idea, or fact.

—ANDREA DWORKIN, *Right-Wing Women*, 1978

Yoo Hoo, Mrs. Bloom!

—GERTRUDE BERG, Catchphrase, *Molly Goldberg* (TV show)

He always said she was smart, but their conversations were a mined field in which at any moment she might make the wrong verbal move and find her ignorance exploding in her face.

—JUDITH ROSSNER, *Looking for Mr. Goodbar*, 1975

I'm not a person who keeps things in. Tell! That opens up the congestion a little—the lungs are for breathing, not secrets. My wife never tells, she coughs, coughs. All night. Wakes up. Ai, Iz, open up the window, there's no air. You poor woman, if you want to breathe, you got to tell.

—GRACE PALEY, "Zagrowsky Tells," *Later the Same Day*, 1985

Men have always detested women's gossip because they suspect the truth: their measurements are being taken and compared.

—ERICA JONG, *Fear of Flying*, 1973

The lying tongue's deceit with silence blight,
Protect me from its venom, you, my Rock,
And show the spiteful sland'rer by this sign
That you will shield me with your endless might.
—SARAH COPIA SULLAM, "My Inmost Hope," A *Treasury of Jewish Letters*, 1953

Overtaken by silence

But this same silence
Is become speech
With the speed of darkness.
—MURIEL RUKEYSER, "The Speed of Darkness," *The Speed of Darkness*, 1968

No foreign tongue, no jargon! We are Israelites, but we are Americans as well.
—REBEKAH BETTELHEIM KOHUT, Papers of the Jewish Women's Congress, 1893

Wherever the relevance of speech is at stake, matters become political by definition, for speech is what makes man a political being.
—HANNAH ARENDT, *The Human Condition*, 1958

Any woman who can't say a four-letter word sometimes is deceitful.
—FANNY BRICE in *Funny Woman* by Barbara W. Grossman, 1991

Tact is the art of making people feel at home when that's where you wish they were.
—ANN LANDERS, Advice Column, 22 December 1998

"But the fun of talking, Ruthy. What about that? It's as good as fucking lots of times. Isn't it?"

"Oh boy," Ruth said, "if it's that good, then it's got to be that bad."
—GRACE PALEY, *Later the Same Day*, 1985

One never discusses anything with anybody who can understand, one discusses things with people who cannot understand.
                          —GERTRUDE STEIN, *Everybody's Autobiography*, 1937

Understanding is a very dull occupation.
                          —GERTRUDE STEIN, *Everybody's Autobiography*, 1937

Roseanne [Roseannadanna] never picks her nose—just talks about it.
                          —GILDA RADNER, *Women in Comedy*, Martin, 1986

In the beginning was the Word. The Word was with God, signified God's Word, the word that was Creation. But over the centuries of human culture the word has taken on other meanings, secular as well as religious. To have the word has come to be synonymous with ultimate authority, with prestige, with awesome, sometimes dangerous persuasion, to have Prime Time, a TV talk show, to have the gift of the gab as well as that of speaking in tongues. The word flies through space, it is bounced from satellites, now nearer than it has ever been to the heaven from which it was believed to have come. But its most significant transformation occurred for me and my kind long ago, when it was first scratched on a stone tablet or traced on papyrus, when it materialized from sound to spectacle, from being heard to being read as a series of signs, and then a script; and traveled through time from parchment to Gutenberg. For this is the genesis story of the writer. It is the story that wrote her or him into being.
                          —NADINE GORDIMER, *Nobel Lectures*, 1991

There are worse words than cuss words, there are words that hurt.
                          —TILLIE OLSEN, "Hey Sailor, What Ship?," *Tell Me a Riddle*, 1960

One must be chary of words because they turn into cages.
                          —VIOLA SPOLIN in *Los Angeles Times*, 26 May 1974

The opposite of talking isn't listening. The opposite of talking is waiting.
—FRAN LEBOWITZ, *Social Studies*, 1981

—

Moral: In saying what is obvious, never choose cunning. Yelling works better.
—CYNTHIA OZICK, "We Are the Crazy Lady and Other
Feisty Feminist Fables," *The First Ms. Reader*, 1972

—

I'm always on the phone because I'm usually not with the people I want to be with.
—NATALIE PORTMAN in *Mademoiselle*, November 1999

COMMUNITY & CITIZENSHIP
(*also see* Civil Rights, Social Movements & Activism)

No one class of people can be independent of each other.
—LILLIAN D. WALD in *The "Mutuality" of Society* by Marjorie N. Feld, 1995

—

Man is not only an animal with a body and a being with a brain but also a social creature who is so ineluctably interconnected with his social group that he is hardly comprehensible outside it.
—FREDA ADLER, *Sisters in Crime*, 1975

—

I alone stand here
ankle-deep
and I sing, I sing,
until the lands
sing to each other.

—MURIEL RUKEYSER, "Searching/Not Searching,"
The Poetic Vision of Muriel Rukeyser by Louise Kertesz, 1980

If we look long enough and hard enough...we will begin to see the connections that bind us together, and when we recognize those connections, we will begin to change the world.

—MURIEL RUKEYSER in *Writing beyond the Ending* by Rachel B. du Plessis, 1995

You do have a choice to become *consciously* historical—that is, a person who tries for memory and connectedness against amnesia and nostalgia—or to become a technician of amnesia and nostalgia, one who loses the imagination by starving it or feeding it junk food.

—ADRIENNE RICH, *Blood, Bread, and Poetry*, 1986

Opinions are formed in a process of open discussion and public debate, and where no opportunity for the forming of opinions exists, there may be moods— moods of the masses and moods of individuals, the latter no less fickle and unreliable than the former—but no opinion.

—HANNAH ARENDT, *On Revolution*, 1963

The Jew knows no sectarianism in communal work.

—REBEKAH BETTELHEIM KOHUT, NCJW Proceedings, 1896

Nothing defines the quality of life in a community more clearly than people who regard themselves, or whom the consensus chooses to regard, as mentally unwell.

—RENATA ADLER, *Toward a Radical Middle*, 1969

Wherever groups of women come together to define their own visions, economic and personal, and make connections with other groups of women working in our own interests, politically accountable to our own needs and wants, we are affirming a network of change. We are building the future.

—BLANCHE WEISEN COOK, *Women and Support Networks*, 1979

A Jew's identity is rooted in community.
> —Rabbi Sharon Kleinbaum, *The Journey Home* by Joyce Antler, 1997

One must apply one's reason to everything here, learning to obey, to shut up, to help, to be good, to give in, and I don't know what else. I'm afraid I shall use up all my brains too quickly, and I haven't got so very many.
> —Anne Frank, *The Diary of a Young Girl*, 1947

The kernel of the Torah is: "Thou shalt love thy neighbour as thyself." But in our days we seldom find it so, and few are they who love their fellow men with all their heart. On the contrary, if a man can contrive to ruin his neighbour nothing pleases him more.
> —Glückel of Hameln, *Memoirs*, 1692

Too many Americans have twisted the sensible right to pursue happiness into the delusion that we are entitled to a guarantee of happiness. If we don't get exactly what we want, we assume someone must be violating our rights. We're no longer willing to write off some of life's disappointments to simple bad luck.
> —Susan Jacoby, *Inside Soviet Schools*, 1974

COURAGE, CHARACTER & INTEGRITY

(*also see* Individuals, Self-Realization & Human Nature *and* Morality & Ethics)

The best index to a person's character is (a) how he treats people who can't do him any good, and (b) how he treats people who can't fight back.
> —Abigail Van Buren, "Dear Abby" Advice Column, 16 May 1974

The real test of class is how you treat people who cannot possibly do you any good.

—ANN LANDERS, Advice Column, 22 January 1999

—

"You are so afraid of losing your moral sense that you are not willing to take it through anything more dangerous than a mud puddle."

—GERTRUDE STEIN, "Adele," *Q.E.D.*, 1903

—

We made the smell of Banana in chemistry once, and I nearly cried because it actually smelled like Bananas and was so simple and so fake.

—EVE BABITZ, *Eve's Hollywood*, 1974

—

...ardent, intelligent, sweet, sensitive, cultivated, erudite. These are the adjectives of praise in an androgynous world. Those who consider them epithets of shame or folly ought not to be trusted with leadership, for they will be men hot for power and revenge, certain of right and wrong.

—CAROLYN G. HEILBRUN, *Toward a Recognition of Androgyny*, 1973

—

Don't be humble. You're not that great.

—GOLDA MEIR, Remark

—

Insecure people don't fry my burger.

—WINONA RYDER in "Hot Actress" by David Handelman, *Rolling Stone*, May 1989

—

"Any piece of furniture, I don't care how beautiful it is, has got to be lived with, kicked about, and rubbed down, and mistreated by servants, and repolished, and knocked around and dusted and sat on or slept in or eaten off of before it develops its real character," Salina said. "A good deal like human beings."

—EDNA FERBER, *So Big*, 1924

While men represent powerful activity as assertion and aggression, women in contrast portray acts of nurturance as acts of strength.

—CAROL GILLIGAN, *In a Different Voice*, 1982

"Well, there are people who eat the earth and eat all the people on it like in the Bible with the locusts. And other people who stand around and watch them eat it. Sometimes I think it ain't right to stand an' watch them do it."

—LILLIAN HELLMAN, *The Little Foxes*, 1939

The accomplice to the crime of corruption is frequently our own indifference.

—BESS MYERSON in *Redbook*, April 1974

What it comes down to is this: the grocer, the butcher, the baker, the merchant, the landlord, the druggist, the liquor dealer, the policeman, the doctor, the city father and the politician—these are the people who make money out of prostitution, these are the real reapers of the wages of sin.

—POLLY ADLER, *A House Is Not a Home*, 1953

Are we really courageous, we who do not know fear, if we remain firm in the face of danger?

—EMMA GOLDMAN, *Living My Life*, 1939

My favorite thing is to go where I've never been.

—DIANE ARBUS, *Diane Arbus*, 1972

...catch courage.

—CAROLYN G. HEILBRUN, *The Last Gift of Time: Life Beyond Sixty*, 1997

My father [Moshe Dayan, Israeli political and military leader; 1915–1981], I remembered, had no fears at all. In that he differed greatly from me. But he could not be called a courageous man because he had no fears to overcome.

—YAËL DAYAN, *New Face in the Mirror*, 1959

⁓

I now think of this courage to challenge unjust authority from a position of love rather than hate as spiritual courage. I think of it as the courage to question our most hallowed and sanctified norms—as the young Jew named Jesus did almost two thousand years ago when he defied the religion and secular authorities of his day.

—RIANE EISLER, *Sacred Pleasure*, 1995

⁓

"Carry in your own valise, son. It is not seemly for a man to load his goods on other men, black or white."

—LILLIAN HELLMAN, *Another Part of the Forest*, 1946

⁓

Courage in women always catches me up, moves me to compassion, and the desire [to offer women] succor, sustenance, if possible.

—CAROLYN G. HEILBRUN, *The Last Gift of Time: Life Beyond Sixty*, 1997

⁓

He never regarded himself as crazy. The world was.

—ERICA JONG, *Fear of Flying*, 1973

⁓

I love getting crazy over and over.

—SANDRA BERNHARD in *Women in Comedy*, Martin, 1986

⁓

I understand you undertake to overthrow my undertaking.

—GERTRUDE STEIN, *Everybody's Autobiography*, 1937

The word which can never die on this earth, for it is the heart of it and the meaning and the glory. The sacred word: EGO.

—AYN RAND, *Anthem*, 1946

Those who have mastered etiquette, who are entirely, impeccably right, would seem to arrive at a point of exquisite dullness.

—DOROTHY PARKER, "Mrs. Post Enlarges on Etiquette,"
New Yorker, 31 December 1927

But gentleness is active
gentleness swabs the crusted stump
invents more merciful instruments
to touch the wound beyond the wound

—ADRIENNE RICH, "Natural Resources," *The Dream of a Common Language*, 1978

Honesty is a selfish virtue. Yes, I am honest enough.

—GERTRUDE STEIN, "Adele," *Q.E.D.*, 1903

Honor wears different coats to different eyes.

—BARBARA TUCHMAN, *The Guns of August*, 1962

What makes it so plausible to assume that hypocrisy is the vice of vices is that integrity can indeed exist under the cover of all other vices except this one.

—HANNAH ARENDT, *On Revolution*, 1963

To say yes, over and over, to our integrity, we need to know where we have been: we need our history.

—ADRIENNE RICH, *Blood, Bread, and Poetry*, 1986

But I prefer to fall innocent into your power than to sin in the eyes of the Lord.

—SUSANNA, Book of Daniel, c. 167–164 B.C.E., Bible

I believe in a kind of fidelity to your own early ideas; it's a kind of antagonism in me to prevailing trends.
—GRACE PALEY in *Women Writing in America* by Blanche H. Gelfant, 1984

Dost thou still retain thine integrity? Curse God, and die.
—WIFE OF JOB, Book of Job, c. early fifth century B.C.E., Bible

I sold my integrity for on-the-lot parking at Paramount.
—EMILY LEVINE, Stand-up routine

Speak, ye that ride on white asses, ye that sit in judgment, and walk by the way.
—DEBORAH, with Barak, Book of Judges, c. ninth century B.C.E., Bible

A leader who doesn't hesitate before he sends his nation into battle is not fit to be a leader.
—GOLDA MEIR, *Good as Golda*, 1970

There are lies that glow so brightly we consent to give a finger and then an arm to let them burn.
—MARGE PIERCY, *Sisterhood Is Powerful*, 1970

The manipulator liberates only
the mad bulldozers of the ego to level
the ground.
—MARGE PIERCY, *Sisterhood Is Powerful*, 1970

Toughness doesn't have to come in a pinstripe suit.
—DIANNE FEINSTEIN in *Time*, 4 June 1984

But maybe half a lie is worse than a real lie.
—LILLIAN HELLMAN, *Another Part of the Forest*, 1946

Oh, I wish I were a miser; being a miser must be so occupying.
—GERTRUDE STEIN, Quoted by Thornton Wilder in *Writers at Work* (1st), 1958

Never let men mock at our ruin.
—ESTHER, Book of Esther, c. 199–150 B.C.E., Bible

Upon me be thy curse, my son: only obey my voice, and go fetch me them.
—REBEKAH, Book of Genesis, c. ninth century B.C.E., Bible

I am continually fascinated at the difficulty intelligent people have in distinguishing what is controversial from what is merely offensive.
—NORA EPHRON in *Esquire*, January 1976

It's a fact that it is much more comfortable to be in the position of the person who has been offended than to be the unfortunate cause of it.
—BARBARA WALTERS, *How to Talk with Practically Anybody about Practically Anything*, 1970

If I've offended any of you, you needed it.
—ROBIN TYLER, *Always a Bridesmaid, Never a Groom* (comedy album)

Don't put yourself on a platter. What are you—a roast duck, everything removable with a lousy piece of flatware? Be secret. Turn over on your side. Let them guess if you're stuffed. That's how I got where I am.
—GRACE PALEY, *Just As I Thought*, 1998

Within me I would be the mistress; outside, if necessary, a slave. I would knit my world together, make contact with the outside world, write the right kinds of letters, and be as I thought appropriate to different people.
—YAËL DAYAN, *New Face in the Mirror*, 1959

You lose in the end unless you know how the wheel is fixed or can fix it yourself.
—EDNA FERBER, *Saratoga Trunk*, 1941

Rosiness is not a worse windowpane than gloomy gray when viewing the world.
—GRACE PALEY, *Enormous Changes at the Last Minute*, 1960

I've got a lot of patience, baby
And that's a lot of patience to lose.
—LAURA NYRO, "When I Was a Freeport," 1971

Happy the man who accepts in patience all that God ordains for him or for his children.
—GLÜCKEL OF HAMELN, *Memoirs*, 1692

Like a bird in the butcher's palm you flutter in my hand, insolent pride.
—RACHEL, "Revolt," *Poems from the Hebrew*, 1973

Although a beautiful shock of golden hair swings across her forehead
And love finds nourishment in her eyes
The chaste Susannah never strays from the right path
And harbors not one thought without the Lord.
—DEVORAH ASCARELLI, *Written Out of History*
by Sondra Henry & Emily Taitz, 1990

They sicken of the calm, who knew the storm.
—DOROTHY PARKER, "Fair Weather," *Sunset Gun*, 1928

Pass from one end to the other, batter the air with your magnificent strokes, and listen, since no other noise is heard, to nothing but the sound of your own hoarse trumpet!
—SARAH COPIA SULLAM, "Letter to Baldassar Bonfaccio"
(Venice, 1621), *A Treasury of Jewish Letters*, 1953

Only when human sorrows are turned into a toy with glaring colors will baby people become interested—for a while at least. The people are a very fickle baby that must have new toys every day.
                          —EMMA GOLDMAN, *Anarchism and Other Essays*, 1911

On my surface...there must be no sign showing, no seam—a perfect surface.
                —JOANNE GREENBERG, *I Never Promised You a Rose Garden*, 1964

She found it difficult to make decisions but attributed this to being ambidextrous.
                          —GLORIA DEVIDAS KIRCHHEIMER, *Goodbye, Evil Eye*, 2000

A little thing indeed is a sweetly smelling sacrifice.
                          —JUDITH, Book of Judith, c. 150 B.C.E., Bible

Sitting in America and talking about hard work is easier than doing the work. To deny oneself various comforts is also easier in talk than in deed.
                          —GOLDA MEIR in *Golda Meir*, Syrkin, 1964

There are events without which one's life becomes unimportant, a worthless toy; and there are times when one is commanded to do something, even at the price of one's life.
                          —HANNAH SENESH, *Hannah Senesh*, 1966

"There are only two kinds of people in the world that really count. One kind's wheat and the other kind's emeralds."
                          —EDNA FERBER, *So Big*, 1924

If I am to be one with my people, I must go back to the roots of my people, and be sprouted forth again. I cannot praise one thing, teach one thing, and practice another.… I cannot act a lie in the privacy of my own room.

—JESSIE SAMPTER, *The Speaking Heart* (unpub. autobio.)

To put it rather bluntly, I am not the type who wants to go back to the land; I am the type who wants to go back to the hotel.

—FRAN LEBOWITZ, *Social Studies*, 1981

It is easier to betray than to remain loyal. It takes far less courage to kill yourself than it takes to make yourself wake up one more time. It's harder to stay where you are than to get out. (For everyone but you, that is.)

—JUDITH ROSSNER, *Nine Months in the Life of an Old Maid*, 1969

A lie was something that didn't happen but might just as well have.

—JUDITH ROSSNER, *Looking for Mr. Goodbar*, 1975

Of course, it is easy to turn your eyes from what is happening if it is not happening to *you*. Or if you have not put yourself where it is happening.

—SUSAN SONTAG in *New York Times Magazine*, 2 May 1999

The freakish is no longer a private zone, difficult of access. People who are bizarre, in sexual disgrace, emotionally violent are seen daily on the newsstands, on TV, in the subways. Hobbesian man roams the streets, quite visible, with glitter in his hair.

—SUSAN SONTAG, *On Photography*, 1977

She did not know then that the price of allowing false opinions was the gradual loss of one's capacity for forming true ones.

—MURIEL SPARK, "Bang-Bang You're Dead," *Collected Stories: I*, 1968

CULTURES, NATIONALITY & IMMIGRANTS

(*also see* Nations & the World *and* Society & Social Classes)

The recognition of difference is part of the very appreciation of life.
—MARCIA FALK, *The Book of Blessings*, 1996

The trouble with us [children of immigrants] is that the ghetto of the Middle Ages and the children of the twentieth century have to live under one roof.
—ANZIA YEZIERSKA, "The Fat of the Land," *Hungry Hearts* and *Other Stories*, 1920

He was a Nyasa with a face so black that the blackness was an inverted dazzle—you couldn't see what he was thinking.
—NADINE GORDIMER, "The Pet," *Not for Publication and Other Stories*, 1965

Black people cannot and will not become integrated into American society on any terms but those of self-determination and autonomy.
—GERDA LERNER, *Black Women in White America*, 1972

Black women...are trained from childhood to become workers, and expect to be financially self-supporting for most of their lives. They know they will have to work, whether they are married or single; work to them, unlike to white women, is not a liberating goal, but rather an imposed lifelong necessity.
—GERDA LERNER, *Black Women in White America*, 1972

...the Negroes whose black faces dotted the boards of the Southern wharves as thickly as grace notes sprinkle a bar of lively music.
—EDNA FERBER, *Show Boat*, 1926

We in the West...should be careful of judging whole societies that have survived an epoch when to act morally often involved not only the risk of death, but also the risk of torture.

—EVA HOFFMAN, *Exit Into History*, 1993

I am suspicious—first of all, in myself—of adopted mysticisms of glib spirituality, above all of white people's tendency to...vampirize American Indian, or African, or Asian, or other "exotic" ways of understanding.

—ADRIENNE RICH, *What Is Found There*, 1993

It had no definite expression. It was not in their bearing; it could not be said to look out from the dead, black, Indian eye, nor was it anywhere about the immobile, parchment face. Yet somewhere black implacable resentment smoldered in the heart of this dying race.

—EDNA FERBER, *Cimarron*, 1929

Out they pour, the little hyphenated Americans, more conscious of their patriotism than perhaps any other large group of children, unaware that to some of us they carry on their shoulders our hopes of a finer, more democratic America, when their old-world traditions shall be mingled with the best that lies in our new-world ideals. They bring a hope that a better relationship—even the great brotherhood—is not impossible, and that through living love and understanding we shall come to know the shame of prejudice.

—LILLIAN D. WALD, *The House on Henry Street*, 1915

Give me your tired, your poor,
Your huddled masses yearning to breathe free,
The wretched refuse of your teeming shore,
Send these, the homeless, tempest-tossed to me,
I lift my lamp beside the golden door!

—EMMA LAZARUS, "The New Colossus," c. 1886

So at last I was going to America! Really, really going, at last! The boundaries burst. The arch of heaven soared. A million suns shone out of every star. The winds rushed out into outer space, roaring in my ears, "America! America!"

—MARY ANTIN, *The Promised Land*, 1912

[I remember my passage to America] as six days of weeping, seasickness and fear. No matter what I tried to say and act, deep inside I was mourning. It was a tearing out, a violent uprooting, a voyage of death.

—GERDA LERNER, *A Death of One's Own*, 1978

I saw America—a big idea—a deathless hope—a world still in the making. I saw that it was the glory of America that it was not yet finished. And I, the last comer, had her share to give, small or great, to the making of America, like those Pilgrims who came in the *Mayflower*.

—ANZIA YEZIERSKA, "America and I" (1923),
The Journey Home by Joyce Antler, 1997

What prayers were in this temple offered up,
Wrung from sad hearts that knew no joy on earth,
By these lone exiles of a thousand years,
From the fair sunrise land that gave them birth!

—EMMA LAZARUS, "In the Jewish Synagogue at Newport"
(27 July 1867), *Emma Lazarus*, 1982

Without comprehension, the immigrant would forever remain shut—a stranger in America. Until America can release the heart as well as train the hand of the immigrant, he would forever remain driven back upon himself, corroded by the very richness of the unused gifts within his soul.

—ANZIA YEZIERSKA, "How I Found America,"
Hungry Hearts and Other Stories, 1920

Steadily as I worked to win America, America advanced to lie at my feet.... I was a princess waiting to be led to the throne.

—MARY ANTIN, *The Promised Land*, 1912

DEATH & GRIEF

Excuse my dust.

—DOROTHY PARKER, "Epitaph,"

~

If I perish, I perish.

—ESTHER, Book of Esther, c. 199–150 B.C.E., Bible

~

I hope to die at my post; on the street, or in prison.

—ROSA LUXEMBURG, Letter to Sonia Liebnicht [wife of Karl Liebnicht (1871–1919), German journalist and politician]

~

I shall put on my dead face with a silence free
Of joy and of pain forevermore,
And dawn will trail like a child after me
To play with shells on the shore.

—YOCHEVED BAT-MIRIAM, "Parting," *Poems from the Hebrew*, 1973

~

In the moment before I crossed over, I knew that the priests and magicians of Egypt were fools and charlatans for promising to prolong the beauties of life beyond the world we are given. Death is no enemy, but the foundation of gratitude, sympathy, and art. Of all life's pleasures, only love owes no debt to death.

—ANITA DIAMANT, *The Red Tent*, 1997

Death not merely ends life, it also bestows upon it a silent completeness, snatched from the hazardous flux to which all things human are subject.
—HANNAH ARENDT, *The Life of the Mind*, 1978

For we must needs die, and are as water spilt on the ground, which cannot be gathered up again.
—WOMAN OF TEKOA, Book of 2 Samuel, c. 550 B.C.E., Bible

It's a terrible thing to die young. Still, it saves a lot of time.
—GRACE PALEY, *Just As I Thought*, 1998

An old lady was asked to come to the funeral of her next-door neighbor and she answered, "Why should I go to her funeral? She won't come to mine."
—MOLLY PICON, *Molly!*, 1980

"Are graves breath-space for longing?"
—NELLY SACHS, *The Seeker and Other Poems*, 1970

Do you realize the planning that goes into a death? Probably even more than goes into a marriage. This, after all, really is for eternity.
—GAIL PARENT, *Sheila Levine Is Dead and Living in New York*, 1972

It happens that in the several seconds before we die, the well of the ribs opens, and a crystal pebble is thrown in; then there is a distant tiny splash, no more than the chirp of a droplet. This seeming pebble is the earthly equal of what astrophysicists call a black hole—a dead sun that has collapsed into itself, shrinking from density to deeper density, until it is smaller than the period at the end of this sentence.
—CYNTHIA OZICK, *The Puttermesser Papers*, 1997

Better to die—to rest in shadows folded,
Than thus to grope amid the depths in vain!
> —RAHEL MORPURGO, "And here also I have done nothing…"
> (a.k.a. "The Dark Valley"; 1867), *The Harp of Rachel*, 1890

———

Dying seems less sad than having lived too little.
> —GLORIA STEINEM, *Outrageous Acts and Everyday Rebellions*, 1983

———

And when I die
and when I'm gone
there'll be one child born
and a world to carry on…
> —LAURA NYRO, "And When I Die," 1966

———

I had to make the choice of how I was going to die. Once you've faced that, it's
there for the rest of your life.
> —GERDA LERNER, *A Death of One's Own*, 1978

———

Malach homowes [Angel of Death],…what signal did you follow when, although
conscious of your eternal and universal triumph, you yielded for a while? Is
there still a mission for me to perform, which accomplished, shall complete the
significance of my life? If so I shall rally and seek strength for it and pull myself
together to accomplish whatever is commanded.
> —BERTHA PAPPENHEIM, "Prayers, III," Stephanie Forchheimer, tr., 1946

———

*When two of their sons died on Sabbath, Beruriah did not inform Meir [her husband]
of their children's death upon his return from the academy in order not to grieve him
on the Sabbath! Only after the Havdalah prayer did she broach the matter, saying:
Some time ago a certain man came and left something in my trust; now he has
called for it. Shall I return it to him or not? Naturally Meir replied in the affir-
mative, whereupon Beruriah showed him their dead children. When Meir began to*

weep, she asked: Did you not tell me that we must give back what is given on trust? The Lord gave, and the Lord has taken away.

—BERURIAH in *The Status of Women in Formative Judaism* by Leonard Swidler, 2001

A man may hoard his honors and his gold until the very last, and then comes bitter Death to make all forgotten; his honors and his gold are of no avail.

—GLÜCKEL OF HAMELN, *Memoirs*, 1692

Take off your shoes as by the burning bush,
Before the mystery of death and God.

—EMMA LAZARUS, "In the Jewish Synagogue at Newport," *Emma Lazarus*, 1982

It is so hard for us little human beings to accept this deal that we get. It's really crazy, isn't it? We get to live, then we have to die. What we put into every moment is all we have. You can drug yourself to death or you can smoke yourself to death or eat yourself to death, or you can do everything right and be healthy and then get hit by a car. Life is so great, such a neat thing, and yet all during it we have to face death, which can make you nuts and depressed.

—GILDA RADNER, *It's Always Something*, 1989

I tease and laugh at death, so that it won't get the better of me.

—FRIDA KAHLO in *Frida*, Herrera, 1983

Death is only a physical separation, while love and remembrance are a spiritual union.

—ITKA FRAJMAN ZYGMUNTOWICZ, "Survival and Memory," *Four Centuries*, 1992

"Well, that's what they want, to be dead. I mean, that's why alls they ever do is talk about heaven, the place you go to find lasting peace after everything's dead. Like that's the greatest place you could ever be."

—ROSEANNE BARR, *My Life as a Woman*, 1989

Dying, even agonized dying, generates its own amnesia.
                              —CYNTHIA OZICK, *The Puttermesser Papers*, 1997

"I reckon there's nothing worse than waking up dead one morning, full of regrets."
                                        —SUE MARGOLIS, *Spin Cycle*, 2001

This quality of grief
could bring down
mankind.
                —ROBIN MORGAN, "On the Watergate Women," *Monster*, 1972

Unless grief submits itself to laws and customs, it is wild, uncouth, unhuman, and yet the very customs that restrain, permit and suggest a full expression of the otherwise impotent feeling that takes possession of one—to do something, something more than weep and lament, that will give evidence of the sorrow and sadness pent up within.
                      —HENRIETTA SZOLD in *Lost Love*, Shargel, 1997

There must be a limit to our grief. Yes, it is life affirming to allow ourselves to feel—to feel pain. But it is anti-life to mourn without limit—to consume one's life in sadness.
          —RABBI SHIRA MILGROM, Sermon, "Yom Kippur 5749," *Four Centuries*, 1992

It's a hard thing to mourn someone you love. But a harder thing still, I think, to sit *shivah* for the living.
          —CAROL K. HOWELL, "Tornado Watch Cookbook," *Shaking Eve's Tree*, 1990

When we think of loss we think of the loss, through death, of people we love. But loss is a far more encompassing theme in our life. For we lose not only through death, but also by leaving and being left, by changing and letting go and moving on. And our losses include not only our separations and departures from those we love, but our conscious and unconscious losses of romantic dreams, impossible expectations, illusions of freedom and power, illusions of safety—and the loss of our own younger self, the self that thought it would always be unwrinkled and invulnerable and immortal.

—JUDITH VIORST, *Necessary Losses*, 1986

To see those suffer whom one holds dearer than oneself is to realize the terrible isolation of the human soul.

—HENRIETTA SZOLD in *Lost Love*, Shargel, 1997

No event in this troubled life brings us nearer to our God than the taking away from us of those so loved & cherished.

—REBECCA GRATZ, "Letter to Miriam Moses Cohen," *Four Centuries*, 1992

I was never one to leave anything. I had trouble parting with our old '78 Buick.

—FRAN DRESCHER, *Cancer, Schmancer*, 2002

Razors pain you
Rivers are damp;
Acids stain you;
And drugs cause cramp.
Guns aren't lawful;
Nooses give;
Gas smells awful;
You might as well live.

—DOROTHY PARKER, "Resumé," *Enough Rope*, 1926

If you are of the opinion that the contemplation of suicide is sufficient evidence of a poetic nature, do not forget that actions speak louder than words.

—FRAN LEBOWITZ, *Metropolitan Life*, 1978

Not to be, to be gone—I pray for this.
At the gates of infinity, like a fey child.
—YOCHEVED BAT-MIRIAM, "Distance Spills Itself," *Poems from the Hebrew*, 1973

For those who live neither with religious consolations about death nor with a sense of death (or of anything else) as natural, death is the obscene mystery, the ultimate affront, the thing that cannot be controlled. It can only be denied.
—SUSAN SONTAG, *Illness as Metaphor*, 1978

Once her dying got underway, Anna could not really complain about how the process moved along.
—MERRILL JOAN GERBER, *Anna in the Afterlife*, 2002

Not suffer? What would be left if she didn't have suffering?
—MERRILL JOAN GERBER, *Anna in the Afterlife*, 2002

Life was always life—this trip to death was just more of it.
—MERRILL JOAN GERBER, *Anna in the Afterlife*, 2002

If I had my life over again I should form the habit of nightly composing myself to thoughts of death. I would practise, as it were, the remembrance of death. There is no other practise which so intensifies life. Death, when it approaches, ought not to take one by surprise. It should be part of the full expectancy of life. Without an ever-present sense of death life is insipid. You might as well live on the whites of eggs.
—MURIEL SPARK, *Memento Mori*, 1959

EDUCATION & SCHOOLS

(*also see* Intelligence, Memory & the Mind)

"Hi, teach!"

—BEL KAUFMAN, *Up the Down Staircase*, 1964

〜

I could undertake to be an efficient pupil if it were possible to find an efficient teacher.

—GERTRUDE STEIN, "Adele," *Q.E.D.*, 1903

〜

Outside the doors of study…an angel waits.

—JOANNE GREENBERG, *I Never Promised You a Rose Garden*, 1964

〜

I was fed on dreams, instructed by means of prophecies, trained to hear and see mystical things that callous senses could not perceive. I was taught to call myself a princess, in memory of my forefathers who had ruled a nation…. God needed me and I needed Him, for we two together had a work to do, according to an ancient covenant between him and my forefathers.

—MARY ANTIN, *The Promised Land*, 1912

〜

There is as much to learn from standing on the sidelines watching the other swimmers as there is being right in there, paddling away. It's just another perspective.

—ELAINE BERNSTEIN PARTNOW, *Breaking the Age Barrier*, 1981

〜

In school books, the Dick and Jane syndrome reinforced our emerging attitudes. The arithmetic books posed appropriate conundrums: "Ann has three pies...Dan has three rockets...." We read the nuances between the lines: Ann keeps her eye on the oven; Dan sets his sights on the moon.

—LETTY COTTIN POGREBIN, "Down with Sexist Upbringing,"
The First Ms. Reader, 1972

—

Not too soon and not too late; the secret of education lies in choosing the right time to do things.

—NATALIA GINZBURG, *Little Virtues,* 1985

—

I have always regarded the development of the individual as the only legitimate goal of education.

—SUSAN JACOBY, *Inside Soviet Schools,* 1974

—

I don't love studying. I hate studying. I like learning. Learning is beautiful.

—NATALIE PORTMAN, *Interview* magazine, March 1996

—

I'm going to college. I don't care if it ruins my career. I'd rather be smart than a movie star.

—NATALIE PORTMAN, *USA Today,* November 1994

—

A government's responsibility to its young citizens does not magically begin at the age of six. It makes more sense to extend the free universal school system downward—with the necessary reforms and community control that child care should have from the start.

—GLORIA STEINEM in Ms., April 1974

—

As a country, we have to get serious about education as a keystone of our economy and society. In the past the labor market had much greater diversity. You could drop out of high school and still get a decent-paying job in an auto plant or some other kind of blue-collar work. Those jobs today are few and far between.

—SHOSHANA ZUBOFF in *Omni,* April 1991

His most precious gift, if foreign born, is the absence of class distinction in the public school—the stronghold of democracy.

—LILLIAN D. WALD, *The House on Henry Street*, 1915

The state recognizes its responsibility for the development of citizens. To meet this responsibility, the school is its most efficient agency.

—LILLIAN D. WALD, *The House on Henry Street*, 1915

There is enormous opposition from the religious right, once again on the grounds that to educate young people about sex is immoral. Actually, if we stop to think about it, what is immoral is *not* to educate young people about sex.

—RIANE EISLER, *Sacred Pleasure*, 1995

Educational opportunity for all citizens is as much an article of social faith in the Soviet Union as it is in the United States. Everyone believes in education: party leaders, intellectuals, factory workers, farm laborers. The Soviets have much more faith than Americans in the ability of public institutions to transform their lives; schools—not Marxist-Leninist theory—are seen by parents as the key to a better future for their children.

—SUSAN JACOBY, *Inside Soviet Schools*, 1974

When it comes to education, we don't know how to count what really counts.

—SUSAN PARTNOW, Remark to Editor, 27 October 2000

What are we educating women for? To raise this question is to face the whole problem of women's role in society. We are uncertain about the end of women's education precisely because the status of women in our country is fraught with contradictions and confusion.

—MIRRA KOMAROVSKY, *Women in the Modern World*, 1953

Since every effort in our educational life seems to be directed toward making of the child a being foreign to itself, it must of necessity produce individuals foreign to one another, and in everlasting antagonism with each other.

—EMMA GOLDMAN, *Red Emma Speaks*, 1972

That we have not made any respectable attempt to meet the special educational needs of women in the past is the clearest possible evidence of the fact that our educational objectives have been geared exclusively to the vocational patterns of men.

—BETTY FRIEDAN, *The Feminine Mystique*, 1963

What we must remember above all in the education of our children is that their love of life should never weaken.

—NATALIA GINZBURG, *Little Virtues*, 1985

Partnership education helps students look beyond conventional social categories, such as capitalism versus communism, right versus left, religious versus secular, and even industrial versus preindustrial or postindustrial. They can instead begin to focus on relationships, and on the underlying question of what kinds of beliefs and social structures support or inhibit relations of violence or nonviolence, democracy or authoritarianism, justice or injustice, caring or cruelty, environmental sustainability or collapse.

—RIANE EISLER, *Tomorrow's Children*, 2000

A girl was "finished" when she could read her prayers in Hebrew, following the meaning by the aid of the Yiddish translation especially prepared for women. If she could sign her name in Russian, do a little figuring, and write a letter in Yiddish to the parents of her betrothed, she was called *wohl gelehrent*—well educated.

—MARY ANTIN, *The Promised Land*, 1912

A compulsory universal University education, which means the thorough education of the head, hand and heart of *every individual* human being, can be the only developer of the real divinity in man, of the altruism which can make earth beautiful with its glow.

—MINNIE D. LOUIS in *American Hebrew*, 28 June 1895

Education is not a product: mark, diploma, job, money—in that order; it is a process, a never-ending one.

—BEL KAUFMAN, *Up the Down Staircase*, 1964

The world could maybe come to an end on next Tuesday.
The ceiling could maybe come crashing on my head.
I maybe could run out of things for me to worry about.
And then I'd have to do my homework instead.

—JUDITH VIORST, "Fifteen, Maybe Sixteen Things to Worry About,"
If I Were in Charge of the World and Other Worries..., 1981

I knew Bella would be a success because she always did her homework and practiced her violin.

—ESTHER SAVITSKY [Bella Abzug's mother],
Quoted in *Bella Abzug* by Doris Faber, 1976

School should be from the beginning the first battle which a child fights for himself, without us; from the beginning it should be clear that this is his battlefield and that we can give him only very slight and occasional help there. And if he suffers from injustice there or is misunderstood it is necessary to let him see that there is nothing strange about this, because in life we have to expect to be constantly misunderstood and misinterpreted, and to be victims of injustice; and the only thing that matters is that we do not commit injustices ourselves.

—NATALIA GINZBURG, *Little Virtues*, 1985

The legal answer
to the problem of feeding children
is ten free lunches every month,

being equal, in the child's real life,
to eating lunch every other day.
　　—SUSAN GRIFFIN, "I Like to Think of Harriet Tubman," *Like the Iris of an Eye*, 1976

—

Take your children to the Religious School at a very early age. Select for them
a teacher who loves little ones and who loves God. What do these babies care
about Adam and Eve, or the order of creation? Introduce them to the wonders
of plant and animal life. *Show them God* in the bursting seed, in the budding
flower, in the bird-producing egg, the glorious sunshine. Let them see God and
learn to love Him for His blessings in which they share. Let them be made to
feel that God means protection, that to Him they owe love and respect and
gratitude and loyalty. Make God the starting point and the goal. Love of God,
confidence in God, fear, not of God, but of His disapproval, these are the steps
by which to develop the feeling of moral obligation, first to the world, then to
Judaism.
　　　　　　　　　　　　　—JULIA RICHMAN, NCJW Proceedings, 1896

—

Keep our boys and girls, more especially our boys, in the Religious Schools until
they are full-grown in soul as well as stature.
　　　　　　　　　　　　　—JULIA RICHMAN, NCJW Proceedings, 1896

—

I was a fantastic student until ten, and then my mind began to wander.
　　　　　　　　　　　　　—GRACE PALEY in *Ms.*, March 1974

—

I had very good marks [at the yeshiva], but my conduct was always poor. I was
so impatient. I'd sit there holding up my hand and when the teacher ignored
me, I'd talk anyway. We'd study the Bible and I had questions: why, why, why?
It didn't go over well.
　　　　　　—BARBRA STREISAND in *Streisand: Her Life* by James Spada, 1995

—

Everyone is your teacher.
　　　　　　　　—ELAINE BERNSTEIN PARTNOW, *Hear Us Roar*, 1988

Good teachers, like Tolstoy's happy families, are alike everywhere.
—BEL KAUFMAN, *Up the Down Staircase*, 1964

"If I can teach you something, it may mean that I can count at least some-where."
—JOANNE GREENBERG, *I Never Promised You a Rose Garden*, 1964

I feel nourished by teaching. I have a great sense of vocation about teaching.
—RUTH WEISBERG in *Exposures*, Brown, 1989

Heritage. How have we come from the savages, now no longer to be savages—this to teach. To look back and learn what humanizes man—this to teach. To smash all ghettos that divide us—not to go back, not to go back—this to teach.
—TILLIE OLSEN, "Tell Me a Riddle," *Tell Me a Riddle*, 1960

To me education is a leading out of what is already there in the pupil's soul. To Miss Mackay it is a putting in of something that is not there, and that is not what I call education, I call it intrusion.
—MURIEL SPARK, *The Prime of Miss Jean Brodie*, 1961

First teach a person to develop to the point of his limitations and then—pfft!—break the limitation.
—VIOLA SPOLIN in *Los Angeles Times*, 26 May 1974

FAITH, RELIGION, THE BIBLE & SPIRITUALITY

(*also see* God *and* Jews & Judaism)

Blessed is the flame that set hearts on fire.

Blessed are the hearts that knew how to die with honor,

Blessed is the match that burned, and kindled flames.

—MARGE PIERCY, "Blessed is the Match"

The soul has a different age from that recorded in the register of births and deaths. At your birth, the soul already has an age that never changes. One can be born with a 12-year-old soul. One can also be born with a thousand-year-old soul...I believe the soul is that part of man that he is least aware of.

—ETTY HILLESUM, *An Interrupted Life*, 1983

Beliefs and convictions reach out from the past, and they cannot be altered by fervent desire alone. They possess their own logic and illogic, their own organic existence, their own rhythm of development.

—RAISA DAVYDOVNA ORLOVA, *Memoirs*, 1983

I always found myself more drawn to each religious milieu than I would have anticipated, but in time, a ghoulish threat of being absorbed in alien territory always sent me retreating to the blander and safer ground of home.

—VANESSA L. OCHS, *Words on Fire*, 1999

The best thing for you, my children, is to serve God from your heart without falsehood or deception, not giving out to people that you are one thing while, God forbid, in your heart you are another. Say your prayers with awe and devotion.

—GLÜCKEL OF HAMELN, *Memoirs*, 1692

It is hard to think of conversion as a blinding light on the road to Damascus, or as a highly spiritual or intellectual process, when the light comes from a flickering television; the voice of the deity is Bishop Sheen.... I was troubled at a young age by the idea that pouring water over someone's head could change his relationship to God.

—SUSAN JACOBY, *Half Jew*, 2000

True piety was simple, direct, and earnest. It involved opening one's heart to God and singing God's praises and recognizing that, while moral laws are from God, external forms of worship (i.e., religious ceremonies and observances) are human creations that must be altered to "suit the times" if they are to retain their meaning.

—RAY FRANK in *Ray Frank Litman: A Memoir* by Simon Litman (her husband), 1957

I have engaged in building my own belief structure step by step. They are poems written on the road to an imagined destination of faith. That imagination of faith acts as yeast in my life as a writer: in that sense I do experience "faith that *works*" as well as "work that enfaiths."

—DENISE LEVERTOV, "Work That Enfaiths," *New and Selected Essays*, 1992

I'm not going to have any Bibles in my school. That surprise you all? It's the only book in the world but it's just for grown people, after you know it don't mean what it says.

—LILLIAN HELLMAN, *Another Part of the Forest*, 1946

Even if you don't believe a word of the Bible, you've got to respect the person who typed all that!

—LOTUS WEINSTOCK, Stand-up routine

Deborah became to me not a prophetess but a great political emancipator. Mother Sarah stood for the single standard of wife and mother in the home.

—REBEKAH BETTELHEIM KOHUT, *My Portion: An Autobiography*, 1927

In truth, I think that we should make contact with the supernatural in silence and in a profound and lonely meditation.
—CLARICE LISPECTOR, Profile by Rachel Gutierrez, Carla Sherman, tr., http://www.vidaslusofonas.pt (Lives of the Portuguese-Speaking World), 2000

—

Anyway, what is the soul
But a dream of itself?
—ALICIA SUSKIN OSTRIKER, "Message from the Sleeper at Hell's Mouth,"
A Woman Under the Surface, 1982

—

My proposals, or should I say requirements,
Include at least one image of a god,
Virile, beard optional, one of a goddess
Nubile, breast size approximating mine,
One divine baby, one lion, one lamb,
All nude as figs, all dancing wildly...
—ALICIA SUSKIN OSTRIKER, "Everywoman Her Own Theology,"
The Little Space, 1998

—

baby, there is no
god but
they'll kill you
for him.

—DAPHNE GOTTLIEB, "the jewish atheist mother has her say,"
in toto, Why Things Burn, 2001

—

It must be Sunday
Everybody's telling the truth....
—PHOEBE SNOW, "It must be Sunday," Phoebe Snow, 1973

—

We will certainly be amazed that our most famous story of human origins, the Genesis story of Adam and Eve, has absolutely nothing good to say about sex, love or pleasure, that it presents the human quest for higher consciousness as a curse rather than a blessing, and that it does not even touch on the awe and wonder we humans experience when we behold or touch someone we love.

—RIANE EISLER, *Sacred Pleasure*, 1995

Something went terribly wrong with Christianity's original gospel of love. How otherwise could such a gospel be used to justify all the torture, conquest, and bloodletting carried out by devout Christians against others, and against one another, that makes up so much of our Western history?

—RIANE EISLER, *The Chalice and the Blade*, 1987

Clergy are father figures to many women, and sometimes they are threatened by another woman accomplishing what they see as strictly male goals. But I can see them replacing that feeling with a sense of pride that women can have that role.

—RABBI SALLY PRIESAND, *Women at Work* by Betty Medsger, 1975

Opening the synagogue to more diverse populations, creating sermons and texts that include women, and empowering congregants, women clergy are bringing a new openness and excitement to religious practice.

—JOYCE ANTLER, *The Journey Home*, 1997

Cloister existence is one of unbroken sameness for all.... The rumor of the outside world dies away at the heavy cloister gate.

—SARAH BERNHARDT, *Memories of My Life*, 1907

This reclamation of divinity for Mary is particularly important, since we obviously need to leave behind the idealization of a family in which only the father and the son, and not the mother, are divine. In fact, we also need to add to the pantheon of a holy family a divine daughter.

—RIANE EISLER, *Sacred Pleasure*, 1995

Social Service...can not be a substitute for religion.
—REBEKAH BETTELHEIM KOHUT, *American Hebrew*, 31 December 1897

From the beginning, she sought knowledge; perceive, it does not say wisdom, but knowledge; and this was at the expense of an Eden. She lost Eden, but she gained that wisdom which has made sure of man's immortality.
—RAY FRANK, "Woman in the Synagogue,"
Papers of the Jewish Women's Congress, 5 September 1893

I have just enough faith to believe it exists.
—DENISE LEVERTOV, "Work That Enfaiths," *New and Selected Essays*, 1992

I weep not now as once I wept
At Fortune's stroke severe;
Since faith hath to my bosom crept,
    And placed her buckler there.
—PENINA MOÏSE, *Hymnal of Penina Moïse*, 1856

I learned of Faith by touching earth, I learned of faith by listening to breath move through me.... The faith I found was in my own body as spiritual truth, and my felt "thought" or symbol creation has me imaging my own body as goddess, as earth, as shechinah.
—FANCHON SHUR, "My Dance Work as a Reflection of a
Jewish Woman's Spirituality," *Four Centuries*, 1992

It's an incredible con job when you think about it, to believe something now in exchange for something after death. Even corporations with their reward systems don't try to make it posthumous.
—GLORIA STEINEM, *Revolution from Within*, 1992

Heaven must be an awfully dull place if the poor in spirit live there.
—EMMA GOLDMAN, *Red Emma Speaks*, 1972

I was born from love
and my poor mother worked the mines
I was raised on the good book Jesus
till I read between the lines...

—LAURA NYRO, "Stoney End," 1966

The Vatican came down with a new ruling. They said no surrogate mothers...A good thing they didn't make this rule before Jesus was born.

—ELAYNE BOOSLER, Stand-up routine

"And why shouldn't a girl be the Messiah?"

—JESSIE SAMPTER, *In the Beginning* (unpub. novel)

That was one of the things she held against the missionaries: how they stressed Christ's submission to humiliation, and so had conditioned the people of Africa to humiliation by the white man.

—NADINE GORDIMER, "Not for Publication,"
Not for Publication and Other Stories, 1965

Moses supposes his toeses are roses
But Moses supposes erroneously.

—BETTY COMDEN, "Elocution," with Adolph Green, *Singin' in the Rain*, 1952

"Paradise is only for those who have already been there."

—CYNTHIA OZICK, "Envy; or, Yiddish in America,"
The Pagan Rabbi and Other Stories, 1971

Paradise is a dream bearing the inscription on Solomon's seal: *This, too, will pass.*

—CYNTHIA OZICK, *The Puttermesser Papers*, 1997

Even Paradise was not complete without a woman, and no paradise on earth can be perfectly complete unless we have men and women.
—HANNAH GREENEBAUM SOLOMON, Speech, NCJW Proceedings, 1896

When I still used to say prayers, even as a child, after the "Now I lay me down to sleep" and the Sh'ma Yisrael—I would pray for a "boy to like me best" and a "*work* of my own to do" when I grew up. I did not want to be discontented like my mother was.
—BETTY FRIEDAN in *The Journey* by Joyce Antler, 1997

For prayer is the language of the heart,—needing no measured voice, no spoken tone.
—GRACE AGUILAR, *The Spirit of Judaism*, 1842

What prayers were in this temple offered up,
Wrung from sad hearts that knew no joy on earth,
By these lone exiles of a thousand years,
From the fair sunrise land that gave them birth!
—EMMA LAZARUS, "In the Jewish Synagogue at Newport"
(27 July 1867), *Emma Lazarus*, 1982

To the women who have been the creators I commend the task of becoming preachers and prophets.
—HENRIETTA SZOLD, Address, Women's Day (Tel Aviv), 31 May 1934

But when the Lord said unto Moses, "And ye shall be unto Me a nation of priests and a holy nation," the message was not to one sex; and that the Israelites did not so consider it, is proved by the number of women who were acknowledged prophets, and who exercised great influence on their time and on posterity.
—RAY FRANK, Address, "Woman in the Synagogue," 5 September 1893

Actually, I have only two things to worry about now: afterlife and reincarnation.
—GAIL PARENT, *Sheila Levine Is Dead and Living in New York*, 1972

"Not everybody feels religion the same way. Some it's in their mouth, but some it's like a hope in their blood, their bones."
—TILLIE OLSEN, "O Yes," *Tell Me a Riddle*, 1960

To make your spiritual yearning public, I thought, was to announce that you were wounded. To turn deeply into religion was to admit that your own resources were so weak you had to resort to magic and miracle cures for healing. To acquire faith was to mobilize the powers of an overly active imagination.
—VANESSA L. OCHS, *Words on Fire*, 1999

Religion, like water, may be free, but when they pipe it to you, you've got to help pay for the piping. And the piper!
—ABIGAIL VAN BUREN, "Dear Abby" Advice Column, 28 April 1974

Organized religion has a part in the evolution of personal religion. It is the material upon which personal religion is grafted, but the process of grafting must be individual. Every human soul must, through thought, prayer, and study, cultivate his own religion to suit himself.
—LILY MONTAGU, *Lily Montagu*, 1985

Reader, you forget that economics precedes religion; worship grew out of eating, not the other way around.
—ANNE ROIPHE, *The Pursuit of Happiness*, 1991

I most want to write about: how a modern woman has sought the face of God—not the name nor the fame but the *face* of God—and what adventures came to meet her on this ancient human path.
—MARY ANTIN, *20th Century Authors*, Kunitz, 1942

The difference between our ancestors and ourselves is that they took visions and miracles as a matter of course, as proof of the existence of the supernatural. Omens exist only if you believe in them. We have lost the capacity to recognize any omen or a vision.

—SAVINA J. TEUBAL, "*Simchat Hochmah:* A Crone Ritual," *Four Centuries*, 1992

There would be no value in worship services and symbols did they not, preserved in their Purity and Beauty, serve as aids to right living.

—LILY MONTAGU, *Lily Montagu*, 1985

Religion urges us to fight evil as contrary to the Divine Law. It urges us to combat abject misery, sin and disease because God *is*. In His name we can work, as we believe in co-operation with Him, since through Him goodness must ultimately prevail.

—LILY MONTAGU, "Sermon to the Reform Synagogue, Berlin," *Lily Montagu*, 1985

My heart went out, seeking the God of my people. In thousands of homes those white candles burned tonight. I joined an invisible congregation.

—JESSIE SAMPTER, *The Speaking Heart* (unpub. autobio.)

In our days of prosperity it is more difficult to sustain a religious spirit than in times of adversity, because we are apt to forget that God who has bountifully given may also take away.

—RACHEL SIMON, *Records and Reflections*, 1894

A saint a real saint never does anything, a martyr does something but a really good saint does nothing.... Realistically speaking anybody is more interesting doing nothing than doing anything.

—GERTRUDE STEIN, *Last Operas and Plays* by Carl Van Vechten, 1949

If there's one kind of person in this world who makes other people feel miserable it's a saint.

—RABBI MARCIA TAGER, "Cousins," *Shaking Eve's Tree*, 1990

If you believe only what you see, your world will consist only of molecules and atoms, of inert matter, having little soul and meaning, you yourself will be but a moving mechanism, having neither significance nor permanency, nor connection with the central meaning of things.

—TEHILLA LICHTENSTEIN, "Believing is *Seeing*," *Four Centuries*, 1992

The grandest temples we have ever had or the world has even known were those which had the blue sky for a roof, and the grandest psalms ever sung were those rendered under the blue vaults of heaven.

—RAY FRANK in *Ray Frank Litman: A Memoir* by
Simon Litman (her husband), 1957

When my soul was in the lost-and-found
You came along to claim it.

—CAROLE KING, "A Natural Woman," *Tapestry*, 1967

The human soul is incorruptible, immortal, and divine, and infused by God into our body at that time when the organism is formed and able to receive it within the maternal womb: and this truth is so certainly, infallibly, and indubitably impressed on me, as I believe it is impressed on every Jew and Christian.

—SARAH COPIA SULLAM, Letter to Baldassar Bonfaccio (Venice, 1621),
A Treasury of Jewish Letters, 1953

My soul doth magnify the Lord, And my spirit hath rejoiced in God my Savior.

For he hath regarded the low estate of his handmaiden; for, behold, from henceforth all generations shall call me blessed.

For he that is mighty hath done to me great things; and holy is his name.

And his mercy is on them that fear him from generation to generation.

He hath shewed strength with his arm; he hath scattered the proud in the imagination of their hearts.

He hath put down the mighty from their seats, and exalted them of low degree.

He hath filled the hungry with good things; and the rich he hath sent empty away.

He hath helped his servant Israel, in remembrance of his mercy.

—VIRGIN MARY, Book of Luke, c. 65–80 C.E., New Testament

"Here's your last chance. Mary, the Virgin, is visited by the Angel. He has an announcement to make. Mary will give birth to a baby, a son, who will be the son of God."

"Gee," says Mary, "I wanted a girl."

"That's good, Mother," says my eldest, patting me.

—E. M. BRONER, "Joking Around," *Ghost Stories*, 1995

The tenacity with which for millennia of Western history both women and men have, in the figure of the Christian Virgin Mary, clung to the worship of a compassionate and merciful mother attests to the human hunger for such a reassuring image.

—RIANE EISLER, *The Chalice and the Blade*, 1987

We believe in the oneness of humanity, as all people are children of God.

—LILY MONTAGU, *Lily Montagu*, 1985

The physical is the known; through it we may find our way to the unknown, the intuitive, and perhaps beyond that to man's spirit itself.

—VIOLA SPOLIN in *Los Angeles Times*, 26 May 1974

We must admit that there is a difference between a life touched by infinity and a life limited by that which is perceived by the senses by facts provable by the human mind. We want the unprovable, we want love, truth and beauty, and we can only find these on the spiritual plane.

—LILY MONTAGU, *Lily Montagu*, 1985

Passionate concern may lead to errors of judgment, but the lack of passion in the face of human wrong leads to spiritual bankruptcy.

—JUSTINE WISE POLIER in *The Journey Home* by Joyce Antler, 1997

I think the bottom line of a spiritual journey is to be able to experience your-self as someone of real worth. And I think that's necessary for political expres-sion. I think there's so much overlap between those two realms. I'll flip it the other way: I don't really understand what political activity is about if it's not grounded in some sense of the importance of spirit in people's lives.

—MERLE FELD, "Women Who Dared," Jewish Women's Archive (http://www.jwa.org), August 2003

Have we arrived at our own faith and our own path or simply internalized the beliefs of parents, clergy, spouse, or friends?

—JOAN BORYSENKO, *A Woman's Journey to God*, 1999

Emily Dickinson wrote about faith as a fragile thing, a winged thing. Like a thin diaphanous membrane, it changes the color of the world. Under the spell of faith the ordinary shimmers. The mundane becomes miraculous. The daily sunrise and sunset are a call to celebration. The seasons in their majestic turn-ing, a succession of holy days. Every face holds the possibility of love, and strangers are just friends whom we don't yet know.

—JOAN BORYSENKO, *A Woman's Journey to God*, 1999

"Being a witch is like royalty," I said calmly. "You have to inherit it from some-one."

—JUDITH ROSSNER, *Nine Months in the Life of an Old Maid*, 1969

"Nothing infuriates people more than their own lack of spiritual insight, Sandy, that is why the Moslems are so placid, they are full of spiritual insight."
—MURIEL SPARK, *The Prime of Miss Jean Brodie*, 1961

—

I wouldn't take the Pope too seriously. He's a Pole first, a pope second, and maybe a Christian third.
—MURIEL SPARK in *International Herald Tribune*, 29 May 1989

—

Kathleen, speaking from the Catholic point of view which takes some getting used to, said, "She was at Confession only the day before she died—wasn't she lucky?"
—MURIEL SPARK, "Portobello Road," *Collected Stories: I*, 1968

FAMILY & RELATIVES

(*also see* Children; Fathers & Fatherhood; *and* Mothers & Motherhood)

My mother had eight daughters and no son; and yet never did I hear a word of regret pass the lips of either my mother or my father that one of us was not a son.
—HENRIETTA SZOLD, Letter to Haym Peretz (16 September 1916),
Henrietta Szold, Lowenthal, 1942

—

There is a curiously strong bond in Jewish families. They cling together. Jewish parents are possessive, Jewish sons and daughters are filial to the point of sentimentality.
—EDNA FERBER, *A Peculiar Treasure*, 1939

—

Every adult in the world has to tell the truth to the young, if we are to have a world at all.
—FAY KANIN in *American Women Playwrights*, Shafer, 1995

I've always had time for my children. I went home every day for lunch. When the children were small, if I worked on weekends, they came to the laboratory with me. When they were older, I took them to museums, on trips.

—ROSALYN YALOW in *Les Prix Nobel Yearbook*, Tore Frängsmyr, ed., 1977

Intreat me not to leave thee, or to return from following after thee: for whither thou goest, I will go; and where thou lodgest, I will lodge: thy people shall be my people, and thy God my God.... Where thou diest, will I die, and there will I be buried: the Lord do so to me, and more also, if ought but death part thee and me.

—RUTH, 1:16, 17, Book of Ruth, late fifth–fourth century B.C.E., Bible

The average family exists only on paper and its average budget is a fiction, invented by statisticians for the convenience of statisticians.

—SYLVIA PORTER, *Sylvia Porter's Money Book*, 1975

We must understand the difference between what we mean by family and what the Right Wing means by family.... Women are the means of production, owned by the husband. Children are the labor, owned by the husband. And that's what they mean by family. Consequently, they oppose any direct guarantee of right between wife and the law or children and the law, because that is antithetical to their definition of the family.

—GLORIA STEINEM, Speech, NWPC Conference
(Albuquerque, New Mexico), July 1981

The family is the basic cell of government.

—GLORIA STEINEM, Speech, NWPC Conference
(Albuquerque, New Mexico), July 1981

I'm not a lady, I'm your daughter.

—DOROTHY FIELDS, Remark to her father, Lew Fields, Cotton Club, Harlem, 1927

A family is a little civilization unto itself, with its own history, laws, codes, and discontents.

—CAROL K. HOWELL, "The Cutting," *River City*, Fall 1990

In my family and in others too, it sometimes seemed as if women had all the power.... They certainly ran *our* lives, and they could make life hell for our fathers. It took a new consciousness to realize that women...had to dominate the family for lack of economic and political power in the outside world.

—BETTY FRIEDAN in *New York Times Magazine*, 17 November 1978

The modern mother's dual interests in both briefcases and babies also has a significant influence on the way in which men make the transition to fatherhood.... In this intermediate area a potential space is emerging that provides an opportunity for men to be engaged in the procreation and early care of children.

—JUDITH PARTNOW HYMAN, *Becoming a Father*, 1995

[There] has been an intensive campaign for a return to "traditional family values"—the new code name for an authoritarian, male-dominated, patriarchal family designed to teach both boys and girls to obey orders from above, no matter how unjust or unloving they may be. This campaign has mainly come from fundamentalist and other religious groups who are still told by their leaders that the ranking of man over woman is divinely ordained.

—RIANE EISLER, *Sacred Pleasure*, 1995

As long as fathers rule but do not nurture, as long as mothers nurture but do not rule, the conditions favoring the development of father-daughter incest will prevail.

—JUDITH LEWIS HERMAN, *Father-Daughter Incest*, 1981

Leah grabbed her sister by the shoulders. "Better to put your trust in my hands and Jacob's than in stories made out of wind and fear."

—ANITA DIAMANT, *The Red Tent*, 1997

My childhood world was gone, but not from my heart and mind. Nothing dies as long as it is remembered and transmitted from person to person, from generation to generation. Or, as my beloved grandmother used to say, "My child, you only have what you choose to give away!"

—ITKA FRAJMAN ZYGMUNTOWICZ, "Survival and Memory," *Four Centuries*, 1992

The only life many of the leaders of the anti-family planning movement seem to care about—indeed obsess about—is life *before* birth and *after* death.

—RIANE EISLER, *Sacred Pleasure*, 1995

how sister gazed at sister
reaching through mirrored pupils
back to the mother

—ADRIENNE RICH, "Sibling Mysteries," *The Dream of a Common Language*, 1978

Parents can only give good advice or put them on the right paths, but the final forming of a person's character lies in their own hands.

—ANNE FRANK, *The Diary of a Young Girl*, 1947

Your responsibility as a parent is not as great as you might imagine. You need not supply the world with the next conqueror of disease or major motion-picture star. If your child simply grows up to be someone who does not use the word "collectible" as a noun, you can consider yourself an unqualified success.

—FRAN LEBOWITZ, *Social Studies*, 1981

a monument to love and joy,
to human worth, to faith we kept
for you, my sons, for you.

—ETHEL ROSENBERG, *Death House Letters of Ethel and Julius Rosenberg*, 1953

All they wished for her was that she should turn herself into a little replica of them.

—MIDGE DECTER, *Liberal Parents, Radical Children*, 1975

—

A child's independence is too big a risk for the shaky balance of some parents.

—JOANNE GREENBERG, *I Never Promised You a Rose Garden*, 1964

—

Lifestyles and sex roles are passed from parents to children as inexorably as blue eyes or small feet.

—LETTY COTTIN POGREBIN, "From Beijing to Tikkun Olam,"
The First Ms. Reader, 1972

—

My parents and I are very close...(*genetically*).

—WENDY LIEBMAN, http://www.wendyliebman.com, 27 January 2003

—

In [my parents'] Old World yearnings, I was a stranger who had invented myself.... [But now], for the first time, I was doing something they could understand. I was helping Jews.

—RUTH GRUBER, *Haven*, 1983

—

Re winning her featherweight championship: Tell that to my in-laws. They say, big deal, so when am I getting pregnant?

—JILL MATTHEWS in *The Complete Idiot's Guide to Jewish History and Culture*
by Rabbi Benjamin Blech, 1999

—

A bird once set out to cross a windy sea with its three fledglings. The sea was so wide and the wind so strong, the father bird was forced to carry his young, one by one, in his strong claws. When he was halfway across with the first fledgling the wind turned to a gale, and he said, "My child, look how I am struggling and risking my life in your behalf. When you are grown up, will you do as much for me and provide for my old age?" The fledgling replied, "Only bring me to safety, and when you are old I shall do everything you ask of me."

Whereat the father bird dropped his child into the sea, and it drowned, and he said, "So shall it be done to such a liar as you." Then the father bird returned to shore, set forth with his second fledgling, asked the same question, and receiving the same answer, drowned the second child with the cry, "You, too, are a liar!" Finally he set out with the third fledgling, and when he asked the same question, the third and last fledgling replied, "My dear father, it is true you are struggling mightily and risking your life in my behalf, and I shall be wrong not to repay you when you are old, but I cannot bind myself. This though I can promise: when I am grown up and have children of my own, I shall do as much for them as you have done for me." Whereupon the father bird said, "Well spoken, my child, and wisely; your life I will spare and I will carry you to shore in safety."

—GLÜCKEL OF HAMELN, *Memoirs*, 1692

Parents sighed, shrugged, lifted their eyes heavenward, asking God to witness the madness of their young, asking for the strength to bear the terrible burden of their children's lunacy.

—RABBI MARCIA TAGER, "Cousins," *Shaking Eve's Tree*, 1990

Coming out of the cocoon of child rearing back into the world and into the light I discovered that my parents had suddenly gotten old. It seemed to me that one day they were young or at least only middle-aged and now they were old.

—RABBI MARCIA TAGER, "Cousins," *Shaking Eve's Tree*, 1990

A person who cuts himself off from his people cuts himself off at the roots of his being; he becomes a shell, a cipher, a spiritual suicide.

—ANZIA YEZIERSKA in *Anzia Yezierska: A Writer's Life*
by Louise Levitas Henriksen, 1988

It is within the families themselves where peace can begin. If families can learn to respect their members, and deal with conflict resolution, that would be the first step to keeping peace on a global level.

—SUSAN PARTNOW, "Families for Peace," *Puget Sound Coop Newsletter*, Spring 1986

FASHION & SHOPPING

(*also see* Beauty & Appearance)

Brevity is the soul of lingerie.
—DOROTHY PARKER, *While Rome Burns* by Alexander Woollcott, 1934

I do not believe in God. I believe in cashmere.
—FRAN LEBOWITZ, Remark

My first words: "Can I take it back if I wore it?"
—FRAN DRESCHER, Stand-up routine

I hate fashion. I've always hated it. Fashion is an imposition, a rein on freedom.
—GOLDA MEIR, Quoted by Oriana Fallaci in *L'Eurepeo*, 1973

I think of an evening bag as what I put on top of the table—almost like a piece of jewelry, not a bag.
—DONNA KARAN, Quoted by Elsa Klensch, CNN Interactive, 7 March 1997

Taking the sensibility and the earthiness and the hand that's used in the East and connecting it to what we can do here in the West—I tried to put those two worlds together in a very sensual way.
—DONNA KARAN, Quoted by Elsa Klensch, CNN Interactive, 7 March 1997

Where's the man could ease a heart
Like a satin gown?
—DOROTHY PARKER, "The Satin Dress," *Enough Rope,* 1926

Figure out your hair and wear what you want.
                    —WENDY LIEBMAN, http://www.wendyliebman.com, 2002

Individuality in dressing is not important to men. If they all look alike it means they haven't made a mistake.
                    —RITA RUDNER, http://www.ritafunny.com, 2003

First it was Evita the woman; then came the legend; now *Evita* is a major motion picture and a fabulous fashion concept at Bloomingdale's!
                    —SANDRA BERNHARD, *May I Kiss You on the Lips, Miss Sandra?*, 1998

JUDY HOLLIDAY: I've worn strapless evening gowns since I was twelve years old.

TALLULAH BANKHEAD: Isn't twelve a little young for a strapless evening gown?

JUDY HOLLIDAY: If it stays up, you're old enough.
                    —SELMA DIAMOND in *Funny Women*, Unterbrink, 1987

Buying your own mink coat is real mass rejection.
                    —SELMA DIAMOND in *Funny Women*, Unterbrink, 1987

I base most of my fashion taste on what doesn't itch.
                    —GILDA RADNER, Remark

Yes, I'm wearing Jackie Kennedy's faux pearls, and I feel fantastic. This isn't simply any necklace; these triple strands evoke the feeling of racing through the ocean on my private yacht, the smell of manly sweat, the murmurs of someone cheating, puffs on big cigars, the laughter among men after the telling of a dirty joke.
                    —SANDRA BERNHARD, *May I Kiss You on the Lips, Miss Sandra?*, 1998

Men who have a pierced ear are better prepared for marriage. They've experienced pain and bought jewelry.

—RITA RUDNER, Stand-up routine

—

Listen, when a woman can't have diamonds, she wears rhinestones; and when she can't have rhinestones, she wears glass and holds up her head.

—JOANNE GREENBERG, "Children of Joy" (1966), *Shaking Eve's Tree*, 1990

—

Thank God we're living in a country where the sky's the limit, the stores are open late and you can shop in bed thanks to television.

—JOAN RIVERS in *International Herald Tribune*, 31 May 1989

—

Malls are insular fantasy worlds where the relatively well-off pursue the study and acquisition of superfluous goods as a form of entertainment, in a society in which millions are in desperate need of something to eat and a safe, warm place to sleep.

—LESLIE KANES WEISMAN, *Discrimination by Design*, 1992

—

I went to the mall because I love to shop...(*lift*).

—WENDY LIEBMAN, Stand-up routine

—

Fewer and fewer Americans possess objects that have a patina, old furniture, grandparents' pots and pans—the used things, warm with generations of human touch,...essential to a human landscape. Instead, we have our paper phantoms, transistorized landscapes. A featherweight portable museum.

—SUSAN SONTAG, *On Photography*, 1977

FATHERS & FATHERHOOD

(*also see* Family & Relatives *and* Mothers & Motherhood)

It wasn't just my father but the generations who made my father whose weight was still upon me.

—ANZIA YEZIERSKA, *The Bread Givers*, 1925

—

Our father is old, and there is not a man in the earth to come in unto us after the manner of all the earth; Come let us make our father drink wine, and we will lie with him, that we may preserve seed of our father.

—LOT'S DAUGHTER (the elder), Book of Genesis, c. ninth century B.C.E., Bible

—

If men started taking care of children, the job will become more valuable.

—GLORIA STEINEM in *Time*, 4 December 1989

—

The reawakened nurturance of the actively involved father whose infant is being breastfed is faced with a quandary.... He has to deal with the paradox of being more involved, as he is expected to be, while simultaneously being excluded from the most intimate contact with his new baby.

—JUDITH PARTNOW HYMAN, *Becoming a Father*, 1995

—

He told me he would never do to his son what had been done to him.

—ANNE ROIPHE, *1185 Park Avenue*, 1999

—

That is natural enough when nobody has had fathers they begin to long for them and then when everybody has had fathers they begin to long to do without them.

—GERTRUDE STEIN, *Everybody's Autobiography*, 1937

And what a world goes with a beloved father, what a big chamber is locked after he leaves us!

—HENRIETTA SZOLD in *Lost Love*, Shargel, 1997

My dad took me to Paris for the weekend. We had the most amazing time. On the plane back to London, he asked me, "Do you know why I took you to Paris—only you and me?" And I said, "Why?" And he said, "Because I wanted you to see Paris for the first time with a man who would always love you."

—GWYNETH PALTROW, Quoted by Dotson Rader, *Parade* magazine, 17 January 1999

My childhood was marvelous, because, although my father was a sick man (he had vertigos every month and a half), he was an immense example to me of tenderness, of work (photographer and also painter) and above all of understanding for all my problems.

—FRIDA KAHLO in *Frida*, Herrera, 1983

If Salvo said to Louise, "Correct me if I'm wrong," it meant that any disagreement between father and daughter would seriously undermine the very foundation of Jewish life and might well be the leading cause of heart attacks in Nassau County.

—GLORIA DEVIDAS KIRCHHEIMER, *Goodbye, Evil Eye*, 2000

[There have been] dramatic shifts in the delivery room from the total absence of the expectant father, traditionally pacing back and forth in the alienated bareness of the maternity waiting room, to his ubiquitous presence and emotional involvement in the birthing experience.

—JUDITH PARTNOW HYMAN, *Becoming a Father*, 1995

"I'm not sure if my husband is going to be there when I actually have the baby. He said the only way he's going to be in the room when there's a delivery is if there's a pizza involved."

—RITA RUDNER, *Tickled Pink*, 2001

I saw my father naked once.... But it was okay.... Because I was soooo young…and sooo drunk.

—SARAH SILVERMAN, Stand-up routine

FEELINGS & ATTITUDES

The brain is the seat of the emotions.—Cynthia Ozick, The Puttermesser Papers, 1997

—

Your imagination and your emotions are like a vast ocean from which you wrest small pieces of land that may well be flooded again. That ocean is wide and elemental, but what matter are the small pieces of land you reclaim from it.

—ETTY HILLESUM, *An Interrupted Life*, 1983

—

It is good to have such moments of despair and of temporary extinction; continuous calm would be superhuman.

—ETTY HILLESUM, *An Interrupted Life*, 1983

—

I think when we experience emotion we should delve into it and live through it. We are always trying to shut off pain or control our happiness. Why? To live is to feel.

—GWYNETH PALTROW, "Castaway: Saturday," *Marie-Claire* magazine, January 1998

—

We have lived through the era when happiness was a warm puppy, and the era when happiness was a dry martini, and now we have come to the era when happiness is "knowing what your uterus looks like."

—NORA EPHRON, *Crazy Salad*, 1975

I don't think of all the misery, but of all the beauty that still remains.

—ANNE FRANK, *The Diary of a Young Girl*, 1947

—

Mama's philosophy and approach to life were succinct: If it's good it's not forever, and if it's bad it's not forever.

—MOLLY PICON, *Molly!*, 1980

—

Angels can fly because they take themselves lightly.

—LOTUS WEINSTOCK, Sign-off line, Stand-up routine

—

Curb Your Dogma.

—LOTUS WEINSTOCK, Stand-up routine

—

Portraying a Miss America contestant: What will I do if I win? Well, Bert…before I was helping the poor and ugly. But what I want most of all is to become a human being. I think…I think that human beings are an important part of humanity.

—LOTUS WEINSTOCK, "Miss America," Stand-up routine

—

Throw yourselves at happiness, sisters,
Burst into silvery laughter!

—MIRIAM ULINOVER, "With the *Taytsh-Khumesh*," *Der bobes oyster*
(The Grandmother's Treasure), 1922

—

Happiness is getting a brown gravy stain on a brown dress.

—TOTIE FIELDS, Stand-up routine

—

I hang all my heavy needs
on a bird's wing.

—MALKA HEIFETZ TUSSMAN, "Mild, My Wild," *With Teeth in the Earth*, 1992

Do you know that hope sometimes consists only of a question without an answer?

—CLARICE LISPECTOR, A maçã no escuro [The Apple in the Dark], 1959

—

Oh! My love, don't be afraid of neediness: it is our greatest destiny.

—CLARICE LISPECTOR, A maçã no escuro [The Apple in the Dark], 1959

—

I came to see the Center elderly as in possession of the philosophers' stone—that universally sought, ever-elusive treasure, harboring the secret that would teach us how to transmute base metals into pure gold. The stone, like the blue-bird's feather of happiness, is said to be overlooked precisely because it is so close to us, hidden in the dust at our feet.

—BARBARA MYERHOFF in Jewish Women's Archive (http://www.jwa.org)

—

"Besides, I like an anger that is not fearful and guilty."

—JOANNE GREENBERG, I Never Promised You a Rose Garden, 1964

—

What about being angry at a child who exhausts you, defies you, disappoints you?

—ANNE ROIPHE, Fruitful, 1996

—

She would rather go senile than give up her rage.

—VIVIAN GORNICK, Approaching Eye Level, 1996

—

I soothe my conscience now with the thought that it is better for hard words to be on paper than that Mummy should carry them in her heart.

—ANNE FRANK, The Diary of a Young Girl, 1947

—

She had spent the golden time in grudging its going.

—DOROTHY PARKER, "The Lovely Leave," Laments for the Living, 1929

Instant gratification takes too long.

—CARRIE FISHER, *Postcards from the Edge*, 1987

Singing like a hope, shining like a tear,
Silent the echo of what will befall.

—YOCHEVED BAT-MIRIAM, "Parting," *Poems from the Hebrew*, 1973

It was the old recurrent groan of life. It was the sound of nature turning on its hinge. Everyone had a story to tell him. What resentments, what hatreds, what bitterness, how little good will!

—CYNTHIA OZICK, "The Doctor's Wife," *The Pagan Rabbi and Other Stories*, 1971

And how do you look backward. By looking forward. And what do they see. As they look forward. They see what they had to do before they could look backward. And there we have it all.

—GERTRUDE STEIN, *Reflection on the Atomic Bomb*, 1973

The people are a very fickle baby that must have new toys every day.

—EMMA GOLDMAN, *Anarchism and Other Essays*, 1911

When sleep leaves the body like smoke
and man, sated with secrets,
drives the overworked nag of quarrel
out of its stall,
then the fire-breathing union begins anew ...

—NELLY SACHS, "When Sleep Enters the Body Like Smoke," *O the Chimneys*, 1967

You have to get used to fear,
not fear exactly, but a long unease

—SHIRLEY KAUFMAN, "Bread and Water," *Roots in the Air*, 1996

Express your anger like a swan.
> —ALICIA SUSKIN OSTRIKER, "About Time," *The Little Space*, 1998

You've got to get up every morning with a smile on your face
And show the world all the love in your heart
Then people gonna treat you better
You're gonna find, yes you will
That you're beautiful as you feel.
> —CAROLE KING, "Beautiful," *Tapestry*, 1971

Grab your hat and grab your coat,
Leave your worries on the doorstep.
Just direct your feet
To the sunny side of the street.
> —DOROTHY FIELDS, "The Sunny Side of the Street" with Jimmy McHugh,
> *The International Revue*, 1930

A happy woman is one who has no cares at all; a cheerful woman is one who has cares but doesn't let them get her down.
> —BEVERLY SILLS on *60 Minutes*, CBS-TV, 1975

It requires something more than personal experience to gain a philosophy or point of view from any specific event. It is the quality of our response to the event and our capacity to enter into the lives of others that help us to make their lives and experiences our own.
> —EMMA GOLDMAN, *Red Emma Speaks*, 1972

Lay no flowers on my grave. They are for those who live in the sun, and I have always lived in the shadow.
> —PENINA MOÏSE, Last Words, in *Notable American Women*,
> Edward T. James, ed., 1971

It's never too late to begin a life or a book.

—MOLLY PICON, *Molly!*, 1980

There is no such thing as inner peace. There is only nervousness or death. Any attempt to prove otherwise constitutes unacceptable behavior.

—FRAN LEBOWITZ, *Metropolitan Life*, 1978

Her only enemy was impatience.

—RITA RUDNER, *Tickled Pink*, 2001

I dream and plan as if there was nothing happening in the world, as if there was no war, no destruction, as if thousands upon thousands were not being killed daily.

—HANNAH SENESH, *Hannah Senesh*, 1966

Her mind lives tidily, apart
From cold and noise and pain,
And bolts the door against her heart,
Out wailing in the rain.

—DOROTHY PARKER, "Interior," *Sunset Gun*, 1928

His intelligence was a version of cynicism. He rolled irony like an extra liquid in his mouth.

—CYNTHIA OZICK in *Nation*, 11 May 1998

Jealousy is indeed a poor medium to secure love, but it is a secure medium to destroy one's self-respect. For jealous people, like dope-fiends, stoop to the lowest level and in the end inspire only disgust and loathing.

—EMMA GOLDMAN, *Red Emma Speaks*, 1972

Jealousy is all the fun you think they had.

—ERICA JONG, *How to Save Your Own Life*, 1977

...hot with shame, a loneliness that tells you you're a fool and a loser. Everyone else is feasting, you alone cannot gain a seat at the table.

—VIVIAN GORNICK, *Approaching Eye Level*, 1996

Loneliness was the evaporation of inner life. Loneliness was me cut off from myself. Loneliness was the thing nothing out there could cure.

—VIVIAN GORNICK, *Approaching Eye Level*, 1996

The problem with insight, sensitivity and intuition is that they tend to confirm our biases. At one time people were convinced of their ability to identify witches. All it required was sensitivity to the workings of the devil.

—NAOMI WEISSTEIN in *Psychology Today*, October 1969

I often see through the appearance of things right to the apparition itself.

—GRACE PALEY, *Just As I Thought*, 1998

My tidiness, and my untidiness, are full of regret and remorse and complex feelings.

—NATALIA GINZBURG, "He and I," *Italian Writing Today*, 1967

Kill reverence and you've killed the hero in man.

—AYN RAND, *The Fountainhead*, 1943

Superfluity, excess of custom, and superstition would climb like a choking vine on the Fence of the Law if skepticism did not continually hack them away to make freedom for purity.

—CYNTHIA OZICK, "The Pagan Rabbi," *The Pagan Rabbi and Other Stories*, 1971

Through spontaneity we are re-formed into ourselves. It creates an explosion that for the moment frees us from handed-down frames of reference, memory choked with old facts and information and undigested theories and techniques of other people's findings. Spontaneity is the moment of personal freedom when we are faced with reality, and see it, explore it and act accordingly. In this reality the bits and pieces of ourselves function as an organic whole. It is the time of discovery, of experiencing, of creative expression.

—VIOLA SPOLIN, *Improvisation for the Theater*, 1963

Only to have a grief equal to all these tears!

—ADRIENNE RICH, "Peeling Onions," *Snapshots of a Daughter-in-Law*, 1963

Why am I idiotically timid before such people, while at the same time so critical of their limitations?

—NADINE GORDIMER, *The Late Bourgeois World*, 1966

I have so little mastered the art of tranquil living that wherever go I trail storm clouds of drama around me.

—MARY ANTIN, Letter to Caroline Goodyear, 18 March 1930

Sometimes it's difficult having sympathy with everyone's point of view.

—WENDY WASSERSTEIN, *Uncommon Women and Others*, 1978

My misfortune is my ability to see both sides even of the fundamental religious question.

—HENRIETTA SZOLD, *Summoned to Jerusalem* by Joan Dash, 1979

People who fight fire with fire usually end up with ashes.

—ABIGAIL VAN BUREN, "Dear Abby" Advice Column, 7 March 1974

Re Katharine Hepburn: She runs the gamut of emotions from A to B.
> —DOROTHY PARKER in *Publishers Weekly*, 19 June 1967

Those who do not know how to weep with their whole heart don't know how to laugh either.
> —GOLDA MEIR, Quoted by Oriana Fallaci in *L'Eurepeo*, 1973

By the time we are women, fear is as familiar to us as air. It is our element. We live in it, we inhale it, we exhale it, and most of the time we do not even notice it. Instead of "I am afraid," we say, "I don't want to," or "I don't know how," or "I can't."
> —ANDREA DWORKIN, *Our Blood*, 1976

I intend to do everything that frightens me.
> —GILDA RADNER, *Funny Women*, Unterbrink, 1987

If I embarrass you, tell your friends.
> —BELLE BARTH, Stand-up routine

My own feelings are diverse. Sometimes I am soothed and strengthened and uplifted by the reflection that all goes steadily and unceasingly, no matter how topsy-turvy things were inside of me. And again there are times when I rebel against it, that the trees stand in their majesty, rustling their leaves and undergoing the silent changes of the seasons, and the river speeds on, each wavelet glistening, while I am troubled and disturbed and full of seething, unexpressed feelings.
> —HENRIETTA SZOLD in *Lost Love*, Shargel, 1997

My happiness is not the means to any end. It is the end. It is its own goal. It is its own purpose. Neither am I the means to any end others may wish to accomplish. I am not a tool for their use. I am not a servant of their needs. I am not a bandage for their wounds. I am not a sacrifice on their altars.
> —AYN RAND, *Anthem*, 1946

We all live with the objective of being happy; our lives are all different and yet the same.

—ANNE FRANK, *The Diary of a Young Girl*, 1947

MIRACLE's truck comes down the little avenue, Scott Joplin ragtime strewn behind it like pearls, and, yes, you can feel happy with one piece of your heart.

—ADRIENNE RICH, "Miracle Ice Cream," *Dark Fields of the Republic*, 1995

Hindsight, usually looked down upon, is probably as valuable as foresight, since it does include a few facts.

—GRACE PALEY, *Just As I Thought*, 1998

A new light is coming into the world, as it has always come in moments of darkness and must come as inevitably as the sun rises.... A new synthesis of our hate of war and love of our land, of our social reconstruction and our individual deepening, of radios and music, machines and art, time and eternity, man and God.... This is the burning bush.

—JESSIE SAMPTER in *Opinion*, May 1937

I believe in a kind of fidelity to your own early ideas; it's a kind of antagonism in me to prevailing trends.

—GRACE PALEY, *Women Writing in America* by Blanche H. Gelfant, 1984

Out of rebellion and hope, her parents had been leftists. All that remained of their youthful idealism was their disbelief in God.

—SHARON NIEDERMAN, "A Gift for Languages," *Shaking Eve's Tree*, 1990

Pity is the deadliest feeling that can be offered to a woman.

—VICKI BAUM, *And Life Goes On*, 1932

Her curiosity instructed her more than the answers she was given.
—CLARICE LISPECTOR, *Family Ties*, 1972

Cynicism is an unpleasant way of saying the truth.
—LILLIAN HELLMAN, *The Little Foxes*, 1939

In an ever-changing, incomprehensible world the masses had reached the point where they would…think that everything was possible and that nothing was true.
—HANNAH ARENDT, *Origins of Totalitarianism*, 1951

I was always much too elated to imagine despair.
—EVE BABITZ, *Black Swans*, 1993

Gratitude—the meanest and most sniveling attribute in the world.
—DOROTHY PARKER in *Writers at Work* (1st), 1958

Every day, every day I hear
enough to fill
a year of nights with wondering.
—DENISE LEVERTOV, "Every Day," *Breathing the Water*, 1989

The only things we can share, the only things which we can give to the world without making ourselves poorer, are high thoughts and high aims.
—HANNAH GREENEBAUM SOLOMON, Presidential Address (New York), NCJW Proceedings, 1896

because tiredness at least
you
have always been
faithful.

>   —SUSAN GRIFFIN, "Tiredness Cycle," *Women:*
>   *A Feminist Perspective*, Jo Freeman, ed., 1975

—

I'm awfully scared that everyone who knows me as I always am will discover that I have another side, a finer and better side. I'm afraid they'll laugh at me, think I'm ridiculous and sentimental, not take me seriously.

>   —ANNE FRANK, *The Diary of a Young Girl*, 1947

—

Boredom is just the reverse side of fascination: both depend on being outside rather than inside a situation, and one leads to the other.

>   —SUSAN SONTAG, *On Photography*, 1977

—

If we stay hunkered down defensive and angry, we waste our energies. We act effectively now if we learn to relax into our power, stand upright and leave the foxholes that we have almost begun to consider a permanent home.

>   —NAOMI WOLF, *Fire with Fire*, 1993

—

For her, indignation was a natural reaction. She found it a relief to hold everything against everyone—it was almost her religion. For reasons she did not question, her life energy had been powered by fury. She was actually surprised (now that she was dead) that it hadn't kept her living forever.

>   —MERRILL JOAN GERBER, *Anna in the Afterlife*, 2002

FEMINISM & WOMEN'S LIBERATION

(*also see* Civil Rights, Social Movements & Activism *and* Women)

I don't want anybody calling me Ms.

—ANN LANDERS in *Time*, 21 August 1989

I am a feminist because I feel endangered, psychically and physically, by this society and because I believe that the women's movement is saying that we have come to an edge of history when men—insofar as they are embodiments of the patriarchal idea—have become dangerous to children and other living things, themselves included.

—ADRIENNE RICH, *On Lies, Secrets, and Silence*, 1979

I submit that women's history has been hushed up for the same reasons that black history has been hushed up...and that is that a feminist movement poses a direct threat to the establishment. From the beginning it exposes the hypocrisy of the male power structure.

—SHULAMITH FIRESTONE, *The Dialectic of Sex*, 1970

It is...crucial that we understand lesbian/feminism in the deepest, most radical sense: as that love for ourselves and other women, that commitment to the freedom of all of us, which transcends the category of "sexual preference" and the issue of civil rights, to become a politics of asking women's questions, demanding a world in which the integrity of all women—not a chosen few—shall be honored and validated in every respect of culture.

—ADRIENNE RICH, *On Lies, Secrets, and Silence*, 1979

I have the face of a vampire, but the heart of a feminist.

—THEDA BARA, http://www.imdb.com

If you're a feminist, it means that you've noticed that male ownership of the direction of female lives has been the order of the day for a few thousand years, and it isn't natural.

—GRACE PALEY, *Just As I Thought*, 1998

Anti-feminism is a direct expression of misogyny; it is the political defense of women hating.

—ANDREA DWORKIN, *Right-Wing Women*, 1978

[Within the feminist movement] non-Jewish men treated me the way white men treat black women—as more "sensual," earthy, sexually accessible; as Rebecca of *Ivanhoe*. I experienced the same treatment from feminists, when I was singled out by some comrades as somehow fleshier, earthier, sexier, pushier, more verbal: "Jewish."

—PHYLLIS CHESLER in *Lilith*, Winter 1976/1977

Woman's place is in the house—the House of Representatives.

—BELLA ABZUG, Motto, 1970

Merely external emancipation has made of the modern woman an artificial being.... Now, woman is confronted with the necessity of emancipating herself from emancipation, if she really desires to be free.

—EMMA GOLDMAN, *Anarchism and Other Essays*, 1911

For how can we speak of a free and democratic society with equality and justice for all at the same time that the domination of one half of humanity over the other half is accepted as only proper and right?

—RIANE EISLER, *Sacred Pleasure*, 1995

Great periods of civilization, however much they may have owed their beginning to the aggressive dominance of the male principle, have always been marked by some sort of rise in the status of women. This in its turn is a manifestation of something more profound: the recognition of the importance of the "feminine" principle, not as other, but as necessary to wholeness.

—CAROLYN G. HEILBRUN, *Toward a Recognition of Androgyny*, 1973

Thus changes in women's rights change women's moral judgements, seasoning mercy with justice by enabling women to consider it moral to care not only for others but for themselves.

—CAROL GILLIGAN, *In a Different Voice*, 1982

We don't so much want to see a female Einstein become an assistant professor. We want a woman schlemiel to get promoted as quickly as a male schlemiel.

—BELLA ABZUG in *American Chronicle*, 1987

Our time has come. We will no longer content ourselves with leavings and bits and pieces of the rights enjoyed by men…we want our equal rights, nothing more but nothing less. We want an equal share of political and economic power.

—BELLA ABZUG, *Gullible's Travels* by Jill Johnston, 1974

Women's history is the primary tool for women's emancipation.

—GERDA LERNER in *Ms.*, September 1981

Women's Liberation is just a lot of foolishness. It's the men who are discriminated against. They can't bear children. And no one's likely to do anything about that.

—GOLDA MEIR in *Newsweek*, 23 October 1972

They always said the women's movement had no sense of humor. Well, we do. It's just that we laugh when the joke's not on us.

—ROBIN TYLER in *Women in Comedy*, Martin, 1986

Judaism has always been the keynote of liberty and I cannot conceive of one [Jewish] man voting against the amendment [for women's suffrage].
—MAUD NATHAN in *Philadelphia Record*, 1 November 1915

True, the movement for women's rights has broken many old fetters, but it has also forged new ones.
—EMMA GOLDMAN, *Anarchism and Other Essays*, 1911

There are and always have been two different approaches within feminism. One—"victim feminism," as I define it—casts women as sexually pure and mystically nurturing, and stresses the evil done to these "good" women as a way to petition for their rights. The other, which I call "power feminism," sees women as human beings—sexual, individual, no better or worse than their male counterparts—and lays claim to equality simply because women are entitled to it.
—NAOMI WOLF, *Fire with Fire*, 1993

We are in the midst of a violent backlash against feminism.
—NAOMI WOLF, *The Beauty Myth*, 1990

The old feminism spoke the language of liberation…. The new feminism speaks the language of power.
—GERTRUDE HIMMELFARB in *Seattle Times*, 14 May 1989

The decline of feminism after the First World War is attributable at least in part to the eventual concentration of the women's movements on the single narrow issue of suffrage—which was won.
—MIRIAM SCHNEIR, *Feminism: The Essential Historical Writings*, 1972

FOOD, DRINK & DIET
(*also see* Beauty & Appearance)

I love to drink Martinis,

Two at the very most

Three, I'm under the table;

Four, I'm under the host.

—DOROTHY PARKER, *New Yorker*, 1997

"Are you sick?" my mother would ask if I left a scrap from a twelve-ounce Delmonico. You weren't considered fed unless you were in pain. The more somebody loved you, the more they wanted you to eat.

—PATRICIA VOLK, *Stuffed*, 2001

"What cook can match herself against hunger and memory?"

—JOANNE GREENBERG, "Children of Joy," *Shaking Eve's Tree*, 1990

Today I am a woman cooking
I enjoy the hum of it, the warmth of it
The flaring nostrils-drool of it
Today I am a woman cooking on a day when women cook

—ELAINE BERNSTEIN PARTNOW, "A Woman Cooking," 1978

Having someone else peel your potatoes can be habit-forming.

—LETTY COTTIN POGREBIN, *Deborah, Golda, and Me*, 1991

Diets, like clothes, should be tailored to you.

—JOAN RIVERS in *Los Angeles Times*, 10 May 1974

I'm so compulsive about losing weight, I weigh myself after I cough.
> —ELAYNE BOOSLER, Stand-up routine

"Your idea of a balanced diet is a fried egg sandwich in both hands."
> —SUE MARGOLIS, *Spin Cycle*, 2001

"I daren't give your father the Danish or the cream cheese—he's actually dropped two or three pounds in the last week." "Yeah," Jack said dolefully, as he put the Danish and bagels into Shelley's bread bin, "I'm starving myself to death so that I can live a little longer."
> —SUE MARGOLIS, *Spin Cycle*, 2001

Come sit on the table, dinner is ready.... You'll swallow a cup, darling?... Throw an eye into the ice-box and give me an accounting.
> —GERTRUDE BERG in "The Goldbergs' Jewish Humor" by Charles Angoff, *Congress Weekly 18*, 5 March 1951

I drank, because I wanted to drown my sorrows, but now the damned things have learned to swim, and now decency and good behavior weary me!
> —FRIDA KAHLO in *Frida*, Herrera, 1983

Roast Beef, Medium, is not only a food. It is a philosophy. Seated at Life's Dining Table, with a menu of Morals before you, your eye wandering a bit over the entrées, the hors d'oeuvres, and the things...à la carte though you know that the Roast Beef, Medium, is safe and sane, and sure.
> —EDNA FERBER, *Roast Beef, Medium*, 1911

I hereby affirm my own right as a Jewish American feminist to make chicken soup, even though I sometimes take it out of a can.
> —BETTY FRIEDAN in *Tikkun*, January/February 1988

Once Fang took us out for doughnuts and coffee. The kids loved it—they'd never given blood before.

—PHYLLIS DILLER, Stand-up routine

I was raised on Tabasco and gumbo by my mother at a time in America when onions and garlic were considered a shock.

—EVE BABITZ, *Two by Two*, 1999

I never let myself get over 110. I'm swollen, that's my problem. I have the same measurements as Elizabeth Taylor. Her living room is nine by twelve, and so is mine.

—TOTIE FIELDS, Stand-up routine

I've been on a diet for two weeks and all I've lost is two weeks.

—TOTIE FIELDS, Stand-up routine

Obese, hefty, overweight, rotund. I never knew there were so many ways to say fatty.

—TOTIE FIELDS, Stand-up routine

I read recipes the same way I read science fiction. I get to the end and think, "Well, that's not going to happen."

—RITA RUDNER, http://www.ritafunny.com, 2003

They could not see they were too thin because slenderness had become a statement of power. There could never be too much of it, since more implied that the will had grown even stronger in its relentless struggle to dominate matter.

—KIM CHERNIN, *The Obsession*, 1981

The obsession [of slenderness]…might well be considered one of the most serious forms of suffering affecting women in America today.
—KIM CHERNIN, *The Obsession*, 1981

Drink my lord:…I will draw water for thy camels also, until they have done drinking.
—REBEKAH, Book of Genesis, c. ninth century B.C.E., Bible

To ask women to become unnaturally thin is to ask them to relinquish their sexuality.
—NAOMI WOLF, *The Beauty Myth*, 1990

FREEDOM & DEMOCRACY
(*also see* Government & Political Systems *and* United States of America)

Democracy must first be safe for America before it can be safe for the world.
—EMMA GOLDMAN, *Mother Earth*, April 1916

The freer that women become, the freer will men be. Because when you enslave someone—you *are* enslaved.
—LOUISE NEVELSON in *AFTRA* magazine, Summer 1974

True emancipation begins neither at the polls nor in courts. It begins in woman's soul.
—EMMA GOLDMAN, *Anarchism and Other Essays*, 1911

Each separate soul contains the nation's force,
And both embrace the world.
—EMMA LAZARUS, "Rosh-Hashanah, 5643" (1882), *Emma Lazarus*, 1982

In a culture where approval/disapproval has become the predominant regulator of effort and position, and often the substitute for love, our personal freedoms are dissipated.

—VIOLA SPOLIN, *Improvisation for the Theater*, 1963

Emancipation from every kind of bondage is my principle.

—ERNESTINE LOUISE ROSE in American Jewish Historical Society, http://www.ajhs.org, 2003

Contrary to what we have been taught, freedom and equality are not just a matter of political organization, but of the structure of personal and social life as a whole.

—RIANE EISLER, *Sacred Pleasure*, 1995

Freedom for supporters of the government only, for the members of one party only—no matter how big its membership may be—is not freedom at all. Freedom is always freedom for the man who thinks differently.

—ROSA LUXEMBURG, Quoted in *Die Russische Revolution* by Paul Froelich, 1940

Without general elections, without freedom of the press, freedom of speech, freedom of assembly, without the free battle of opinions, life in every public institution withers away, becomes a caricature of itself, and bureaucracy rises as the only deciding factor.

—ROSA LUXEMBURG, Quoted in *Die Russische Revolution* by Paul Froelich, 1940

There's something contagious about demanding freedom.

—ROBIN MORGAN, *Sisterhood Is Powerful*, 1970

When does a life bend toward freedom? grasp its direction?

—ADRIENNE RICH, *Dark Fields of the Republic*, 1995

When we were told that by freedom we understood free enterprise, we did very little to dispel this monstrous falsehood.... It is a minor blessing compared with the truly political freedoms, such as freedom of speech and thought, of assembly and association, even under the best conditions.

—HANNAH ARENDT, *On Revolution*, 1963

Man cannot be free if he does not know that he is subject to necessity, because his freedom is always won in his never wholly successful attempts to liberate himself from necessity.

—HANNAH ARENDT, *The Human Condition*, 1958

Wars and revolutions...have outlived all their ideological justifications.... No cause is left but the most ancient of all, the one, in fact, that from the beginning of our history has determined the very existence of politics, the cause of freedom versus tyranny.

—HANNAH ARENDT, *On Revolution*, 1963

How did Chinese women, after having their feet bound for many generations, finally discover they could run?

—BETTY FRIEDAN, *The Feminine Mystique*, 1963

Until we are all free, we are none of us free.

—EMMA LAZARUS in *American Hebrew*, 3 November 1882–23 February 1883

Years when the enemy is in our state,
and liberty, safe in the people's hands,
is never safe and peace is never safe.

—MURIEL RUKEYSER, "Ann Burlak," *Waterlily Fire*, 1962

Wherever you turn someone is shouting give me liberty or I give you death.

—GRACE PALEY, *Just As I Thought*, 1998

When women are pessimistic about their political strength and feel hopeless about changing the conditions of their lives, it is almost as if they do not believe that democracy means the country belongs to them. But it's true.

—NAOMI WOLF, *Fire with Fire*, 1993

FRIENDSHIP

(*also see* Love & Desire)

A friend I can trust is the one who will let me have my death. The rest are actors who want me to stay and further the plot.

—ADRIENNE RICH, *Poems: Selected and New*, 1974

~

There's a kind of emotional exploration you plumb with a friend that you don't really do with your family.

—BETTE MIDLER in *Parade* magazine, 5 February 1989

~

Winter, spring, summer or fall
All you have to do is call
And I'll be there,
You've got a friend.

—CAROLE KING, "You've Got a Friend," *Tapestry*, 1971

~

Friends love misery, in fact. Sometimes, especially if we are too lucky or too successful or too pretty, our misery is the only thing that endears us to our friends.

—ERICA JONG, *How to Save Your Own Life*, 1977

~

...my short list of long-term friends.

—CARRIE FISHER, *Postcards from the Edge*, 1987

She was friendless and yet a friend to others and the same intensity with which she ignored the future marked her passionate attitude to the past.

—YAËL DAYAN, *Death Had Two Sons*, 1967

It is one thing to go your separate way, leaving friends and comrades behind in peace and prosperity; it is another thing to fail to remember them when the world is casting them out.

—MARY ANTIN in *Common Ground*, Spring 1941

Friendship of a kind that cannot easily be reversed tomorrow must have its roots in common interests and shared beliefs, and even between nations, in some personal feeling.

—BARBARA TUCHMAN in *Harper's*, December 1972

Anything for a friend.

—SOPHIE TUCKER in *Funny Women*, Unterbrink, 1987

Then if my friendships break and bend,
There's little need to cry
The while I know that every foe
Is faithful till I die.

—DOROTHY PARKER, "The Heel"

I'm not against friendliness, she said, I'm not even against Americans.

—GRACE PALEY, *Enormous Changes at the Last Minute*, 1974

Constant use had not worn ragged the fabric of their friendship.

—DOROTHY PARKER, "The Standard of Living," *The Portable Dorothy Parker*, 1944

[Friendships] are easy to get out of compared to love affairs, but they are not easy to get out of compared to, say, jail.

—FRAN LEBOWITZ, *Mirabella*, 1992

It's very important when making a friend to check and see if they have a private plane. People think a good personality trait in a friend is kindness or a sense of humor. No, in a friend a good personality trait is a Gulfstream.

—FRAN LEBOWITZ, *Travel & Leisure*, 1994

Doesn't anybody stay in one place anymore?

—CAROLE KING, "So Far Away," *Tapestry*, 1971

I have seen how heart cells from different organisms, when placed together in the same petri dish, begin to pulsate in unison. There is a connection between all living things, and more so between all like things.

—ELAINE BERNSTEIN PARTNOW, *Hear Us Roar*, 1988

GOD

(*also see* Faith, Religion, the Bible & Spirituality *and* Jews & Judaism)

If you cannot sound the depths of the heart of man or unravel the arguments of his mind, how can you fathom the God who made all things, or sound his mind or unravel his purposes?

—JUDITH, Book of Judith, c. 150 B.C.E., Bible

God knows (*she* knows) that women try.

—GLORIA STEINEM, "Sisterhood," *The First Ms. Reader*, 1972

"Hear, O Israel! The Lord our God, the Lord is One!" Such is the literal trans-lation of the Hebrew, *sh'ma yisrael adonai elohaynu, adonai ekad*, but it is impos-sible to give the full force of the Hebrew by English words.... It is the avowal of belief, belief in the unparalleled, unchanging, incomprehensible unity of God, the repetition and acknowledgment of which marks us as His chosen peo-ple,—His redeemed, His beloved, His first-born,—separates us from every other nation, every other religion of the world.

—GRACE AGUILAR, *The Spirit of Judaism*, 1842

When I pray, I hold a silly, naïve, or serious *dialogue* with what is deep inside me, which for convenience' sake I call God.

—ETTY HILLESUM, *An Interrupted Life*, 1983

Praying to God for something for yourself strikes me as being too childish for words.... To pray for another's well-being is something I find childish as well; one should only pray that another should have enough strength to shoulder his burden. If you do that, you lend him some of your own strength.

—ETTY HILLESUM, *An Interrupted Life*, 1983

I didn't know what she was saying when she moved her lips in a Baptist church or a Catholic cathedral or, less often, in a synagogue, but it was obvious that God could be found anywhere.

—LILLIAN HELLMAN, *An Unfinished Woman*, 1969

Bless what brought us through
the sea and the fire; we are caught
in history like whales in polar ice.
Yet you have taught us to push against the walls,
to reach out and pull each other along.

—MARGE PIERCY, *The Art of Blessing the Day*, 1999

But you have no right to demand guarantees where the designs of the Lord our God are concerned. For God is not to be coerced as man is, nor is he, like mere man, to be cajoled.

—JUDITH, Book of Judith, c. 150 B.C.E., Bible

Sing ye to the Lord, for he hath triumphed gloriously; the horse and his rider hath he thrown into the sea.

—MIRIAM, Book of Exodus, c. ninth century B.C.E., Bible

So let all thine enemies perish, O Lord: but let them that love him be as the sun when he goeth forth in his might.

—DEBORAH, with Barak, Book of Judges, c. ninth century B.C.E., Bible

My heart rejoiceth in the Lord, mine horn is exalted in the Lord: my mouth is enlarged over mine enemies; because I rejoice in thy salvation.

There is none holy as the Lord: for there is none beside thee: neither is there any rock like our God.

—HANNAH, Book of 1 Samuel, c. 550 B.C.E., Bible

The Lord killeth, and maketh alive: he bringeth down to the grave, and bringeth up.

The Lord maketh poor, and maketh rich: he bringeth low, and lifteth up.

He raiseth up the poor out of the dust, and lifteth up the beggar from the dunghill, to set them among princes, and to make them inherit the throne of glory: for the pillars of the earth are the Lord's, and he hath set the world upon them.

He will keep the feet of his saints, and the wicked shall be silent in darkness; for by strength shall no man prevail.

—HANNAH, Book of 1 Samuel, c. 550 B.C.E., Bible

The God who would do this to him deserved only silence.
—ANNE ROIPHE, *1185 Park Avenue*, 1999

My love, you don't believe in the God, because we made a mistake when we humanized Him. We humanized Him because we did not understand Him, then it didn't work out. I'm certain that He is not human. But although He's not human, He sometimes makes us divine.
—CLARICE LISPECTOR, *Uma aprendizagem ou O livro dos prazeres* [An Apprenticeship or the Book of Pleasures], 1971

God said the only people I like are the atheists 'cause they play hard-to-get.
—LOTUS WEINSTOCK, *The Lotus Position*, 1982

Why wilt thou swallow up the inheritance of the Lord?
—WOMAN OF ABEL OF BETH-MAACAH, Book of 2 Samuel, c. 550 B.C.E., Bible

May your whole creation serve you! For you spoke and things came into being, you sent your breath and they were put together, and no one can resist your voice.
—JUDITH, Book of Judith, c. 150 B.C.E., Bible

No, God's in the wilderness next door—that huge tundra room, no walls and a sky roof—busy at the loom.
—DENISE LEVERTOV, "The Task," *Oblique Prayers*, 1984

The Lord does not take vacations. He is always on the job.
—ANN LANDERS, Advice Column, 17 March 1994

She once heard a skeptic mocking her brother, saying, "Your God is not strictly honest, or He would not have stolen a rib from sleeping Adam,"... She asked him to fetch a police official whereupon he asked her why. We were robbed last night of a silver cruet and the thief left in its place a golden one. *He responded, "If that is all I wish that thief would visit me every day!"*... And yet you object to the removal of the rib from sleeping Adam! Did he not receive in exchange a woman to wait on him?

—IMMA SHALOM in *The Status of Women in Formative Judaism* by Leonard Swidler, 2001

God forgives those who invent what they need.

—LILLIAN HELLMAN, *The Little Foxes*, 1939

He had once demonstrated that, since God had made the world, and since there was no God, the world in all logic could not exist.

—CYNTHIA OZICK, *Trust*, 1966

When I was in rabbinical school I believed in an all-powerful God, but the older I get, the more I believe in a limited God, a God who loves and cares, who weeps with us, but who can't change things. I hope the message I give to my congregants is that we need strength to accept where we find ourselves.

—RABBI SALLY PRIESAND in *New York Times*, 19 September 1993

If God, as we believe, is the God of life, then we must seek to harmonize our lives with His. The task is a difficult one. If God were not the moving force of all life but static, the approach would be less difficult. God demands partnership from us. We must move forward with Him in the creation of joy and righteousness.

—LILY MONTAGU, *Lily Montagu*, 1985

Why have we permitted it that their God seems one of Love and ours one of Vengeance?

—ANNIE NATHAN MEYER, "Prejudice: A Challenge and a Discipline"

I don't believe God is a chauvinist.... When you read the Bible there are two chapters of Genesis that have different interpretations of how woman was created.... I believe that woman was not created from a rib...but was created equally, like it says in one of the chapters: God created Adam and then split him in two so that each side has masculine and feminine qualities. They're different but equal.... Where is it written that women have to be subservient? Men have interpreted the law to serve themselves and society's needs. In other words, it is *not* written!

—BARBRA STREISAND in *Streisand: Her Life* by James Spada, 1995

God has a female presence, [but] the female presence is in exile. It is not until we redeem Her and bring Her home to rest in us that the entire world will be redeemed.

—RABBI LYNN GOTTLIEB in *Jewish Heroes & Heroines of America*
by Seymour Brody, 1996

God needs hearts more than heads in His service.

—JULIA RICHMAN, NCJW Proceedings, 1896

It would have been natural for [our ancient ancestors] to image the universe as an all-giving Mother from whose womb all life emerges and to which, like the cycles of vegetation, it returns after death to be again reborn. It also makes sense that societies with this image of the powers that govern the universe would have a very different social structure from societies that worship a divine Father who wields a thunderbolt and/or sword.

—RIANE EISLER, *The Chalice and the Blade*, 1987

If only she could remember what it was she had done to offend God so, perhaps she could make some sense of what He had done to her.

—FAYE MOSKOWITZ, "A Leak in the Heart," *Shaking Eve's Tree*, 1990

"I'm telling you plain, everything is God. Are you looking, Hayim? Are you using your eyes? The Baal Shem Tov, of blessed memory, spent days in the fields

and the woods, and there he saw the Holy One arising from every living thing
and also the stones."

—LILIAN NATTEL, *The River Midnight*, 1999

"Let's put it this way. You'd better hope there is no God. Because a God who
presides over Auschwitz is either evil himself or psychotic."

—CAROL K. HOWELL, *Defying Gravity*, 1995

"What does He want? Blindly obedient and faithful pets? Why didn't He just
populate the earth with golden retrievers?"

—CAROL K. HOWELL, "The Islands Laugh Exultant," *Other Voices*, Spring 2001

God had been present all along but I had never noticed.

—RABBI LAURA GELLER, "Encountering the Divine Presence," *Four Centuries*, 1992

God is the Thou I discover through my encounter with the human thous in my
life, people of whom I can say "for seeing your face is like seeing the face of
God."

—RABBI LAURA GELLER, "Encountering the Divine Presence," *Four Centuries*, 1992

We believe in one moving force through which we and all the universe are created. God is manifested in us and in all our doings.

—LILY MONTAGU, *Lily Montagu*, 1985

[There is a] depth and urgency of the search of Jewish and Christian women for
connection to the Divine, which found expression in more than 1000 years of
feminist Bible criticism and religious re-visioning.

—GERDA LERNER, *The Creation of Feminist Consciousness*, 1993

Hear O Israel—
The divine abounds everywhere

and dwells in everything;
the many are One.

—MARCIA FALK, *The Book of Blessings*, 1996

GOOD & EVIL

(*also see* Courage, Character & Integrity *and* Morality & Ethics)

We will try to be holy,
We will try to repair the world given to us to hand on.
Precious is this treasure of words and knowledge and deeds
    that moves inside us.
Holy is the hand that works for peace and for justice,
Holy is the mouth that speaks for goodness
Holy is the foot that walks toward mercy.

—MARGE PIERCY, *The Art of Blessing the Day*, 1999

It's really a wonder that I haven't dropped all my ideals because they seem so absurd and impossible to carry out. Yet, I keep them, because in spite of everything I still believe that people are really good at heart. I simply can't build up my hopes on a foundation consisting of confusion, misery, and death. I see the world gradually being turned into a wilderness, I hear the ever-approaching thunder, which will destroy us too, I can feel the sufferings of millions and yet, if I look up into the heavens, I think that it will all come right, that this cruelty too will end, and that peace and tranquility will return again.

—ANNE FRANK, *The Diary of a Young Girl*, 1947

Religion urges us to fight evil as contrary to the Divine Law. It urges us to combat abject misery, sin and disease because God is. In His name we can work, as we believe in co-operation with Him, since through Him goodness must ultimately prevail.

—LILY MONTAGU, *Lily Montagu*, 1985

And finally I twist my heart round again, so that the bad is on the outside and the good is on the inside, and keep on trying to find a way of becoming what I would so like to be, and could be, if...there weren't any other people living in the world.

—ANNE FRANK, *The Diary of a Young Girl*, 1947

How do you make out [that such a prayer should be permitted]? Because it is written "Let *hattaim* [sins] cease"? Is it written *hottim* [sinners]? It is written *hattaim!* Further, look to the end of the verse "and let the wicked men be no more." Since the sins will cease, there will be no more wicked men! Rather pray for them that they should repent, and there will be no more wicked.

—BERURIAH in *The Jewish Woman*, Elizabeth Koltun, ed., 1976

Fashions in sin change.

—LILLIAN HELLMAN, *Watch on the Rhine*, 1941

The serpent beguiled me, and I did eat.

—EVE, Book of Genesis, c. ninth century B.C.E., Bible

Behold therefore, I will gather thee unto thy fathers, and thou shalt be gathered into thy grave in peace; and thine eyes shall not see all the evil which I will bring upon this place.

—HULDAH, Book of 2 Kings, c. 550 B.C.E., Bible

Trouble is a great equalizer. No matter what our differences, in time of trouble the differences fade, and we become brothers and sisters. We want to reach out and help one another.

—ANN LANDERS, Advice Column, 17 November 1998

"Trouble has a mind of its own."

—CAROL K. HOWELL, "Tornado Watch Cookbook," *Shaking Eve's Tree*, 1990

Evil is obvious only in retrospect.

—GLORIA STEINEM, *Outrageous Acts and Everyday Rebellions*, 1983

They did not know...that the same force that had made him tolerant, was now the force that made him ruthless—that the justice which would forgive miles of innocent errors of knowledge, would not forgive a single step taken in conscious evil.

—AYN RAND, *Atlas Shrugged*, 1957

The banality of evil.

—HANNAH ARENDT [Referring to Adolf Eichmann, German Nazi official who, as head of the Gestapo's Jewish section, was responsible for the slaughter of millions of Jews during World War II; tried and hanged in Israel in 1962], *Eichmann in Jerusalem*, 1963

We sinful men are in the world as if swimming in the sea and in danger of being drowned. But our great, merciful and kind God, in his great mercy, has thrown ropes into the sea that we may take hold of them and be saved. These are our holy Torah where is written what are the rewards and punishments for good and evil deeds.

—GLÜCKEL OF HAMELN, *Memoirs*, 1692

Whatever we stand against
We will stand feeding and seeding.

—MURIEL RUKEYSER, "Wherever," *Breaking Open*, 1973

GOOD TIMES

(*also see* Show Biz, Sports & Entertainment)

At every party there are two kinds of people—those who want to go home and those who don't. The trouble is, they are usually married to each other.

—ANN LANDERS, Advice Column, 19 June 1991

—

"Most people don't know how to have a good time, any more than spoiled children. I show them. I spend their money for them, and they're grateful for it. I've got nothing to lose, because I live by my wits. They can't take that away from me."

—EDNA FERBER, *Saratoga Trunk*, 1941

—

Fun was all the truth we needed.

—EVE BABITZ, *Black Swans*, 1993

—

I gave myself the intention that although I am lame, it is preferable not to pay much attention to sickness, because in any case one can kick the bucket simply by stumbling against a banana peel. Tell me what you are doing, try not to work so many hours, have more fun, since the way the world is going we are all on death's door and it is not worth while to leave this world without having had a little fun in life.

—FRIDA KAHLO in *Frida*, Herrera, 1983

—

The radio…goes on early in the morning and is listened to at all hours of the day, until nine, ten and often eleven o'clock in the evening. This is certainly a sign that the grown-ups have infinite patience, but it also means that the power of absorption of their brains is pretty limited, with exceptions, of course—I don't want to hurt anyone's feelings. One or two news bulletins would be ample per day! But the old geese, well—I've said my piece!

—ANNE FRANK, *The Diary of a Young Girl*, 1947

Tango is such torture that I was glad to discover the Texas two-step, which was much more fun.

> —EVE BABITZ, Quoted by Ron Hogan, Beatrice Interview (online), 2000

I don't want to jitterbug. I want to do slow dances. Nobody wants to slow dance anymore, because guys don't know how and they don't think they can do it.

> —EVE BABITZ, Quoted by Ron Hogan, Beatrice Interview (online), 2000

I wanted to go somewhere
  the brain had not yet gone

> —ADRIENNE RICH, "Letters to a Young Poet," *Midnight Salvage*, 1999

I misremember who first was cruel enough to nurture the cocktail party into life. But perhaps it would be not too much too say, in fact it would be not enough to say, that it was not worth the trouble.

> —DOROTHY PARKER in *Esquire*, November 1964

The party's over—
It's time to call it a day—
No matter how you pretend
You knew it would end this way.
It's time to wind up the masquerade—
Just make your mind up—
The piper must be paid.

> —BETTY COMDEN, "The Party's Over," with Adolph Green, *Bells Are Ringing*, 1960

The origin of a modern party is anthropological: humans meet and share food to lower hostility between them and indicate friendship.

> —BARBARA WALTERS, *How to Talk with Practically Anybody*
> *about Practically Anything*, 1970

But how many of us ever enter into *real* rest—not going on vacations or spending time on hobbies but practicing a regular discipline that can change our very selves?

　　　　　　　　　　　—RABBI NAOMI LEVY, *To Begin Again*, 1998

Drink, and dance and laugh and lie,
Love the reeling midnight through,
For tomorrow we shall die!
(But, alas, we never do.)

　　　　　　　　　　　—DOROTHY PARKER, "The Flaw in Paganism"

This was my first continental holiday by car…and it confirmed my impression that cars are undesirable…. Traveling around in a little tin box isolates one from the people and the atmosphere of the place in a way that I have never experienced before. I found myself eyeing with envy all rucksacks and tents.

　　　　　　　　　—ROSALIND FRANKLIN in *Saint Elizabeth* by Anne Sayre, 1975

To Salvo, the shortest distance between New York and California was the number of relatives one could count on for accommodations.

　　　　　　　　　—GLORIA DEVIDAS KIRCHHEIMER, *Goodbye, Evil Eye*, 2000

Traveling, each day is several.

　　　　　　　　　—BONNIE FRIEDMAN in *New York Times*, 14 March 1999

I'm flying, and there's a guy sitting next to me, and I could tell he really wanted me…(*to shut up*).

　　　　　　　　　　　—WENDY LIEBMAN, Stand-up routine

The mind of a traveler has only one spotlight, and it is always trained on the present scene.

　　　　　　　　　—EMILY "MICKEY" HAHN, *Nobody Said* Not *to Go*, Ken Cuthbertson, 1998

Travel is the best education you can have in life, learning that your life and the world you live in is just a very small part of the world.
                    —DEBRA MESSING in *USA Weekend Online*, 17 September 1999

Fact: Girls who are having a good sex thing stay in New York. The rest want to spend their summer vacations in Europe.
                    —GAIL PARENT, *Sheila Levine Is Dead and Living in New York*, 1972

And if there were a ship to take over the mantle of the *Titanic*, what would it be? What about the entire Carnival cruise line for starters? Have people lost their minds? Can someone possibly think that sitting out on a stinking, floating Vegas hotel for five days, running into the same people all day, could be interpreted as a vacation? Waking up in a cabin the size of a closet?
                    —SANDRA BERNHARD, *May I Kiss You on the Lips, Miss Sandra?*, 1998

There is a cruise ship out in the distance, all lit up at night.... It's comfy and neat, and no confusion is involved. Isn't it great to sail the seas and have everyone the same? Boat + romance – iceberg = *Love Boat*. In the meantime, all the dreams have sunk to the bottom: rusted, broken, and resting in the dark.
                    —SANDRA BERNHARD, *May I Kiss You on the Lips, Miss Sandra?*, 1998

I love walking my feet off. Gimme a map and a box of Band-Aids and I'm all set!
                    —FRAN DRESCHER, *Cancer, Schmancer*, 2002

The dream of automation remains a powerful one—the idea of a clockwork world running without human intervention but generating enough wealth that everyone can go fishing, read books, and study art.
                    —SHOSHANA ZUBOFF in *Omni*, April 1991

The discovery of the good taste of bad taste can be very liberating. The man who insists on high and serious pleasures is depriving himself of pleasure; he continually restricts what he can enjoy; in the constant exercise of his good taste he will eventually price himself out of the market, so to speak. Here Camp taste supervenes upon good taste as a daring and witty hedonism. It makes the man of good taste cheerful, where before he ran the risk of being chronically frustrated. It is good for the digestion.

—SUSAN SONTAG, *Against Interpretation*, 1966

Using a camera appeases the anxiety which the work-driven feel about not working when they are on vacation and supposed to be having fun. They have something to do that is like a friendly imitation of work: they can take pictures.

—SUSAN SONTAG, *On Photography*, 1977

GOVERNMENT & POLITICAL SYSTEMS

(*also see* Civil Rights, Social Movements & Activism; Law & Order; *and* Society & Social Classes)

Capitalism…has…grown into a huge insatiable monster.

—EMMA GOLDMAN in *Mother Earth*, April 1916

The authority of any governing institution must stop at its citizen's skin.

—GLORIA STEINEM in *Ms.*, November 1981

There's never been a good government.

—EMMA GOLDMAN, Quoted by Katherine Anne Porter in
Los Angeles Times, 7 July 1974

The strongest bulwark of authority is uniformity; the least divergence from it is the greatest crime.

—EMMA GOLDMAN, *Red Emma Speaks*, 1983

At all levels of government, the question is one of priorities and money. The contradiction between what consumers (the bulk of whom are low-income) pay out in taxes and what they receive in goods and services is simply sharper the closer it is to home.

—SUSAN WITKOVSKY, "The Impediments to Public Day Care Programs in San Francisco," Master's Thesis, San Francisco State University (now California State University), 1974

The experience of Russia, more than any theories, has demonstrated that *all* government, whatever its forms or pretenses, is a dead weight that paralyzes the free spirit and activities of the masses.

—EMMA GOLDMAN, *My Disillusionment in Russia*, 1923

If we get a government that reflects more of what this country is really about, we can turn the century—and the economy—around.

—BELLA ABZUG in *Redbook*, April 1974

The soldier's business is to take life. For that he is paid by the State, eulogized by political charlatans and upheld by public hysteria. But woman's function is to give life, yet neither the State nor politicians nor public opinion have ever made the slightest provision in return for the life woman has given.

—EMMA GOLDMAN in *Mother Earth*, April 1916

No government which is for the profiteers can be also for the people, and I am for the people, while the government is for the profiteers.

—ROSE PASTOR STOKES (1917) in *Fire and Grace*, Zipser, 1989

Is a shift from a system leading to chronic wars, social injustice, and ecological imbalance to one of peace, social justice, and ecological balance a realistic possibility?

—RIANE EISLER, *The Chalice and the Blade*, 1987

—

The critical factors in politically repressive societies are, first, the repression of female sexual freedom and, second, the distortion of both male and female sexuality through the erotization of domination and violence.

—RIANE EISLER, *Sacred Pleasure*, 1995

—

Revolution is a process and not an event.

—BLANCHE WEISEN COOK, *Women and Support Networks*, 1979

—

Communists are people who fancied that they had an unhappy childhood.

—GERTRUDE STEIN, Quoted by Thornton Wilder in *Writers at Work* (1st), 1958

—

Anarchism is the only philosophy which brings to man the consciousness of himself; which maintains that God, the State, and society are non-existent, that their promises are null and void, since they can be fulfilled only through man's subordination. Anarchism is therefore the teacher of the unity of life; not merely in nature, but in man.

—EMMA GOLDMAN, *Anarchism and Other Essays*, 1911

—

Whether you believe in a creed, or what you call religion, or not, there is something in Socialism that must move you. How can you love God, whom you have not seen, if you do not love your fellow man, whom you have seen?

—ROSE PASTOR STOKES in "Daughters of the Book," Sigerman, 1992

—

However sugar-coated and ambiguous, every form of authoritarianism must start with a belief in some group's greater right to power, whether that right is justified by sex, race, class, religion, or all four. However far it may expand, the progression inevitably rests on unequal power and airtight roles within the family.

—GLORIA STEINEM, *Revolution from Within*, 1992

We are one in all and all in one. There are no men but only the great WE. One, indivisible and forever.

—AYN RAND, *Anthem*, 1946

Communism is fascism with a human face.

—SUSAN SONTAG, Speech, Forum for Poland's Solidarity, New York City, 1982

Authoritarian political ideologies have a vested interest in promoting fear, a sense of the imminence of takeover by aliens—and real diseases are useful material.

—SUSAN SONTAG, *AIDS and Its Metaphors*, 1989

The ideology of capitalism makes us all into connoisseurs of liberty—of the indefinite expansion of possibility.

—SUSAN SONTAG, *AIDS and Its Metaphors*, 1989

GUILT, INNOCENCE & CONSCIENCE

(*also see* Courage, Character & Integrity; Good & Evil; *and* Truth, Lies & Superstitions)

"Mama, let me tell you, I feel awful [for not writing you]."

"Oh, God, sonny, if I could only believe that, I'd be the happiest mother in the world."

—ELAINE MAY, Stand-up routine, with Mike Nichols

As if there could be a world
Of absolute innocence
In which we forget ourselves
            —ALICIA SUSKIN OSTRIKER, "The Dogs at Live Oak Beach, Santa Cruz,"
                                                    The Little Space, 1998

You,…the inexperienced, who learn nothing in the nights.
Many angels are given you
But you do not see them.
            —NELLY SACHS, "Chorus of Clouds," *The Seeker and Other Poems*, 1970

I am not willing, now or in the future, to bring bad trouble to people who, in
my past association with them, were completely innocent of any talk or any
action that was disloyal or subversive…. I cannot and will not cut my conscience to fit this year's fashions, even though I long ago came to the conclusion that I was not a political person and could have no comfortable place in
any political group.
                            —LILLIAN HELLMAN in *Nation*, 31 May 1952

But I prefer to fall innocent into your power than to sin in the eyes of the Lord.
            —SUSANNA, Book of Daniel, c. 167–164 B.C.E., Bible

Guilt: Although it is sometimes better to sin and feel guilty than never to sin
at all, it is pretty ratty to sin and not feel guilty.
                —JUDITH VIORST, *Love and Guilt and the Meaning of Life*, 1979

But the neurotic conscience behaves like a gestapo headquarters within the
personality, mercilessly tracking down dangerous or potentially dangerous ideas
and every remote relative of these ideas, accusing, threatening, tormenting in
an interminable inquisition to establish guilt for trivial offenses or crimes committed in dreams.
                            —SELMA FRAIBERG, *The Magic Years*, 1959

Conscience: These internal tyrants…these busybodies, moral detectives, jailers of the human spirit, what will they say?
—EMMA GOLDMAN, *Anarchism and Other Essays*, 1911

It is quite gratifying to feel guilty if you haven't done anything wrong: how noble! Whereas it is rather hard and certainly depressing to admit guilt and to repent.
—HANNAH ARENDT, *Eichmann in Jerusalem*, 1963

There may be repentance at the eleventh hour, but who can say which hour may not be the eleventh one?
—RAY FRANK, Speech, Yom Kippur sermon (Spokane Falls, Washington), 1890

In former days, everyone found the assumption of innocence so easy; today we find fatally easy the assumption of guilt.
—CAROLYN G. HEILBRUN, *Poetic Justice* by Amanda Cross, 1970

You can't chase away guilt with a political slogan.
—ANNE ROIPHE, *Fruitful*, 1996

HEALTH & DISEASE
(*also see* The Human Body…& Its Parts)

Few of us have responded with enough urgency to meet this crisis of catastrophic proportions…. And a disease that has infected far more heterosexuals than homosexuals throughout the world was dismissed as a gay disease with that official, homophobic wink—implying that those deaths didn't really matter.
—BARBRA STREISAND in *Streisand: Her Life* by James Spada, 1995

I think of my illness [ovarian cancer] as a school, and finally I've graduated.
—GILDA RADNER, *Life*, 1988

—

But the world doesn't change itself because you have cancer. The only world that changes is yours!
—FRAN DRESCHER, *Cancer, Schmancer*, 2002

—

Laughter is one of the strongest medicines on the planet.... If it's strong enough to kill an orgasm, surely it's strong enough to kill cancer.
—LOTUS WEINSTOCK, Stand-up routine

—

Was I succulent? Was I juicy?
—ALICIA SUSKIN OSTRIKER, "Mastectomy," *The Crack in Everything*, 1996

—

Like one of those trees with a major limb lopped, I'm a shade more sublime today than yesterday
—ALICIA SUSKIN OSTRIKER, "Normal," *The Little Space*, 1998

—

Re a woman who suffers from aphasia (the loss of the ability to use words): Is she going to be "all there"? I don't know. But during a solar eclipse, the sun is still there, isn't it? And when a star collapses in on itself, isn't that star still there?
—SUSAN YANKOWITZ, *Night Sky*, 1991

—

When we began to see the results of our efforts [in research] in the form of new drugs which filled real medical needs and benefited patients in very visible ways, our feeling of reward was immeasurable.
—GERTRUDE B. ELION, *Les Prix Nobel*, 1988

—

There is a double standard of mental health—one for men, another for women—existing among most clinicians.... For a woman to be healthy, she must "adjust" to and accept the behavioral norms of her sex—passivity, acquiescence, self-sacrifice, and lack of ambition—even though these kinds of "loser" behaviors are generally regarded as socially undesirable (i.e. nonmasculine).

—PHYLLIS CHESLER, *Women and Madness*, 1972

There is no creativity in madness; madness is the opposite of creativity, although people may be creative in spite of being mentally ill.

—JOANNE GREENBERG, Comment, National Association for
Rights Protection and Advocacy, 1998

Our basic idea was that the nurse's peculiar introduction to the patient and her organic relationship with the neighborhood should constitute the starting point for a universal service to the region…. We planned to utilize, as well as to be implemented by all agencies and groups of whatever creed which were working for social betterment, private as well as municipal. Our scheme was to be motivated by a vital sense of the interrelation of all these forces…we considered ourselves best described by the term "public health nurses."

—LILLIAN D. WALD, *The House on Henry Street*, 1915

Of all the tyrannies which have usurped power over humanity, few have been able to enslave the mind and body as imperiously as drug addiction.

—FREDA ADLER, *Sisters in Crime*, 1975

In her drugged state, she felt only a euphoria, as if all the pain of her life had become a vast salty water, buoying up, where she floated on the great blue waves of a vast, melodramatic sea.

—SUSAN FROMBERG SCHAEFFER, *Falling*, 1973

To heal ourselves we also have to heal society.

—RIANE EISLER, *Sacred Pleasure*, 1995

Nothing cures like time and love…

—LAURA NYRO, "Time and Love," 1970

The work of healing is in peeling away the barriers of fear and past conditioning that keep us unaware of our true nature of wholeness and love.
　　　　　—JOAN BORYSENKO, *Minding the Body, Mending the Mind*, 1987

But the Divine Mind, and the divine attributes of God, have residence within man, they are within yourself, and therefore, healing, too, is within yourself; the healing that you seek is within yourself.
　　　　　—TEHILLA LICHTENSTEIN, "Believing is *Seeing*," *Four Centuries*, 1992

My friend healed. She began to push her troubles off her chest. They became smaller. Sometimes she could fit them in her pocket. Sometimes she could pluck them from her arm and keep them from burrowing into her skin, and squash them like ticks on her dog.
　　　　　—E. M. BRONER, "Body Memories," *Four Centuries*, 1992

What we call "madness" can also be caused or exacerbated by injustice and cruelty, within the family and society; and that freedom, radical legal reform, political struggle, and kindness are crucial to psychological and moral health.
　　　　　—PHYLLIS CHESLER, *Women and Madness*, 25th Anniversary Ed., 1997

Without the context of a political movement, it has never been possible to advance the study of psychological trauma.
　　　　　—JUDITH LEWIS HERMAN, *Trauma and Recovery*, 1992

My HMO is so expensive, they charge me for a self-breast exam. It's a flat fee.
　　　　　—WENDY LIEBMAN, http://www.wendyliebman.com, 9 June 2003

Next to gold and jewelry, health is the most important thing you can have.
　　　　　—PHYLLIS DILLER, Stand-up routine

She's so dumb that she studies for her Pap test.
                    —JOAN RIVERS in *Funny Women*, Unterbrink, 1987

Everyone knows the sound of heels clicking in hospital corridors. Everyone knows the tread of the heart.
                    —BETTE HOWLAND, *Things to Come and Go*, 1983

"Make yourself a nice hot toddy, and while you sip it, read Proust. Proust is the only thing when you're sick."… I skipped the hot toddy, but by God it worked. Saved me. Was the antibiotic which wouldn't "touch" the Thing I had. Marvelous crazy poet. Marvelous Proust.
                    —SUE KAUFMAN, *Diary of a Mad Housewife*, 1967

A man's illness is his private territory and, no matter how much he loves you and how close you are, you stay an outsider. You are healthy.
                    —LAUREN BACALL, *Lauren Bacall: By Myself*, 1978

Illness is the night-side of life, a more onerous citizenship. Everyone who is born holds dual citizenship, in the kingdom of the well and in the kingdom of the sick. Although we all prefer to use only the good passport, sooner or later each of us is obliged, at least for a spell, to identify ourselves as citizens of that other place.
                    —SUSAN SONTAG, *Illness as Metaphor*, 1978

The fact that illness is associated with the poor—who are, from the perspective of the privileged, aliens in one's midst—reinforces the association of illness with the foreign: with an exotic, often primitive place.
                    —SUSAN SONTAG, *Illness as Metaphor*, 1978

The usefulness of madmen is famous: they demonstrate society's logic flagrantly carried out down to its last scrimshaw scrap.
                    —CYNTHIA OZICK, "The Hole/Birth Catalog," *The First Ms. Reader*, 1972

Now I realised the distinction between neurosis and madness, and in my agitation I half-envied the woman beyond my bedroom wall, the sheer cool sanity of her behaviour within the limits of her impracticable mania.
—MURIEL SPARK, "Come Along, Marjorie," *Collected Stories: I*, 1968

You were asked to mistrust even the reality to which you were closest and which you could discern as clearly as daylight. Small wonder that mental patients have so low a tolerance for lies.
—JOANNE GREENBERG, *I Never Promised You a Rose Garden*, 1964

Later, they began to explore the secret idea that Deborah shared with all the ill—that she had infinitely more power than the ordinary person and was at the same time also his inferior.
—JOANNE GREENBERG, *I Never Promised You a Rose Garden*, 1964

While [women] live longer than ever before, and longer than men, there is less and less use for them in the only place they have been given—within the family. Many newly useless women are emerging more publicly and visibly into insanity and institutions.
—PHYLLIS CHESLER, *Women and Madness*, 1972

Nothing defines the quality of life in a community more clearly than people who regard themselves, or whom the consensus chooses to regard, as mentally unwell.
—RENATA ADLER, *Toward a Radical Middle*, 1969

The girl…was a gentle, generous veteran of mechanical psychiatry in a dozen other hospitals. Her memory had been ragged, but her sickness was still intact.
—JOANNE GREENBERG, *I Never Promised You a Rose Garden*, 1964

I don't romanticize mental illness. But at the same time, I wonder what will happen if we are able to lighten the load of memory. Would we end up with a drug to make loss "lite," to speed up "closure," to make horrors "manageable"? At some point reducing human suffering is editing human experience. For better or for worse.

—ELLEN GOODMAN, Syndicated Column, 15 November 2002

In a way, retarded children are satisfying. Everything is a triumph. Even getting Bucky to manage to get a spoon to his mouth was a triumph. God compensates.

—BEVERLY SILLS in *Divas*, Sargeant, 1959

The hysteria of women and the combat neurosis of men are one. Recognizing the commonality of affliction may even make it possible at times to transcend the immense gulf that separates the public sphere of war and politics—the world of men—and the private sphere of domestic life—the world of women.

—JUDITH LEWIS HERMAN, *Trauma and Recovery*, 1992

While patients with simple [post traumatic stress syndrome] fear they may be losing their minds, patients with the complex disorder often feel they have lost themselves.

—JUDITH LEWIS HERMAN, *Trauma and Recovery*, 1992

I would willingly give up my whole career if I could have just one normal child.

—BEVERLY SILLS in *Divas*, Sargeant, 1959

She always says she dislikes the abnormal, it is so obvious. She says the normal is so much more simply complicated and interesting.

—GERTRUDE STEIN, *The Autobiography of Alice B. Toklas*, 1933

"Psychiatry shmuckiatry," my father says. "A racket. They make money so families can split up. Look at the divorce rate."

—GLORIA DEVIDAS KIRCHHEIMER, *Goodbye, Evil Eye*, 2000

He had been in analysis for seven years and he regarded life as a long disease, alleviated by little fifty-minute bloodlettings of words from the couch.

—ERICA JONG, *How to Save Your Own Life*, 1977

Re *analysis*: It would straighten me out—and there goes the act.

—JOAN RIVERS in *Funny Women*, Unterbrink, 1987

Psychology has nothing to say about what women are really like, what they need and what they want, for the simple reason that psychology does not know. Yet psychologists will hold forth endlessly on the true nature of woman, with dismaying enthusiasm and disquieting certitude.

—NAOMI WEISSTEIN in *Psychology*, October 1969

Until psychologists realize that it is they who are limiting discovery of human potential...by their assumption that people move in a context-free ether, with only their innate dispositions and their individual traits determining what they will do, then psychology will have nothing of substance to offer in this task.

—NAOMI WEISSTEIN, Address, "'Kinder, Kuche, Kirche' as Scientific Law," American Studies Association (California), 26 October 1968

A large part of the popularity and persuasiveness of psychology comes from its being a sublimated spiritualism: a secular, ostensibly scientific way of affirming the primacy of "spirit" over matter.

—SUSAN SONTAG, *Illness as Metaphor*, 1978

I was like a social worker for lepers. My clients had a chunk of their body they wanted to give away; for a price I was there to receive it. Crimes, sins, nightmares, hunks of hair: it was surprising how many of them had something to dispose of. The more I charged, the easier it was for them to breathe freely once more.

—TAMA JANOWITZ, "Modern Saint 271," *Slaves of New York*, 1986

Psychotherapy, unlike castor oil, which will work no matter how you get it down, is useless when forced on an uncooperative patient.
—ABIGAIL VAN BUREN, "Dear Abby" Advice Column, 11 July 1974

What does a feminist therapist do that's different? A feminist therapist tries to *believe* what women say. Given the history of psychiatry and psychoanalysis, this alone is a radical act.
—PHYLLIS CHESLER, *Women and Madness*, 25th Anniversary Ed., 1997

I am not sure that even with a leader, encounter therapy works; without a leader, it is dangerous.
—NORA EPHRON, *Crazy Salad*, 1975

Depression is melancholy minus its charms—the animation, the fits.
—SUSAN SONTAG, *Illness as Metaphor*, 1978

Any important disease whose causality is murky, and for which treatment is ineffectual, tends to be awash in significance.
—SUSAN SONTAG, *Illness as Metaphor*, 1978

AIDS obliges people to think of sex as having, possibly, the direst consequences: suicide. Or murder.
—SUSAN SONTAG, *AIDS and Its Metaphors*, 1989

I envy paranoids; they actually feel people are paying attention to them.
—SUSAN SONTAG in *Time Out* (London), 19 August 1992

Pain is real when you get other people to believe in it. If no one believes in it but you, your pain is madness or hysteria.
—NAOMI WOLF, *The Beauty Myth*, 1990

Oh, the trifles, the people, that get on your nerves when you have a neurosis!
—MURIEL SPARK, "Come Along, Marjorie," *Collected Stories: I*, 1968

HOME & HOUSEKEEPING
(*also see* Mothers & Motherhood)

Cleaning your house while your kids are still growing
Is like shoveling the walk before it stops snowing.
—PHYLLIS DILLER, *Phyllis Diller's Housekeeping Hints*, 1966

"Woman's work! Housework's the hardest work in the world. That's why men won't do it."
—EDNA FERBER, *So Big*, 1924

Instilling habits of cleanliness promotes ideas of economy and exactness in the recipient, awakens dormant ambitions, and instills a feeling of self-respect. With a pure soul must be a clean body.
—REBEKAH BETTELHEIM KOHUT, Papers of the Jewish Women's Congress, 1893

My mother was such a fanatic that when there was nothing left in the house to clean, she'd go stand on the sidewalk and swat ants.
—CAROL K. HOWELL, "Saving Soviet Jewelry," *Nebraska Review*, Spring 1988

I'm not going to vacuum 'til Sears makes one you can ride on.
—ROSEANNE BARR on *Roseanne* (TV show)

My mother talked about "redoing"—as if anything had ever been done.
—BETTE HOWLAND, *Things to Come and Go*, 1983

Go, return each to her mother's house.
> —NAOMI, Book of Ruth, late fifth–early fourth century B.C.E., Bible

My home is in whatever town I'm booked.
> —POLLY ADLER, *A House Is Not a Home*, 1953

I ran away from [the ghetto in Hartford]. But I've been running back to it [and] to Mama [ever since].
> —SOPHIE TUCKER in *The Journey Home* by Joyce Antler, 1997

Re her two homes in New Jersey and Beverly Hills: One keeps us real, the other keeps us phony.
> —RENEE TAYLOR in *Funny Women*, Unterbrink, 1987

Re the family maid: She used to come over and make tuna salad and we'd watch *Let's Make a Deal* while my mom cleaned the house.
> —SANDRA BERNHARD in *Funny Women*, Unterbrink, 1987

To housekeep, one had to plan ahead and carry items of motley nature around in the mind and at the same time preside, as mother had, at table, just as everything, from the liver and bacon, to the succotash, to the French toast and strawberry jam, had not been matters of forethought and speculation.
> —FANNIE HURST, *Imitation of Life*, 1932

What can be wrong
That some days I hug this house
Around me like a shawl, and feel
Each window like a tatter in its skin,
Or worse, bright eyes I must not look through?
—SUSAN FROMBERG SCHAEFFER, "Housewife," *The Witch and the Weather Report*, 1972

I'm nine years behind in my ironing. I bury a lot in the backyard.

—PHYLLIS DILLER, Stand-up routine

I hate housework! You make the beds, you do the dishes—and six months later you have to start all over again.

—JOAN RIVERS, "Work," *Woman Talk*, Michèle Brown & Ann O'Connor, eds., 1984

The definition of women's work is shitwork.

—GLORIA STEINEM in *Writer's Digest*, February 1974

"Honey-chile, it will shore seem a funny world up dar widout washin'. If de Lawd's robes only needed launderin', I'd do his tucks de way He's never seen 'em done."

—FANNIE HURST, *Imitation of Life*, 1932

My tidiness, and my untidiness, are full of regret and remorse and complex feelings.

—NATALIA GINZBURG, "He and I," *Italian Writing Today*, 1967

A house in which there are no people—but with all the signs of tenancy—can be a most tranquil good place.

—MURIEL SPARK, "Portobello Road," *Collected Stories: I*, 1968

With four walk-in closets to walk in,
Three bushes, two shrubs, and one tree,
The suburbs are good for the children,
But no place for grown-ups to be.

—JUDITH VIORST, "The Suburbs Are Good for the Children,"
It's Hard to Be Hip Over Thirty..., 1968

But Lilo never seemed to understand that you have to have things before you can throw them away. It's easy for Lilo to turn up her nose at the suburbs. To

Lilo the word suburban is pejorative. But Lilo grew up in a suburb, in a white house guarded by a velvet lawn. I think you have to grow up on city streets to want lawns for your children.

—RABBI MARCIA TAGER, "Cousins," *Shaking Eve's Tree*, 1990

—

I need not say to a single woman within reach of my voice that never should any secondary duty take away from us the sacredness of the first, the near duty,...When such a conflict of duties presents itself, home and love are ever the magnets that draw us on, promising peace and rest.

—HANNAH GREENEBAUM SOLOMON, Presidential Address
(New York), NCJW Proceedings, 1896

THE HUMAN BODY...
& ITS PARTS
(*also see* Beauty & Appearance *and* Health & Disease)

It is the avant-garde teachers who...have come to realize that body release, not body control, is what is needed for natural grace to emerge, as opposed to artificial movement.

—VIOLA SPOLIN, *Improvisation for the Theater*, 1963

—

"You and I both have livers, large and small intestines, kidneys, spines, blood vessels, nerves, spleens, stomachs, hearts and, I had thought, brains in common. What conclusions do you draw from anatomy? That I am about to take you to the cleaners?"

—MARGE PIERCY, *Small Changes*, 1973

For the theatre one needs long arms; it is better to have them too long than too short. An artiste with short arms can never, never make a fine gesture.

—SARAH BERNHARDT, *Memories of My Life*, 1907

We need to cultivate the skill of sustaining a *calm body* with an *alert mind*. Many of us have forgotten, or have never known, how to achieve this balance. We are either awake, alert, and wired for action, or we are relaxed, lethargic, and possibly sleepy.

—SUSAN PARTNOW, *Everyday Speaking*, 1998

Whatever happens with us, your body will haunt mine

—ADRIENNE RICH, "(The Floating Poem, Unnumbered),"
The Dream of a Common Language, 1978

Acknowledging the body is acknowledging what is real…. It's such a strain, a struggle, to appear to be without physical blemish…to remain young as the relentless years add up. It's time consuming and emotionally depleting.

—ROSALYN DREXLER, *Contemporary Women Playwrights*, Betsko, 1987

This broad goes to an eye doctor. He holds up a chart with letters and says, "Can you read this?" She says, "No." He holds up another chart with bigger letters. "Can you see this?" "No," she says. He holds up another chart with huge letters. "Can you see this?" "No," she says. He takes out his schlong and says, "Can you see this?" "That I can see," she says. "Oh, that's your problem," he says. "You're cockeyed."

—PEARL WILLIAMS, Stand-up routine

I think it's time for a real woman who has led a real life to re-design Barbie. Let's start with her nose. I think a bump where her brother hit her with a base-ball bat while she was sleeping is a nice touch. Breasts. How about the kind that face east and west, wanting nothing to do with each other? Her hips could start out at a normal size and then quietly expand over the years while she remained powerless to do anything about it. I want little girls to grow up thinking, "Why should I go to the gym? My body may not be perfect but it's better than Barbie's." Are you listening, Mattel?

—RITA RUDNER, http://www.ritafunny.com, 2003

~

The Spanish have the right idea when it comes to talking about bodies: they say "the," not "my," distancing themselves. I am not my wattle.

—CAROL K. HOWELL, A *Fool at the Feast*, 2002

~

I don't know what my mother-in-law's measurements are. We haven't had her surveyed yet.

—PHYLLIS DILLER, Stand-up routine

~

I don't believe that science has proved the existence of male menopause, but if it did exist, my philosophy would be the same as for female menopause: You should do everything possible not to let your body dictate your actions. You can either give in to negative feelings or fight them, and I'm of the belief that you should fight them. To risk wrecking a marriage because you allow some supposed chemical change to rule your life is just not worth it!

—DR. RUTH WESTHEIMER, http://www.drruth.com,1997

~

When we ignore human movement we ignore our innate ability to perceive and respond to the process of becoming. We are naturally expressive through our bodies, and our rituals either build spontaneity or inhibit that option.

—FANCHON SHUR, "My Dance Work as a Reflection of a Jewish Woman's Spirituality," *Four Centuries*, 1992

~

Our tissues, our cells remember. . . .

—FANCHON SHUR, "My Dance Work as a Reflection of a Jewish Woman's Spirituality," *Four Centuries*, 1992

Why had no one told me that my body would become a battlefield, a sacrifice, a test? Why did I not know that birth is the pinnacle where women discover the courage to become mothers?

—ANITA DIAMANT, *The Red Tent*, 1997

"Are you there God? It's me, Margaret.
I just told my mother I want a bra.
Please help me grow God. You know where.
I want to be like everyone else."

—JUDY BLUME, *Are You There God? It's Me, Margaret*, 1970

If you are a girl, worry that your breasts are too round. Worry that your breasts are too pointed. Worry that your nipples are the wrong color. Worry that your breasts point in different directions.

If you are a boy, worry that you will get breasts.

If you are a boy, worry that you'll never be able to grow a mustache.

If you are a girl, worry that you have a mustache.

—DELIA EPHRON, *Teenage Romance*, 1981

Re her reasons for rejecting the flattening bandeau of the 1920s and devising the modern day bra in 1922: Nature made woman a bosom, so nature thought it was important. Why argue with nature?... A sister shouldn't look like a brother.

—IDA ROSENTHAL in *Women Inventors* by Linda Jacobs Altman, 1997

Re her breasts: Two reasons why I didn't become a ballerina.

—BETTE MIDLER in *Women in Comedy*, Martin, 1986

Re her breasts: I won't tell you how much they weigh, but it costs $87.50 to send them to Brazil.

—BETTE MIDLER, Concert patter

My breasts have fed three children, nurtured and sustained their bodies and built them up in twelve ways. If they wanna lay down after that, by god they deserve the rest. These tits are being donated to Madison Ave. after I die, to help sell cars and stereos and keep up the gross national product for you folks, so show a little fucking respect for me there kimosabe.

—ROSEANNE BARR, *My Life as a Woman*, 1989

After a certain number of years our faces become our biographies. We get to be responsible for our faces.

—CYNTHIA OZICK in *Writers at Work* (8th), 1988

I think your whole life shows in your face and you should be proud of that.

—LAUREN BACALL in *Daily Telegraph*, 2 March 1988

How does an inexpressive face age? More slowly, one would suppose.

—SUSAN SONTAG, *Death Kit*, 1967

Denial, grief, and then ultimately acceptance...those are the three stages I go through whenever I get a haircut.

—RITA RUDNER, *Tickled Pink*, 2001

She examines his body minutely and without shame, and he wakes to see her at it, and smiles without telling her why: she is the first not to pretend the different colours and textures of their being is not an awesome fascination. How can it be otherwise? The laws that have determined the course of life for them are made of skin and hair, the relative thickness and thinness of lips...Skin and hair. It has mattered more than anything else in the world.

—NADINE GORDIMER, *A Sport of Nature*, 1987

Washing the hands, we call to mind the holiness of body.

—MARCIA FALK, *The Book of Blessings*, 1996

Everything about me has stopped growing except my nose.
—FANNY BRICE in *The Fabulous Fanny* by Norman Katkov, 1953

On our wedding night, my husband said, "Can I help you with the buttons?" I was naked at the time.
—JOAN RIVERS, Stand-up routine

The senses are not discreet!
—JOANNE GREENBERG, *I Never Promised You a Rose Garden*, 1964

HUMOR & COMEDY
(*also see* Actors, Comedians & Performers *and* Show Biz, Sports & Entertainment)

God hath made me to laugh, so that all that hear will laugh with me.
—SARAH, Book of Genesis, c. ninth century B.C.E., Bible

Assertion is taking your own power, aggression is taking your power over others. I'm going to take power from the people who took power from me. A comic must be aggressive with an audience. It's not assertive, it's not sharing. Social satirists and people who deal with political analysis have to be very strong. They're not just getting up there and doing self-deprecating jokes.
—ROBIN TYLER in *The Body Politic*, September 1979

Nothing in our personal lives was sacred. We used all of it for material on the show. The most important thing was those ninety minutes live on Saturday night. So what if your whole world was falling apart as long as you could find a joke in it and make up a scene. Millions of Americans saw what we did, and it was a charmed time. We thought we were immortal, at least for five years. But that doesn't exist anymore.
—GILDA RADNER, *It's Always Something*, 1989

Men do not want women to be funny.... Men want women to be fluffy little air-heads. Men don't want women to be aggressive, but to become a real comic, you *have* to be aggressive.... To be aggressive and yet stay feminine, that's the trick.

—PHYLLIS DILLER in *Funny Women*, Unterbrink, 1987

I'm not afraid to do anything comedically. I don't worry about femininity. I see that being funny...frightens some men. But...it just won't shut me up.

—GILDA RADNER in *Funny Women*, Unterbrink, 1987

If you're a comic you have to be nice. And the audience has to like you. You have to have a softness about you, because if you do comedy and you are harsh, there is something offensive about it.

—FANNY BRICE in *Women in Comedy*, Martin, 1986

Men have this silly, witchy...attitude that a woman who is a comic has lost her femininity.

—PHYLLIS DILLER in *Women in Comedy*, Martin, 1986

The real reason for comedy is to hide the pain.

—WENDY WASSERSTEIN in *Contemporary Women Playwrights*, Betsko, 1987

Your anger can be 49 percent and your comedy 51 percent, and you are okay. If the anger is 51 percent, the comedy is gone.

—JOAN RIVERS, *Enter Talking*, 1986

My routines come out of total unhappiness. My audiences are my group therapy.

—JOAN RIVERS on BBC 2, 23 February 1990

Andy [Kaufman] had taught me a valuable lesson. The deeper the comedy came from within you, the funnier it was.

—ELAYNE BOOSLER in *Funny Women*, Unterbrink, 1987

My comedy is an observance of life. And so to start observing it too seriously would be the end of it.

—GILDA RADNER in *Women in Comedy*, Martin, 1986

You have to be basically an elegant person to succeed in comedy. If you don't have taste, your comedy will never make it. That's one of the true secrets of comedy.

—PHYLLIS DILLER in *Funny Women*, Unterbrink, 1987

If I thought I hurt anybody, I'd go crazy. That's why I pick on the biggies—they can take it.... Comedy should be on that very fine line of going too far.... Otherwise it's pap.

—JOAN RIVERS in *Funny Women*, Unterbrink, 1987

Comedy is tragedy revisited or hostility. It is mock hostility, of course, or it would be ugly.... Everybody has got to be bad. See, if everything is good, you've got Grace Kelly and that's not funny.

—PHYLLIS DILLER in *Women in Comedy*, Martin, 1986

It was no accident that Lenny [Bruce] had chosen comedy. It is the last "free speech" art form and, like my father said, it is mightier than the pen *and* the sword.

—ROSEANNE BARR, *My Life as a Woman*, 1989

Humor as a weapon in the social arsenal constructed to maintain caste, class, race, and sex inequalities is a very common thing.

—NAOMI WEISSTEIN, *She Needs*, 1973

Humor comes from pain.

—ROBIN TYLER in *Women in Comedy*, Martin, 1986

In anything Jewish I ever did, I wasn't standing apart, making fun of the race. I *was* the race, and what happened to me on the stage is what could happen to them. They identified with me, and then it was all right to get a laugh, because they were laughing at me as well as themselves.

—FANNY BRICE in *The Fabulous Fanny* by Norman Katkov, 1953

⁓

That was so funny I almost forgot to laugh.

—GILDA RADNER, as Geek Queen Lisa Lupner on *Saturday Night Live*

⁓

There is good taste in humor like there is good taste in clothes or furniture. It is okay for one Irishman to call another Irishman anything, any kind of name. But if you are not an Irishman, keep the mouth shut. The same with all people.

—FANNY BRICE in *Funny Women*, Unterbrink, 1987

⁓

What was most striking about [Woody] Allen's humor…is that this Jewish anxiety at the center of his wit touched something alive in America at the moment and went out beyond us…. It made Jews of gentiles.

—VIVIAN GORNICK in *Village Voice*

⁓

Humor fills the vacuum caused by taboo.

—PENINA V. ADELMAN, "The Womb and the Word," *Four Centuries*, 1992

⁓

A good laugh is good for the spirits it's true,
But a good cry is good for the soul.

—BETTE MIDLER, *The Saga of Baby Divine*, 1983

⁓

I laugh that I may not weep.

—ROBIN TYLER in *Women in Comedy*, Martin, 1986

I heard someone say, and so I said it too, that ridicule is the most effective weapon. Well, now I know. I know that there are things that never have been funny, and never will be. And I know that ridicule may be a shield, but it is not a weapon.

—DOROTHY PARKER in *You Might As Well Live* by John Keats, 1970

INDIVIDUALS, SELF-REALIZATION & HUMAN NATURE
(*also see* Life & Events)

We must believe in ourselves or no one else will believe in us.

—ROSALYN YALOW, *Les Prix Nobel Yearbook*, Tore Frängsmyr, ed., 1977

No matter where I run,
I meet myself there.

—DOROTHY FIELDS, "Where Am I Going?" *Sweet Charity*, 1966

You are translucent, and the world's own understanding and love shine through you.... You suffer from striving, but it is unnecessary. *You are already.*

—ANZIA YEZIERSKA, *All I Could Never Be*, 1932

Let me listen to me and not to them.

—GERTRUDE STEIN, Remark

I was born, I have lived, and I have been made over.

—MARY ANTIN, *The Promised Land*, 1912

Cherish forever what makes you unique,
   'cuz you're really a yawn if it goes.
                      —BETTE MIDLER, *The Saga of Baby Divine*, 1983

—

When you get older, you realize it's a lot less about your place in the world but your place in you. It's not how everyone views you, but how you view yourself.
             —NATALIE PORTMAN in *Star Wars Insider*, August 2002

—

All the process of uprooting, transportation, replanting, acclimatization, and development took place in my own soul.
                    —MARY ANTIN, *The Promised Land*, 1912

—

"Has any act of selfishness ever equaled the carnage perpetrated by disciples of altruism?"
                    —AYN RAND, *The Fountainhead*, 1943

—

Humility is no substitute for a good personality.
                    —FRAN LEBOWITZ, Remark

—

The day's blow
rang out, metallic—or it was I, a bell awakened,
and what I heard was my whole self
saying and singing what it knew: I *can*.
   —DENISE LEVERTOV, "Variation on a Theme by Rilke," *Breathing the Water*, 1989

—

Paradoxically, the more integrated we become as we strive to fashion our own life scripts, the more open we are to further changes in consciousness. And the more we dare to try out new paths, like all explorers of new territory, the more we open up further paths that make it possible for us to experience life in ways we never thought possible.
                    —RIANE EISLER, *Sacred Pleasure*, 1995

If sex and creativity are often seen by dictators as subversive activity, it's because they lead to the knowledge that you own your own body (and with it your own voice), and that's the most revolutionary insight of all.

—ERICA JONG, "The Artist as Housewife: The Housewife as Artist,"
The First Ms. Reader, 1972

If humans could be
that intensely whole, undistracted, unhurried,
swift from sheer
unswerving impetus! If we could blossom
out of ourselves, giving
nothing imperfect, withholding nothing!

—DENISE LEVERTOV, "The Métier of Blossoming," *This Great Unknowing*, 1998

What lets us be who we most are?
Suppose we only had to know
the climate, what grows where,
how rich or shallow the soil is.
A kind of field guide
for dislocated souls.

—SHIRLEY KAUFMAN, "Lemon Sponge," *Roots in the Air*, 1996

I read *The Magic of Believing* over and over for two solid years, and I began to believe.... And my belief in myself changed the entire course of my life.

—PHYLLIS DILLER in *Funny Women*, Unterbrink, 1987

One needs something to believe in, something for which one can have whole-hearted enthusiasm. One needs to feel that one's life has meaning, that one is needed in this world.

—HANNAH SENESH, *Hannah Senesh*, 1966

But by the time I'd grown up, I naturally supposed that I'd grown up.

—EVE BABITZ, *Eve's Hollywood*, 1974

You see, I have this tendency to confusion. It runs in the family. Goes back generations. My grandmother was the worst. When she heard ninety percent of crime happens in the home, she moved the house.
—SUE MARGOLIS, *Spin Cycle*, 2001

But the individual was not a tool for something. He was the maker of tools. He was the one who must build. Even for the best purpose it is criminal to turn an individual into simply a means for some ultimate end. A society in which the dignity of the individual is destroyed cannot hope to be a decent society.
—GOLDA MEIR, "The Zionist Purpose," Speech at Dropise College, 26 November 1967

If you live an autonomous life you never really are repressed.
—GRACE PALEY in *Ms.*, March 1974

No one had missed him, no one was in pursuit.
He himself must be
the key, now, to the next door,
the next terrors of freedom and joy.
—DENISE LEVERTOV, "St. Peter and the Angel," *Oblique Prayers*, 1984

The struggle to maintain my own individuality and freedom was always more important to me than the wildest love affair.
—EMMA GOLDMAN, *Emma Goldman in America* by Alice Wexler, 1984

I have deliberately chosen the uncertain path whenever I had a chance.
—EMILY "MICKEY" HAHN, *Nobody Said Not to Go* by Ken Cuthbertson, 1998

Now that she held this tremulous but growing conviction that she was alive, she began to be in love with the new world.
—JOANNE GREENBERG, *I Never Promised You a Rose Garden*, 1964

Every time you take the opportunity to speak from your deep convictions, you will learn more about yourself.

—SUSAN PARTNOW, *Everyday Speaking*, 1998

"And if I fight, then for *what?*"

"For nothing easy or sweet, and I told you that last year and the year before that. For your own challenge, for your own mistakes and the punishment for them, for your own definition of love and sanity—a good strong self with which to begin to live."

—JOANNE GREENBERG, *I Never Promised You a Rose Garden*, 1964

Sometimes I wonder if we were those two people nearly twenty years ago along via Nazionale; two people who talked so politely, so urbanely, in the sunset; who chatted about everything, and nothing; two pleasant talkers, two young intellectuals out for a walk; so young, so polite, so distracted, so ready to judge each other with absent kindliness, so ready to say goodbye for ever, in that sunset, on that street corner.

—NATALIA GINZBURG, *Little Virtues*, 1985

Looking at yourself in a mirror isn't exactly a study of life.

—LAUREN BACALL in *Daily Mail*, 1 November 1990

This anatomy of me is serving the double purpose of revealing me to myself.

—FANNIE HURST, *Anatomy of Me*, 1958

And when is there time to remember, to sift, to weigh, to estimate, to total?

—TILLIE OLSEN, "I Stand Here Ironing," *Tell Me a Riddle*, 1960

How long it takes us to gather the component parts of our memory—the problems, self-appraisals, the self-analysis, our little daily dilemmas, petty quests for comfort. And how quickly they can all disappear.

—YAËL DAYAN in *Israel Journal*, June 1967

She takes daily walks on the land that was once the bottom of the sea, marking and classifying, sifting through her thoughts the meaning of the jagged edge of discontent that have begun to make inroads anew inside her.

—VIVIAN GORNICK in Ms., October 1973

—

Lotus wants to be totally free; Weinstock will settle for a discount.

—LOTUS WEINSTOCK, Stand-up routine

—

I never looked at myself as a nitwit. I never looked at anything I did as vacant or dumb or bubble-headed. There was always a sensibility about what I did. Because someone is hopeful, because someone likes to have fun, because someone is trusting and open, does not necessarily mean that someone is stupid.

—GOLDIE HAWN in Women in Comedy, Martin, 1986

—

"I'm going to be independent like Misha was before she got herself into trouble. And who brought her down?" Ruthie asked agitatedly. "Nobody knows for sure, but it wasn't an angel, I can tell you. It was some man."

—LILIAN NATTEL, The River Midnight, 1999

—

If I talk, everyone thinks I'm showing off; when I'm silent they think I'm ridiculous; rude if I answer, sly if I get a good idea, lazy if I'm tired, selfish if I eat a mouthful more than I should, stupid, cowardly, crafty, etc.

—ANNE FRANK, The Diary of a Young Girl, 1947

—

Self-image is not created in a vacuum.

—ELAINE BERNSTEIN PARTNOW, Breaking the Age Barrier, 1981

—

It is easier to live through someone else than to become complete yourself.

—BETTY FRIEDAN, The Feminine Mystique, 1963

You lose in the end unless you know how the wheel is fixed or can fix it yourself.
—EDNA FERBER, *Saratoga Trunk*, 1941

Solitude is un-American.
—ERICA JONG, *Fear of Flying*, 1973

I want to be alone.
—VICKI BAUM, *Grand Hotel* (play), 1930

A world is locked up with every human being that passes beyond our physical ken.
—HENRIETTA SZOLD in *Lost Love*, Shargel, 1997

To write with my heart. To think and speak with my heart. To be adventurous, to be an activist, to be a rebel, to be compassionate, and most of all, to be a *mensch*—a decent human being.
—RUTH GRUBER, *Haven*, 1983

Poor human nature, what horrible crimes have been committed in thy name!
—EMMA GOLDMAN, *Anarchism and Other Essays*, 1911

The goat's business is none of the sheep's concern.
—EDNA FERBER, *Saratoga Trunk*, 1941

One must either accept some theory or else believe one's instinct or follow the world's opinion.
—GERTRUDE STEIN, "Helen," *Q.E.D.*, 1903

You have an opinion. I have an opinion. Life don't have no opinion.
—GRACE PALEY, "Zagrowsky Tells," *Later the Same Day*, 1985

I feel in opposition to almost everything.
—ELAINE MAY in *Women in Comedy*, Martin, 1986

I have never had the home-feeling anywhere since I was twelve years old; perhaps I never shall. I seem always to be standing on tiptoe at the edge of another, a different world. Perhaps Palestine, like the world of my childhood, will be nearer that world.
—JESSIE SAMPTER in *The Journey Home* by Joyce Antler, 1997

She tried to be respectable because respectability kept away the chaos that sometimes overwhelmed her, causing her to call out in her sleep, screaming wild sounds, a warning to the future, a mourning for the past.
—ANNE ROIPHE, *Long Division*, 1972

I read in a French book that there was nothing so abandoned as a respectable young girl.
—LILLIAN HELLMAN, *Toys in the Attic*, 1959

I think something is only dangerous if you are not prepared for it or if you don't have control over it or if you can't think through how to get yourself out of a problem.
—JUDITH RESNIK in *Time*, 10 February 1986

Every time I deny myself I commit a kind of suicide.
—SUSAN GRIFFIN, *Pornography and Silence*, 1981

We keep secrets from ourselves that all along we know.
—SUSAN GRIFFIN, *A Chorus of Stones*, 1992

It can be less painful for a woman not to hear the strange, dissatisfied voice stirring within her.
—BETTY FRIEDAN, *The Feminine Mystique*, 1963

Woe to the individual who attempts to ingratiate himself with the enemy instead of following his own route.

—HANNAH SENESH, *Hannah Senesh*, 1966

To keep anything the way you like it for yourself, you have to have the stomach to ignore—dead and hidden—whatever intrudes.

—NADINE GORDIMER, *The Conservationist*, 1975

It is distraction, not meditation, that becomes habitual; interruption, not continuity; spasmodic, not constant toil.

—TILLIE OLSEN, *Silences*, 1965

It was to take me almost half a lifetime of the Biblical three score and ten to evaluate properly the richness of that heritage.

—FANNIE HURST, *Anatomy of Me*, 1958

Identity is a bag and a gag. Yet it exists for me with all the force of a fatal disease. Obviously I am here, a mind and a body. To say there's no proof my body exists would be arty and specious and if my mind is more ephemeral, less provable, the solution of being a writer with solid (touchable, tearable, burnable) books is as close as anyone has come to a perfect answer. The obvious reason that every asshole in the world wants to write.

—JUDITH ROSSNER, *Nine Months in the Life of an Old Maid*, 1969

"The point is," Evelyn said, "we're taught that we have to be perfect. Like objects in a museum, not people. People don't have to be perfect, only objects do."

—JUDITH ROSSNER, *Looking for Mr. Goodbar*, 1975

It is not to be supposed that Miss Brodie was unique…. There were legions of her kind during the nineteen-thirties, women from the age of thirty and upward who crowded their war-bereaved spinsterhood with voyages of discovery into new ideas and energetic practices in art or social welfare, education or religion.

—MURIEL SPARK, *The Prime of Miss Jean Brodie*, 1961

INTELLIGENCE, MEMORY & THE MIND

(*also see* Education & Schools)

Humans, the only self-regarding animals, blessed or cursed with this torturing higher faculty, have always wanted to know why.

—NADINE GORDIMER in *Nobel Lectures*, 1991

Facts could be kept separate by a convention; that was what made childhood possible. Now knowledge finds me out; in all its risible untidiness.

—ADRIENNE RICH, "From Morning-Glory to Petersburg," *Snapshots of a Daughter-in-Law*, 1963

But what parent can tell when some such fragmentary gift of knowledge or wisdom will enrich her children's lives? Or how a small seed of information passed from one generation to another may generate a new science, a new industry— a seed which neither the giver nor the receiver can truly evaluate at the time.

—HELENA RUBINSTEIN, *My Life for Beauty*, 1966

The most elusive knowledge of all is self-knowledge and it is usually acquired laboriously through experience outside the classroom.

—MIRRA KOMAROVSKY, *Women in the Modern World*, 1953

Because nothing the mind leapt to was imperfect. Nothing was an accident.
                              —BONNIE FRIEDMAN, *The Thief of Happiness*, 2003

I was into pain reduction and mind expansion, but what I've ended up with is pain expansion and mind reduction.
                              —CARRIE FISHER, *Postcards from the Edge*, 1987

Four be the things I am wiser to know:
Idleness, sorrow, a friend, and a foe.

Four be the things I'd be better without:
Love, curiosity, freckles, and doubt.
                              —DOROTHY PARKER, "Inventory," *Enough Rope*, 1926

Woe! my knowledge is weak,
My wound is desperate.
                              —RAHEL MORPURGO, *The Harp of Rachel*, 1890

Once I had tasted of the fruit of the tree of knowledge, there was no going back.
                    —BLU GREENBERG in *The Journey Home* by Joyce Angler, 1997

We are always in search of the redeeming formula, the crystallising thought....
                              —ETTY HILLESUM, *An Interrupted Life*, 1983

I Brake for Insights.
                              —LOTUS WEINSTOCK, Stand-up routine

You will be a blessing to me, magic spell that is in the heart,
for bringing me to the fruit,
through it I will be redeemed,
Though I will no longer know flighty pleasure.
                              —ANDA AMIR, "Eve," *Land of Israel*, 1987

"Don't you believe 'em when they say that what you don't know won't hurt you. Biggest lie ever was. See it all and go your own way and nothing'll hurt you. If what you see ain't pretty, what's the odds! See it anyway. Then next time you don't have to look."

—EDNA FERBER, *Show Boat*, 1926

Why do you study so much? What secret are you looking for? Life will reveal it to you soon. I already know it all, without reading or writing. A little while ago, not much more than a few days ago, I was a child who went about in a world of colors, of hard and tangible forms. Everything was mysterious and something was hidden, guessing what it was was a game for me. If you knew how terrible it is to know suddenly, as if a bolt of lightning elucidated the earth. Now I live in a painful planet, transparent as ice; but it is as if I had learned everything at once in seconds. My friends, my companions became women slowly, I became old in instants and everything today is bland and lucid. I know that nothing lies behind, if there were something I would see it....

—FRIDA KAHLO in *Frida*, Herrera, 1983

"All you know is what you remember; pardon me, what you think you remember; pardon me, what you've been telling yourself you remember. All this time you've been talking to yourself. That's what you know."

—CAROL K. HOWELL, *A Fool at the Feast*, 2002

I have always felt that I've lived my life with all these extra images and experiences from other minds. I've got Goya's mind and Rembrandt's mind, Kathe Kollwitz's mind. I have access to all those other great visions of humanity, of nature, of order. I want to be among them. I want to add my voice, my vision.

—RUTH WEISBERG in *Exposures*, Brown, 1989

God has given us the physical eye, a miraculous instrument, with which to behold reality, the world about us, but he has given us the still more miraculous instrument of the imagination, he has given us the power of visualization, with which to create new and greater realities....

—TEHILLA LICHTENSTEIN, "Believing is *Seeing*," *Four Centuries*, 1992

Imagination is the highest kite one can fly.

—LAUREN BACALL, Remark

The first problem for all of us, men and women, is not to learn, but to unlearn.

—GLORIA STEINEM in *New York Times*, 26 August 1971

So who's to know?

—GERTRUDE BERG, *Me and Molly*, 1948

"I know it, and when I know a thing wid my knowin', I knows it."

—FANNIE HURST, *Imitation of Life*, 1932

Everybody gets so much information all day long that they lose their common sense.

—GERTRUDE STEIN, *Reflection on the Atomic Bomb*, 1973

I haven't managed to become learned about anything, even the things I've loved most in life: in me they remain scattered images, which admittedly feed my life of memories and feelings, but fail to fill my empty cultural wasteland.

—NATALIA GINZBURG in *Italian Writing Today*, 1967

We learn through experience and experiencing, and no one teaches anyone anything. This is as true for the infant moving from kicking to crawling to walking as it is for the scientist with his equations. If the environment permits it, anyone can learn whatever he chooses to learn; and if the individual permits it, the environment will teach him everything it has to teach.

—VIOLA SPOLIN, *Improvisation for the Theater*, 1963

The most beautiful thing in the world is, precisely the conjunction of learning and inspiration. Oh, the passion for research and the joy of discovery!

—WANDA LANDOWSKA, *Landowska on Music*, 1964

Learning is the new form of labor.

—SHOSHANA ZUBOFF in *Omni*, April 1991

Rebuking a student for muttering his lessons: Is it not written, "ordered in all things and sure?" If it [the Torah] is "ordered" in your 248 limbs it will be "sure," otherwise it will not be "sure."

—BERURIAH in *The Status of Women in Formative Judaism* by Leonard Swidler, 2001

As for logic, it's in the eye of the logician.

—GLORIA STEINEM in *The First Ms. Reader*, 1972

A love for mathematics is a rare thing; it's a terrible thing to waste wherever it is found.

—AMY COHEN in *Women's Review of Books*, November 1998

Doing mathematics requires a tolerance for frustration.

—AMY COHEN in *Women's Review of Books*, November 1998

Memory is a nutriment, and seeds stored for centuries can still germinate.

—ADRIENNE RICH, Lecture, *Blood, Bread, and Poetry*, 1986

I want to visit Memory Lane, I don't want to live there.

—LETTY COTTIN POGREBIN, *Deborah, Golda, and Me*, 1991

Bless the gift of memory
that breaks unbidden, released
from a flower or a cup of tea
so the dead move like rain through the room.

—MARGE PIERCY, *The Art of Blessing the Day*, 1999

Not for one second
will my self hold still, but wanders
anywhere,
everywhere it can turn...

—DENISE LEVERTOV, "Flickering Mind," *A Door in the Hive*, 1989

Just as having opposable thumbs differentiates us primates from all other
species, enabling us to grasp and wield tools and other objects in our hands,
having "opposable minds," if you will, enables Homo sapiens, unlike our pri-
mate cousins, to develop logic, self-argument, inner opposition, so that we can
grasp any situation and mold it into an agreeable and useful shape with our
minds.

—ELAINE BERNSTEIN PARTNOW, *Breaking the Age Barrier*, 1981

The mind makes its own business.

—GRACE PALEY, *Later the Same Day*, 1985

The mind's passion is all for singling out. Obscurity has another tale to tell.

—ADRIENNE RICH, "Focus," *Necessities of Life*, 1966

A rational process is a moral process.

—AYN RAND, *Atlas Shrugged*, 1957

The will to be totally rational
is the will to be made out of glass and steel:
and to use others as if they were glass and steel.

—MARGE PIERCY, *Sisterhood Is Powerful*, 1970

Evidence and reason: my heroes and my guides.

—NAOMI WEISSTEIN in *Women Look at Biology Looking at Women*, 1979

For a research worker the unforgotten moments of life are those rare ones, which come after years of plodding work, when the veil over nature's secret seems suddenly to lift and when what was dark and chaotic appears in a clear and beautiful light pattern.

—GERTY THERESA CORI in *Notable American Women*, 1980

Let men of understanding now arise
And teach us by their calculations wise
How long till our redemption's Star shall come

—RAHEL MORPURGO, Untitled (1859), *Four Centuries*, 1992

Boys don't make passes at female smart-asses.

—LETTY COTTIN POGREBIN, "Down with Sexist Upbringing," *The First Ms. Reader*, 1972

There's nothing worse than feeling dumb and having millions.

—SANDRA BERNHARD, *May I Kiss You on the Lips, Miss Sandra?*, 1998

He [Diego Rivera, renowned Mexican muralist and Kahlo's husband] has said many times that he would rather have many intelligent enemies than one stupid friend.

—FRIDA KAHLO in *Frida*, Herrera, 1983

She's so stupid, when she sees a sign that says "Wet Floor" she does.

—JOAN RIVERS, Stand-up routine

What is the use of thinking if after all there is to be organization.

—GERTRUDE STEIN, *Everybody's Autobiography*, 1937

There were people made to think and people made to listen. I ain't sure either you or Lundee were made to do either.

—LILLIAN HELLMAN, *Days to Come*, 1936

There are no dangerous thoughts; thinking itself is dangerous.

—HANNAH ARENDT, *The Life of the Mind*, 1978

"What is the meaning of this noise?"

"It's the sound of thinking, Mr. McCabe," I said.

—BEL KAUFMAN, *Up the Down Staircase*, 1964

Thought…is still possible, and no doubt actual, wherever men live under the conditions of political freedom. Unfortunately…no other human capacity is so vulnerable, and it is in fact far easier to act under conditions of tyranny than it is to think.

—HANNAH ARENDT, *The Human Condition*, 1958

Yet I cannot accept the politically dangerous doctrine that some sex-linked characteristic of females leads them to avoid rigorous thought.

—AMY COHEN in *Women's Review of Books*, November 1998

My wisdom came too late.

—TILLIE OLSEN, "I Stand Here Ironing," *Tell Me a Riddle*, 1960

Then I saw you, tree,
I recognized you by that apple,
you have stored it in the wisdom of all your juices.

And I knew the secret, for which you had grown,
for which you have grown tall, and even branched out,
I too have grown up,

I too have grown tall—
like you I carry my fruit.
                              —ANDA AMIR, "Eve," *Land of Israel*, 1987

—

Wisdom is the process by which visions are realized.
                              —SAVINA J. TEUBAL in *Four Centuries*, 1992

—

There's a helluva distance between wisecracking and wit. Wit has truth in it;
wisecracking is simply calisthenics with words.
                              —DOROTHY PARKER in *Writers at Work* (1st), 1958

—

It takes a lot of time to be a genius, you have to sit around so much doing nothing, really doing nothing.
                              —GERTRUDE STEIN, *Everybody's Autobiography*, 1937

—

I'm not afraid of facts, I welcome facts *but a congeries of facts is not equivalent to
an idea*. This is the essential fallacy of the so-called "scientific" mind. People
who mistake facts for ideas are incomplete thinkers; they are gossips.
          —CYNTHIA OZICK, "We Are the Crazy Lady and Other Feisty Feminist Fables,"
                                                        The First Ms. Reader, 1972

—

Ideas move fast when their time comes.
                              —CAROLYN G. HEILBRUN, *Toward a Recognition of Androgyny*, 1973

—

Ideas are powerful things, requiring not a studious contemplation but an action,
even if it is only an inner action. Their acquisition obligates each man in some
way to change his life, even if it is only his inner life. They demand to be stood
for. They dictate where a man must concentrate his vision. They determine his
moral and intellectual priorities. They provide him with allies and make him
enemies. In short, ideas impose an interest in their ultimate fate which goes far
beyond the realm of the merely reasonable.
                              —MIDGE DECTER, *The Liberated Woman and Other Americans*, 1971

Undernourished, intelligence becomes like the bloated belly of a starving child: swollen, filled with nothing the body can use.

—ANDREA DWORKIN, *Right-Wing Women*, 1978

A great many people think that polysyllables are a sign of intelligence.

—BARBARA WALTERS, *How to Talk with Practically Anybody about Practically Anything*, 1970

Intelligence at the service of poor instinct is really dangerous.

—GLORIA STEINEM in *Writer's Digest*, February 1974

Wild intelligence abhors any narrow world; and the world of women must stay narrow, or the woman is an outlaw. No woman could be Nietzsche or Rimbaud without ending up in a whorehouse or lobotomized.

—ANDREA DWORKIN, *Right-Wing Women*, 1978

Intellectuals can tell themselves anything, sell themselves any bill of goods, which is why they were so often patsies for the ruling classes in nineteenth-century France and England, or twentieth-century Russia and America.

—LILLIAN HELLMAN, *An Unfinished Woman*, 1969

Professional intellectuals are the voice of a culture and are, therefore, its leaders, its integrators and its bodyguards.

—AYN RAND, *For the New Intellectual*, 1961

Ever since Kant divorced reason from reality, his intellectual descendants have been diligently widening the breach.

—AYN RAND, *The New Left*, 1968

Original thought is like original sin: both happened before you were born to people you could not have possibly met.

—FRAN LEBOWITZ, *Social Studies*, 1981

She had opened her mind to the words the way an eye used to darkness, veiled with its lashes, opens cautiously to the light, and, finding it even a little blinding, closes itself too late. The light had come, and come invincibly, even after the eye had renounced it. It was too late to unsee.

—JOANNE GREENBERG, *I Never Promised You a Rose Garden*, 1964

I...stretch my hands
With an entreaty...
To show me the light
And give light to my eyes,
To each worm that glows in the darkness at night,
That it shall bring its wonder before my heart
And redeem the darkness that is enclosed in me.

—KADYA MOLODOWSKY, "Prayers," *Paper Bridges*, 1999

I have forgotten what it was
that I have been trying to remember.

—MURIEL RUKEYSER, "Women as Market," *The Speed of Darkness*, 1968

We must use what we have to invent what we desire.

—ADRIENNE RICH, *What Is Found There*, 1993

Remember your advice, easy to keep your head above water, empty things float. Float.

—TILLIE OLSEN, *Tell Me a Riddle*, 1960

In this obstinate race after the original—while avoiding thoroughly that which has already been said and taking refuge on an island that we thought was uninhabited—do we not risk running into a good old acquaintance who has just been dropped?

—WANDA LANDOWSKA, *Landowska on Music*, 1964

Interpretation is the revenge of the intellect upon art.
—SUSAN SONTAG, *Against Interpretation*, 1966

Intelligence…is really a kind of taste: taste in ideas.
—SUSAN SONTAG, *Against Interpretation*, 1966

Action was always better than rumination.
—FAYE KELLERMAN, *Stalker*, 2000

ISRAEL & ZIONISM

(*also see* Jews & Judaism)

Still on Israel's head forlorn,
Every nation heaps its scorn.
—EMMA LAZARUS, "The World's Justice," c. 1882

We hope for friendship with our Arab neighbors, we want to develop the country for the good of both the Jews and the Arabs…. We do not know what the future will bring but we pray and work for healing and peace.
—HENRIETTA SZOLD, Letter to her sister, *Pride of Our People* by David C. Gross, 1979

We intend to remain alive. Our neighbors want to see us dead. This is not a question that leaves much room for compromise.
—GOLDA MEIR in *Reader's Digest*, July 1971

We desire nothing more than peace, but we cannot equate peace merely with an apathetic readiness to be destroyed. If hostile forces gather for our proposed destruction, they must not demand that we provide them with ideal conditions for the realization of their plans.

—GOLDA MEIR, "The Israeli Action in Sinai: 1956," General Assembly of the United Nations, 5 December 1956

———

Let me tell you something that we Israelis have against Moses. He took us forty years through the desert in order to bring us to the one spot in the Middle East that has no oil!

—GOLDA MEIR, Remark

———

We have not the slightest doubt that eventually there will be peace and co-operation between us. This is a historic necessity for both peoples. We are prepared; we are anxious to bring it about now.

—GOLDA MEIR, "A Solemn Appeal to the Arabs," Statement, General Assembly of the United Nations, 7 October 1957

———

There is no Zionism except for the rescue of Jews.

—GOLDA MEIR, As Good as Golda, 1970

———

[As the years of World War II progressed, the children reaching Palestine as Youth Aliyah wards] seemed to become more sick, more bitter, without hope for the future.... It took months of patient effort for our social workers and nurses and doctors to restore their self-confidence, and to give them back their hope in the future.

—HENRIETTA SZOLD in Pride of Our People by David C. Gross, 1979

———

The action Israel needs now is social equalization, democratization, and a complete change of gatekeepers.... As long as Orthodoxy is the only legally recognized form of Judaism, as long as the army remains the perceived savior of the nation, and as long as men reign supreme in the state, synagogue, and military, complete freedom is impossible for those who are not Jewish, not Orthodox, or not male.

—LETTY COTTIN POGREBIN, Deborah, Golda, and Me, 1991

O you chimneys,
O you fingers
And Israel's body as smoke through the air!
                              —NELLY SACHS, "O the Chimneys," O the Chimneys, 1967

I'll tell you what Zionism is. It is a liberation movement for a people who have
been persecuted all their lives and throughout human history.
                              —BELLA ABZUG in The Journey Home by Joyce Antler, 1997

[Zionism is] Jewish messianism in a practical form. It is Jewish hope, aspiration,
dream, prayer made practical.
                              —HENRIETTA SZOLD, The Journey Home by Joyce Antler, 1997

If we are Zionists, as we say we are, what is the good of meeting and talking and
drinking tea? Let us do something real and practical—let us organize the Jewish
women of America and send nurses and doctors to Palestine.
                              —HENRIETTA SZOLD in Pride of Our People by David C. Gross, 1979

I certainly didn't expect to be affected so deeply, but the minute the plane landed I was overwhelmed with an indescribable feeling about being there. I didn't
have any kind of strong Zionist background, but going there changed my point
of view. [Israel] is now one of the deepest things in my life.
—ANNA SOKOLOW in Jewish Women's Archive (http://www.jwa.org), August 20, 2003

We only want that which is given naturally to all peoples of the world, to be
masters of our own fate, only of our fate, not of others', and in cooperation and
friendship with others.
                              —GOLDA MEIR in Golda Meir, Syrkin, 1984

Woe to the nations
    who rise against my race!
                              —JUDITH, Book of Judith, c. 150 B.C.E., Bible

When peace comes we will perhaps in time be able to forgive the Arabs for killing our sons, but it will be harder for us to forgive them for having forced us to kill their sons.

—GOLDA MEIR, Press conference, London, 1969

...you, lord, chose
Israel out of all the nations
and our ancestors out of all the people of old times
to be your heritage for ever.

—ESTHER, Book of Esther, c. 199–150 B.C.E., Bible

According to civil law, women are equal to men. But I have to go to a religious court as far as personal affairs are concerned. Only men are allowed to be judges there—men who pray every morning to thank God He did not make them women.

—SHULAMIT ALONI in *Crazy Salad* by Nora Ephron, 1975

Thus the Israeli woman, like her American counterpart, pushes aside all youthful enthusiasm and ambition to develop an active personality and instead copies the model with which she is presented—an agreeable beautiful doll and cheap servant. One day, when the children have grown up, she comes face to face with the emptiness and looks for fulfillment in language courses, ceramics and art circles, volunteer work and charity, wrapped around a cup of coffee watching a fashion show.

—SHULAMIT ALONI in *Israel* magazine, April 1971

Even today, in its mutilated form, Palestine is big enough to be an island in the sea of seemingly hopeless Jewish destiny, an island upon which we can peacefully build a lighthouse to beam its light into the darkness, a light of everlasting human values, the light of the one God.

—HANNAH SENESH, *Hannah Senesh*, 1966

Responding to this remark made by Sadducees: "It is written: 'Sing, O barren, thou that didst not bear.' Because she did not bear, she should sing?": Fool! Look at the end of the verse, where it is written, "for more are the children of the desolate than the children of the married wife, saith the Lord." Rather, what is the meaning of "O barren, thou didst not bear"?—Sing O community of Israel, who resembles a barren woman, for not having borne children like you, who are damned to hell.

—BERURIAH in *The Status of Women in Formative Judaism*
by Leonard Swidler, 2001

Judaism must be perpetuated and can be perpetuated only by their repatriation in the land of the fathers.... It will yield sanctuary, refuge, and protection in the days of readjustment soon to dawn, we hope.

—HENRIETTA SZOLD in *Henrietta Szold*, Lowenthal, 1942

On Friday a bomb exploded in the Jaffa marketplace killing as many persons as are killed, according to the newspaper reports, in a regular pitched battle in the Chinese or the Spanish war. Nevertheless, we are having "disturbances"—not a war—in Palestine!... It's no use warning me not to overwork; it's no use telling anybody in Palestine to take precautions. One has to grit one's teeth and take a chance.

—HENRIETTA SZOLD in *Henrietta Szold*, Lowenthal, 1942

I want to say to you, friends, that the Jewish community in Palestine is going to fight to the very end. If we have arms to fight with, we will fight with those, and if not, we will fight with stones in our hands.

—GOLDA MEIR, "In the Midst of Battle: 1948," Speech,
Council of Jewish Chicago, 21 January 1948

To me the mention of Israel is like the clang of a fire bell to a fireman.

—SOPHIE TUCKER in *The Journey Home* by Joyce Antler, 1997

Your Holiness, do you know what my earliest memory is? A *pogrom* in Kiev. When we were merciful and when we had no homeland and when we were weak, we were led to the gas chambers.
—GOLDA MEIR, Remark to Pope Paul VI, 19 January 1973

＿

Blow, Israel, the sacred cornet! Call
Back to thy courts whatever faint heart throb
With thine ancestral blood, thy need craves all.
—EMMA LAZARUS, "The New Year, Rosh-Hashanah, 5643 (1882),"
Emma Lazarus, 1982

＿

There is no city in the world which can bear comparison in point of interest with Jerusalem,—fallen, desolate, and abject even as it appears—changed as it has been since the days of its glory.
—JUDITH MONTEFIORE in *Essays in Jewish History*, Cecil Roth, ed., 1934

＿

No place has ever suffered like Jerusalem:—it is more than probable that not a single relic exists of the city that was the joy of the whole earth....
—JUDITH MONTEFIORE in *Essays in Jewish History*, Cecil Roth, ed., 1934

＿

During centuries of dislocation and powerlessness, we kept our soul. Now, we have a homeland and an army but our soul is in mortal danger.
—LETTY COTTIN POGREBIN, *Deborah, Golda, and Me*, 1991

JEWS & JUDAISM
(*also see* Faith, Religion, the Bible & Spirituality; God; *and* Israel & Zionism)

From time immemorial the Jewish woman has remained in the background, quite content to let the fathers and brothers be the principals in a picture wherein she shone only by a reflected light. And it is well that it has been so; for while she has let the strong ones do battle for her throughout centuries of darkness and opposition, she has gathered strength and courage to come forward in an age of progressive enlightenment to battle for herself if necessary, or prove by being a noble helpmeet how truly she appreciates the love which has shielded her in the past.

—RAY FRANK, Speech, Yom Kippur sermon, Spokane Falls, Washington, 1890

Re her role as the first female sofer stam *[Jewish ritual scribe] and her first commission to inscribe a Torah:* It's a very strong statement for women to be empowered to tell the story of our people.... This, I hope, will have permanent, long-term, positive impact on the role of women not only within traditional Judaism but globally, God willing.

—AVIEL BARCLAY in *Moment* (online), 2003

One of the things that has kept my inspiration for the service of God and the Jewish people has been what Rabbi Jacob Joseph Isaac Horowitz, the Lubliner Rebbe, said: "One cannot tell another which way to follow.... Each one must see to which way he is attracted, and in this way he is to serve with all his strength." That and the knowledge deep in the core of my soul that I am supposed to do this.

—AVIEL BARCLAY in *Moment* (online), 2003

I do believe that women must open Torah wide and seize it for themselves, though they know full well that the consequences may even be dangerous.

—VANESSA L. OCHS, *Words on Fire*, 1999

The purity of Jewish upbringing—the restrictions that one carries through life being a "nice Jewish girl"—what a burden.

—LAUREN BACALL, *Lauren Bacall: By Myself*, 1978

I'm just a little Jewish girl trying to be cute.

—DOROTHY PARKER, Remark

"They Don't Make Jews Like Jesus Anymore"

—PATSY ABBOT, song title

~

There was two little minks in the woods. A hunter comes by and shoots one and aims at the other. The first mink turns to his friend and says, "See you in shul."

—BELLE BARTH, Stand-up routine

~

I heard a rumor that [male rock star] Marilyn Manson's Jewish.... That must mean that somewhere there's 20 or 30 people who can say, "Oh yeah, Marilyn Manson, I went to Hebrew School with that guy."

—SARAH SILVERMAN, Stand-up routine

~

I come from a real rabbinical dynasty, and it couldn't help but have fashioned my life. It's given me so much inner peace and inner strength.

—GWYNETH PALTROW in "How Judaism Helped Gwyneth Paltrow" by Ivor Davis, JewZ.com

~

We might say she [woman] is the synagogue.

—REBEKAH BETTELHEIM KOHUT in *American Hebrew*, 31 December 1897

~

The woman for centuries was held in subjection because she was female; the Jew because of his religious belief in one God only, rejecting the Jew Jesus as a divinity. Hounded and bedeviled and persecuted, granted few rights and fewer privileges, they learned—the rejected Female and the rejected Jew—perforce to see through the back of their heads as well as through the front of their heads.

—EDNA FERBER, *A Kind of Magic*, 1963

~

If a Jew or Jewess who uses firearms to defend himself against firearms is a criminal, then many new prisons will be needed.

—GOLDA MEIR in *Golda Meir*, Syrkin, 1964

Those that perished in Hitler's gas chambers were the last Jews to die without standing up to defend themselves.
—GOLDA MEIR, "In the Hour of Deliverance: 1967" Speech, United Jewish Appeal rally at Madison Square Garden, New York, 11 June 1967

Judaism has no dying god, no embalming of dead bodies, above all no slightest version of death-instinct.
—CYNTHIA OZICK, "Choose Life," *The First Ms. Reader*, 1972

I had this idea that Jews *were* supposed to be better. I'm not saying they were, but they were *supposed* to be, and it seemed to me on my block that they often were. I don't see any reason in being in this world actually if you can't in some way be better, repair it somehow…. So to be like all the other nations seems to me a waste of nationhood, a waste of statehood, a waste of energy, and a waste of life.
—GRACE PALEY, *Just As I Thought*, 1998

"Young man, I am a Jew and a socialist. I think that's more than enough for one lifetime, don't you?"
—VIVIAN GORNICK, *Fierce Attachments*, 1987

Being a Jew, one learns to believe in the reality of cruelty and one learns to recognize indifference to human suffering as a fact.
—ANDREA DWORKIN, *Letters from a War-Zone*, 1989

Half-Jews do have a place in Jewish life whether the ultra-Orthodox like it or not.
—SUSAN JACOBY, *Half Jew*, 2000

I believe two qualities are necessary for engaging in *tikkun olam* [repairing the world]: one, that you have the ability to see the other, to see a problem, to see pain, to see injustice—not the theory of it, but the actual face of it, to see the face of the other. And secondly, that you are able to see yourself as a person capable of creating change....

> —MERLE FELD, "Women Who Dared," Jewish Women's Archive
> (http://www.jwa.org), August 2003

⁓

The Jewish world—and I mean the intensely Jewish world, not the usual secular circles that I move in—have more resources.... [They] have rituals, they have ceremonies, they have knowledge, they have things to do that other people do not in the cases of illness or emergency or a crisis like this.

> —BARBARA MYERHOFF in *In Her Own Time* (documentary film), 1986

⁓

The ordination of women was just the beginning of our journey. What would Jewish institutions look like if they were shaped in response to the values that seem to be shared by so many women—balance, intimacy, empowerment?... What will Jewish communities be like when rabbis stop being surrogate Jews and instead enable their communities to take responsibility for their Jewish lives? What will Jewish institutions be like when we make room for the many different kinds of Jews we know there are...?

> —RABBI LAURA GELLER, "From Equality to Transformation,"
> *Gender and Judaism*, T. M. Rudavsky., ed., 1995

⁓

I learned first hand what it means to be defined as "the Other," the deviant. I was a respectable, bourgeois person, with class privileges...and then within weeks I was defined as a Jew, nothing else.

> —GERDA LERNER, *Why History Matters: Life and Thought*, 1997

⁓

Why had this religion of ours once been so fixated on secret parts of women? I was sure the menstrual practices, like animal sacrifice, had long been abandoned.

> —VANESSA L. OCHS, *Words on Fire*, 1999

⁓

From my early youth I believed in two things: one, the need for Jewish sovereignty, so that Jews...can be masters of their own fate; and two, a society based

on justice and equality without exploitation. But I was never so naïve or foolish as to think that if you merely believe in something it happens. You must
struggle for it.

—GOLDA MEIR in *Twentieth-Century Women*
Political Leaders by Claire Price-Groff, 1998

We [in Israel] are not a better breed; we are not the best Jews of the Jewish people. It so happened that we are there and you are here. I am certain that if you
were there and we were here, you would be doing what we are doing there, and
you would ask us who are here to do what you will have to do.

—GOLDA MEIR in *Twentieth-Century Women*
Political Leaders by Claire Price-Groff, 1998

Q: Why does a Jew always answer a question with a question?

A: And why should a Jew *not* answer a question with a question?

—ERICA JONG, *Fear of Flying*, 1973

Is discord going to show itself while we are still fighting, is the Jew once again
worth less than another? Oh, it is sad, very sad, that once more, for the
umpteenth time, the old truth is confirmed: "What one Christian does is his
own responsibility, what one Jew does is thrown back at all Jews."

—ANNE FRANK, *The Diary of a Young Girl*, 1947

The Wandering Jew in me seeks forgetfulness…[but] I can never forget, for I
bear the scars. But I want to forget…. I want to be now of to-day.

—MARY ANTIN, *The Promised Land*, 1912

I can no more return to the Jewish fold that I can return to my mother's womb.

—MARY ANTIN in *Common Ground*, Spring 1941

I have found my wider world of the spirit, and nothing can dislodge me.... In all those places where race lines are drawn, I shall claim the Jewish badge; but in my Father's house of many mansions I shall continue a free spirit.

—MARY ANTIN in *Common Ground*, Spring 1941

I am a historian because of my Jewish experience.

—GERDA LERNER, *Why History Matters*, 1997

Back to square one. The Jew remains "the Other." [But] I am a Jewish woman, I am an immigrant, and I will no longer permit others to define me.

—GERDA LERNER, *A Death of One's Own*, 1978

We can't forget that Judaism's worldview rests on a hierarchical paradigm (God over man, man over woman-child-animal-plant) that sanctifies male supremacy and diminishes the female in its theology, history, and daily ritual.

—LETTY COTTIN POGREBIN, *Deborah, Golda, and Me*, 1991

I feel successful when we—the congregation and I—are Jewish together.

—RABBI SALLY PRIESAND in *New York Times*, 19 September 1993

I was pained but not surprised to feel invisible as a lesbian among Jews. I was terribly disappointed and confused to feel invisible as a Jew among lesbians.

—EVELYN TORTON BECK, Introduction, *Nice Jewish Girls*, 1989

We have an obligation to do this, offering a place where homosexuals and their families can worship. Critics say that homosexuality destroys the family, but we reconstruct families that have been shattered.

—RABBI SHARON KLEINBAUM in *The Journey Home*, by Joyce Antler, 1997

We want a Jewish community where people participate, one that truly welcomes all people, and different people, in our midst. The Torah tells us over and

over...about the stranger in Egypt.... For us, exile is not a literary metaphor or a convenient refrain. It has genuine meaning every day in our lives.
—RABBI SHARON KLEINBAUM in *New York Times*, 5 May 1993

—

[I was taught] to speak quietly in public, to dress without ostentation, to repress all vividness or spontaneity, to assimilate with a world which might see us as too flamboyant.... If you did not effectively deny family and community, there would always be a cousin claiming kinship with you, who was the wrong kind of Jew.
—ADRIENNE RICH, "Split at the Root," *Nice Jewish Girls*, 1989

—

I think the world has to be startled a little bit. While being reverent about Jewish tradition, at the same time we have to be creative and bold.
—RABBI SHARON KLEINBAUM in *The Journey Home* by Joyce Antler, 1997

—

Our two-thousand-year history justifies us, the present compels us, the future gives us confidence.
—HANNAH SENESH, *Hannah Senesh*, 1966

—

To be a Jew is to care—not only about ourselves, but about others.
—BELLA ABZUG in *The Journey Home* by Joyce Antler, 1997

—

Women could get into Heaven because they were wives and daughters of men. Women had no brains for study of God's Torah, but they could be the servants of men who studied the Torah. Only if they cooked for the men, and washed for the men, and didn't nag or curse the men out of their homes; only if they let the men study the Torah in peace, then, maybe, they could push themselves into Heaven with the men, to wait on them there.
—ANZIA YEZIERSKA, *The Bread Givers*, 1925

"Poverty becomes a Jew like a red ribbon on a white horse. But you're no longer a Jew. You're a *meshumeides*, an apostate, an enemy of your own people. And even the Christians will hate you."

—ANZIA YEZIERSKA, *Red Ribbon on a White Horse*, 1950

Down with the wall that divides us from our Christian brother! High up with the standard of Judaism in the other camp. Act in every sense of the word as *American Jews*.... It is a glorious privilege to be a Jew, but it is also glorious to be an American.

—REBEKAH BETTELHEIM KOHUT, Papers of the Jewish Women's Congress, 1893

We are not Jews first and Americans afterward, we are American Jews.

—JULIA RICHMAN in *Julia Richman* by Selma C. Berrol, 1993

I believe...that the Jewish people, because of the ancient and historic struggle for social and economic justice, should be peculiarly fitted to recognize a special Jewish mission in the cause of the modern socialist movement.

—ROSE PASTOR STOKES in *Daughters of the Book*, Sigerman, 1992

Most of [Jewish] laws seem to me good, wise and beautiful. But some do not. Shall I break those? For me the answer lies in Zionism, in Palestine. We are a democratic people that has kept its identity for two thousand years through the preservation of its laws; but in recent centuries our developing law has stood still; it needs revisions.

—HENRIETTA SZOLD in *The Journey Home* by Joyce Antler, 1997

Women, Jewish women among them, have conquered a place in public life where it was not accorded to them. That place they will occupy, let the reactionary say what he will.

—HENRIETTA SZOLD in *The Maccabaean*, July 1903

We [Hadassah] are an organization of Jewish women who believe in the "healing of the daughter of the people," in the healing of the soul of the Jewish people as well as its body.

—HENRIETTA SZOLD, Speech to Hadassah, New York City

The Kaddish means to me that the survivor publicly and markedly manifests his wish and intention to assume the relation to the Jewish community which his parent had, and that so the chain of tradition remains unbroken from generation to generation, each adding its own link.

—HENRIETTA SZOLD in *Henrietta Szold*, Lowenthal, 1942

Wherever Jews have lived, no matter how trying the circumstances, they established *yeshivot* [schools].

—VANESSA L. OCHS, *Words on Fire*, 1999

Why isn't there one *Techninnah* [supplication or prayer] in all the books to fit my modern case—not one to raise up the spirit of a so-called emancipated woman, Heaven save the mark!

—HENRIETTA SZOLD in *Lost Love*, Shargel, 1997

I have felt that to be a Jew was, in some ways at least, to be especially privileged. Two thousand years of persecution have made the Jew quick to sympathy, quick-witted (he'd better be), tolerant, humanly understanding. The highest compliment we can pay a Christian is to say of him that he has a Jewish heart.

All this makes life that much more interesting. It also makes life harder, but I am perverse enough to like a hard life.... I like overcoming things. Maybe a psychiatrist could tell me why, and it might not prove flattering. Being a Jew makes it tougher to get on, and I like that.

—EDNA FERBER, A *Peculiar Treasure*, 1939

The denial of woman's ability to serve the synagogue in every part of its work is cruel and dangerous.

—REBEKAH BETTELHEIM KOHUT in *American Hebrew*, 31 December 1897

I realized that even if we were born Jews, there was a moment in our lives when we *became* Jews.

—RUTH GRUBER, *Haven*, 1983

Jewishness was my home, and God sitting up in the sky, was my friend.

—RUTH GRUBER, *Ahead of Time: My Early Years as a Foreign Correspondent*, 1991

To be a Jew in the twentieth century
Is to be offered a gift. If you refuse,
Wishing to be invisible, you choose
Death of the spirit, the stone insanity.

—MURIEL RUKEYSER, "Letter to the Front," *Beast in View*, 1944

Just as it took our people forty years of wandering in the desert to reach a rich and fertile promised land, the journey toward the promised land of an egalitarian Judaism is far from over.

—RABBI LAURA GELLER, "From Equality to Transformation,"
Gender and Judaism, T. M. Rudavsky., ed., 1995

The gentlemen here tell me, it is not considered essential for ladies to observe that strict piety which is required of themselves; but surely at a place of devotion the mind ought to testify due respect and gratitude toward the Omnipotent.

—JUDITH MONTEFIORE in *Essays in Jewish History*, Cecil Roth, ed., 1934

We must not remain Hebrews only because our fathers were.

—GRACE AGUILAR, *The Spirit of Judaism*, 1842

As descendants of the great nation to whom God entrusted his Holy Law, which was to enlighten all the people of the earth, and the living witnesses of His sacred Legacy, the Jews ought to be among the purest and wisest of the sons of men, and the most faithful adherents to their religious duties; therefore it is incumbent on them to "teach their children diligently."

—REBECCA GRATZ, *Occident and American Jewish Advocate* 16, 1858

—

Although our stock is naturally so vigorous that in Europe the Jews remain after incalculable suffering and privation the healthiest of races, yet close confinement and sedentary occupations have undeniably stunted and debilitated us in comparison with our normal physical status. For nearly nineteen hundred years we have been living on an idea; our spirit has been abundantly fed, but our body has been starved, and has become emaciated past recognition, bearing no likeness to its former self.

Let our first care to-day be the re-establishment of our physical strength, the reconstruction of our national organism, so that in future, where the respect due to us cannot be won by entreaty, it may be commanded, and where it cannot be commanded, it may be enforced.

—EMMA LAZARUS in *American Hebrew*, 3 November 1882–23 February 1883

—

Every true Jewess is a priestess, and by the very strength of her unobtrusive belief is a witness for religion; and when faith in God is the source of her virtues, truth and integrity, gentleness and purity the foundation stones of her life, then truly is she a blessing in Israel.

—REBEKAH BETTELHEIM KOHUT, NCJW Proceedings, 1896

—

The Jewish religion is purest Monotheism. It knows no dogmas, no church, no sects, no proselytes, no mission, no worldly or political ambitions. It is in the best sense a matter of private conscience; it has and needs no outward forms and authorities to bind its members together.

—BERTHA PAPPENHEIM in *Jewish Review*, January 1913

—

The house of study—the home and nursery of specifically Jewish culture—has ever been closed to the woman, and wherever Jewish learning is transmitted in the traditional way, so it will remain in the future.

—BERTHA PAPPENHEIM in *Jewish Review*, January 1913

There is only one domain which the Jewish woman shares equally with the man, and that is in the fulfillment of that command, which was said by one of our sages to contain the whole of the Jewish religion, "Love thy neighbor as thyself."

—BERTHA PAPPENHEIM in *Jewish Review*, January 1913

My father is not a strictly observant Orthodox Jew. He does as others do. Sometimes he Observes. Sometimes he Looks the Other Way.

—BETTE HOWLAND, *Things to Come and Go*, 1983

...for her religion had nothing to do with it. This was hard for the family to accept. Religion, they think, has everything to do with everything. If it was not for their religion, they ask, why else were six million Jews killed?

—RABBI MARCIA TAGER, "Cousins," *Shaking Eve's Tree*, 1990

It is almost difficult to remember God amid all the rules and bustle of everyday Jewish life. We have appropriated Jewish observance so well that we take it for granted, just as we often take the ones we hold most dear for granted because we are already comfortable with them.

—RABBI SUSAN C. GROSSMAN, "On *Tefillin*," *Four Centuries*, 1992

"If we forget the Jews in Auschwitz, they died for nothing. If we forget the Jews in Russia, they suffer for nothing. That is what makes a Jew a Jew. He remembers."

—CAROL K. HOWELL, "Saving Soviet Jewelry," *Nebraska Review*, Spring 1988

One shouldn't have to choose between Jewish skills and Jewish values, but I realized through my jealousy that as an adult one can learn how to *daven* and *lain* and speak Hebrew, but it is much harder as an adult to learn that being Jewish means being involved with *tikkun olam*.

—RABBI LAURA GELLER in *Four Centuries*, 1992

Many people accuse Jews of loving money.... Let me set you straight. Jews do not love money, Jews love food and Jews love stories and Jews love life. The food and life parts are the reason we acquire money because we comprehend that those piles of quarters may buy us our lives at any given time in any given country with any given peoples who really believe that money and God are the same thing.
—ROSEANNE BARR, *My Life as a Woman*, 1989

We cannot be asked to fragment ourselves. We are women. And we are Jews. We are feminists. And we are Zionists. And we just take all parts of ourselves with us...wherever there is work to be done in the struggle for freedom, justice and dignity.
—LETTY COTTIN POGREBIN in *The Journey Home* by Joyce Antler, 1997

"Jews don't think about heaven—we think about history."
—CAROL K. HOWELL, "Tornado Watch Cookbook," *Shaking Eve's Tree*, 1990

"That's the difference between us and them," Sven said. "Gentiles are on such chummy terms with the unknown."
—LAURIE COLWIN, "A Big Storm Knocked It Over," *Shaking Eve's Tree*, 1990

Oh that the sound of the Shofar might rouse the congregation...that a generation would arise, born of strength and love and reverence for the holy Schechina [sic], who blesses those who live and govern with a pure heart.
—BERTHA PAPPENHEIM, "Prayers, II, A Prayer for Women,"
Stephanie Forchheimer, tr., 1946

[Keeping kosher was] the symbol of an initiation, like the insignia of a secret brotherhood, that set her apart and gave her freedom and dignity. Every law whose yoke she accepted willingly seemed to add to her freedom: she herself had chosen...to enter that brotherhood. Her Judaism was no longer a stigma, a meaningless accident of birth from which she could escape.... It had become a distinction, the essence of her self-hood, what she was, what she wanted to be, not merely what she happened to be.
—JESSIE SAMPTER, *In the Beginning* (unpub. novel)

Think of it, ye Israelites, the chosen of the earth, so divided as to how you will worship Jehovah that you forget to worship at all!

—RAY FRANK, Yom Kippur sermon (Spokane Falls, Washington), 1890

To be a Jew is a destiny.

—VICKI BAUM, *And Life Goes On*, 1932

Why must I give them
Victory anew
The laughing tormentors
In their graves
Who rise to assault my calendar

—BLU GREENBERG, "Resisting Yom Hashoah 1985," *Four Centuries*, 1992

He lived in a village where the goyim lined up at dawn to watch their Jewish neighbors being crammed into cattle cars, then occupied their houses, ate from their plates, wore their clothing, slept in their beds. Abel has no doubt their sleep was sound and their digestion good.

—CAROL K. HOWELL, "Gittel's Golem," *Story Quarterly*, October 2001

But the consciousness of the people was saved by the *Torah*, that invisible but all-powerful mobile State.

—HANNAH SENESH, *Hannah Senesh*, 1966

We have only our holy Torah in which we may find and learn all that we need for our journey through this world to the world to come. It is like a rope which the great and gracious God has thrown to us as we drown in the stormy sea of life, that we may seize hold of it and be saved.

—GLÜCKEL OF HAMELN, *Memoirs*, 1692

Torah is the source of Jewish wisdom *(hochmah)*, whose roots are our foundations and whose branches spread out to infinity.

—SAVINA J. TEUBAL, *"Simchat Hochmah:* A Crone Ritual," *Four Centuries,* 1992

There is a Torah of our lives as well as the Torah that was written down. Both need to be listened to and wrestled with: both unfold through interactive commentary.

—RABBI LAURA GELLER in *Four Centuries,* 1992

Wrestling with Torah is like making love. I get close enough to be wounded—and the texts often hurt. But I've gotten close enough to be blessed—the astonishing moment of blinding insight when the world suddenly looks forever different, when we discover wholeness in what had seemed to be disparate and unconnected.

—RABBI LAURA GELLER in *Four Centuries,* 1992

The Covenant is silent about women; the Covenant consorts with the world at large.

—CYNTHIA OZICK, *Lilith,* Spring/Summer 1979

There was none of the chaos of our own services—women waving and talking in the balconies, men swaying and chanting and beating their breasts below. This service was orderly. It didn't seem Jewish at all.

—LYNN FREED, "Foreign Student," *Shaking Eve's Tree,* 1990

The shul needed a new roof. It needed a lot of other things besides, primarily new blood, but a roof was easier to find.

—CAROL K. HOWELL, "Tornado Watch Cookbook," *Shaking Eve's Tree,* 1990

I had spent the New Year itself with a family who filled my spiritual emptiness with pancakes; who thought the Diaspora would be ended through the sheer force of their hospitality.

—NIKKI STILLER, "A State of Emergency," *Shaking Eve's Tree,* 1990

LANGUAGE, LANGUAGES & WORDS

(*also see* Communication)

By making literature in *mame-loshn* patrilineal rather than matrilineal, Sholom Aleichem instantly created a male Yiddish literary dynasty.... Just when Yiddish was being championed as an authentic national *mame-loshn* [he] declared—and everyone agreed—its literature now belonged to the fathers.

—IRENA KLEPFISZ, *Found Treasures*, 1994

As the Yiddish lessons continue, Jack's reading to me has become, along with dreams and old photographs, another key to memories squirreled away for over half a century. It is as if I have unlocked a trunk where the words had been stored like wedding linens, too precious for everyday use, or velvet draperies, no longer in fashion, but too good to give away.

—FAYE MOSKOWITZ, "Learning Yiddish," *Peace in the House*, 2002

They had learned Yiddish at home; their first language, the primary language, the expression of feeling and family life. For them it meant a separation between that life and the rest. (What they called "this cockeyed world.") But for us it meant a division within the family itself; barriers between parents and children; bitterness fated.

—BETTE HOWLAND, *Things to Come and Go*, 1983

There's only two Yiddish words you need to know. *Gelt* and *schmuck*. If a man has no *gelt* he is.

—BELLE BARTH, Stand-up routine

I don't mean to be vulgar, but it's profitable!

—BELLE BARTH, Stand-up routine

Euphemisms, like fashions, have their day and pass, perhaps to return at another time. Like the guests at a masquerade ball, they enjoy social approval only so long as they retain the capacity for deception.

—FREDA ADLER, *Sisters in Crime*, 1975

If the men in the room would only think how they would feel graduating with a "spinster of arts" degree they would see how important this [language reform] is.

—GLORIA STEINEM, Speech, Yale University, 23 September 1981

Only where there is language is there world.

—ADRIENNE RICH, "The Demon Lover," *Leaflets*, 1969

This is the oppressor's language, yet I need it to talk to you.

—ADRIENNE RICH in *Yearning* by bell hooks, 1990

Finding language that will allow people to act together while cherishing each other's individuality is probably the most feminist and therefore truly revolutionary function of writers.

—GLORIA STEINEM, *Outrageous Acts and Everyday Rebellions*, 1983

A language is a map of our failures.

—ADRIENNE RICH, "The Burning of Paper Instead of Children,"
The Will to Change, 1971

Language makes culture, and we make a rotten culture when we abuse words.

—CYNTHIA OZICK, "We Are the Crazy Lady and Other Feisty Feminist Fables,"
The First Ms. Reader, 1972

No foreign tongue, no jargon! We are Israelites, but we are Americans as well.

—REBEKAH BETTELHEIM KOHUT, Papers of the Jewish Women's Congress, 1893

Only what is written in French is poetry, and only what is sung in Italian is music. The rest is holy—the Hebrew—or harsh—the German.
                    —GLORIA DeVIDAS KIRCHHEIMER, *Goodbye, Evil Eye*, 2000

I stand and listen to people speaking French in the stores and in the street. It's such a pert, crisp language, elegant as rustling taffeta.
                                          —BELVA PLAIN, *Evergreen*, 1978

This language [oppressive patriarchy] makes me sleepy. It makes my ankles swell.

                                          —ANNE ROIPHE, *Fruitful*, 1996

It is the nature of aphoristic thinking to be always in a state of concluding; a bid to have the final word is inherent in all powerful phrase-making.
                         —SUSAN SONTAG, *Barthes: Selected Writings*, 1982

Though collecting quotations could be considered as merely an ironic mimetism—victimless collecting, as it were…in a world that is well on its way to becoming one vast quarry, the collector becomes someone engaged in a pious work of salvage. The course of modern history having already sapped the traditions and shattered the living wholes in which precious objects once found their place, the collector may now in good conscience go about excavating the choicer, more emblematic fragments.
                                —SUSAN SONTAG, *On Photography*, 1977

LAW & ORDER

(*also see* Civil Rights, Social Movements & Activism)

No great idea in its beginning can ever be within the law. How can it be within the law? The law is stationary. The law is fixed. The law is a chariot wheel which binds us all regardless of conditions or place or time.
> —EMMA GOLDMAN, "Address to the Jury," *Mother Earth,* April 1916

In commercial law, the person duped was too often a woman. In a section on land tenure, one 1968 textbook explains that "land, like women, was meant to be possessed."
> —RUTH BADER GINSBURG in Ms., April 1974

The phenomenon of female criminality is but one wave in this rising tide of female assertiveness—a wave which has not yet crested and may even be seeking its level uncomfortably close to the high-water mark set by male violence.
> —FREDA ADLER, *Sisters in Crime,* 1975

Crime is naught but misdirected energy.
> —EMMA GOLDMAN, *Anarchism and Other Essays,* 1911

Stripped of ethical rationalizations and philosophical pretensions, a crime is anything that a group in power chooses to prohibit.
> —FREDA ADLER, *Sisters in Crime,* 1975

I think women often get not so much an unfair deal as an illogical one. Once in the Cabinet we had to deal with the fact that there had been an outbreak of assaults on women at night. One minister (a member of an extreme religious party) suggested a curfew. Women should stay home after dark. I said: "But it's the men who are attacking the women. If there's to be a curfew, let the men stay at home, not the women."

—GOLDA MEIR, Speech

—

No punishment has ever possessed enough power of deterrence to prevent the commission of crimes. On the contrary, whatever the punishment, once a specific crime has appeared for the first time, its reappearance is more likely than its initial emergence could ever have been.

—HANNAH ARENDT, Eichmann in Jerusalem, 1963

—

If I were a good judge it was because I felt I might have committed every crime or offense charged against the children brought before me. That I had not was largely a matter of luck, privilege, and always feeling loved.

—JUSTINE WISE POLIER in The Journey Home by Joyce Antler, 1997

—

Explaining why she never wore her heavy judicial robes in Family Court: There is nothing about a black robe that encourages a child to talk to me like a human being.

—JUSTINE WISE POLIER in Jewish Heroes and Heroines of America by Seymour Brody, 1996

—

But even judges sometimes progress.

—EMMA GOLDMAN in Mother Earth, April 1916

—

A judge steps out of the proper judicial role most conspicuously and dangerously when he or she flinches from a decision that is legally right because the decision is not the one the home crowd wants.

—RUTH BADER GINSBURG in Women in American Law, Berry, 1996

—

Laws are extremely useful indicators of the behaviors that are at a particular time and place considered acceptable or unacceptable.

—RIANE EISLER, Sacred Pleasure, 1995

Her heart beat for law, even for tax law.
                          —CYNTHIA OZICK, *The Puttermesser Papers*, 1997

The long history of antiobscenity laws makes it very clear that such laws are most often invoked against political and life-style dissidents.
                          —GLORIA STEINEM in *Ms.*, October 1973

After all, that is what laws are for, to be made and unmade.
                          —EMMA GOLDMAN in *Mother Earth*, April 1916

In the United States we have a society pervaded from top to bottom by contempt for the law.
                          —BARBARA TUCHMAN in *Newsweek*, 12 July 1976

I don't follow precedent, I establish it.
                          —FANNY ELLEN HOLTZMAN in *Women in American Law*, Berry, 1996

There are enough high hurdles to climb, as one travels through life, without having to scale artificial barriers created by laws or silly regulations.
                          —GLORIA ALLRED in *Los Angeles Times Home Magazine*, 7 January 1979

That man is a creature who needs order yet yearns for change is the creative contradiction at the heart of the laws which structure his conformity and define his deviancy.
                          —FREDA ADLER, *Sisters in Crime*, 1975

Woman throughout the ages has been mistress to the law, as man has been its master. The controversy between rule of law and rule of men was never relevant to women—because, along with juveniles, imbeciles, and other classes of legal nonpersons, they had no access to law except through men.
                          —FREDA ADLER, *Sisters in Crime*, 1975

Gentlemen, women have the vote. Further progress is inevitable. Our common concern should be to attract the best types of women to the law, to set honorable standards. Why admit a woman to the practice of law if you're going to ban her from the Bar Building? A tolerant approach will reflect greater dignity on all of us.

—FANNY ELLEN HOLTZMAN in *The Lady and the Law* by Ted Berkman, 1976

In the strange heat all litigation brings to bear on things, the very process of litigation fosters the most profound misunderstandings in the world.

—RENATA ADLER in *Lawyer's Wit and Wisdom*, 1995

A verbal agreement is not worth the paper it's written on.

—FANNY BRICE in *Funny Women*, Unterbrink, 1987

There is no privacy more inviolable than that of the prisoner. To visualize that cell in which he is thinking, to reach what he alone knows; that is a blank in the dark.

—NADINE GORDIMER, *The House Gun*, 1997

Together we hunted down the answers to all the seemingly insoluble riddles which a complex and callous society presented.... And yet for the sake of these answers, for the sake of American democracy, justice and brotherhood, for the sake of peace and bread and roses, and children's laughter, we shall continue to sit here [in prison] in dignity and in pride—in the deep abiding knowledge of our innocence before God and man, until the truth becomes a clarion call to all decent humanity.

—ETHEL ROSENBERG, *Death House Letters of Ethel and Julius Rosenberg*, 1953

Justice is a performance.

—NADINE GORDIMER, *The House Gun*, 1997

who would have thought
that JUSTICE
GOD'S TORTOISE
would be so slow
> —NIKKI STILLER, "Apocalyptic Thursday," *Newark Review*, Vol. 2, set 1

I do think that being the second woman is wonderful, because it is a sign that being a woman in a place of importance is no longer extraordinary.
> —RUTH BADER GINSBURG [the second woman appointed to the U.S. Supreme Court; Sandra Day O'Connor was the first] in *Women in American Law*, Berry, 1996

Her sandal ravished his eyes,
her beauty took his soul prisoner...
and the scimitar cut through his neck!
> —JUDITH, Book of Judith, c. 150 B.C.E., Bible

We Americans seem to be obsessed with the brilliance of the devious criminal mind. In reality, most felons are just plain dumb.
> —FAYE KELLERMAN, *Stalker*, 2000

LIFE & EVENTS

(*also see* Individuals, Self-Realization & Human Nature)

The preciousness of every ordinary moment is emphasized with every tick of the clock. Isn't it a magnificent day?
> —BEL KAUFMAN, *Up the Down Staircase*, 1964

Keep me from saying right now in the ripeness of my years.
Unharness the horses, Mitika, I don't want to go anywhere.
Keep me from saying such things.
> —MALKA HEIFETZ TUSSMAN, "Keep Me," *With Teeth in the Earth*, 1992

There are events without which one's life becomes unimportant, a worthless toy; and there are times when one is commanded to do something, even at the price of one's life.
> —HANNAH SENESH, Diary Entry (25 December 1943), *Hannah Senesh*, 1966

There are lives that are shut and should stay shut.
> —LILLIAN HELLMAN, *Toys in the Attic*, 1959

You have to learn to do everything, even to die.
> —GERTRUDE STEIN, Remark

Is the whole of life stripping ourselves of cliché after cliché?
> —BONNIE FRIEDMAN in *New York Times*, 14 March 1999

Life is a negotiation.
> —WENDY WASSERSTEIN, Remark

Life may be hated or wearied of, but never despised.
> —TILLIE OLSEN, "Tell Me a Riddle," *Tell Me a Riddle*, 1960

Make sure that your Life is a Rare Entertainment!
It doesn't take anything drastic.
You needn't be gorgeous or wealthy or smart
Just Very Enthusiastic!
> —BETTE MIDLER, *The Saga of Baby Divine*, 1983

living in the orchard and being
hungry, and plucking
the fruit

—DENISE LEVERTOV, "O Taste and See," O *Taste and See*, 1963

—

Nobody lives without a personal life.

—GRACE PALEY in *Women Writing in America* by Blanche H. Gelfant, 1984

—

"How do I save my own life?" the poet asked.

"By being a fool," God said.

—ERICA JONG, *How to Save Your Own Life*, 1977

—

Find comfort in your daily walk my child
and say hello to things you've never known
and lift yourself to touch their hands
and love them, for all time,
For soon again, you know
you'll have to walk alone.

—LOTUS WEINSTOCK, "Find Comfort," 1987

—

Be loyal to life, don't create fiction but accept what life is giving you, show
yourself worthy of whatever it may be by recollecting and pondering over it,
thus repeating it in imagination: "this is the way to remain alive."

—HANNAH ARENDT, *Men in Dark Times*, 1968

—

As the hours dragged by, we were beckoned into the mysteries of Indian time.
Things happen when they happen. There is no rush. Nothing to do, no place
to go better than where you are. This is a great clinical exercise for type A personalities. You either learn to go with the flow here or resign yourself to drop-
ping dead from a heart attack.

—JOAN BORYSENKO, *A Woman's Journey to God*, 1999

Two girls discover
the secret of life
in a sudden line of
poetry.

I who don't know the
secret wrote
the line.

—DENISE LEVERTOV, "The Secret," *Poems 1960–1967*, 1964

It's all an experiment, isn't it? Aren't we just one great big petri dish in the cosmos?

—ELAINE BERNSTEIN PARTNOW, *Hear Us Roar*, 1988

The human condition is such that pain and effort are not just symptoms which can be removed without changing life itself; they are the modes in which life itself, together with the necessity to which it is bound, makes itself felt. For mortals, the "easy life of the gods" would be a lifeless life.

—HANNAH ARENDT, *The Human Condition*, 1958

The mute inglorious Millions: those whose waking hours are all struggle for existence; the barely educated; the illiterate; women—their silence the silence of centuries as to how life was, is, for most of humanity.

—TILLIE OLSEN, *Silences*, 1965

What at one time one refuses to see never vanishes but returns, again and again, in many forms.

—SUSAN GRIFFIN, *A Chorus of Stones*, 1992

Dying seems less sad than having lived too little.

—GLORIA STEINEM, *Outrageous Acts and Everyday Rebellions*, 1983

My life has been a tapestry of rich and royal hue.
An everlasting vision of the ever-changing view.

—CAROLE KING, "Tapestry," *Tapestry*, 1971

I am one of those people who can't help getting a kick out of life—even when it's a kick in the teeth.

—POLLY ADLER, *A House Is Not a Home*, 1953

And if the central religious image [in Neolithic times] was a woman giving birth and not, as in our time, a man dying on a cross, it would not be unreasonable to infer that life and the love of life—rather than death and the fear of death—were dominant in society as well as art.

—RIANE EISLER, *The Chalice and the Blade*, 1987

She was thinking about it she was thinking about life. She knew it was just like that through and through.

She never did not want to leave it.

She did not want to stop thinking about it thinking about life, so that is what she was thinking about.

—GERTRUDE STEIN, "Ida," 1941

Life after life after life goes by
without poetry,
without seemliness,
without love.

—DENISE LEVERTOV, "The Mutes," *The Sorrow Dance*, 1966

All is pattern, all life, but we can't always see the pattern when we're part of it.

—BELVA PLAIN, *Crescent City*, 1984

Sow in me your living breath,
As you sow a seed in the earth.

—KADYA MOLODOWSKY, "Prayers," *Paper Bridges*, 1999

My life is made up of so many, many routine, confused details that there is no pattern to it. Occasionally there arises from the swirling mass of "categorical imperatives" that keep me submerged spiritually, a momentary, blue electric shaft, in the light of which I see my plans for myself made oh! So many years ago. The plans were for something so different from that which has come about, and they were so much finer than this incessant wrestling with projects, organizations, details, and defensive tactics.

—HENRIETTA SZOLD in *The Journey Home* by Joyce Antler, 1997

It just goes to show you, it's always something.

—GILDA RADNER, "Roseanne Rosannadanna" on *Saturday Night Live*

Life is a series of delicate meetings held together by a spider's thread strong as a steel span, tender as the wind blowing it all away.

—SANDRA BERNHARD, *May I Kiss You on the Lips, Miss Sandra?*, 1998

For a long time it seemed to me
that real life was about to begin,
but there was always some obstacle in the way.

Something had to be got through first,
some unfinished business;
time still to be served,
a debt to be paid.

Then life would begin.

At last it dawned on me
that these obstacles were my life.

—BETTE HOWLAND, "Obstacles"

If logic tells you that life is a meaningless accident, don't give up on life. Give up on logic.

—RABBI SHIRA MILGROM in *Four Centuries*, 1992

But suppose we viewed life not as using up our limited supply but as the accumulation of moments—moments like treasures.

—RABBI SHIRA MILGROM in *Four Centuries*, 1992

Often, the truly great and valuable lessons we learn in life are learned through pain. That's why they call it "growing pains." It's all about yin and yang. And that's not something you order off column A at your local Chinese restaurant.

—FRAN DRESCHER, *Cancer, Schmancer*, 2002

Life has a way of distracting you. One minute you're contemplating absolute evil, and the next you're rinsing out your hosiery and checking the roast.

—CAROL K. HOWELL, *Defying Gravity*, 1995

If life is the problem—short, arbitrary, unfair—then life is also the solution: life is what distracts you from the awful and essential fact of life.

—CAROL K. HOWELL in *Oxford* magazine, Vol. XVI, 2002

Life is a do-it-yourself kit, so do it yourself. Work. Practice.

—PHYLLIS DILLER in *Funny Women*, Unterbrink, 1987

Let us bless the source of life that nurtures fruit on the vine as we weave the branches of our lives into the tradition.

—FANCHON SHUR, *The Book of Blessings*, 1992

I don't understand how a woman who survived the McCarthy Period, the Russian Revolution, and my own adolescence can tremble at the sight of a cockroach or be rattled by a trip on the crosstown bus. Perhaps the kind of

character shaped by waiting in a cellar for the latest pogrom to pass enables you
to deal with catastrophes but makes waiting for a cab a melodrama.

—NIKKI STILLER, "A State of Emergency," *Shaking Eve's Tree*, 1990

It's not the tragedies that kill us, it's the messes.

—DOROTHY PARKER in *Writers at Work* (1st), 1958

However confused the scene of our life appears,
however torn we may be who now do face that scene,
it can be faced, and we can go on to be whole.

—MURIEL RUKEYSER, *The Life of Poetry*, 1949

We must live for the few who know and appreciate us, who judge and absolve
us, and for whom we have the same affection and indulgence. The rest I look
upon as a mere crowd, lively or sad, loyal or corrupt, from whom there is nothing to be expected but fleeting emotions, either pleasant or unpleasant, which
leave no trace behind them.

—SARAH BERNHARDT, *The Memoirs of Sarah Bernhardt*, 1977

This living, this living, this living,
Was never a project of mine.

—DOROTHY PARKER, "Coda," *Sunset Gun*, 1928

In order to live a fully human life we require not only control of our bodies
(though control is a prerequisite); we must touch the unity and resonance of
our physicality, our bond with the natural order, the corporeal grounds of our
intelligence.

—ADRIENNE RICH, *Of Woman Born*, 1976

We have almost succeeded in leveling all human activities to the common
denominator of securing the necessities of life and providing for their abundance.

—HANNAH ARENDT, *The Human Condition*, 1958

So one chamber after the other is locked up in our hearts as we go through life, and sometimes the very key is lost.

—HENRIETTA SZOLD in *Lost Love*, Shargel, 1997

~

I am an instrument in the shape of a woman
trying to translate pulsations into images
for the relief of the body and the reconstruction of the mind.

—ADRIENNE RICH, "The Burning of Paper Instead of Children,"
The Will to Change, 1971

~

Immortality is what nature possesses without effort and without anybody's assistance, and immortality is what the mortals must therefore try to achieve if they want to live up to the world into which they were born, to live up to the things which surround them and to whose company they are admitted for a short while.

—HANNAH ARENDT, *Between Past and Future*, 1961

~

There is no magic to immortality.

—ANITA DIAMANT, *The Red Tent*, 1997

~

But I do not believe that the banks of a river suffer for letting the water run, or that the art suffers because it rains, or the atom suffers discharging its energy.... For me everything has a natural compensation.

—FRIDA KAHLO in *Frida*, Herrera, 1983

~

Considering how dangerous everything is nothing is really very frightening.

—GERTRUDE STEIN, *Everybody's Autobiography*, 1937

~

Much happens when we're not there.

—DENISE LEVERTOV, "Window-Blind," *Breathing the Water*, 1989

Certain national and international events decided the work and friendships of my daily life.... Of course I didn't realize it at the time. It just seemed like more bad news.

—GRACE PALEY, *Just As I Thought*, 1998

It's the frames which make some things important and some things forgotten. It's all only frames from which the content rises.

—EVE BABITZ, *Eve's Hollywood*, 1974

The new always happens against the overwhelming odds of statistical laws and their probability, which for all practical, everyday purposes amounts to certainty; the new therefore always appears in the guise of a miracle.

—HANNAH ARENDT, *The Human Condition*, 1958

You do too much. Go and do nothing for a while. Nothing.

—LILLIAN HELLMAN, *Toys in the Attic*, 1959

When you got nothin' to do, we can't do it for you.

—LILLIAN HELLMAN, *Days to Come*, 1936

It was easy enough to kill yourself in a fit of despair. It was easy enough to play the martyr. It was harder to do nothing. To endure your life. To wait.

—ERICA JONG, *Fear of Flying*, 1973

A nightmare is terrifying because it can never be undone.... While in the beautiful well-ordered lie of our everyday lives there was almost nothing we could not do.

—JUDITH ROSSNER, *Nine Months in the Life of an Old Maid*, 1969

Existence is no more than the precarious attainment of relevance in an intensely mobile flux of past, present, and future.
—SUSAN SONTAG, *Styles of Radical Will*, 1969

How can I say it, if not timidly like this: life is it self my self. Life is it self my self, and I don't understand what I say. And then I adore.
—CLARICE LISPECTOR, A *Paixão segundo G. H.*
(The Passion According to G. H.), 1967

I was not looking for my dreams to interpret my life, but rather for my life to interpret my dreams.
—SUSAN SONTAG, *The Benefactor*, 1963

Persons who merely have-a-life customarily move in a dense fluid. That's how they're able to conduct their lives at all. Their living depends on not seeing.
—SUSAN SONTAG, *Death Kit*, 1967

Although none of the rules for becoming more alive is valid, it is healthy to keep on formulating them.
—SUSAN SONTAG, *I, Etcetera*, 1979

"Art and religion first; then philosophy; lastly science. That is the order of the great subjects of life, that's their order of importance."
—MURIEL SPARK, *The Prime of Miss Jean Brodie*, 1961

LOVE & DESIRE

(*also see* Friendship *and* Relationships & the Sexes)

When love is out of your life, you're through in a way. Because while it's there it's like a motor that's going, you have such vitality to do things, big things, because love is goosing you all the time.
> —FANNY BRICE in *The Fabulous Fanny* by Norman Katkov, 1953

Man has bought brains, but all the millions in the world have failed to buy love. Man has subdued bodies, but all the power on earth has been unable to subdue love. Man has conquered whole nations but all his armies could not conquer love. Man has chained and fettered the spirit, but he has been utterly helpless before love. High on a throne, with all the splendor and pomp his gold can command, man is yet poor and desolate, if love passes him by. And if it stays, the poorest hovel is radiant with warmth, with light and color. Thus love has the magic power to make of a beggar a king. Yes, love is free; it can dwell in no other atmosphere. In freedom it gives itself unreservedly, abundantly, completely.
> —EMMA GOLDMAN, *Anarchism and Other Essays*, 1910

Gee, I'd like to give you something swell, baby,
Diamond bracelets Woolworth's doesn't sell, baby.
Till that lucky day, you know darn well, baby,
That I can't give you anything but love.
> —DOROTHY FIELDS, "I Can't Give You Anything but Love,"
> with Jimmy McHugh, 1920s

Love is much nicer to be in than an automobile accident, a tight girdle, a higher tax bracket or a holding pattern over Philadelphia.
> —JUDITH VIORST in *Redbook*, February 1975

just when i think i'm getting the knack
i see you and have a panic attack
now i'm an acrobat on the channel changer
and it seems i'm out of danger
—JUSTINE FRISCHMANN, "In the City," *The Radio One Sessions*, 2001

Sometimes people fall in love with people they shouldn't marry.
—GWYNETH PALTROW, Quoted by Dotson Rader in *Parade* magazine, 17 January 1999

Love, by its very nature, is unworldly, and it is for this reason rather than its rarity that it is not only apolitical but antipolitical, perhaps the most powerful of all antipolitical human forces.
—HANNAH ARENDT, *The Human Condition*, 1958

Do you want me to tell you something really subversive? Love *is* everything it's cracked up to be. That's why people are so cynical about it.
—ERICA JONG, *How to Save Your Own Life*, 1977

Love, the strongest and deepest element in all life, the harbinger of hope, of joy, of ecstasy; love, the defier of all laws, of all conventions; love, the freest, the most powerful molder of human destiny; how can such an all-compelling force be synonymous with that poor little State and Church-begotten weed, marriage?
—EMMA GOLDMAN, *Anarchism and Other Essays*, 1911

It's true love because
If he said quit drinking martinis but I kept on drinking them
and the next morning I couldn't get out of bed,
He wouldn't tell me he told me.
—JUDITH VIORST, "True Love"

They say your fist
is roughly
the size of your heart.
I'm looking for
the well-hung woman.

—DAPHNE GOTTLIEB, "Personal Ad," St. 2, *Pelt*, 1999

—

I kept my age, my gray hair, my lined face before me all the time, even when
that peculiar young happy feeling took possession of me in his presence.... I
kept myself well in hand. Of course, there were times when my passion
absorbed and mastered me. One evening, it had been snowing and raining and
sleeting, but it stopped, and a high whistling wind arose. I could not stay in, the
pain at my heart drew me out at eight o'clock in the evening, and I raced
around Morningside Park screaming at the top of my voice whenever the wind
was noisy enough to drown my agony. That calmed me, and I came back to my
desk, feeling as though I could never again give way. What a mistake! How
many nights since then I have prayed and wrestled with myself, and writhed on
my bed, and been in utter blank despair for days at a time.

—HENRIETTA SZOLD in *Lost Love*, Shargel, 1997

—

The most vital right is the right to love and be loved.

—EMMA GOLDMAN, *Anarchism and Other Essays*, 1911

—

But young love thrives on colour, warmth, beauty. It becomes prosaic and inar-
ticulate when forced to begin its day at four in the morning...and to end that
day at nine, numb and sodden with weariness, after seventeen hours of physical labor.

—EDNA FERBER, *So Big*, 1924

—

If love does not know how to give and take without restrictions, it is not love,
but a transaction that never fails to lay stress on a plus and a minus.

—EMMA GOLDMAN, *Anarchism and Other Essays*, 1911

Love, our subject:
we've trained it like ivy to our walls
baked it like bread in our ovens
worn it like lead on our ankles

—ADRIENNE RICH, *Poems*, 1974

Bless the teaching of how to open
in love so all the doors and windows of the
body swing wide on their rusty hinges
and we give ourselves with both hands.

—MARGE PIERCY, "She'ma, 2," *The Art of Blessing the Day*, 1999

Oh, life is a glorious cycle of song,
A medley of extemporanea;
And love is a thing that can never go wrong;
And I am Marie of Roumania.

—DOROTHY PARKER, "Comment," *Enough Rope*, 1926

oh baby
i want to be your direct object.
you know, that is to say
i want to be on the other
side of all the verbs i know
you know how to use.

—DAPHNE GOTTLIEB, "watch your tense and case," St. 1, *Pelt*, 1999

Suddenly, I see that the diffused love, which is the deepest lesson of the East,
has within it the seeds of nonpossessive love. And with a surprised weariness I
remember my own country. For God knows, those clutched, nonseparating
marriages of the West don't indicate *love*.

—VIVIAN GORNICK, *In Search of Ali-Mahmoud*, 1973

When my soul was in the lost-and-found
You came along to claim it.

—CAROLE KING, "A Natural Woman," *Tapestry*, 1967

Obviously, love is an old established track.
Ten million suckers walk the plank.
If you land on your tail
Every time that you fall
There must be a reason for it all.
Love is the reason for it all.

—DOROTHY FIELDS, "Love Is the Reason," with Arthur Schwartz,
A Tree Grows in Brooklyn (musical), 1951

I'm in the mood for love
Simply because you're near me;
Funny, but when you're near me
I'm in the mood for love.

—DOROTHY FIELDS, "I'm in the Mood for Love," with Jimmy McHugh, 1935

I ain't had no lovin' since January, February, June or July…

—NORA BAYES, "Shine On, Harvest Moon," 1907

Nothing is real but love…. Nothing so false as ambition.

—ANZIA YEZIERSKA, *The Open Cage*, 1979

I had begun to preach to myself that my feelings were absurd in a woman of my age, and in relation to him, so many years my junior. I examined my face in the mirror, and went away saying, never again shall this foolish, hopeless feeling master me—only to succumb the next time I saw him.

—HENRIETTA SZOLD in *Lost Love*, Shargel, 1997

I cannot love him for what he is not.

—FRIDA KAHLO in *Frida*, Herrera, 1983

Love is friendship that has caught fire.

—ANN LANDERS, Advice Column, 23 April 2002

There are those who claim that love is blind, but it seems to me that hatred is blind.

—ITKA FRAJMAN ZYGMUNTOWICZ, "Survival and Memory," *Four Centuries*, 1992

Love is the ultimate giving, an expression of one's best self.

—BEL KAUFMAN, *Up the Down Staircase*, 1964

We who were loved will never
unlive that crippling fever.

—ADRIENNE RICH, "After a Sentence in 'Malte Laurids Brigge,'"
Snapshots of a Daughter-in-Law, 1963

Falling in love was the worst thing that could happen to a woman. Hadn't she seen this disaster repeated often enough? No matter how gifted or accomplished the woman…love provided a socially condoned route to self-destruction. Love automatically took precedence over work, money, reputation, ambition—the entire professional life that a woman had struggled so hard and honorably to create. Love succeeded where the world had failed to knock you out of the game.

—SHARON NIEDERMAN, "A Gift for Languages," *Shaking Eve's Tree*, 1990

Brevity may be the soul of wit, but not when someone's saying, "I love you."

—JUDITH VIORST in *Redbook*, February 1975

How come smart women like us keep falling in love with schmucks?

—JUDY BLUME, *Smart Women*, 1983

It was possible for brains to break the heart.

—CYNTHIA OZICK, *The Puttermesser Papers*, 1997

Scratch a lover, and find a foe.
>   —DOROTHY PARKER, "Ballade of a Great Weariness," *Enough Rope*, 1926

⁓

When my fiancé proposed it was very romantic. He turned off the TV. Well, he muted it. During the commercial.
>   —WENDY LIEBMAN, http://www.wendyliebman.com, 30 December 2002

⁓

"I had a girlfriend in Italy, and it was going really well until I learned to speak Italian."
>   —RITA RUDNER, *Tickled Pink*, 2001

⁓

Desire. Desire. The nebula
opens in space, unseen
your heart utters its great beats
in solitude.
>   —ADRIENNE RICH, "The Demon Lover," *Leaflets*, 1969

⁓

How helpless we are, like netted birds, when we are caught by desire!
>   —BELVA PLAIN, *Evergreen*, 1978

⁓

Love is the direct opposite of hate. By *definition* it's something you can't feel for more than a few minutes at a time, so what's all this bullshit about loving somebody for the rest of your life?
>   —JUDITH ROSSNER, *Nine Months in the Life of an Old Maid*, 1969

⁓

The love of the famous, like all strong passions, is quite abstract. Its intensity can be measured mathematically, and it is independent of persons.
>   —SUSAN SONTAG, *The Benefactor*, 1963

⁓

By the time you swear you're his,
Shivering and sighing,

And he vows his passion is
Infinite, undying—
Lady, make a note of this:
One of you is lying.
—DOROTHY PARKER, "Unfortunate Coincidence," *Enough Rope*, 1926

MARRIAGE, HUSBANDS, WIVES & DIVORCE

(*also see* Family & Relatives *and* Relationships & the Sexes)

Marriage involves big compromises all the time. International-level compromises. You're the U.S.A., he's the USSR, and you're talking nuclear warheads.
—BETTE MIDLER in *Parade*, 5 February 1989

Chains do not hold a marriage together. It is threads, hundreds of tiny threads which sew people together through the years. That is what makes a marriage last—more than passion or even sex!
—SIMONE SIGNORET in *Daily Mail*, 4 July 1978

It was so cold I almost got married.
—SHELLEY WINTERS in *New York Times*, 29 April 1956

The subjection of women, in my view, lies most deeply in the ingrained conviction—shared by both men and women—that for women marriage is the pivotal experience. It is this conviction, primarily, that reduces and ultimately destroys in women that flow of psychic energy that is fed in men from birth by the anxious knowledge given them that one is alone in this world; that one is never taken care of; that life is a naked battle between fear and desire, and that fear is kept in abeyance only through the recurrent urge of desire.
—VIVIAN GORNICK in *Village Voice*, 31 May 1973

An old couple came to a rabbi for a divorce. They had been married for sixty-five years. The rabbi, astounded, asked the wife, "Why, after sixty-five years, would you want a divorce?" And the old lady answered, "Because enough is enough!"

—MOLLY PICON, *Molly!*, 1980

The women who take husbands not out of love but out of greed, to get their bills paid, to get a fine house and clothes and jewels; the women who marry to get out of a tiresome job, or to get away from disagreeable relatives, or to avoid being called an old maid—these are whores in everything but name. The only difference between them and my girls is that my girls gave a man his money's worth.

—POLLY ADLER, *A House Is Not a Home*, 1953

"Always been my downfall…underestimating the gray matter of women. That's why my ex[-wife] has a new Mercedes and I'm driving a ten-year-old Plymouth."

—FAYE KELLERMAN, *Stalker*, 2000

Why does a woman work for ten years to change a man's habits and then complain that he's not the man she married?

—BARBRA STREISAND, Remark

As complicated as joint custody is, it allows the delicious contradiction of having children and maintaining the intimacy of life-before-kids.

—DELIA EPHRON, *Funny Sauce*, 1986

What's the difference between the Italian wife, the French wife, and the Jewish wife? When the Italian wife is having an affair, she says, "Mamma mia." When the French wife is having an affair, she says, "Ooh-la-la." When the Jewish wife is having an affair, she says, "Jake, the ceiling needs painting."

—PEARL WILLIAMS, Stand-up routine

What I'm doing in this car flying down these screaming highways is getting my tail to Juarez so I can legally rid myself of the crummy son-of-a-bitch who promised me a tomorrow like a yummy fruitcake and delivered instead wilted lettuce, rotted cucumber, a garbage of a life.

—ANNE ROIPHE, *Long Division*, 1972

I married "Mr. Right." Mr. Always Fucking Right!

—LOTUS WEINSTOCK, Stand-up routine

If divorce has increased one thousand percent, don't blame the women's movement. Blame our obsolete sex roles on which our marriages were based.

—BETTY FRIEDAN, Speech, 20 January 1974

Divorce makes its mark on children both in the short term and the long term…. Long after the divorce is final, children of divorce often have trouble entering into committed relationships of their own, fearing their relationships will end as their parents' did.

—ANN LANDERS, Advice Column, 3 February 1999

The honeymoon is over
And we find that dining by candlelight makes us squint,
And that all the time
I was letting him borrow my comb and hang up his wet raincoat in my closet,
I was really waiting
To stop letting him.

—JUDITH VIORST, "The Honeymoon Is Over,"
It's Hard to Be Hip Over Thirty…, 1968

I have too many fantasies to be a housewife…. I guess I *am* a fantasy.

—MARILYN MONROE, Quoted by Gloria Steinem in *The First Ms. Reader*, 1972

The suburban housewife—she was the dream image of the young American women and the envy, it was said, of women all over the world. The American housewife—freed by science and labor-saving appliances from the drudgery, the dangers of childbirth, and the illnesses of her grandmother...had found true feminine fulfillment.

—BETTY FRIEDAN, *The Feminine Mystique*, 1963

The role of the housewife is, therefore, analogous to that of the president of a corporation who would not only determine policies and make over-all plans but also spend the majority of his time and energy in such activities as sweeping the plant and oiling the machines.... For a woman to get a rewarding sense of total creation by way of the multiple monotonous chores that are her daily lot would be as irrational as for an assembly line worker to rejoice that he had created an automobile because he tightened a bolt.

—EDITH MENDEL STERN, "Women Are Household Slaves,"
American Mercury, January 1949

The problem lay buried, unspoken for many years in the minds of American women. It was a strange stirring, a sense of dissatisfaction, a yearning that women suffered in the middle of the twentieth century in the United States. Each suburban housewife struggled with it alone. As she made the beds, shopped for groceries, matched slipcover material, ate peanut butter sandwiches with her children, chauffeured Cub Scouts and Brownies, lay beside her husband at night, she was afraid to ask even of herself the silent question: "Is this all?"

—BETTY FRIEDAN, *The Feminine Mystique*, 1963

There is something dangerous about being a housewife.

—BETTY FRIEDAN, *The Feminine Mystique*, 1963

The considerate exemption of woman from duties outside the home is not the only reason for her having become a sort of domestic recluse; the important precept of early marriage, and a certain fear of sexual passion in man, have cut the woman off from free intercourse with the male world, and thereby from all intellectual life.

—BERTHA PAPPENHEIM in *Jewish Review*, January 1913

"Housewives" is a term I employ that means anybody who has ever had to clean up somebody else's shit and not been paid for it.

—ROSEANNE BARR, *My Life as a Woman*, 1989

I wanted to have been married forever to one person, my ex-husband or my present one. Either has enough character for a whole life, which as it turns out is really not such a long time. You couldn't exhaust either man's qualities or get under the rock of his reasons in one short life.

—GRACE PALEY, "Wants," *The Collected Stories*, 1994

My husband said he needed more space, so I locked him out of the house.

—ROSEANNE BARR, Stand-up routine

Only a marriage with partners strong enough to risk divorce is strong enough to avoid it.

—CAROLYN G. HEILBRUN in *Ms.*, August 1974

Marriage today must be concerned not with the inviolable commitment of constancy and unending passion, but with the changing patterns of liberty and discovery.

—CAROLYN G. HEILBRUN in *Ms.*, August 1974

Never go to bed mad. Stay up and fight.

—PHYLLIS DILLER, *Phyllis Diller's Housekeeping Hints*, 1966

Coupling doesn't always have to do with sex.... Two people holding each other up like flying buttresses. Two people depending on each other and babying each other and defending each other against the world outside. Sometimes it was worth all the disadvantages of marriage just to have that: one friend in an indifferent world.

—ERICA JONG, *Fear of Flying*, 1973

For forty-seven years they had been married. How deep back the stubborn, gnarled roots of the quarrel reached, no one could say—but only now, when tending to the needs of others no longer shackled them together, the roots swelled up visible, split the earth between them, and the tearing shook even the children, long since grown.

—TILLIE OLSEN, "Tell Me a Riddle," *Tell Me a Riddle*, 1960

Marriage is lonelier than solitude.

—ADRIENNE RICH, "Paula Becker to Clare Westhoff,"
The Dream of a Common Language, 1978

During the 1970s when the women's movement was taking hold, everyone was divorcing. Women were afraid that if they upset the barrel...they would be standing in front of a house with a little suitcase, not knowing what to do.

—MIRIAM SCHAPIRO in *Parade* magazine, 1998

All married couples should learn the art of battle as they should learn the art of making love. Good battle is objective and honest—never vicious or cruel. Good battle is healthy and constructive, and brings to a marriage the principle of equal partnership.

—ANN LANDERS, *Ann Landers Says "Truth Is Stranger,"* 1968

The important and only God of practical American life: Can the man make a living? Can he support a wife? That is the only thing that justifies marriage.

—EMMA GOLDMAN, *Anarchism and Other Essays*, 1911

In a bad marriage, friends are the invisible glue. If we have enough friends, we may go on for years, intending to leave, talking about leaving—instead of actually getting up and leaving.

—ERICA JONG, *How to Save Your Own Life*, 1977

Wasn't marriage, like life, unstimulating and unprofitable and somewhat empty when too well ordered and protected and guarded? Wasn't it finer, more splendid, more nourishing, when it was, like life itself, a mixture of the sordid and the magnificent; of mud and stars; of earth and flowers; of love and hate and laughter and tears and ugliness and beauty and hurt?

—EDNA FERBER, *Show Boat*, 1926

There is a rhythm to the ending of a marriage just like the rhythm of a courtship—only backward. You try to start again but get into blaming over and over. Finally you are both worn out, exhausted, hopeless. Then lawyers are called in to pick clean the corpses. The death has occurred much earlier.

—ERICA JONG, *How to Save Your Own Life*, 1977

"Men often marry their mothers."

—EDNA FERBER, *Saratoga Trunk*, 1941

I'm getting married on April 12th. My fiancé and I still haven't decided on the year.

—WENDY LIEBMAN, http://www.wendyliebman.com, 20 January 2003

Our marriage exists for a higher purpose, to write comedy. We see our marriage as comedy, and we're observers of that comedy.

—RENEE TAYLOR in *Funny Women*, Unterbrink, 1987

Re secrets of a good marriage: Fidelity and pasta.

—RENEE TAYLOR in *Funny Women*, Unterbrink, 1987

Marriage is the only state to be in. I believe a woman should have as many love affairs as she likes, but only one at a time.

—NORA BAYES, Stand-up routine

I don't want to be a star! I just want to get married.

—GOLDIE HAWN in *Women in Comedy*, Martin, 1986

I was part of a mixed marriage. I'm human; he's a Klingon.

—CAROL LEIFER, Stand-up routine

Marry rich. Buy him a pacemaker, then stand behind him and say "boo."

—JOAN RIVERS, Stand-up routine

I always say the most difficult thing for a woman to do is try to act naïve—on the first night of her second marriage.

—BELLE BARTH, Stand-up routine

I realized on our first wedding anniversary that our marriage was in trouble. Fang gave me luggage. It was packed. My mother damn near suffocated in there.

—PHYLLIS DILLER, Stand-up routine

My husband walks in the door one night, he says to me, "Roseanne, don't you think it's time we sat down and had a serious talk about our sex life?" I say to him, "You want me to turn off *Wheel of Fortune* for that?"

—ROSEANNE BARR, Stand-up routine

Now I know why mother
Taught me to be true
She knew I'd meet someone
Exactly like you.

—DOROTHY FIELDS, "Exactly Like You," with Jimmy McHugh,
International Revue, 1930

Can we today measure devotion to husband and children by our indifference to everything else? Is it not often true that the woman who has given up all the external world for her husband and her children has done it not out of a sense of duty, out of devotion and love, but out of incapacity, because the soul is not able to take into itself the many-sidedness of life, with its sufferings but also with its joys?

—GOLDA MEIR, *The Plough Woman*, c. 1930

Now you girls have careers and *you* want a wife.

—WENDY WASSERSTEIN, *Isn't It Romantic?*, 1984

Women often choose a spouse who will express just those traits and qualities they most need to deny within themselves, or those qualities they wish they could express themselves but can't. A woman may then rage against her spouse as he expresses the very qualities she chose him for.

—HARRIET GOLDHOR LERNER in *Viewpoint*, Vol. 16, No. 5

In taking out an insurance policy one pays for it in dollars and cents, always at liberty to discontinue payments. If, however, woman's premium is a husband, she pays for it with her name, her privacy, her self-respect, her very life, "until death doth part."

—EMMA GOLDMAN, *Anarchism and Other Essays*, 1911

Marriage always demands the greatest understanding of the art of insincerity possible between two human beings.

—VICKI BAUM, *And Life Goes On*, 1932

It's late, Jake, and time to expire.

—GERTRUDE BERG, *Molly Goldberg* (TV show)

There was altogether too much candor in married life; it was an indelicate modern idea, and frequently led to upsets in a household, if not divorce.

—MURIEL SPARK, *Memento Mori*, 1959

two by two in the ark of
the ache of it.

—Denise Levertov, "The Ache of Marriage," *O Taste and See*, 1963

Men

(*also see* Relationships & the Sexes *and* Women)

There was nothing more fun than a man!

—Dorothy Parker, "The Little Old Lady in Lavender Silk," *Death and Taxes*, 1931

The only problem with menstruation for men is that some sensitive schmuck could write about it for the *Village Voice*, and become the new expert on women's inner life.

—Wendy Wasserstein, *Uncommon Women and Others*, 1978

Beware of the man who praises women's liberation; he is about to quit his job.

—Erica Jong in *Time* Special Issue, Fall 1990

I have yet to hear a man ask for advice on how to combine marriage and a career.

—Gloria Steinem, Remark

There is another side to chivalry. If it dispenses leniency, it may with equal justification invoke control.

—Freda Adler, *Sisters in Crime*, 1975

It is funny the two things most men are proudest of is the thing that any man can do and doing does in the same way, that is being drunk and being the father of their son.

—Gertrude Stein, *Everybody's Autobiography*, 1937

Normal men aren't going to love anyone who looks forward to anything but them.

—EVE BABITZ, *Black Swans*, 1993

Men always fall for frigid women because they put on the best show.

—FANNY BRICE in *A Child of the Century* by Ben Hecht, 1954

Femininity pleases men because it makes them appear more masculine by contrast; and, in truth, conferring an extra portion of unearned gender distinction on men, an unchallenged space in which to breathe freely and feel stronger, wiser, more competent, is femininity's special gift.

—SUSAN BROWNMILLER, *Femininity*, 1984

We think that we live in a heterosexual society because most men are fixated on women as sexual objects; but, in fact, we live in a homosexual society because all credible transactions of power, authority, and authenticity take place among men; all transactions based on equity and individuality take place among men. Men are real; therefore, all real relationship is between men; all real communication is between men; all real reciprocity is between men; all real mutuality is between men.

—ANDREA DWORKIN, *Our Blood*, 1976

The bar is the male kingdom. For centuries it was the bastion of male privilege, the gathering place for men away from their women, a place where men could go to freely indulge in the Bull Session…a serious political function: the release of the guilty anxiety of the oppressor class.

—SHULAMITH FIRESTONE, "The Bar as Microcosm," *Voices for Women's Liberation*, Leslie B. Tanner, ed., 1970

No man can be friends with a woman he finds attractive. He always wants to have sex with her. Sex is always out there. Friendship is ultimately doomed and that is the end of the story.

—NORA EPHRON, *When Harry Met Sally* (screenplay), 1989

And you think that I belong to you too, and that's why you want me. You want me and my art reproduction. You want my art reproduction and my entire reproduction system. You hate both my systems. The HOW TO LIE FOREVER System and the HOW TO LIVE HARMONIOUSLY AS A WOMAN system.

—ROSALYN DREXLER, *Skywriting*, 1968

Lots of men, you see, simply aren't ready for assertive women. They expect us to tiptoe in, trembling and pleading for our rights and when those rights are denied, they expect us not to cause a furor but to tiptoe away quietly.

—GLORIA ALLRED in *Los Angeles Times Home Magazine*, 7 January 1979

What is the use of being a little boy if you are going to grow up to be a man.

—GERTRUDE STEIN, *Everybody's Autobiography*, 1937

What is man that woman lies down to adore him?

—GRACE PALEY, *Just As I Thought*, 1998

Men renounce whatever they have in common with women so as to experience no commonality with women; and what is left, according to men, is one piece of flesh a few inches long, the penis. The penis is sensate; the penis is the man; the man is human; the penis signifies humanity.

—ANDREA DWORKIN, *Pornography: Men Possessing Women*, 1981

A man is allowed to blaspheme the world because it belongs to him to damn.

—SHULAMITH FIRESTONE, *The Dialectic of Sex*, 1970

Men chart the stars, create language and culture as we know it, record history as they see it, build and destroy the world around us, and continue to run every major institution that generates power, policy, and wealth. Men define the very "reality" that—until the current feminist movement—I, for one, accepted as a given, and although women throughout history have exercised a certain power

as mothers, we have not created the conditions in which we mother, nor have we constructed the predominant myths and theories about "good mothering."
—HARRIET GOLDHOR LERNER, *The Dance of Intimacy*, 1989

You can be replaced by a tampon.
—ROBIN TYLER, Stand-up routine

Don't accept rides from strange men,
and remember that all men are strange as hell.
—ROBIN MORGAN, "Letter to a Sister Underground," *Sisterhood Is Powerful*, 1970

Gentlemen don't love love. They just like to kick it around.
—SOPHIE TUCKER in *Funny Women*, Unterbrink, 1987

Men want you to scream "You're the best" while swearing you've never done this with anyone before.
—ELAYNE BOOSLER, Stand-up routine

Men don't live well by themselves. They don't even live like people. They live like bears with furniture.
—ELAYNE BOOSLER, Stand-up routine

A man assumes that a woman's refusal is just part of a game. Or, at any rate, a lot of men assume that. When a man says no, it's no. When a woman says no, it's yes, or at least maybe. There is even a joke to that effect. And little by little, women begin to believe in this view of themselves.
—ERICA JONG, *Fear of Flying*, 1973

"It is impossible to persuade a man who does not disagree, but smiles."
—MURIEL SPARK, *The Prime of Miss Jean Brodie*, 1961

MONEY, BUSINESS & ECONOMICS

(*also see* Advertising, Image & the Media *and* Work & Working)

I've been rich and I've been poor. Rich is better.

—SOPHIE TUCKER, Remark

Money…is really the difference between men and animals, most of the things men feel animals feel and vice versa, but animals do not know about money, money is a purely human conception and that is very important to know very very important.

—GERTRUDE STEIN, *Everybody's Autobiography*, 1937

Money is always there but the pockets change.

—GERTRUDE STEIN, Remark

When you earn it and spend it you do know the difference between three dollars and a million dollars, but when you say it and vote it, it all sounds the same.

—GERTRUDE STEIN, Remark

You can't have everything. Where would you put it?

—ANN LANDERS, Advice Column

Women were the sacrificial lambs of the Depression, but amid the collective pain of the nation's empty bellies, they scarcely felt the knife.

—MARJORIE ROSEN, *Popcorn Venus*, 1973

Is there yet a portion or inheritance for us in our father's house? Are we not counted of him strangers? For he hath sold us, and hath quite devoured also our money. For all the riches which God hath taken from our father, that is ours, and our children's.

—LEAH, Book of Genesis, c. ninth century B.C.E., Bible

—

When we were young enough to have children, we had no money. And when we had money, we were too old.

—HANNAH ARENDT in *For Love of the World*
by Hannah Elisabeth Young-Bruehl, 1981

—

Economic growth may one day turn out to be a curse rather than a good, and under no conditions can it either lead into freedom or constitute a proof for its existence.

—HANNAH ARENDT, *On Revolution*, 1963

—

Profits are springing, like weeds, from the fields of the dead.

—ROSA LUXEMBURG, *The Crisis in the German Social Democracy*, 1919

—

I don't want to make money. I just want to be wonderful.

—MARILYN MONROE, Quoted by Gloria Steinem in *The First Ms. Reader*, 1972

—

We are into an "era of aspirations" in our economy. In this era, most of us will spend a shrinking share of our income on the traditional necessities of food, clothing, shelter, and transportation while we spend a steadily increasing share of our income for goods and services which reflect our hopes and wants.

—SYLVIA PORTER, *Sylvia Porter's Money Book*, 1975

—

When we elevate money into a prize, a goal, an object to be striven for, we give it a position, an importance, a nobility, which it should not have in our children's eyes. We implicitly affirm the principle—a false one—that money is the crowning reward for work, its ultimate objective.

—NATALIA GINZBURG, *Little Virtues*, 1985

—

Some of us would like to ignore the institutions and the money problems. I do not see how that is possible. The provision of child care on even a moderate scale requires the use of institutional money, public money. I have no trouble with using public money. Child care and other services [are] exactly what it should be used for.

—SUSAN WITKOVSKY, Address, University of California Conference
on Child Care, Berkeley, April 1975

—

For millions, the retirement dream is in reality an economic nightmare. For millions, growing old today means growing poor, being sick, living in substandard housing, and having to scrimp merely to subsist. And this is the prospect not for the one out of every ten Americans now over sixty-five…but also for the sixty-five million who will reach retirement age within the next thirty-three years.

—SYLVIA PORTER, *Sylvia Porter's Money Book*, 1975

—

The true defense against wealth is not a fear of wealth—of its fragility and of the vicious consequences that it can bring—the true defense against wealth is an indifference to money.

—NATALIA GINZBURG, *Little Virtues*, 1985

—

When you have lived for years on end without any sense of the future or any real feeling for the reality of the morrow, the whole idea of putting something aside, of saving, goes clean out of your head.

—EUGENIA GINZBURG, *Within the Whirlwind*, 1979

—

Money never remains just coins and pieces of paper. It is constantly changing into the comforts of daily life. Money can be translated into the beauty of living, a support in misfortune, an education, or future security. It also can be translated into a source of bitterness.

—SYLVIA PORTER, *Sylvia Porter's Money Book*, 1975

It is true that money attracts; but much money repels.

—CYNTHIA OZICK, *Trust*, 1966

Some people are more turned on by money than they are by love.... In one respect they're alike. They're both wonderful as long as they last.

—ABIGAIL VAN BUREN, "Dear Abby" Advice Column, 26 April 1974

money money money
do you feel like a pawn
in your own world?
you found the system
and you lost the pearl...

—LAURA NYRO, "Money," 1975

Hollywood money isn't money. It's congealed snow, melts in your hand, and there you are.

—DOROTHY PARKER in *Writers at Work* (1st), 1958

The man has the burden of the money. It's needed day after day. More and more of it. For ordinary things and for life. That's why holidays are a hard time for him. Another hard time is the weekend, when he's not making money or furthering himself.

—GRACE PALEY, *Enormous Changes at the Last Minute*, 1960

Money has screwed me up in my relationships with men.

—GOLDIE HAWN in *Women in Comedy*, Martin, 1986

Jake wants the children to have everything money can buy, and I want them to have everything money can't buy.
—GERTRUDE BERG in "The Goldbergs' Jewish Humor" by Charles Angoff, *Congress Weekly 18*, 5 March 1951

—

You lose your manners when you're poor.
—LILLIAN HELLMAN, *Another Part of the Forest*, 1946

—

Nowadays nobody is ready to lend anything to other people, from one hand into the other. When I needed something for living, I was obliged to offer double pledges and to pay high interest. What shall I do? I wriggled about like a worm before I was prepared to borrow money on pawn in such a time. The saying goes: Need breaks iron, if you will or not. You must eat, domestics must eat, you may be as careful as you like, you must have money anyhow.
—SAREL GUTMANS, Letter to her Husband, Prague (November 1619), in *A Treasury of Jewish Letters*, 1953

—

If you have in hand money or goods belonging to other people, give more care to them than if they were your own, so that, please God, you do no one a wrong.
—GLÜCKEL OF HAMELN, *Memoirs*,1692

—

I've got all the money I need.... So long as I die before Monday.
—SUE MARGOLIS, *Spin Cycle*, 2001

—

She [her mother] did not know how to read or write. She only knew how to count money.
—FRIDA KAHLO in *Frida*, Herrera, 1983

—

TALLULAH BANKHEAD: I can't get used to this French money.

FRED ALLEN: Yes, it's printed on the thinnest paper I've ever seen in public.
—SELMA DIAMOND in *Funny Women*, Unterbrink, 1987

I knew so little about money I used to sign my checks, "Love, Rita."

—RITA RUDNER, Stand-up routine

Those drinks are gonna be six bucks, and it'll cost you three more to have me take 'em off the tray and put 'em on the table.

—ROSEANNE BARR in *The Haunted Smile*, Epstein, 2001

"Disunity, that's the trouble. It's my absolute opinion that in our complex industrial society, no business enterprise can succeed without sharing the burden of the problems of other enterprises."

—AYN RAND, *Atlas Shrugged*, 1957

The cosmetic business is interesting among modern industries in its opportunities for women. Here they have found a field that is their own province—working for women with women, and giving that which only women can give—an intimate understanding of feminine needs and feminine desires.

—HELENA RUBINSTEIN, "Manufacturing—Cosmetics," *Careers for Women*, 1928

I would give the woman a sample of whatever she did not buy as a gift. It might be a few teaspoonfuls of powder in a wax envelope. I just knew, even though I had not yet named the technique, that a gift with a purchase was very appealing.

—ESTÉE LAUDER, *Estée: A Success Story*, 1985

I will tell thee an idea that has come into mind that "oil from the flinty rock" is *petroleum*, and there is nothing new under the sun.

—RAHEL MORPURGO, Letter to Isaac Luzzatto, *The Harp of Rachel*, 1890

As case after case came up, I saw the vast chasms between our rhetoric of freedom, equality and charity, and what we were doing to, or not doing for poor people, especially children.

—JUSTINE WISE POLIER in *The Journey Home* by Joyce Antler, 1997

Give a beggar a dime and he'll bless you. Give him a dollar and he'll curse you for withholding the rest of your fortune. Poverty is a bag with a hole at the bottom.

—ANZIA YEZIERSKA, *Red Ribbon on a White Horse*, 1950

Until we end the masculinization of wealth, we will not end the feminization of poverty.

—GLORIA STEINEM, Women of Power Conference, 6 April 2000

If you have never been poor, you don't know what life is worth.

—JESSIE SAMPTER, *The Speaking Heart* (unpub. autobio.)

I do want to get rich but I never want to do what there is to do to get rich.

—GERTRUDE STEIN, *Everybody's Autobiography*, 1937

Man gets his daily bread
in sweat, but no one said
in daily death. Don't eat
those nice green dollars your wife
gives you for breakfast.

—DENISE LEVERTOV, "The Parts," *The Jacob's Ladder*, 1961

In short, prostitution is inevitably a transaction between *un*equals: one where the buyers set the price, deciding what kinds of women (or little girls or boys) are worth paying for, and the sellers have little if any power to determine how their bodies will be used. This is why prostitution is not amenable to reform—and why it is inevitable in a society where women's bodies are still essentially commodities for sale to men, as is all too vividly reflected in television ads for everything from cars to Coca-Cola, where women's bodies are used as marketing come-ons.

—RIANE EISLER, *Sacred Pleasure*, 1995

Counting is the religion of this generation it is its hope and its salvation.
—GERTRUDE STEIN, *Everybody's Autobiography*, 1937

MORALITY & ETHICS

(*also see* Courage, Character & Integrity; Guilt, Innocence & Conscience; *and* Truth, Lies & Superstitions)

Violent outrage and equally violent despair seem inevitable responses to our era. All the horrors committed in the name of national honor or the sanctity of the family or individual integrity have caught up with us.
—HARRIET ROSENSTEIN, "Reconsidering Sylvia Plath," *The First Ms. Reader*, 1972

While an ethic of justice proceeds from the premise of equality—that everyone should be treated the same—an ethic of care rests on the premise of nonviolence—that no one should be hurt.
—CAROL GILLIGAN, *In a Different Voice*, 1982

The blind willingness to sacrifice people to truth, however, has always been the danger of an ethics abstracted from life. This willingness links Gandhi to the biblical Abraham, who prepared to sacrifice the life of his son in order to demonstrate the integrity and supremacy of his faith. Both men, in the limitations of their fatherhood, stand in implicit contrast to the woman who comes before Solomon and verifies her motherhood by relinquishing truth in order to save the life of her child.... The ethics of...adulthood...has become principled at the expense of care.
—CAROL GILLIGAN, *In a Different Voice*, 1982

We must make our business ethics...correspond with Bible ethics.
—MAUD NATHAN in *The Review 11*, No. 4, March 1907

We brought you up to know that people are more important than things.
—SUSAN HERMAN, to her son, in *Startup.com* (documentary film), 2001

The strength, the grossness, spirit and gall of choice.
—MURIEL RUKEYSER, "Nine Poems for the Unborn Child," *Waterlily,* 1962

For one of the greatest challenges we face today is to create and disseminate new myths and images that make it possible for us to see that we *do* have choices, that we are not doomed to eternal misery by "selfish genes" or "original sin"—and most important, that in the last analysis the choice of our future is up to us.
—RIANE EISLER, *Sacred Pleasure,* 1995

There is nothing here I would ever choose—and nothing I can ever part with.
—BETTE HOWLAND, *Things to Come and Go,* 1983

The only real moral crime that one man can commit against another is the attempt to create, by his words or actions, an impression of the contradictory, the impossible, the irrational, and thus shake the concept of rationality in his victim.
—AYN RAND, *Atlas Shrugged,* 1957

"Look here," Furii said. "I never promised you a rose garden. I never promised you perfect justice."
—JOANNE GREENBERG, *I Never Promised You a Rose Garden,* 1964

If I were to speak your kind of language, I would say that man's only moral commandment is: Thou shalt think. But a "moral commandment" is a contradiction in terms. The moral is the chosen, not the forced; the understood, not the obeyed. The moral is the rational, and reason accepts no commandments.
—AYN RAND, *Atlas Shrugged,* 1957

we move
but our words stand
become responsible
and this is verbal privilege
—ADRIENNE RICH, "North American Time," *Your Native Land, Your Life*, 1986

Fairness is an abstract concept with no foundation in reality.
—SUSAN HERMAN, Remark to Editor, Interlocken
(Antrim, New Hampshire), 16 February 1984

The type of fig leaf which each culture employs to cover its social taboos offers a twofold description of its morality. It reveals that certain unacknowledged behavior exists and it suggests the form that such behavior takes.
—FREDA ADLER, *Sisters in Crime*, 1975

During the rest of my screen career, I am going to continue doing vampires as long as people sin. For I believe that humanity needs the moral lesson and it needs it in repeatedly large doses.
—THEDA BARA, Quoted in *Theda Bara: A Biography of the Silent Screen Vamp*
by Ronald Genini, 1996

A rational process is a moral process.
—AYN RAND, *Atlas Shrugged*, 1957

Thus changes in women's rights change women's moral judgements, seasoning mercy with justice by enabling women to consider it moral to care not only for others but for themselves.
—CAROL GILLIGAN, *In a Different Voice*, 1982

The most important effect of transcending those old sex roles may be an evolution of morality and religious thought.
—BETTY FRIEDAN, *The Second Stage*, 1981

We [women] are not more moral, we are only less corrupted by power.
—GLORIA STEINEM in *New York Times Book Review*, 26 August 1971

Promises are the uniquely human way of ordering the future, making it predictable and reliable to the extent that this is humanly possible.
—HANNAH ARENDT, *Crises of the Republic*, 1972

Rather would I have the love songs of romantic ages, rather Don Juan and Madame Venus, rather an elopement by ladder and rope on a moonlight night, followed by the father's curse, mother's moans, and the moral comments of neighbors, than correctness and propriety measured by yardsticks.
—EMMA GOLDMAN, *Anarchism and Other Essays*, 1922

What if women's voices tell us things we would rather not hear, or simply cannot hear—because they express values and priorities that are different from those we espouse?
—ROSALIND PETCHESKY, *Negotiating Reproductive Rights*, with Karen Judd, eds., 1998

Our sins in the twentieth century—greed, violence, inhumanity—have been profound, with the result that the pride and self-confidence of the nineteenth century have turned to dismay and self-disgust.
—BARBARA TUCHMAN in *Newsweek*, 12 July 1976

We endeavor to raise wages instead of spreading knowledge. We clean streets instead of our hearts, we build better houses, instead of better homes.
—ANNIE NATHAN MEYER, "Spreadhenism"

In your young life, you rebel against values you think are square. After a while, you realize they are good values and there's a reason they've been around for thousands of years.
—BETTE MIDLER in *Funny Women*, Unterbrink, 1987

...here is a city, Chaldean Ur,
Whence come a race of most upright men,
Who are ever right-minded and their works good.
They are neither concerned for the sun's course,
Nor the moon's, nor for monstrosities on earth,
Nor for satisfaction from ocean's depths,
Nor for signs of sneezing and the augury from birds;
Nor for soothsaying, nor sorcery, nor incantations;
Nor for deceitful follies of ventriloquists.
They do not, Chaldean fashion, astrologize,
Nor watch the stars.
But they are concerned about rightness and virtue.

—SIBYL, the Jewish, *The Fourth Book of Sibylline Oracles*, c. 100 B.C.E.

As far as the education of children is concerned I think they should be taught not the little virtues but the great ones. Not thrift but generosity and an indifference to money; not caution but courage and a contempt for danger; not shrewdness but frankness and a love of truth; not tact but love for one's neighbour and self-denial; not a desire for success but a desire to be and to know.

—NATALIA GINZBURG, *Little Virtues*, 1985

The little virtues also arise from our deepest instincts, from a defensive instinct; but in them reason speaks, holds forth, displays its arguments as the brilliant advocate of self-preservation. The great virtues well up from an instinct in which reason does not speak, an instinct that seems to be difficult to name.

—NATALIA GINZBURG, *Little Virtues*, 1985

"If the world knew virtue when it saw virtue, wouldn't *men* be Torah?"

—JOANNE GREENBERG, "Children of Joy," *Shaking Eve's Tree*, 1990

MOTHERS & MOTHERHOOD

(*also see* Home & Housekeeping *and* Population & Birth Control)

Mummy herself has told us that she looked upon us more as her friends than her daughters. Now that is all very fine, but still, a friend can't take a mother's place.

—ANNE FRANK, *The Diary of a Young Girl*, 1947

She, who had no worldly goods to leave, yet left to me an inexhaustible legacy. Inherent in it, this heritage of summoning resources to make out of song, food and warmth, expressions of human love—courage, hope, resistance, belief....

—TILLIE OLSEN, "Dream Vision," *Shaking Eve's Tree*, 1990

How can one accept crazy creatures who deem it a misfortune to get pregnant and a disaster to give birth to children? When it's the greatest privilege we women have compared with men!

—GOLDA MEIR, Quoted by Oriana Fallaci in *L'Eurepeo*, 1973

Most women should do what they did best, and which men did not do at all—bear babies.... Of course, it is not meant that there are not a few women in every generation who are exceptions to the rule.

—GERTRUDE STEIN, "Degeneration in American Women"

You tell me who has to leave the office when the kid bumps his head or slips on a milk carton.

—WENDY WASSERSTEIN, *Isn't It Romantic?*, 1984

Only a mother remembers her children's landmarks as her own.

—LETTY COTTIN POGREBIN, *Deborah, Golda, and Me*, 1991

Even now
in this sweet flesh
isn't there something starting to withdraw?
—SHIRLEY KAUFMAN, "Milk," *Roots in the Air*, 1996

I slipped into the world while my mother was on her knees, scrubbing the floor.
—ROSE PASTOR STOKES, *I Belong to the Working Class*, 1992

We begin life with loss. We are cast from the womb without an apartment, a charge plate, a job or a car. We are sucking, sobbing, clinging, helpless babies. Our mother interposes herself between us and the world, protecting us from overwhelming anxiety. We shall have no greater need than this need for our mother.
—JUDITH VIORST, *Necessary Losses*, 1986

Gender might not require a woman to stay home and raise the kids but it was clear that biology could not be erased just like that.... The pull to reproduce was not a political decision but deeply primordial, a response to rhythms and tides not always accessible to reason.
—ANNE ROIPHE, *Fruitful*, 1996

I was born in New York City on a cold January night when the water pipes in our apartment froze and burst. Fortunately, my mother was in the hospital rather than at home at the time.
—GERTRUDE B. ELION in *Les Prix Nobel*, 1988

Wondrous hole! Magical hole! Dazzlingly influential hole! Noble and effulgent hole! From this hole everything follows logically: first the baby, then the placenta, then, for years and years and years until death, a way of life. It is all logic, and she who lives by the hole will live also by its logic. It is, appropriately, logic with a hole in it.
—CYNTHIA OZICK, "The Hole/Birth Catalog," *The First Ms. Reader*, 1972

I've been inside institutions,
my family,
kindergarten,
grammar school, high
school, college and then
marriage, waiting
to be
grown up...
> —SUSAN GRIFFIN, "Letters to the Outside," *Dear Sky*, 1973

Let it be neither mine nor thine, but divide it.
> —PROSTITUTE OF JERUSALEM [mother of the dead child],
> Book of 1 Kings, c. 550 B.C.E., Bible

O my lord, give her the living child, and in no wise slay it: she is the mother thereof.
> —PROSTITUTE OF JERUSALEM [mother of the living child],
> Book of 1 Kings, c. 550 B.C.E., Bible

The woman I needed to call my mother was silenced before I was born.
> —ADRIENNE RICH, "Reforming the Crystal," *Poems: Selected and New*, 1974

Through every night we hate,
preparing the next day's war...
> —SHIRLEY KAUFMAN, "Mothers, Daughters," *The Floor Keeps Turning*, 1970

before
I could be her daughter,
she turned me into her mother.
Taught me the names of love
in her language: grief
and sorrow, sorrow and grief.
> —SHIRLEY KAUFMAN, "Leftovers," *Roots in the Air*, 1996

Even during the hardest economic times [my mother] made sure that Susan [my sister] and I had four things that she believed were essential to our later success: good shoes (I don't mean stylish); a firm, quality mattress; a top pediatrician (none other than Doctor Benjamin Spock); and a therapist.

—HARRIET GOLDHOR LERNER in online biography

What woman doesn't die in childbirth
What child doesn't murder the mother.

—ALICIA SUSKIN OSTRIKER, "Surviving," *The Little Space*, 1998

For, of course, the natural childbirth-breastfeeding movement Margaret Mead helped to inspire was not at all a return to primitive earth-mother maternity. It appealed to the independent, educated, spirited…woman…because it enabled her to experience childbirth not as a mindless female animal, an object manipulated by the obstetrician, but as a whole person, able to control her own body with her aware mind.

—BETTY FRIEDAN, *The Feminine Mystique*, 1963

No phallic hero, no matter what he does to himself or to another to prove his courage, ever matches the solitary, existential courage of the woman who gives birth.

—ANDREA DWORKIN, *Our Blood*, 1976

Obviously there is pain in childbirth. But giving birth is also a moment of awe and wonder, a moment when the true miracle of aliveness, and of a woman's amazing part in that miracle, is suddenly experienced in every cell of one's body. It is in that sense truly an altered state of consciousness.

—RIANE EISLER, *Sacred Pleasure*, 1995

Why had no one told me that my body would become a battlefield, a sacrifice, a test? Why did I not know that birth is the pinnacle where women discover the courage to become mothers?

—ANITA DIAMANT, *The Red Tent*, 1997

A chance acquaintance in an English railway carriage, a member of the peerage, once said to me in four unadorned words: I hate my mother. It was the first time I had heard such blasphemy uttered. Surely God would strike him dead. But God did not take action, and the lovely countryside through which we were riding kept smiling.

—FANNIE HURST, *Anatomy of Me*, 1958

Many of us are living out the unlived lives of our mothers, because they were not able to become the unique people they were born to be.

—GLORIA STEINEM in *Wise Women* by Joyce Tenneson, 2002

From the hour that I gave mama my first stare from her bed of my birth, I must have braced my new spine against being overpowered by the rush of her personality.

—FANNIE HURST, *Anatomy of Me*, 1958

It seems we came to an agreement long ago: she suffers for me, I live out her fantasies.

—NIKKI STILLER, "A State of Emergency," *Shaking Eve's Tree*, 1990

The more a daughter knows about her mother's life—without flinching or whining—the stronger the daughter.

—ANITA DIAMANT, *The Red Tent*, 1997

Maternal feelings are a splendid rationale for misbehavior.

—EUGENIA GINZBURG, *Within the Whirlwind*, 1979

Years rolled by like unstrung pearls,
Peninah kept having more boys and girls,
Hannah kept waiting for one seed to grow,
But her belly was filled with darkness and woe.

—PENINA V. ADELMAN, "Ballad of Hannah," *Miriam's Well*, 1986

If I can't give birth to a live human being, I can give birth to the ideas and struggles within me.

—PENINA V. ADELMAN, *Miriam's Well*, 1986

I heard the names of Rebecca, Rachel and Leah as early as the names of father, mother, and nurse.

—MARY ANTIN, *The Promised Land*, 1912

We were squeezed between that proverbial rock and hard place. Motherhood by definition requires tending of the other, a sacrifice of self-wishes for the needs of a helpless, hapless human being, and feminism by definition insists on attention being paid to the self, to the full humanity, wishes, desires, capacities of the self. This basic contradiction is not simply the nasty work of a sexist society. It is the lay of the land, the mother of all paradoxes, the irony we cannot bend with mere wishing or might of will. Here are the ingredients of our private and public human tragedy. Nevertheless I still wanted more children.

—ANNE ROIPHE, *Fruitful*, 1996

...on second cry I woke
fully and gave to feed and fed on feeding.

—MURIEL RUKEYSER, "Night Feeding," *Selected Poems*, 1951

I wanted so much to make it work, to nourish my child with my own body—it seemed like the essential act of mother love, surely what little girls yearn for when they instinctively clutch their dolls to their chests.

—CAROL K. HOWELL, *A Fool at the Feast*

Mama, Mama, my regrets for all the pain I caused you crowd in on me in these after-years. Your virtues transcended your faults. Papa knew that and bent his neck to your storms. I had neither his sweet humility nor fortitude.... If only—I could live it over again.

—FANNIE HURST, *Anatomy of Me*, 1958

NATIONS & THE WORLD

(*also see* Cities & States; Cultures, Nationality & Immigrants; Israel & Zionism; *and* United States of America)

The way I look at the world—it's suffering a global nervous breakdown.
—BELLA ABZUG in Interview, *GEMNETGIST* Fall issue, April 1997

Come to think of it all the earth is a graveyard, you never know when you're walking over heads—particularly this continent [Africa], cradle of man, prehistoric bones and the bits of shaped stone…that were weapons and utensils.
—NADINE GORDIMER, *The Conservationist*, 1975

[In Mexico] one always has to go around with one's thorns sharp…to defend oneself from all the *cabrones* [bastards]…who get into hot arguments wanting always to get ahead and to screw the next person.
—FRIDA KAHLO in *Frida*, Herrera, 1983

Each separate soul contains the nation's force,
And both embrace the world.
—EMMA LAZARUS, "Rosh-Hashanah, 5643" (1882), *Emma Lazarus*, 1982

There is a desperate lack of variety to the poverty here [Egypt], a kind of stupor of simplicity, an aimlessness that covers the people in a thick expressionless haze.
—VIVIAN GORNICK, *In Search of Ali-Mahmoud*, 1973

Europe is dusty plush,
First-class carriages
with first-class dust.

—ERICA JONG, *Fear of Flying*, 1973

Oh, lovely Europe, your flowers and your wine, your bread, your music.
—BELVA PLAIN, *Evergreen*, 1978

All foreigners regard other societies through the prisms of their own value systems.
—SUSAN JACOBY, *Inside Soviet Schools*, 1974

In America if they do not do it right away they do not do it at all in France they very often seem not to be going to do it at all but if it has ever really been proposed at all sometimes it really is done.
—GERTRUDE STEIN, *Everybody's Autobiography*, 1937

There is not a German writer left in Germany who is worth thinking about. The gifted writers and enterprising publishers who had any independence had left Germany. Only the Nazi writers and publishers remain so as to please the Nazi government.
—BLANCHE WOLF KNOPF in *New York Times*, 14 July 1936

The deserts of the Middle East are in need of water, not bombers.
—GOLDA MEIR, Address, "The Israeli Action in Sinai: 1956," General Assembly of the United Nations, 7 October 1957

Every country gets the circus it deserves. Spain gets bullfights. Italy gets the Catholic Church. America gets Hollywood.
—ERICA JONG, *How to Save Your Own Life*, 1977

I ask myself, have nations ever declined from a loss of moral sense rather than from physical reasons or the pressure of barbarians? I think that they have.
—BARBARA TUCHMAN in *A World of Ideas* by Bill Moyers, 1989

Liberalism has a future in South Africa, but fundamental changes will take a lot longer than most people think.

—HELEN SUZMAN in *Time*, 29 May 1989

—

Though the world cannot be changed by talking to one child at a time, it may at least be known.

—GRACE PALEY, *Just As I Thought*, 1998

—

Heaven and earth observe how we cherish or spoil our world.

—MARGE PIERCY, *The Art of Blessing the Day*, 1999

—

"We did make a new world. Just not exactly the one we intended. It's a bigger job than we realized, to make things good and fair. It won't be us who finish it. But we gave it a pretty good start before we lost our way."

—MARGE PIERCY, *City of Darkness, City of Light*, 1996

—

Like the effects of industrial pollution and the new system of global financial markets, the AIDS crisis is evidence of a world in which nothing important is regional, local, limited; in which everything that can circulate does and every problem is, or is destined to become, worldwide.

—SUSAN SONTAG, *AIDS and Its Metaphors*, 1989

—

Nations are communities that are always being imagined, reconceived, reasserted, against the pressure of a defining Other. The specter of a nation without borders, an infinitely porous nation, is bound to create anxiety. Europe needs its overbearing America.

—SUSAN SONTAG in *New York Times Magazine*, 2 May 1999

Nature & the Environment

The best remedy for those who are afraid, lonely or unhappy is to go outside, somewhere where they can be quiet, alone with the heavens, nature and God. Because only then does one feel that all is as it should be and that God wishes to see people happy, amidst the simple beauty of nature. As long as this exists, and it certainly always will, I know that then there will always be comfort for every sorrow, whatever the circumstances may be. And I firmly believe that nature brings solace in all troubles.

—ANNE FRANK, *The Diary of a Young Girl*, 1947

I lived once in the American desert. The solitude opens up. It becomes an enormous surrounding comfort. But the solitude in the city is a confusing and painful thing.

—VIVIAN GORNICK, *In Search of Ali-Mahmoud*, 1973

As I kneel to put the seeds in
careful as stitching, I am in love.
You are the bed we all sleep on.
You are the food we eat, the food
we ate, the food we will become.
We are walking trees rooted in you.

—MARGE PIERCY, "The Common Living Dirt," *Stone, Paper, Knife*, 1983

The sky is reduced,
A narrow blue ribbon banding the lake.
Someone is wrapping things up.

—SUSAN FROMBERG SCHAEFFER, " "Post Mortem,"
The Witch and the Weather Report, 1972

Some have named this space where we are rooted
a place of death.
We fix them with our callous eyes
and call it, rather, a terrain of resurrection.
> —ROBIN MORGAN, "Easter Island, I: Embarcation," *Monster*, 1972

For leaves don't fall. They descend
Longing for earth, they come winging.
> —MALKA HEIFETZ TUSSMAN, "Leaves," *With Teeth in the Earth*, 1992

The earth is the very quintessence of the human condition.
> —HANNAH ARENDT, *The Human Condition*, 1958

Countries are starting to see that they can't have economic growth without
protecting their resource base. The economic growth disappears as the fisheries
disappear, as the forest disappears, as soil erosion progresses. They can't have
real growth without environmental management.
> —JESSICA TUCHMAN MATHEWS in *A World of Ideas* by Bill Moyers, 1989

Fully occupied with growing—that's the amaryllis.
> —DENISE LEVERTOV, "The Métier of Blossoming," St. 1,
> *This Great Unknowing: Last Poems*, 1998

To take care of the world demands also a lot of patience: I have to wait for the
day in which an ant will show up.
> —CLARICE LISPECTOR, *Água Viva* [Live Water], 1974

We call it "Nature"; only reluctantly admitting ourselves to be "Nature" too.
> —DENISE LEVERTOV, "Sojourns in the Parallel World," *Sands of the Well*, 1996

We know ourselves to be made from this earth. We know this earth is made from our bodies. For we see ourselves. And we are nature. We are nature seeing nature. We are nature with a concept of nature. Nature weeping. Nature speaking of nature to nature.

—SUSAN GRIFFIN, *Women and Nature*, 1980

Nature is commonplace. Imitation is more interesting.

—GERTRUDE STEIN in *My Autobiography* by Charlie Chaplin, 1964

I used to think that communing with nature was a healing, positive thing. Now, I think I'd like to commune with other things—like room service and temperature control.

—ROSEANNE BARR, *My Life as a Woman*, 1989

You fellows have got to get this [phosphate-pollution problem] straightened out, because the laundry's piling up.

—BETTY FURNESS in *Bella!* by Bella Abzug, 1972

Can we really expect adequate funding for programs to clean up our environment and care for people's basic needs as long as the socially essential work of caretaking and cleaning is relegated to women for little or no pay?

—RIANE EISLER, *Sacred Pleasure*, 1995

Land of low clouds, I belong to you.
I carry in my heart your every drop of rain.

—LEA GOLDBERG, "Song of the Strange Woman," *Poems from the Hebrew*, 1973

I'm singing in the rain,
Just singing in the rain.
What a glorious feeling,
I'm happy again.

—BETTY COMDEN, "Singin' in the Rain," with Adolph Green, 1952

He picked up some earth and poured it into the boy's palm. "Grasp it, feel it, taste it. There is your God. If you want to pray, boy, pray to the sky to bring rain to our land and not virtue to your souls."

—YAËL DAYAN, *Envy the Frightened*, 1960

"Rose is a rose is a rose is a rose."

—GERTRUDE STEIN, "Sacred Emily," 1913

The night sky, like the God of Moses, was unending, incomprehensible, full of enormous, indecipherable messages. Who wouldn't be anxious in the face of this?

—LAURIE COLWIN, "A Big Storm Knocked It Over," *Shaking Eve's Tree*, 1990

Spring comes softly to Michigan; winter is more outspoken. The wind grows quiet and sun cuts through gray snow to warm the earth below. Overnight a few tender snowdrops appear in dark, wet patches where the snow has melted. The wet places grow; ice chunks relax and fall apart. One day the pavements are dry and little girls in sweaters come out to chalk hopscotch squares on the sidewalks.

—FAYE MOSKOWITZ, "A Leak in the Heart," *Shaking Eve's Tree*, 1990

Not like the country. My. I never heard anybody say a thing like that before. It takes courage to just up and say you don't like the country. Everybody likes the country.

—LILLIAN HELLMAN, *Toys in the Attic*, 1959

We lack the knowledge we showed ten
thousand years past, that you live
a goddess but mortal, that what we take
must be returned; that the poison we drop
in you will stunt our children's growth.

—MARGE PIERCY, "The Common Living Dirt," *Stone, Paper, Knife*, 1983

this wounded
World that we cannot heal, that is our bride.
—ALICIA SUSKIN OSTRIKER, "The Eighth and Thirteenth," *The Little Space*, 1998

The ocean, whose tides respond, like women's menses, to the pull of the moon, the ocean which corresponds to the amniotic fluid in which human life begins, the ocean on whose surface vessels (personified as female) can ride but in whose depths sailors meet their death and monsters conceal themselves...it is unstable and threatening as the earth is not; it spawns new life daily, yet swallows up lives; it is changeable like the moon, unregulated, yet indestructible and eternal.

—ADRIENNE RICH, *Of Woman Born*, 1976

Skies ever-blue, daily sunshine, disgusted us like smile-buttons.
—DENISE LEVERTOV, "In California During the Gulf War," *Evening Train*, 1992

But ours is a time when "man's conquest of nature" threatens all life on our planet, when a dominator mind-set and advanced technology are a potentially lethal mix, when all around us institutions designed to maintain domination and exploitation are proving incapable of coping with the massive social, economic, and ecological problems they have created.

—RIANE EISLER, *Sacred Pleasure*, 1995

Guns have metamorphosed into cameras in this earnest comedy, the ecology safari, because nature has ceased to be what it always had been—what people needed protection from. Now nature tamed, endangered, mortal—needs to be protected from people.

—SUSAN SONTAG, *On Photography*, 1977

Nature in America has always been suspect, on the defensive, cannibalized by progress. In America, every specimen becomes a relic.

—SUSAN SONTAG, *On Photography*, 1977

Darkness in the woods was more than just lack of light; it was something tangible. It enveloped and smothered.

—FAYE KELLERMAN, *Stalker*, 2000

PETS & ANIMALS

Pigeons on the grass alas.

—GERTRUDE STEIN, *Four Saints in Three Acts* (opera), 1927

The bees
care for the allium, if you don't—
hear them now, doing their research,
humming the arias
of a honey opera...

—DENISE LEVERTOV, "In Praise of Allium," *Breathing the Water*, 1989

Oh yes, I care
My great big bear
Despite the eye that blackened
The bloody nose
The tooth that chipped
The lip that split
The vet, the bills
The food, the spills
The wallet bare
Oh yes, I care
My lovely bear
My Samson

—ELAINE BERNSTEIN PARTNOW, "Ode to my German Shepherd," 1972

My husband and I are either going to buy a dog or have a child. We can't decide whether to ruin our carpet or ruin our lives.

—RITA RUDNER, Stand-up routine

"I'm just a dog. Look, no opposable thumb."

—ROSALYN DREXLER, *The Cosmopolitan Girl*, 1975

It had proved impossible to anthropomorphize him into a handsome, dignified, well-behaved bully-boy; and somewhere along the unsuccessful process, he had lost the instincts of a dog, into the bargain.

—NADINE GORDIMER, "The Pet," *Not for Publication and Other Stories*, 1965

I think dogs are the most amazing creatures; they give unconditional love. For me they are the role model for being alive.

—GILDA RADNER, *It's Always Something*, 1989

How sad it is that a turtle can live to 150, or a parrot can live as long as a human, but man's best friend can only live for a decade or two. With some things there's little justice.

—FRAN DRESCHER, *Cancer, Schmancer*, 2002

You enter into a certain amount of madness when you marry a person with pets.

—NORA EPHRON, *Heartburn*, 1983

I used to think all cats were she's
But now I think that they're all he's
They love to lounge and stretch and nuzzle
And lie relaxed, with brow unpuzzled
They hunt with glee, whether mouse or chickadee
And show them off for the world to see
They come only when and if they please
Yes, I'm quite sure—all cats are he's

—ELAINE BERNSTEIN PARTNOW, "Cat Gender," 1973

There are three basic personality factors in cats: The kind who run up when you say hello and rub against you in cheap romance; the kind who run away certain that you mean to ravish them; and the kind who just look back and don't move a muscle. I love all three kinds.

—EVE BABITZ, *Eve's Hollywood*, 1974

Cockroach knows it's been
Naughty. Scrambles across the
Floor so stealthily.

Better hide, cockroach.
Got a rolled up magazine
Like the jaws of death.

Missed. Where are you now?
On the ceiling! Headline reads:
Roach outsmarts woman.

—ELAINE BERNSTEIN PARTNOW, "Cockroach Haiku X3," 1983

POLITICS, POLITICIANS & LEADERSHIP

(*also see* Civil Rights, Social Movements & Activism *and* Government & Political Systems)

The first woman President will have to show that she has all of the marbles required to run the government on her own.

—DIANNE FEINSTEIN in *Parade* magazine, 7 February 1999

The political arena leaves one no alternative, one must either be a dunce or a rogue.

—EMMA GOLDMAN, *Anarchism and Other Essays*, 1911

Re the legislative ban on assault weapons, which Dianne Feinstein championed, that was signed into law in 1994: It really comes down to a question of blood or guts—the blood of innocent people or the Senate of the United States having the guts to do what we should do when we take that oath to protect the welfare of our citizens.

—DIANNE FEINSTEIN in *Politics in America* 1998, 1999

There is no hope even that woman, with her right to vote, will ever purify politics.

—EMMA GOLDMAN, *Anarchism and Other Essays*, 1911

In a world where authority is equated with ownership of information, sharing that information becomes very threatening.

—SHOSHANA ZUBOFF in *Omni*, April 1991

I was running [for Congress] not because I happened to be a woman but because I was a woman.

—BELLA ABZUG, Induction Speech, National Women's Hall of Fame, Seneca Falls, New York, 24 September 1994

One thing that crystallized for me like nothing else this year is that Congress is a very *unrepresentative* institution…. Those men in Congress…represent their *own* point of view—by reason of their sex, background, and class.

—BELLA ABZUG, *Bella!*, 1972

I want to be able to live without a crowded calendar. I want to be able to read a book without feeling guilty, or go to a concert when I like…. But I do not intend to retire to a political nunnery.

—GOLDA MEIR, Statement of Resignation, *Good as Golda*, 1970

We have made tremendous strides since 1920. Women have a stronger voice in our communities and in our workplaces. I am proud to serve as one of the 14 women, Republican and Democrat, in the United States Senate, and now we have 62 women in the House of Representatives. We have made progress, but much more needs to be done.

—BARBARA BOXER, Letter re the Anniversary of the Ratification of the 19th Amendment, 18 August 2003

the Conquerors.
They're always watching,
invisibly electroded in our brains,
to be certain we implode our rage against each other
and not explode it against them.

—ROBIN MORGAN, *Sisterhood Is Powerful*, 1970

I think the Democratic emblem should be changed from a donkey to a pro-phylactic. It's perfect. It supports inflation, keeps production down, helps a bunch of pricks and gives a false sense of security when one is being screwed.

—ROBIN TYLER, Stand-up routine

...the deep-seated American distrust that still prevailed of diplomacy and diplomats.... Diplomacy means all the wicked devices of the Old World, spheres of influence, balances of power, secret treaties, triple alliances, and, during the interwar period, appeasement of Fascism.

—BARBARA TUCHMAN in *Foreign Affairs*, October 1972

Diplomacy is kind of like a basketball game. An awful lot can happen in the last 30 seconds.

—JESSICA TUCHMAN MATHEWS in *Knight Ridder Tribune*, 9 March 2003

Liberals! They're not leaders! If they were real leaders they'd understand that their style of politicking and self-aggrandizement is what's destroying the capacity of any of us to get anywhere.

—BELLA ABZUG, *Bella!*, 1972

I'm also very proud to be a liberal. Why is that so terrible these days? The liberals were liberating. They fought slavery, fought for women to have the right
to vote…fought to end segregation, fought to end apartheid. Thanks to liberals, we have Social Security, public education, consumer and environmental
protection, Medicare, Medicaid, the minimum-wage law, unemployment compensation. Liberals put an end to child labor. They even gave us the five-day
work week. What's to be ashamed of?
                        —BARBRA STREISAND in *Streisand: Her Life* by James Spada, 1995

It was the Catskills [a popular, upstate New York, mountain resort area frequented in large part by Jews; often referred to as the Borscht Belt], not early
socialist teaching at my father's knee, that made me a Marxist.
                                    —VIVIAN GORNICK, *Approaching Eye Level*, 1996

Queens may rule either as monarchs or as nationalized angels in the house.
                —CAROLYN G. HEILBRUN, *Toward a Recognition of Androgyny*, 1973

But the establishment is made up of little men, very frightened.
                                                —BELLA ABZUG, *Bella!*, 1972

Our tradition of political thought had its definite beginning in the teachings of
Plato and Aristotle. I believe it came to a no less definite end in the theories
of Karl Marx.
                                —HANNAH ARENDT, *Between Past and Future*, 1961

You can't govern without having the training in it. Even Plato said that a long
time ago. You need to be trained in government, to exercise it, to practice it.
But the American public is now satisfying itself with entertainers.
                        —BARBRA TUCHMAN in *A World of Ideas* by Bill Moyers, 1989

I've been the first [woman] four times now…. What I've learned is there is a
testing period that goes on—particularly in an executive capacity. I think it

[takes someone] with the ability to run a campaign well, put together a plat-form that resounds with the American people and someone with the stamina, the staying power, the determination and enthusiasm to carry it off.
—DIANNE FEINSTEIN in *Parade* magazine, 7 February 1999

Corruption of politics has nothing to do with the morals, or the laxity of morals, of various political personalities. Its cause is altogether a material one.
—EMMA GOLDMAN, *Anarchism and Other Essays,* 1911

Women must continue to invade the domains of power in order to change institutions as we know them, in order to offer places to other women...and to do justice to themselves.
—CAROLYN G. HEILBRUN, *Reinventing Womanhood,* 1979

A thoughtful husband, the [candidate's] manual said, should squelch any rumors that his wife is running for office because their marriage is on the skids. (Why else would a woman want to be in Congress?)
—BELLA ABZUG in *Ms.,* April 1974

If American politics are too dirty for women to take part in, there's something wrong with American politics.
—EDNA FERBER, *Cimarron,* 1929

Re the damage done to Geraldine Ferraro's candidacy due to her husband's financial misdeeds: What has the women's movement learned from [Geraldine Ferraro's] candidacy for vice president? Never get married.
—GLORIA STEINEM in *Boston Globe,* 14 May 1987

The word "revolution" itself has become not only a dead relic of Leftism, but a key to the deadendedness of male politics: the "revolution" of a wheel which returns in the end to the same place; the "revolving door" of a politics which has "liberated" women only to use them, and only within the limits of male tolerance.

—ADRIENNE RICH, Introduction to *The Work of a Common Woman:*
The Collected Poetry of Judy Grahn, 1977

—

You can't have a Congress that responds to the needs of the workingman when there are practically no people here who represent him. And you're not going to have a society that understands its humanity if you don't have more women in government.

—BELLA ABZUG in *Redbook*, April 1974

—

If we could harness the destructive energy of disagreements over politics, we wouldn't need the bomb.

—BARBARA WALTERS, *How to Talk with Practically Anybody*
about Practically Anything, 1970

—

Politics is the reflex of the business and industrial world.

—EMMA GOLDMAN, *Anarchism and Other Essays*, 1911

—

People in politics are not very kind to each other.

—YAËL DAYAN in *Los Angeles Times*, 7 March 1974

—

The new women in politics seem to be saying that we already know how to lose, thank you very much. Now we want to learn how to win.

—GLORIA STEINEM in *Ms.*, April 1974

—

Politics is about power: about who has it, how it is defined, and how it is exercised. Since these are issues in all relationships—be they sexual or nonsexual, between parents and children, between women and men, or between different racial, religious, economic, and national groups—human relations are always political.

—RIANE EISLER, *Sacred Pleasure*, 1995

Revolution is but thought carried into action.
>—EMMA GOLDMAN in *The Feminist Papers* ed. by Alice Rossi, 1973

The ultimate end of all revolutionary social change is to establish the sanctity of human life, the dignity of man, the right of every human being to liberty and well-being.
>—EMMA GOLDMAN, *My Further Disillusionment in Russia*, 1924

I remember and I make sure my daughters know, it was old biddies like we are now and young women who brought the King down. We are the Revolution, ladies, and we carry it in our blood to the future.
>—MARGE PIERCY, *City of Darkness, City of Light*, 1996

the revolutionary look
that says I am in the world
to change the world.
>—MURIEL RUKEYSER, "Woman as Market," *The Speed of Darkness*, 1968

The most radical revolutionary will become a conservative the day after the revolution.
>—HANNAH ARENDT, *Crises of the Republic*, 1972

The revolutionaries are those who know when power is lying in the street and when they can pick it up.
>—HANNAH ARENDT, *Crises of the Republic*, 1972

If you learn how to rule one single man's soul, you can get the rest of mankind.
>—AYN RAND, *The Fountainhead*, 1943

The will to domination is a ravenous beast. There are never enough warm bodies to satiate its monstrous hunger.
>—ANDREA DWORKIN, *Our Blood*, 1976

POPULATION &
BIRTH CONTROL

(*also see* Feminism & Women's Liberation)

No, it is not because woman is lacking in responsibility, but because she has too much of the latter that she demands to know how to prevent conception.
—EMMA GOLDMAN in *Mother Earth*, April 1916

~

...a very large family. Four brothers and three sisters, they wouldn't touch birth control with a basement beam. Orthodox. Constructive fucking. Builders, baby.
—GRACE PALEY, *Enormous Changes at the Last Minute*, 1960

~

[The decades before *Roe* were] years of terror, of silently fearing pregnancy, of sneaking off to possible sterility or death, and of sex ridden with shame.
—ROSALIND PETCHESKY, *Abortion and Woman's Choice*, 1990

~

Although every organized patriarchal religion works overtime to contribute its own brand of misogyny to the myth of woman-hate, woman-fear, and woman-evil, the Roman Catholic Church also carries the immense power of very directly affecting women's lives everywhere by its stand against birth control and abortion, and by its use of skillful and wealthy lobbies to prevent legislative change. It is an obscenity—an all-male hierarchy, celibate or not, that presumes to rule on the lives and bodies of millions of women.
—ROBIN MORGAN, *Sisterhood Is Powerful*, 1970

~

In the middle-class United States, a veneer of "alternative lifestyles" disguises the reality that, here as everywhere, women's apparent "choices" whether or not to have children are still dependent on the far from neutral will of male legislators, jurists, a male medical and pharmaceutical profession, well-financed lobbies, including the prelates of the Catholic Church, and the political reality that women do not as yet have self-determination over our bodies and still live mostly in ignorance of *our* authentic physicality, our possible choices, our eroticism itself.

—ADRIENNE RICH, *On Lies, Secrets, and Silence*, 1979

On being asked if she would favor birth control laws: I will if you make it retroactive.

—FLORENCE PRAG KAHN in *San Francisco Chronicle*, August 1926

The male morning-after pill, yeah. The moment the paternity suit's filed, it changes their blood group.

—SUE MARGOLIS, *Spin Cycle*, 2001

Frankly, I think it's a good law [24-hour waiting period before getting an abortion]. The other day I wanted to go get an abortion. I really wanted an abortion, but then I thought about it and it turned out I was just thirsty.

—SARAH SILVERMAN on *Saturday Night Live*, 1993

By any humane, and rational, standards, doing everything possible to dramatically reduce birthrates should be a top moral priority for all the world's secular and religious leaders—particularly since both maternal and infant mortality rates are highest precisely in those areas where women are forced by lack of contraception and abortion to bear children that cannot be adequately cared for.

—RIANE EISLER, *Sacred Pleasure*, 1995

What happened to the good old days of homemade ice cream and Trojans?... When did it become the woman's chore?

—GAIL PARENT, *Sheila Levine Is Dead and Living in New York*, 1972

The White House and both houses of Congress are all securely in Republican hands, and all hands are ready to chip away at reproductive rights—one law, one rule, one regulation, one case at a time.

—ELLEN GOODMAN, Syndicated Column, 21 January 2003

Considering that I was to become famous as an advocate of contraception, it's somewhat ironic that my parents didn't use it at precisely the point when they should have.

—Dr. Ruth Westheimer, http://www.drruth.com, 1997

At any hour God may open the sealed womb.

—Kadya Molodowsky, "Songs of Women," *Paper Bridges*, 1999

"But I've been miserable ever since I came back. From Puerto Rico, that's where I had it [the abortion], it was like a vacation. It's almost like—it's not supposed to be that easy. It's too big a sin to get off that lightly."

—Judith Rossner, *Looking for Mr. Goodbar*, 1975

The emphasis must not be on the right to abortion but on the right to privacy and reproductive control.

—Ruth Bader Ginsburg in Ms., April 1974

Racism, Sexism & Other Prejudices

(*also see* Anti-Semitism)

I believe there are a couple of gross injustices in the world: against African blacks and against Jews. Moreover, I think these two instances of injustice can only be remedied by Socialist principles.

—Golda Meir, Quoted by Oriana Fallaci *in L'Eurepeo*, 1973

Racism is a bacterium, potentially curable but presently deadly; anti-Semitism is a virus, potentially deadly but presently contained.

—Letty Cottin Pogrebin, *Deborah, Golda, and Me*, 1991

There can be no doubt that our Nation has had a long and unfortunate history of sex discrimination. Traditionally, such discrimination was rationalized by an attitude of "romantic paternalism" which, in practical effect, put women, not on a pedestal, but in a cage.

—RUTH BADER GINSBURG, Supreme Court decision (1973) in
The Encyclopedia of Women's History by K. Cullen-DuPont, 1987

Ageism in language can be very subtle and may not be as immediately apparent as racist or sexist terms. Like its counterparts, however, it is equally necessary to rid our language of ageist expressions.

—ELAINE BERNSTEIN PARTNOW, *Breaking the Age Barrier*, 1981

But how to burn it out—to purify one's mind of worms and grubs and frights of strangers, and a fear of the black Walpurgisnacht, when all the demons will run loose over the suburban lawns saying "You must now be slaves. Take your turn. It's only fair. The master must grovel in the dirt." I mean to say that despite my concern for civil liberties, for equality, for justice in Mississippi—I am blond, and blond is still beautiful, and if I have one life to lead it will be as a white, and I am a mass of internal contradictions, all of which cause me to finally attempt some rite which will bring salvation, save me from a system I despise but still carry within me like any other of my vital organs.

—ANNE ROIPHE, *Up the Sandbox!*, 1970

Shifts in prejudice can work both ways.

—MIDGE DECTER, *The Liberated Woman and Other Americans*, 1971

When we achieve a minimum of acceptance within the community, we often tend to take on the prejudice and discrimination of the community, not necessarily against our own group, but against racial and minority groups who have incurred the displeasure of the dominant groups. Our guilt is the greater because we fail to realize that in showing prejudice against any minority group we endanger all, including our own. When and if society turns against its minorities, it turns against them all, the Negro, the Catholic, and the Jew.

—"Cultural Democracy—Pattern for America," Official statement of National Council of Jewish Women, September 1947

Jew-baiting and Negro lynching are two blunders well worth being freed from; *Kishineffing* outside the land of Kishineff is a greater blot upon civilization than in that "hell's kitchen," Russia.

—ROSE PASTOR STOKES, "Kishineffing It," *I Belong to the Working Class*, 1992

Re meeting of the Jewish Woman's Congress at the Columbian Exposition in Chicago, 1893: The only part of the program they [the men] wished us to fill was the chairs.

—HANNAH GREENEBAUM SOLOMON in *The Journey Home* by Joyce Antler, 1997

Perhaps we should first take time to contemplate why tending to relationships, like changing diapers, is predominantly women's work.... *In relationships between dominant and subordinate groups, the subordinate group members always possess a far greater understanding of dominant group members and their culture than vice versa.*

—HARRIET GOLDHOR LERNER, *The Dance of Intimacy*, 1989

I earn and pay my own way as a great many women do today. Why should unmarried women be discriminated against....

—DINAH SHORE in *Los Angeles Times*, 16 April 1974

I submit that women's history has been hushed up for the same reasons that black history has been hushed up...and that is that a feminist movement poses a direct threat to the establishment. From the beginning it exposes the hypocrisy of the male power structure.

—SHULAMITH FIRESTONE, *The Dialectic of Sex*, 1970

...a typical minority-group stereotype—woman as nigger—if she knows her place (home), she is really a quite lovable, loving creature, happy and childlike.

—NAOMI WEISSTEIN in *Psychology Today*, October 1969

~

The crossroads of racism and sexism had to be a violent meeting place. There is no use pretending it doesn't exist.

—SUSAN BROWNMILLER, *Against Our Will*, 1975

~

Perhaps as a Jew I feel some special kinship with those persecuted for their religious beliefs.

—JOAN BORYSENKO, *A Woman's Journey to God*, 1999

~

The white race *is* the cancer of human history.

—SUSAN SONTAG, *Styles of Radical Will*, 1969

~

I do not think white America is committed to granting equality to the American Negro.... This is a passionately racist country; it will continue to be so in the foreseeable future.

—SUSAN SONTAG, *Styles of Radical Will*, 1969

~

Too many Geminis at one school? Bus them! Let them mingle with a Taurus or a Sagg! Get to know the other half of the zodiac.

—LOTUS WEINSTOCK, Stand-up routine

RELATIONSHIPS & THE SEXES

(*also see* Marriage, Husbands, Wives & Divorce *and* Sex & Sexuality)

If I was required to give up my work for a relationship, that would mean I'd give up the relationship.

—MADELINE KAHN in *Drama-Logue*, 1984

Relationship—that silk purse turned sow's ear.
                                    —CARRIE FISHER, *Postcards from the Edge*, 1987

I can live without it all—
love with its blood pump,
sex with its messy hungers.
men with their peacock strutting,
their silly sexual baggage,
their wet tongues in my ear
and their words like little sugar suckers
with sour centers.
                    —ERICA JONG, "Becoming a Nun," *About Women*, Stephen Berg and
                                    S. J. Marks, eds., 1973

Perhaps it is true that a presentation of only the female side of things…is limited. But…is it any more limited than the prevailing male view of things, which—when not taken as absolute truth—is at least seen as "serious," relevant and important.
                                    —SHULAMITH FIRESTONE, *The Dialectic of Sex*, 1970

Everything else in my life I ever wanted, if I tried for it, I got it. But with men, the harder I tried, the harder I flopped.
                                    —FANNY BRICE in *Women in Comedy*, Martin, 1986

Our greatest compatibility was in how we complemented each other's neuroses.
                                    —FRAN DRESCHER, *Cancer, Schmancer*, 2002

JUDGE: Now, where were we? Oh, yes, plaintiff and defendant were in bed—talking.
                                    —FAY KANIN, *His and Hers*, with Michael Kanin, 1948

He and I had an office so tiny that an inch smaller and it would have been adultery.

—DOROTHY PARKER, Remark

Never have a love affair with a man whose friendship you value. Because there's nothing like sex to make people hate and misunderstand one another.

—EMILY "MICKEY" HAHN, *Nobody Said Not to Go* by Ken Cuthbertson, 1998

This is a population in a permanent state of intermittent attachment. Inevitably, the silent apartment waits.

—VIVIAN GORNICK, *Approaching Eye Level*, 1996

To think the highest-brow,
Which I must say is he,
Should pick the lowest-brow,
Which there's no doubt is me...

—DOROTHY FIELDS, "If My Friends Could See Me Now," *Sweet Charity*, 1966

What is exciting is not for one person to be stronger than the other...but for two people to have met their match and yet they are equally as stubborn, as obstinate, as passionate, as crazy as the other.

—BARBRA STREISAND in *Streisand: Her Life* by James Spada, 1995

Everyone wanted to take me out to dinner.... Many of them were those mon-eyed men looking for romance and full of bicarbonate.

—MOLLY PICON, *Molly!*, 1980

So there I was licking jelly off my boyfriend...and I thought: Oh my God, I'm turning into my mother!

—SARAH SILVERMAN, Stand-up routine

Smart women love smart men more than smart men love smart women.
—NATALIE PORTMAN in *USA Weekend*, May 2002

With new and old patterns both in the air, it is all too human for each partner to reach out for the double dose of privileges, those of the old and those of the new role, leaving to the mate the double dose of obligation.
—MIRRA KOMAROVSKY, *Women in the Modern World*, 1953

Hookers! How do they do it? How could any woman sleep with a man without having a dinner and a movie first?
—ELAYNE BOOSLER, Stand-up routine

This double standard has for millennia been justified by the teachings that in the eyes of God men are of a higher spiritual order than women. It manifests itself in the fact that although men are in Christian dogma deemed to be more spiritual than women, women are in actual practice expected to be far more spiritual than men—more noble, giving, and self-sacrificing. Under this double standard, no matter how kind and caring a woman is, unless she completely sacrifices her own welfare (even her life) for that of others (particularly her husband and children), she can never hope to be considered the spiritual equal of man. And even then, she will only be looked on as the exception to the rule that woman is less spiritually and morally evolved than man.
—RIANE EISLER, *Sacred Pleasure*, 1995

Men seldom make passes
At girls who wear glasses.
—DOROTHY PARKER, "News Item," *Enough Rope*, 1926

Never move to Maine for a man.
—RAVEN SNOOK, *How I Became a Drag Queen Trapped in a Woman's Body*, 1997

I am uncomfortable flirting, it requires a great deal of energy and ego, and I manage to do it only a couple of times a year, and not with interview subjects.

—NORA EPHRON, *Crazy Salad*, 1975

Once you start carrying your own suitcases, paying your own bills, running your own show, you've done something to yourself that makes you one of those women men may like and call "pal" and a "good sport," the kind of woman they tell their troubles to. But you've cut yourself off from the orchids and the diamond bracelets, except those you buy yourself.

—SOPHIE TUCKER, *Some of These Days*, 1945

Guys in Manhattan have the worst lines to try to meet you. It's not their fault—it's just an awkward situation. I'd be walking down the street in cut-offs, with a newspaper, cup of coffee and a dog. A guy would say, "Hey, live around here?"

—ELAYNE BOOSLER, Stand-up routine

On construction workers: They say to five thousand women a day, "Ey, can I go witch you?" And they get rejected five thousand times, get a good night's sleep, and they're ready to start all over again.

—ELAYNE BOOSLER, *Funny Women*, Unterbrink, 1987

It is in opposition (the disputed territory of the argument, the battle for self-definition that goes on beneath the words)...that intimacy takes place.

—NADINE GORDIMER, *The Conservationist*, 1975

The genuine solitaries of life fear intimacy more than loneliness. The married are those who have taken the terrible risk of intimacy and, having taken it, know life without intimacy to be impossible.

—CAROLYN G. HEILBRUN in *Ms.*, August 1974

Long-term commitment to an intimate relationship with one person of whatever sex is an essential need that people have in order to breed the qualities out of which nurturant thought can rise.

—GERDA LERNER in *Ms.*, September 1981

What is important to a relationship is a harmony of emotional roles and not too great a disparity in the general level of intelligence.

—MIRRA KOMAROVSKY, *Women in the Modern World*, 1953

Were our knowledge of human relationships a hundredfold more reliable than it is now, it would still be foolish to seek ready-made solutions for problems of living in the index of a book.

—MIRRA KOMAROVSKY, *Women in the Modern World*, 1953

She was always pleased to have him come and never sorry to see him go.

—DOROTHY PARKER, "Big Blonde," *Laments for the Living*, 1929

Long after you have swung back
away from me
I think you are still with me

—DENISE LEVERTOV, "Losing Track," *Poems 1960–1967*, 1964

He had not bound himself to me by an explicit word, only by those thousand intangible threads that may possibly not be what I thought them, what outsiders thought them.

—HENRIETTA SZOLD in *Lost Love*, Shargel, 1997

"I've had so many failed blind dates, my mates joined to buy me a guide dog."

—SUE MARGOLIS, *Spin Cycle*, 2001

Would you have slept with Onassis for $26 million?

—JOAN RIVERS, Stand-up routine

—

"Be careful.... There's a reason he's still available."

—ANNE ROIPHE, *If You Knew Me*, 1993

—

The worse the boyfriend, the more stunning your American Express bill.

—WENDY WASSERSTEIN, *Bachelor Girls*, 1990

—

Except for their genitals, I don't know what immutable differences exist between men and women. Perhaps there are some other unchangeable differences; probably there are a number of irrelevant differences. But it is clear that until social expectations for men and women are equal, until we provide equal respect for both sexes, answers to this question will simply reflect our prejudices.

—NAOMI WEISSTEIN in *Psychology Today*, October 1969

—

Men and women, women and men. It will never work.

—ERICA JONG, *Fear of Flying*, 1973

—

Destiny is something men select; women achieve it only by default or stupendous suffering.

—HARRIET ROSENSTEIN in *Ms.*, July 1974

—

Today the survival of some...stereotypes is a psychological straitjacket for both sexes.

—MIRRA KOMAROVSKY, *Women in the Modern World*, 1953

—

The only difference between men and women is that women are able to create new little human beings in their bodies while simultaneously writing books, driving tractors, working in offices, planting crops—in general, doing everything men do.

—ERICA JONG in *Redbook*, November 1978

Men and women think differently. Men think in terms of dollars and cents while women think along the lines of conservation of human life. Just as a party of men is called a stag party so is a nation with men serving alone stag-nation.

—MAUD NATHAN in *Philadelphia Record*, 1 November 1915

One thing for sure is that we can't have it both ways. We can't complain end-lessly about their sins, their predatory powers and at the same time encourage them to make nice to our babies.

—ANNE ROIPHE, *Fruitful*, 1996

It is only as women rise in status that men can more comfortably themselves exhibit stereotypically feminine styles of behavior without feeling a loss in their own status.

—RIANE EISLER, *Sacred Pleasure*, 1995

I don't mean that there should be no relationship between the sexes. But let there be various relationships.

—EMILY "MICKEY" HAHN, *Nobody Said* Not *to Go* by Ken Cuthbertson, 1998

"Thank you, Agatha, for the lovely bracelet, but I still haven't changed my mind. I have no desire to touch you in places that I already own. Sincerely, Sheila Levine."

—GAIL PARENT, *Sheila Levine Is Dead and Living in New York*, 1972

The higher the mental development of woman, the less possible it is for her to meet a congenial male who will see in her, not only sex, but also the human being, the friend, the comrade and strong individuality, who cannot and ought not lose a single trait of her character.

—EMMA GOLDMAN, *Anarchism and Other Essays*, 1911

(All your life you wait around for some damn man!)

—DOROTHY PARKER, "Chant for Dark Hours," *Enough Rope*, 1926

I want to be alone.

—VICKI BAUM, *Grand Hotel* (play), 1930

I have always required a man to be dependent on, even when it appeared that I had one already. I won two small boys whose dependence on me takes up my lumpen time and my bourgeois feelings.

—GRACE PALEY, *Enormous Changes at the Last Minute*, 1960

Practically all my boyfriends have missed the things that are really important to me—my birthday, the anniversary of when we met...my clitoris.

—SUE MARGOLIS, *Spin Cycle*, 2001

Why is it no one ever sent me yet
One perfect limousine, do you suppose?
Ah no, it's always just my luck to get
One perfect rose.

—DOROTHY PARKER, "One Perfect Rose"

When sleep leaves the body like smoke
and man, sated with secrets,
drives the overworked nag of quarrel
out of its stall,
then the fire-breathing union begins anew...

—NELLY SACHS, "When Sleep Enters the Body Like Smoke," *O the Chimneys*, 1967

It's only through our relations with others that we develop the outlook of hardiness and come to believe in our own capabilities and inner goodness.

—JOAN BORYSENKO, *Minding the Body, Mending the Mind*, 1987

The message about sex and relationships that she had gotten as a child...was confused, contradictory. Sex was for men, and marriage, like lifeboats, was for women and children.

—CARRIE FISHER, *Postcards from the Edge*, 1987

SCIENCE & HISTORY

To embrace an epoch in all its splendor and truth, to understand the fluctuations of taste, one needs perspective.

—WANDA LANDOWSKA, *Landowska on Music*, 1964

I will never know the experience of others, but I can know my own, and I can approximate theirs by entering their world. This approximation marks the tragic, perpetually inadequate aspect of social research.

—SHULAMIT REINHARZ, *On Becoming a Social Scientist*, 1984

[History] tends to dissolve as you get closer, to fragment into a billion bits of ordinariness.

—EVA HOFFMAN, *Exit Into History*, 1993

The group entrusted with history-making remembers itself. Those who keep the books determine who is authorized to write in them and what is worth writing about. Authority means being the author of one's own reality as it is recorded for posterity. Remembering is not a neutral act.

—LETTY COTTIN POGREBIN, *Deborah, Golda, and Me*, 1991

Controversy both within and between disciplines is an inevitable feature of scientific development.... But not all intellectual controversy is equally beneficial. Pseudo-issues produced by verbal and logical ambiguities are much too frequent and waste our resources.

—MIRRA KOMAROVSKY, *Common Frontiers of the Social Sciences*, 1957

Computerization is part of a long-term historical process in which work has become increasingly abstract.

—SHOSHANA ZUBOFF in *Omni*, April 1991

The entire history of science is a progression of exploded fallacies, not of achievements.

—AYN RAND, *Atlas Shrugged*, 1957

I believe that in art and science are the glories of the human mind. I see no conflict between them.

—GERTY THERESA CORI in *Notable American Women*, 1980

What has robbed us of such simplicity—the telephone or the Darwinian theory?

—HENRIETTA SZOLD in *Lost Love*, Shargel, 1997

Indeed, if we view evolution as a giant creative experiment—of which we humans are one of the latest, and most amazing, results—we see an extraordinary pageant in which the evolution of both sex and consciousness plays an important part.

—RIANE EISLER, *Sacred Pleasure*, 1995

If the fish had stuck to its gills there would have been no movement up to the land.

—CYNTHIA OZICK, "The Hole/Birth Catalog," *The First Ms. Reader*, 1972

For perhaps we are like stones; our own history and the history of the world embedded in us, we hold a sorrow deep within and cannot weep until that history is sung.

—SUSAN GRIFFIN, *A Chorus of Stones*, 1992

Everything that explains the world has in fact explained a world that does not exist, a world in which men are at the center of the human enterprise and women are at the margin "helping" them. Such a world does not exist.

—GERDA LERNER in *Ms.*, September 1981

History as taught in most schools is largely a matter of the struggle for power among men and nations. It is the dates of battles and the names of kings and generals noted for alternately constructing and destroying fortresses, palaces, and religious monuments.

—RIANE EISLER, *The Chalice and the Blade*, 1987

It is hardly surprising that our conventional histories systematically omit anything relating to women or "femininity" when only a very short time ago not one American university even had a women's studies program.... It is thus also not surprising that most "educated" people still find it hard to believe there were any women who mattered in history.

—RIANE EISLER, *The Chalice and the Blade*, 1987

We as women know that there are no disembodied processes; that all history originates in human flesh; that all oppression is inflicted by the body of one against the body of another; that all social change is built on the bone and muscle, and out of the flesh and blood, of human creators.

—ANDREA DWORKIN, *Our Blood*, 1976

In facing history we look at each other, and in facing our entire personal life, we look at each other.

—MURIEL RUKEYSER, *Breaking Open*, 1973

Women are the majority of humankind and have been essential in the making of history.

—GERDA LERNER, *The Majority Finds Its Past*, 1979

I am reading James Psychology [and] a history of Germany. The history I cannot abide; it deals only with wars and dates and kings; those are matters that do not interest me and that I cannot remember. History does not tell the real things.

—JESSIE SAMPTER, *The Speaking Heart* (unpub. autobio.)

I have never aspired to have, nor do I now want, a laboratory or a cadre of investigators-in-training which is more extensive than I can personally interact with and supervise.

—ROSALYN YALOW, Autobiographical entry,
Les Prix Nobel Yearbook, Tore Frängsmyr, ed., 1977

Technological change defines the horizon of our material world as it shapes the limiting conditions of what is possible and what is barely imaginable. It erodes...assumptions about the nature of our reality, the "pattern" in which we dwell, and lays open new choices.

—SHOSHANA ZUBOFF, *In the Age of the Smart Machine*, 1988

The becoming of man is the history of the exhaustion of his possibilities.

—SUSAN SONTAG, *Styles of Radical Will*, 1969

The past itself, as historical change continues to accelerate, has become the most surreal of subjects—making it possible...to see a new beauty in what is vanishing.

—SUSAN SONTAG, *On Photography*, 1977

SEX & SEXUALITY

(*also see* Relationships & the Sexes *and* Racism, Sexism & Other Prejudices)

Dear Abby: Is it wrong to fake orgasm during masturbation?

—LOTUS WEINSTOCK, Stand-up routine

She was sensual without being jaded, accomplished without a hint of whorishness...but she did not admire him as he liked to be admired.... She had a critical eye he disliked in a woman.... She was good at sex, but he did not think she would be good at loving.

—MARGE PIERCY, *City of Darkness, City of Light*, 1996

Women's Liberation calls it enslavement but the real truth about the sexual revolution is that it has made of sex an almost chaotically limitless and there-fore unmanageable realm in the life of women.

—MIDGE DECTER, *The New Chastity*, 1972

The only reason I had a kid is because my husband tossed and turned in his sleep.

—JOAN RIVERS in *Women in Comedy*, Martin, 1986

It's been so long since I made love I can't even remember who gets tied up.

—JOAN RIVERS, Stand-up routine

"Have I Had You Before"

—PATSY ABBOTT, Album title

Girls who put out are tramps. Girls who don't are ladies. This is, however, a rather archaic usage of the word. Should one of you boys happen upon a girl who doesn't put out, do not jump to the conclusion that you have found a lady. What you have probably found is a lesbian.

—FRAN LEBOWITZ, *Metropolitan Life*, 1978

Erotica is simply high-class pornography; better produced, better conceived, better executed, better packaged, designed for a better class of consumer.

—ANDREA DWORKIN, *Pornography: Men Possessing Women*, 1981

Erotic is about sexuality, but pornography is about power and sex-as-weapon—
in the same way we have come to understand that rape is about violence, and
not really about sex at all.

—GLORIA STEINEM in Ms., November 1978

There's a fine line between eroticism and nausea. When a man twists my breast
nonstop for an hour like a computer game, I wanna throw up.

—SANDRA BERNHARD, Women in Comedy, Martin, 1986

What is important now is that we free ourselves from the prison of gender and,
before it is too late, deliver the world from the almost exclusive control of the
masculine impulse.

—CAROLYN G. HEILBRUN, Toward a Recognition of Androgyny, 1973

Androgyny suggests a spirit of reconciliation between the sexes; it suggests, further, a full range of experience open to individuals who may as women be
aggressive, as men, tender; it suggests a spectrum upon which human beings
choose their places without regard to propriety or to custom.

—CAROLYN G. HEILBRUN, Toward a Recognition of Androgyny, 1973

My brother's gay. My parents don't mind as long as he marries a doctor.

—ELAYNE BOOSLER, Stand-up routine

If homosexuality is a disease, let's all call in queer to work. "Hello, can't work
today. Still queer."

—ROBIN TYLER, Stand-up routine

She never felt much in common with gay men; it was like telling her she ought
to feel empathy with child molesters because they were both defined by the law
as sexual deviants.

—MARGE PIERCY, The High Cost of Living, 1978

Lesbian existence comprises both the breaking of a taboo and the rejection of a compulsory way of life. It is also a direct or indirect attack on the male right of access to women.

—ADRIENNE RICH, *Blood, Bread, and Poetry*, 1986

I'd call it love if love
didn't take so many years
but lust too is a jewel
a sweet flower...

—ADRIENNE RICH, "Two Songs," *Necessities of Life*, 1966

Today we do know that from a scientific point of view that for many women masturbation is the best way for them to learn how to give themselves permission to have an orgasm.

—DR. RUTH WESTHEIMER, http://www.drruth.com, 1997

Pornography is not a safety valve, it is a writ of permission.

—ROSALYN DREXLER in *Contemporary Women Playwrights*, Betsko, 1987

She is the pinup, the centerfold, the poster, the postcard, the dirty picture, naked, half-dressed, laid out, legs spread, breast or ass protruding. She is the thing she is supposed to be: the thing that makes him erect.

—ANDREA DWORKIN, *Pornography: Men Possessing Women*, 1981

Women, for centuries not having access to pornography and now unable to bear looking at the muck on the supermarket shelves, are astonished. Women do not believe that men believe what pornography says about women. But they do.

—ANDREA DWORKIN, *Pornography: Men Possessing Women*, 1981

What pornographic literature does is precisely to drive a wedge between one's existence as a full human being and one's existence as a sexual being.

—SUSAN SONTAG, *Styles of Radical Will*, 1969

Re her promiscuous sister: It took a driving instructor two days to teach her how to sit up in a car.

—PHYLLIS DILLER, Stand-up routine

⌐

She had more hands up her dress than the Muppets.

—JOAN RIVERS, Stand-up routine

⌐

When the rabbi said, "Do you take this woman?" sixteen guys said, "We have."

—JOAN RIVERS, Stand-up routine

⌐

Seduction is often difficult to distinguish from rape. In seduction, the rapist often bothers to buy a bottle of wine.

—ANDREA DWORKIN, *Letters from a War-Zone*, 1989

⌐

Sex is to a very large degree socially constructed.

—RIANE EISLER, *Sacred Pleasure*, 1995

⌐

That woman speaks eighteen languages and can't say No in any of them.

—DOROTHY PARKER in *While Rome Burns* by Alexander Woollcott, 1934

⌐

How to put the libido back, restore the lost spontaneity, drive, love of life, the individuality, that sex in America seems to lack?

—BETTY FRIEDAN, *The Feminine Mystique*, 1963

⌐

The view that sex has a spiritual dimension is so alien to everything we have been taught that it takes most people completely aback. But actually this view is rooted in ancient traditions vividly expressed in prehistoric art that earlier scholars often found too embarrassing to deal with, and in some cases to even fully see.

—RIANE EISLER, *Sacred Pleasure*, 1995

"No hanky, no panky. At my age, foreplay is brushing my teeth…when I can remember where I put 'em."

—RITA RUDNER, *Tickled Pink*, 2001

Like should never get together with like. Men should marry women. Jews should marry gentiles. Americans and Europeans. Blacks and whites. People are *against* each other. That's what sex is about—the great bridge across.

—LAURIE COLWIN, "A Big Storm Knocked It Over," *Shaking Eve's Tree*, 1990

Don't cook. Don't clean. No man will ever make love to a woman because she waxed the linoleum—"My God, the floor's immaculate. Lie down, you hot bitch."

—JOAN RIVERS, Stand-up routine

If you love to eat steak, you still wouldn't want to eat it every night for dinner, even if you didn't like the other foods as much. Why? Because if you ate steak every day, you'd become bored with it and there would come a time you'd never want to eat it again. The same effect can happen with sex, which is why it is good to throw in some variety, even if only once in a while.

—DR. RUTH WESTHEIMER, http://www.drruth.com, 1997

No woman needs intercourse; few women escape it.

—ANDREA DWORKIN, *Right-Wing Women*, 1978

Sex is like eating. Sometimes you have fast food, and sometimes you eat a gourmet meal.

—MONICA LEWINSKY in *Time*, 22 March 1999

To people who saw sex as a sacramental act of communion with nature and one another, our sexual images of men humiliating, degrading, mutilating, enslaving, and even killing women in the name of sexual pleasure would have been totally incomprehensible—and patently insane.

—RIANE EISLER, *Sacred Pleasure*, 1995

Sexual war against men is an irrelevant, self-defeating acting out of rage.

—BETTY FRIEDAN, *The Second Stage*, 1981

...the first sexual stirrings of little girls, so masked, so complex, so foolish as compared with the sex of little boys.

—LILLIAN HELLMAN, *An Unfinished Woman*, 1969

It is essential that we realize once and for all that man is much more of a sex creature than a moral creature. The former is inherent, the other is grafted on.

—EMMA GOLDMAN, *Red Emma Speaks*, 1972

After I am waxed old shall I have pleasure, my lord being old also?

—SARAH, Book of Genesis, ninth century B.C.E., Bible

Women complain about sex more often than men. Their gripes fall into two major categories: (1) Not enough. (2) Too much.

—ANN LANDERS, *Ann Landers Says "Truth Is Stranger,"* 1968

Once upon a time sex was romance.... Today, however, to be clinical is to be in.

—MARJORIE ROSEN, *Popcorn Venus*, 1973

Instead of fulfilling the promise of infinite orgastic bliss, sex in the America of the feminine mystique is becoming a strangely joyless national compulsion, if not a contemptuous mockery.

—BETTY FRIEDAN, *The Feminine Mystique*, 1963

"At seventy-two," Jack said with a wicked smile, "I still feel like a twenty-year-old. The thing is, there's never one around."

—SUE MARGOLIS, *Spin Cycle*, 2001

I read for the part of Elizabeth, the virgin queen. I thought they said they were looking for a virgin from Queens. The only virgin in my house is the olive oil.
—FRAN DRESCHER in http://www.perfectpeople.com, 2003

Fear of sexuality is the new, disease-sponsored register of the universe of fear in which everyone now lives.
—SUSAN SONTAG, *AIDS and Its Metaphors*, 1989

Tamed as it may be, sexuality remains one of the demonic forces in human consciousness—pushing us at intervals close to taboo and dangerous desires, which range from the impulse to commit sudden arbitrary violence upon another person to the voluptuous yearning for the extinction of one's consciousness, for death itself.
—SUSAN SONTAG, *Styles of Radical Will*, 1969

Experiences aren't pornographic; only images and representations—structures of the imagination—are.
—SUSAN SONTAG, *Styles of Radical Will*, 1969

I have done abject deeds for sexual passion. So, I am sure, has Norman Schwarzkopf.
—NAOMI WOLF, *Fire with Fire*, 1993

Confucius, in his Book of Rites, held that it was a husband's duty to take care of his wife or concubine sexually as well as financially and emotionally.
—NAOMI WOLF, *Promiscuities*, 1997

For some years she had been thinking she was not much inclined towards sex…. It is not merely a lack of pleasure in sex, it is dislike of the excitement. And it is not merely dislike, it is worse, it is boredom.
—MURIEL SPARK, "Bang-Bang You're Dead," *Collected Stories: I*, 1968

"Sex," she says, "is a subject like any other subject. Every bit as interesting as agriculture."

—MURIEL SPARK, *The Hothouse by the East River*, 1973

SHOW BIZ, SPORTS & ENTERTAINMENT

(*also see* Artists, the Arts & Creativity *and* Celebrities, Heroes & Sheroes)

The audience is the most revered member of the theater. Without an audience there is no theater.... They are our guests, our evaluators, and the last spoke in the wheel which can then begin to roll. They make the performance meaningful.

—VIOLA SPOLIN, *Improvisation for the Theater*, 1963

There is no director who can direct you like an audience.

—FANNY BRICE in *The Fabulous Fanny* by Norman Katkov, 1953

[Audiences] all applaud, but none of them will come home with you and look at your back someplace to see if you have a pimple.

—GILDA RADNER in *Rolling Stone*, 2 November 1978

Re radio: You can't do this, you can't do that. I couldn't even say "hell or damn," and nothing, honey, is more expressive than the way I say "hell or damn."

—SOPHIE TUCKER in *Women in Comedy*, Martin, 1986

It is impossible to improve on reality. The good radio story should never escape reality and the problems of real people.

—GERTRUDE BERG in *Who's Who in Comedy* by Ronald L. Smith, 1992

The television is shadows, Mrs. Enlightened! Mrs. Cultured! A world comes into your house—and it is shadows. People you would never meet in a million lifetimes. Wonders.

—TILLIE OLSEN, *Tell Me a Riddle*, 1960

War toys and [children's television] cartoons dehumanize the enemy, really glamorizing war. The opponent has a legitimate point-of-view, too, and these cartoons don't resolve issues of conflict. There are no treaties, and no solutions in cartoons. There is no consideration given to the opponent.

—SUSAN PARTNOW in *North Seattle Press*, 30 December 1987–12 January 1988

Television was earthbound, but the movies were up in the stars.

—GILDA RADNER, *It's Always Something*, 1989

Theater is a democratic art form—it speaks to the myriad complexities of mood, intellect, station, age, and social status that make up an audience. If it succeeds in moving that amorphous body, whether to laughter, tears, reflection, or anger, it is good theater. If it happens to speak particularly to the members of "the ruling class"—upper class, white, powerful—it may garner the reputation of great theater.

—ELAINE BERNSTEIN PARTNOW, *The Female Dramatist*, 1998

Success in theater is most often measured by box office receipts.

—ELAINE BERNSTEIN PARTNOW, *The Female Dramatist*, 1998

[My parents believed] the theater and all its works represented the lowest damnation and mortal sin.

—NORA BAYES in *Women in Comedy*, Martin, 1986

[My characters] have all been invented only in order to rush madly around, armed to the teeth with language and also with the capacity to be quick-change artists, con men and false prophets, wolves in sheep's clothing and the reverse, so that they might do nothing else than establish an atmosphere of freedom.... They make up new worlds of farce whose highly serious intention, as in all true examples of the genre, is to liberate us from the way things are said to be.

—ROSALYN DREXLER, *The Line of Least Existence*, 1967

I've done everything in the theater except marry the property man.

—FANNY BRICE in *Funny Women*, Unterbrink, 1987

Last year my husband decided a mere television was no longer enough for us. We needed surround sound. It was imperative we go into immediate debt over two side-speakers, a center speaker, and a subwoofer. A man who doesn't listen to anything I say wanted to hear strangers talk to him from four different angles.

—RITA RUDNER, http://www.ritafunny.com, 2003

I have never thought of participating in sports just for the sake of doing it for exercise or as a means to lose weight. And I've never taken up a sport just because it was a social fad. I really enjoy playing. It is a vital part of my life.

—DINAH SHORE in *Los Angeles Times*, 16 April 1974

We gals were babes in the wood then and clung to that old cliché about sports for sports sake.

—BOBBIE ROSENFELD, "Lamp Shades and Ribbon," 1950

Athletic maids to arms!... We are taking up the sword, and high time it is, in defense of our so-called athletic bodies to give the lie to those pen flourishers who depict us not as paragons of feminine physique, beauty and health, but rather as Amazons and ugly ducklings all because we have become sports-minded....

—BOBBIE ROSENFELD, "Crashing the Sacred Sanctum,"
Jewish Women's Archive (http://www.jwa.org)

I'd like to cause a little riot in skating.

—SASHA COHEN, Remark to Reporter at Olympics,
http://www.geocities.com/scchinadoll/Sashas_quotes.html

—

In basketball you can miss a throw and still win. In gymnastics, if a gymnast falls off the beam, she's out of the competition.

—KERRI STRUG, quoted by Eran Lahav in *Ma'ariv Sport*, 13 July, 1997

—

Volleyball is a Jewish sport. It's fun, and nobody can get hurt.

—GAIL PARENT, *Sheila Levine Is Dead and Living in New York*, 1972

—

I...doubt that film can ever argue effectively against its own material: that a genuine antiwar film, say, can be made on the basis of even the ugliest battle scenes.... The medium is somehow unsuited to moral lessons, cautionary tales or polemics of any kind. If you want to make a pacifist film, you must make an exemplary film about peaceful men.

—RENATA ADLER, *A Year in the Dark*, 1970

—

It struck me that the movies had spent more than half a century saying, "They lived happily ever after" and the following quarter-century warning that they'll be lucky to make it through the weekend. Possibly now we are now entering a third era in which the movies will be sounding a note of cautious optimism: You know it just might work.

—NORA EPHRON in *Los Angeles Times*, 27 July 1989

—

Movies have always been a form of popular culture that altered the way women looked at the world and reflected how men intended to keep it.

—MARJORIE ROSEN, *Popcorn Venus*, 1973

—

Studios, purporting to ease the anguish of Depression reality, transformed movies into the politics of fantasy, the great black-and-white opiate of the masses.

—MARJORIE ROSEN, *Popcorn Venus*, 1973

It is ironic that sixties' and seventies' women have seized on a more productive lifestyle than ever before, but the [film] industry has turned its back on reflecting it in any constructive or analytical way.

—MARJORIE ROSEN, *Popcorn Venus*, 1973

If proof were needed of the power of woman's film image on women in life, the number of platinum heads tells the story.

—MARJORIE ROSEN, *Popcorn Venus*, 1973

BENSON: Boy meets girl. Boy loses girl. Boy gets girl.

LAW: The great American fairy-tale. Sends the audience back to the relief rolls in a happy frame of mind.

BENSON: And why not?

LAW: The greatest escape formula ever worked out in the history of civilization…

C. F.: Of course, if you put it that way…but, boys, it's hackneyed.

LAW: You mean classic.

C. F.: *Hamlet* is a classic—but it isn't hackneyed!

LAW: *Hamlet* isn't hackneyed? Why, I'd be ashamed to use that poison gag. He lifted that right out of the Italians.

—BELLA SPEWACK, *Boys Meets Girl*, 1935

But the cinema is a shallow art. It has no—no—no fourth dimension.

—LILLIAN HELLMAN, *The Children's Hour*, 1934

Women's films [in the fifties] became "how-to's" on catching and keeping a man. Veneer. Appearance. Sex Appeal. Hollywood descended into mammary madness.

—MARJORIE ROSEN, *Popcorn Venus*, 1973

Does art reflect life? In movies, yes. Because more than any other art form, films have been a mirror held up to society's porous face.

—MARJORIE ROSEN, *Popcorn Venus*, 1973

If a [movie] scene isn't well written they'll drop your neckline to fill the void.

—MADELINE KAHN in *Newsweek*, 1974

Hit films are the great Hollywood deodorants. Nobody notices the stink of an evaporating few million if there are hits happening at the same time.

—RITA RUDNER, *Tickled Pink*, 2001

Though films become more daring sexually, they are probably less sexy than they ever were. There haven't been any convincing love scenes or romances in the movies in a while. (Nobody even seems to neck in theaters any more.)...when the mechanics and sadism quotients go up, the movie love interest goes dead, and the film just lies there, giving a certain amount of offense.

—RENATA ADLER, *A Year in the Dark*, 1969

Everyone dances, and sings and draws and acts, or knows to a degree what these involve. It is precisely because so few people make films that they belong more or less equally to everyone.

—RENATA ADLER, *A Year in the Dark*, 1969

Which is strongest—the reality out of which the illusion is created, the celluloid illusion itself, or the need for illusion? Do we hold the mirror up and dive in? And if we do, what are the consequences? And what are the responsibilities of the illusion makers?

—MARJORIE ROSEN, *Popcorn Venus*, 1973

Sometimes she thought that the TV wasn't so much an escape as a filter through which he saw and heard everything but was kept from being affected by it too much.

—JUDITH ROSSNER, *Looking for Mr. Goodbar*, 1975

In good films, there is always a directness that entirely frees us from the itch to interpret.

—SUSAN SONTAG, *Against Interpretation*, 1966

SOCIETY & SOCIAL CLASSES

(*also see* Civilization & Progress *and* Community & Citizenship)

I simply contend that the middle-class ideal which demands that people be affectionate, respectable, honest and content, that they avoid excitements and cultivate serenity is the ideal that appeals to me, it is in short the ideal of affectionate family life, of honorable business methods.

—GERTRUDE STEIN, "Adele," *Q.E.D.*, 1903

The ruling class isn't dissatisfied: they are healthy, well-fed, live in beauty, enjoy their own importance: fun-loving cannibals.

—MARGE PIERCY, "The Grand Coolie Damn," *Sisterhood Is Powerful*, 1970

Polite and blind, we lived.

—LILLIAN HELLMAN, *Days to Come*, 1936

There are even born-again bikers. They're the ones with the chains and tattoos that say "Born Again to Lose."

—EMILY LEVINE, Stand-up routine

We've become such highly transient consumers of people, emotions, things that we are psychically hyperventilating. Like the cookie monster, we eat more, buy more, love and lose more, and have more heart attacks.

—ELAINE BERNSTEIN PARTNOW, *Breaking the Age Barrier*, 1981

I've lived in a preindustrial (rural Argentina) as well as an industrial world. You experience a different sense of time in a community that works the land. Human relationships aren't professionalized or contractualized; family and friends take primacy. Life has much more continuity than discontinuity. There's a great deal of poetry in everyday life.

—SHOSHANA ZUBOFF in *Omni*, April 1991

A lot of people, when they hear the word commune, connect it with, like, everyone's on acid and running around naked. This was like this weird suburb, if suburbs were really cool.... We didn't have electricity; which was weird, but it was great to grow up that way. We didn't have TV, so you'd have to do stuff.

—WINONA RYDER, Quoted by David Handelman, *Rolling Stone*, May, 1989

Anthropologists continue to turn up examples which prove that competitive, aggressive, warlike cultures are those in which sexual stereotypes are most polarized, while those social structures allowing for an overlap of roles and functions between men and women (in tasks, child rearing, decision-making, etc.) tend to be collectivist, cooperative and peaceful.

—ROBIN MORGAN, *Sisterhood Is Powerful*, 1970

There is thus no question that those who lead and finance the contemporary "culture wars" in the West are dangerous, not only in the short run but in the long run. Their goal is nothing less than a return to the "good old days," when all women and most men still knew their place in a system based on the ranking of man over woman, man over man, nation over nation, and man over nature—one in which, if they succeed, there will be neither freedom nor equality, as they will have absolute "divinely ordained" control.

—RIANE EISLER, *Sacred Pleasure*, 1995

The ordinary response to atrocities is to banish them from consciousness. Certain violations of the social compact are too terrible to utter aloud: this is the meaning of the word unspeakable.

—JUDITH LEWIS HERMAN, *Trauma and Recovery*, 1992

Commonality carries with it all the meaning of the word *common*. It means belonging to a society, having a public role, being part of that which is universal. It means having a feeling of familiarity, of being known, of communion. It means taking part in the everyday. It also carries with it a feeling of smallness,...of insignificance, a sense that one's own troubles are "as a drop of rain in the sea."

—JUDITH LEWIS HERMAN, *Trauma and Recovery*, 1992

High society is, of course, mainly habit.

—YAËL DAYAN, *New Face in the Mirror*, 1959

High society here [in New York City] turns me off and I feel a bit of rage against all these rich guys here, since I have seen thousands of people in the most terrible misery without anything to eat and with no place to sleep, that is what has most impressed me here, it is terrifying to see the rich having parties day and night while thousands and thousands of people are dying of hunger.

—FRIDA KAHLO in *Frida*, Herrera, 1983

When a society becomes so benevolent that there can be no legitimate confusion between personal insufficiencies and social grievances, the armed rebel has simply lost his cause to the good citizen, and his arms to the sick man of violence, in exile or in crime.

—RENATA ADLER, *Toward a Radical Middle*, 1971

The hippies were taught by their parents, their neighbors, their tabloids, and their college professors that faith, instinct and emotion are superior to reason—and they obeyed. They were taught that material concerns are evil, that the State or the Lord will provide, that the Lilies of the Field do not toil—and they obeyed. They were taught that love, indiscriminate love, for one's fellow-men is the highest virtue—and they obeyed. They were taught that the merging of one's self with a herd, a tribe or a community is the noblest way for men to live—and they obeyed. There isn't a single basic principle of the Establishment which they do not share—there isn't a belief which they have not accepted.

—AYN RAND, *The New Left*, 1968

Jews and homosexuals are the outstanding creative minorities in contemporary urban culture. Creative, that is, in the truest sense: they are creators of sensibilities. The two pioneering forces of modern sensibility are Jewish moral seriousness and homosexual aestheticism and irony.

—SUSAN SONTAG, *Against Interpretation*, 1966

It is doubtful if in all its hothouse garden of women the Hotel Bon Ton boasted a broken finger-nail or that little brash place along the forefinger that tattles so of potato peeling or asparagus scraping.

—FANNIE HURST, *Cosmopolitan*, 1921

In an elitist world, it's always "women and children last."

—MARGE PIERCY, "The Grand Coolie Damn," *Sisterhood Is Powerful*, 1970

Elitism, the polar opposite of "open access," has respectable and ancient antecedents.

—GERDA LERNER, *Why History Matters*, 1997

I am of the philosophy that it's always wise to be nice to working-class people because they're the ones who can make you or break you—your mechanic, electrician, gardener, plumber.

—SANDRA BERNHARD, *May I Kiss You on the Lips, Miss Sandra?*, 1998

STORIES & MYTHS

(*also see* Books, Writers & Poetry)

The universe is made of stories, not of atoms.

—MURIEL RUKEYSER, "The Speed of Darkness," *The Speed of Darkness*, 1968

That the human psyche seems to have a built-in need for a system of stories and symbols that "reveal" to us the order of the universe and tell us what our place within it is is a hunger for meaning and purpose seemingly beyond the power of any rationalistic or logical system to provide.

—RIANE EISLER, *The Chalice and the Blade*, 1987

But to change our realities, we also have to change our myths. As history amply demonstrates, myths and realities go hand in hand.

—RIANE EISLER, *Sacred Pleasure*, 1995

Family stories are not morality plays, although they are about morality.... Perhaps we are all here to make good stories.

—ANNE ROIPHE, *The Pursuit of Happiness*, 1991

The slightest story ought to contain the facts of money and blood in order to be interesting to adults.

—GRACE PALEY, *Just As I Thought*, 1998

I had wanted to wrap this book up in a neat little package. I wanted a perfect ending. Now I've learned the hard way that some poems don't rhyme, and some stories don't have a clear beginning, middle, and end.

—GILDA RADNER, *It's Always Something*, 1989

Myth...has made a whirling comeback out of Space, an Icarus in the avatar of Batman and his kind, who never fall into the ocean of failure to deal with the gravity forces of life. These new myths, however, do not seek so much to enlighten and provide some sort of answers as to distract, to provide a fantasy escape route for people who no longer want to face even the hazard of answers to the terrors of their existence.

—NADINE GORDIMER in *Nobel Lectures*, 1991

No more masks! No more mythologies!
—MURIEL RUKEYSER, "The Poem as Mask," *The Speed of Darkness*, 1968

The streets attest to the power of the narrative drive: its infinite capacity for adaptation in the most inhospitable of times.
—VIVIAN GORNICK, *Approaching Eye Level*, 1996

SUCCESS, DREAMS & ACHIEVEMENT

(*also see* Individuals, Self-Realization & Human Nature)

Invisible wings are given to us too, by which, if we would dare to acknowledge and use them, we might transcend the dualities of time and matter—might be upheld to walk on water. Instead, we humans persistently say no, and persistently experience our wings only as a dragging weight on our backs.
—DENISE LEVERTOV, "Work That Enfaiths," *New and Selected Essays*, 1992

You may be disappointed if you fail, but you are doomed if you don't try.
—BEVERLY SILLS, Remark

Remarking on the secret of her success: Have dreams, have visions, and let no obstacle stop you.
—RUTH GRUBER, Remark, 2001

It stands to reason that if we direct all our efforts towards reaching a goal, we stand in grave danger of losing everything on which we have based our daily activities. For when a goal is superimposed on an activity instead of evolving out of it, we often feel cheated when we reach it.
—VIOLA SPOLIN, *Improvisation for the Theater*, 1963

I've been accused of selling out so often that it's made me realize what extraordinary resources people saw in me in the first place. It's why I can afford to sell out my ideas; I know something new'll spring up to replace the ones I'm unloading.

—JUDITH ROSSNER, *Nine Months in the Life of an Old Maid*, 1969

He could not, could not turn away from this desire: to have the troubling of responsibility, the fretting with money, over and done with; to be free, to be *care*free where success was not measured by accumulation.

—TILLIE OLSEN, "Tell Me a Riddle," *Tell Me a Riddle*, 1960

When I lie awake at night, surrounded by women and girls snoring softly, dreaming loudly, crying into their pillows, tossing and turning, who say during the day, "We don't want to think, to feel anything, otherwise we'll go crazy," then I am often incredibly moved. I lie awake and let the far too many events of a day that's been far too long pass before my eyes, and I think, "Let me be the thinking heart of this barracks."

—ETTY HILLESUM, *An Interrupted Life*, 1983

Success to me is having ten honeydew melons and eating only the top half of each one.

—BARBRA STREISAND in *Life*, 20 September 1963

Success isn't everything but it makes a man stand straight.

—LILLIAN HELLMAN, *Toys in the Attic*, 1959

One of my goals is to be the most non-competitive woman in the world.

—LOTUS WEINSTOCK, *Lotus Position*, 1982

My goal is to be able to say: "Fame and fortune just didn't bring me happiness."

—LOTUS WEINSTOCK, Stand-up routine

It may be lonely at the top, but it's so fucking crowded at the bottom.

—LOTUS WEINSTOCK, Stand-up routine

Opportunities are usually disguised as hard work, so most people don't recognize them.

—ANN LANDERS, Advice Column

I was never afraid of failure after that [a near brush with death] because, I think, coming that close to death, you get kissed. With the years, the actual experience of course fades, but the flavor of it doesn't.

—DEBRA WINGER in *Parade* magazine, 6 March 1994

Throughout the centuries there were men who took first steps down new roads armed with nothing but their own vision. Their goals differed, but they all had this in common: that the step was first, the road new, the vision unborrowed, and the response they received—hatred. The great creators—the thinkers, the artists, the scientists, the inventors—stood alone against the men of their time.

—AYN RAND, *The Fountainhead*, 1943

But it is not hind-sight that makes the world go forward. Edison saw an electric bulb lighting up a room, *before* ever it had occurred…. He saw what was not there, because he believed it could be there, and he brought it about through his vision.

—TEHILLA LICHTENSTEIN, "Believing is *Seeing*," *Four Centuries*, 1992

There was about her—or them—nothing of genius, or greatness, of the divine fire. But the dramatic critics of the younger school who were too late to have seen past genius in its hey-day and for whom the theatrical genius of their day was yet to come, viewed her performance and waxed hysterical, mistaking talent and intelligence and hard work and ambition for something more rare.

—EDNA FERBER, *Show Boat*, 1926

I am always running into people's unconscious.

—MARILYN MONROE in *Marilyn* by Norman Mailer, 1973

Nothing succeeds like address.

—FRAN LEBOWITZ, *Metropolitan Life*, 1978

Fame always brings loneliness. Success is as ice cold and lonely as the North Pole.

—VICKI BAUM, *Grand Hotel* (novel), 1931

A woman who is loved always has success.

—VICKI BAUM, *Grand Hotel* (novel), 1931

It is a mark of many famous people that they cannot part with their brightest hour.

—LILLIAN HELLMAN, *Pentimento*, 1973

[I began to unload] the pyramid of honors, civic and literary, which had been heaped on me by the usual headlong process of rewarding a popular success. One day, I sat down and wrote a wholesale lot of letters of resignation. When I finished, I didn't belong to a single author's club or patriotic society. I was myself again, whatever that was.

—MARY ANTIN in *20th Century Authors*, Kunitz, 1942

I just want to become famous so I can have a nervous breakdown.

—SANDRA BERNHARD in *Funny Women*, Unterbrink, 1987

The point, as Marx saw it, is that dreams never come true.

—HANNAH ARENDT, *Crises of the Republic*, 1972

When she was this great soaring creature it seemed as if it was the earth ones who were damned and wrong, not she, who was so complete in beauty and anger. It seemed to her that they slept and were blind.

—JOANNE GREENBERG, *I Never Promised You a Rose Garden*, 1964

—

Only she who attempts the absurd can achieve the impossible.

—ROBIN MORGAN, *Sisterhood Is Global*, 1984

—

You have to be…aggressive here if you wanna get somethin'.

—KERRI STRUG on the *Rosie O'Donnell Show*, 9 August 1996

—

And I'm working all day and I'm working all night
To be good-looking, healthy, and wise.
And adored.
And contented.
And brave.
And well-read.
And a marvelous hostess,
Fantastic in bed…

—JUDITH VIORST, "Self-Improvement Program," *How Did I Get to Be Forty and Other Atrocities*, 1973

—

My whole career has been one rejection after another.… And then going back and back and pushing against everything and everybody. Getting ahead by small, ugly steps.

—JOAN RIVERS in *Women in Comedy*, Martin, 1986

—

I cannot understand any woman's wanting to be the first woman to do anything. It is a devastating burden and I could not take it, could not be a pioneer, a Symbol of Something Greater.

—NORA EPHRON, *Crazy Salad*, 1975

sleep leads to dreaming
waking to imagination and to
imagine what we
could be, o,
what we could be.

—SUSAN GRIFFIN, "To Gather Ourselves," *Dear Sky*, 1973

"Creation comes before distribution—or there will be nothing to distribute."

—AYN RAND, *The Fountainhead*, 1943

I can honestly say that I was never affected by the question of the success of an undertaking. If I felt it was the right thing to do, I was for it regardless of the possible outcome.

—GOLDA MEIR in *Golda Meir*, Syrkin, 1964

When shall we dare to fly?

—DENISE LEVERTOV, "Standoff," *Breathing the Water*, 1987

Whether we like it or not, women, even now, must exert greater total effort than men for the same degree of success.

—ROSALYN YALOW in *The Lady Laureates* by Olga S. Opfell, 1978

It is a peaceful thing to be one succeeding.

—GERTRUDE STEIN, *Everybody's Autobiography*, 1937

Success can make you go one of two ways. It can make you a prima donna, or it can smooth the edges, take away the insecurities, let the nice things come out.

—BARBARA WALTERS in *Newsweek*, 6 May 1974

Success in show business depends on your ability to make and keep friends.

—SOPHIE TUCKER, *Some of These Days*, with Dorothy Giles, 1945

Everyone has talent. What is rare is the courage to follow the talent to the dark place where it leads.
—ERICA JONG, "The Artist as Housewife: The Housewife as Artist," *The First Ms. Reader*, 1972

The most precious thing in this world is talent; to be gifted.
—FANNY BRICE in *Funny Women*, Unterbrink, 1987

The engineering is secondary to the vision.
—CYNTHIA OZICK, "The Hole/Birth Catalog," *The First Ms. Reader*, 1972

I take me eagles' wings, with vision flying
And brow upraised to look upon the sun.
—RAHEL MORPURGO, Untitled Poem, Nina Davis Salaman, tr., *Four Centuries*, 1992

There is something in me—I just can't stand to admit defeat.
—BEVERLY SILLS, Interview on CBS-TV, 1975

Ambition if it feeds at all, does so on the ambition of others.
—SUSAN SONTAG, *The Benefactor*, 1963

Sisyphus, I. I cling to my rock, you don't have to chain me. Stand back! I roll it up—up, up. And...down we go. I knew that would happen. See, I'm on my feet again. See, I'm starting to roll it up again. Don't try to talk me out of it. Nothing, nothing could tear me away from this rock.
—SUSAN SONTAG, *I, Etcetera*, 1979

TIME—PAST, FUTURE & OTHER DIMENSIONS

It's later than it's ever been.

—LOTUS WEINSTOCK, Stand-up routine

~

I've been on a calendar, but never on time.

—MARILYN MONROE in *Look*, 16 January 1962

~

Sex, drugs, rapping, a passion for total independence to "do their thing" forced renunciation of traditional values—the popular artifice of clothing, purchasing power, education, employment. Looking "natural," they created costumes out of odds and ends and nodded off in the name of peace and love. They were flower children.

—MARJORIE ROSEN, *Popcorn Venus*, 1973

~

Still, we chiefly remember the Fifties, not for the horror of civil defense drills or witch hunts, but for kitschy fads like hoola hoops and poodle cuts and crinolines. For Lucy and Miltie and Howdy and Kukla. One of the few constants during the decade was the direction women were heading: backward.

—MARJORIE ROSEN, *Popcorn Venus*, 1973

~

Because she fears the past she distrusts the future—it, too, will turn into the past. As a result she has nothing.

—CYNTHIA OZICK, *The Shawl*, 1989

~

The future reconnoiters in dirty boots
along the cranberry-dark horizon.

—ADRIENNE RICH, "Autumn Sequence," *Necessities of Life*, 1966

The working morning. Now I love the morning more than the evening, the spring more than the fall. The promise more than the fulfillment.

—RAISA DAVYDOVNA ORLOVA, *Memoirs*, 1983

—

If you ask a member of this generation two simple questions: "How do you want the world to be in fifty years?" and "What do you want your life to be like five years from now?" the answers are quite often preceded by "Provided there is still a world" and "Provided I am still alive."

—HANNAH ARENDT, *Crises of the Republic*, 1972

—

at night the vestiges
of other ages influence us.

—IRENA KLEPFISZ, "dinosaurs and larger issues," *periods of stress*, 1975

—

The idea of the future is our greatest entertainment, amusement, and time-killer. Take it away and there is only the past—and a windshield spattered with dead bugs.

—ERICA JONG, *Fear of Flying*, 1973

—

But how shall time be drawn
from the golden threads of the sun?
Wound
from the cocoon of the silken butterfly
night?

—NELLY SACHS, "Hunter," *The Seeker and Other Poems*, 1970

—

Humans have not the power to dive into futurity, therefore cannot say what will be, but trusting in God Almighty and ever keeping reason in view, I have as good a prospect for future happiness as I at present enjoy.

—JUDITH MONTEFIORE in *Essays in Jewish History*, Cecil Roth, ed., 1934

All their lives they believed in the Future; they struggled and slaved and sacrificed for the Future. Not that they had much choice; it was understood they had been born too soon. Things were going to get better. In the Future. The everlasting Future. And now all of a sudden they see the truth. The Future? What Future?

—BETTE HOWLAND, "The Life You Gave Me," *Things to Come and Go*, 1983

"You must live in the present, be conscious of the past, and not be more than thirty-five minutes late for the future."

—RITA RUDNER, *Tickled Pink*, 2001

With the loss of tradition we have lost the thread which safely guided us through the vast realms of the past, but this thread was also the chain fettering each successive generation to a predetermined aspect of the past. It could be that only now will the past open up to us with unexpected freshness and tell us things that no one as yet has ears to hear.

—HANNAH ARENDT in *Nomos I: Authority*, Carl J. Frederich, ed., 1958

The past was only my cradle, and now it cannot hold me, because I am grown too big.

—MARY ANTIN, *The Promised Land*, 1912

I am drunk on yesterday.
Its murmuring is preserved with every pounding of my blood
—ANDA AMIR, "Lot's Wife," *Land of Israel*, 1987

I will stand like a stone in my place,
forever will I look on the footsteps of my past
—ANDA AMIR, "Lot's Wife," *Land of Israel*, 1987

Every journey into the past is complicated by delusions, false memories, false namings of real events.

—ADRIENNE RICH, *Of Woman Born*, 1976

Nothing from the past could be more remote than this present.
—NADINE GORDIMER, *The House Gun*, 1997

Ù

From the critics of the past I have learned the futility of concerning oneself with the present.
—CAROLYN G. HEILBRUN, *Toward a Recognition of Androgyny*, 1973

Ù

Nothing cures like time and love…
—LAURA NYRO, "Time and Love," 1970

Ù

"Time is only a force; it is neither good nor evil, only necessary."
—SUSAN FROMBERG SCHAEFFER, *Falling*, 1973

Ù

She's gathered up all the time in the world—
nothing else—and waits for scanty trophies,
complete in herself as a heron
—DENISE LEVERTOV, "The Great Black Heron," *Sands of the Well*, 1996

Ù

Time turns out to be far more precious than any other thing. I have a heightened awareness that I might not have all the time in the world. I don't want to waste it.
—RUTH WEISBERG in *Exposures*, Brown, 1989

Ù

Time granted does not necessarily coincide with time that can be most fully used.
—TILLIE OLSEN, *Silences*, 1965

Ù

An unhurried sense of time is in itself a form of wealth.
—BONNIE FRIEDMAN in *New York Times*, 14 March 1999

There was nothing separate about her days.
Like drops upon a window-pane, they ran together and trickled away.
—DOROTHY PARKER, "Big Blonde," *Laments for the Living*, 1929

I must govern the clock, not be governed by it.
—GOLDA MEIR, quoted by Oriana Fallaci in *L'Eurepeo*, 1973

We must breathe time as fishes breathe water.
—DENISE LEVERTOV, "Variation and Reflection on a Theme by Rilke,"
Breathing the Water, 1989

Time is change; we measure its passage by how much things alter.
—NADINE GORDIMER, *The Late Bourgeois World*, 1966

From supper to bedtime is twice as long as from breakfast to supper.
—EDNA FERBER, *Roast Beef, Medium*, 1911

Timing is everything. Time is everything else.
—WENDY LIEBMAN, http://www.wendyliebman.com, 2002

In 1905, one of the soundest principles of humankind—the measurement of time—was tossed into the air like a flapjack, where it disappeared. Albert Einstein...was telling us we could no longer measure time and space in terms of absolutes, but only in terms of an object's frame of reference. The space of one day represents a much greater chunk of time to a boy of 13 than it does to an adult of 36, and so, for the boy, his day *is* longer.
—ELAINE BERNSTEIN PARTNOW, *Breaking the Age Barrier*, 1981

When people say: she's got everything, I've only one answer: I haven't had tomorrow.
—ELIZABETH TAYLOR, *Elizabeth Taylor*, 1965

Today's shocks are tomorrow's conventions.
—CAROLYN G. HEILBRUN, *Toward a Recognition of Androgyny*, 1973

A distraction is to avoid the consciousness of the passage of time.
—GERTRUDE STEIN, *Everybody's Autobiography*, 1937

Finality broods upon the things that pass.
—ADRIENNE RICH, "Walk by the Charles," *Poems: Selected and New*, 1974

Since she had thought about nothing, she did not realize how the time had slipped by.
—CLARICE LISPECTOR, *Family Ties*, 1972

It's a pleasure to share one's memories. Everything remembered is dear, endearing, touching, precious. At least the past is safe—though we didn't know it at the time. We know it now. Because it's in the past; because we have survived.
—SUSAN SONTAG, *I, Etcetera*, 1979

To some degree, everyone is a prisoner of the past.
—JUDITH LEWIS HERMAN, *Trauma and Recovery*, 1992

So far as I knew to date, forever was slip-stitch, split-stitch, cross-stitch, back-stitch; and also buttonhole and running stitches…all along the dipping and rising hemline, as if for always and always.
—MURIEL SPARK, "The Dragon," *The Stories of Muriel Spark*, 1985

TRUTH, LIES & SUPERSTITIONS

(*also see* Guilt, Innocence & Conscience *and* Morality & Ethics)

I have, thanks to my travels, added to my stock all the superstitions of other countries. I know them all now, and in any critical moment of my life, they all rise up in armed legions for or against me.
—SARAH BERNHARDT, *The Memoirs of Sarah Bernhardt,* 1977

My bravado masks the strain of superstition which prevents me from ever breaking a chain letter *(the last person who broke this chain suffered a cerebral hemorrhage)*. Why take a chance?
—GLORIA DEVIDAS KIRCHHEIMER, *Goodbye, Evil Eye,* 2000

Rules, superstitions, *bubbe meises*—maybe it's all the same: we do it because we do it, because we've been doing it this way for five thousand years, because we think that's what makes us who we are. It's hard to give up, this notion of who we are.
—CAROL K. HOWELL, *The Make-up Lesson*

For the trouble with lying and deceiving is that their efficiency depends entirely upon a clear notion of the truth that the liar and deceiver wishes to hide. In this sense, truth, even if it does not prevail in public, possesses an eradicable primacy over all falsehoods.
—HANNAH ARENDT, *Crises of the Republic,* 1972

No one ever asked me to lie, and I was never promised a job for my silence.
—MONICA LEWINSKY in the Starr Report, 9 September 1998

The lying tongue's deceit with silence blight,
Protect me from its venom, you, my Rock,
And show the spiteful sland'rer by this sign
That you will shield me with your endless might.
  —SARAH COPIA SULLAM, "My Inmost Hope," A *Treasury of Jewish Letters*, 1953

Images
split the truth
in fractions.
  —DENISE LEVERTOV, "A Sequence," *The Jacob's Ladder*, 1961

It is safe to say that no other superstition is so detrimental to growth, so enervating and paralyzing to the minds and hearts of the people, as the superstition of Morality.
  —EMMA GOLDMAN, *Red Emma Speaks*, 1972

What would happen if one woman told the truth about her life?
The world would split open.
  —MURIEL RUKEYSER, "Käthe Kollwitz," *The Speed of Darkness*, 1968

Halfway "between truth and endless error," the mold of the species is permanent.
  —BARBARA TUCHMAN, *The First Salute*, 1988

There are lies that glow so brightly we consent to give a finger and then an arm to let them burn.
  —MARGE PIERCY, *Sisterhood Is Powerful*, 1970

But maybe half a lie is worse than a real lie.
  —LILLIAN HELLMAN, *Another Part of the Forest*, 1946

Do you want to live in a world where a man lies about calories?
                    —GAIL PARENT, *Sheila Levine Is Dead and Living in New York*, 1972

The truth is always something that is told, not something that is known. If there were no speaking or writing, there would be no truth about anything. There would only be what is.
                                        —SUSAN SONTAG, *The Benefactor*, 1963

The truth is balance, but the opposite of truth, which is unbalance, may not be a lie.
                                —SUSAN SONTAG, *Against Interpretation*, 1966

UNITED STATES OF AMERICA
(*also see* Cultures, Nationality & Immigrants; Freedom & Democracy; *and* Nations & the World)

"The difference in America is that the women have always gone along. When you read the history of France you're peeking through a bedroom key-hole. The history of England is a joust. The womenfolks were always Elaineish and anemic, it seems.... But here in this land, Sabra, my girl, the women, they've been the real hewers of wood and drawers of water. You'll want to remember that."
                                        —EDNA FERBER, *Cimarron*, 1929

The continent in its voices is full of song; it is not to be heard easily, it must be listened for; among its shapes and weathers, the country is singing, among the lives of its people, its industries, its wild flamboyant ventures, its waste, its buried search. The passion is sung, beneath the flatness and the wild sexual fevers, contorted gothic of the Middle West; the passion is sung, under the regret and violence and fiery flowers of the south; the passion is sung, under the size and range and golden bareness of the Western Coast, and the split acute seasons of the cities standing east.

—MURIEL RUKEYSER, *The Life of Poetry*, 1949

—

The heritage of the American Revolution is forgotten, and the American government, for better and for worse, has entered into the heritage of Europe as though it were its patrimony—unaware, alas, of the fact that Europe's declining power was preceded and accompanied by political bankruptcy, the bankruptcy of the nation-state and its concept of sovereignty.

—HANNAH ARENDT, *Crises of the Republic*, 1972

—

In April 1917 the illusion of isolation was destroyed, America came to the end of innocence, and of the exuberant freedom of bachelor independence. That the responsibilities of world power have not made us happier is no surprise. To help ourselves manage them, we have replaced the illusion of isolation with a new illusion of omnipotence.

—BARBARA TUCHMAN in *New York Times Magazine*, 5 May 1967

—

America—rather, the United States—seems to me to be the Jew among the nations. It is resourceful, adaptable, maligned, envied, feared, imposed upon. It is warm-hearted, overfriendly; quick-witted, lavish, colorful; given to extravagant speech and gestures; its people are travelers and wanderers by nature, moving, shifting, restless; swarming in Fords, in ocean liners; craving entertainment; volatile. The *schnuckle* among the nations of the world.

—EDNA FERBER, *A Peculiar Treasure*, 1939

—

America is my country and Paris is my hometown. And it is as it has come to be. After all anybody is as their air and land is. Anybody is as the sky is low or high, the air heavy or clear and anybody is as there is wind or no wind there. It is that which makes them and the arts they make and the work they do and the way they eat and the way they drink and the way they learn and everything. And so I am an American and I have lived half my life in Paris, not the half that made me but the half in which I made what I made.

—GERTRUDE STEIN, "An American and France," 1936

The unreal is natural, so natural that it makes of unreality the most natural of anything natural. That is what America does, and that is what America is.

—GERTRUDE STEIN, "I Came and Here I Am," *Writers at Work* (1st), 1974

"I am not belittling the brave pioneer men, but the sunbonnet as well as the sombrero has helped to settle this glorious land of ours."

—EDNA FERBER, *Cimarron*, 1929

The open frontier, the hardships of homesteading from scratch, the wealth of natural resources, the whole vast challenge of a continent waiting to be exploited, combined to produce a prevailing materialism and an American drive bent as much, if not more, on money, property, and power than was true of the Old World from which we had fled.

—BARBARA TUCHMAN in *Newsweek*, 12 July 1976

More great Americans were failures than they were successes. They mostly spent their lives in not having a buyer for what they had for sale.

—GERTRUDE STEIN, *Everybody's Autobiography*, 1937

Americans are very friendly and very suspicious, that is what Americans are and that is what always upsets the foreigner, who deals with them, they are so friendly how can they be so suspicious they are so suspicious how can they be so friendly but they just are.

—GERTRUDE STEIN, "The Capital and Capitals of the United States of America," *Writers at Work* (1st), 1974

They want to be like Americans—well, they are like Americans. But I don't want to be like anybody else. I am truly American—free.

—JESSIE SAMPTER, *In the Beginning* (unpub. novel)

In spite of the fact that I understand the advantages that the United States have for any work or activity, I don't like the gringos with all their qualities

and their defects which are very great, their manner of being, their disgusting
Puritanism, their Protestant sermons, their endless pretension, the way that
for everything one must be "very decent" and "very proper" seems to me rather
stupid.

—FRIDA KAHLO in *Frida*, Herrera, 1983

"The gaudiest star-spangled cosmic joke that ever was played on a double-deal-
ing government burst into fireworks today when, with a roar that could be
heard for miles around, thousands of barrels of oil shot into the air on the miserable desert land known as the Osage Indian reservation and occupied by
those duped and wretched—!"

—EDNA FERBER, *Cimarron*, 1929

Although I am very interested in all the industrial and mechanical development of the United States, I find that Americans completely lack sensibility
and good taste.

—FRIDA KAHLO in *Frida*, Herrera, 1983

Americans live in an increasingly violent society that is…inured to violence
(as eighteenth-century France was) and one in which the top is growing ever
richer and further in every way from the vast bulk of the population. I thought
looking at a society in crisis so very strange in some ways and so familiar in others might illuminate our own situation.

—MARGE PIERCY, *City of Darkness, City of Light*, 1996

Catch if you can your country's moment, begin
where any calendar's ripped-off: Appomattox
Wounded Knee, Los Alamos
Selma, the last airlift from Saigon
          —ADRIENNE RICH, *An Atlas of the Difficult World: Poems 1988–1991*, 1991

What better spokesman for the Taliban [than Jerry Falwell and Pat Robertson]? Our fundamentalists agree with theirs. God is on their side. America's sins are to blame.

What better allies for the men who call America the Great Satan?
                    —ELLEN GOODMAN, Syndicated Column, 21 September 2001

This is a very dangerous time when emotion can sweep us up into giving away our precious freedoms and rights for safety—for example, giving too much power to the police and military. This is my greatest fear. Personally I would prefer enduring the risk of terrorists to giving up my freedom and legal protections and living in a repressive police state.
                    —SUSAN PARTNOW, Letter to Editor, 18 September 2001

Where is the acknowledgment that this was not a "cowardly" attack on "civilization" or "liberty" or "humanity" or "the free world" but an attack on the world's self-proclaimed superpower, undertaken as a consequence of specific American alliances and actions?
                    —SUSAN SONTAG, *New Yorker*, September 2001

If you're going to America, bring your own food.
                    —FRAN LEBOWITZ, *Social Studies*, 1981

Our government...learns no lessons, employs no wisdom and corrupts all who succumb to the Potomac fever.
                    —BARBARA TUCHMAN in *Newsweek*, 12 July 1976

The moral immune system of this country has been weakened and attacked, and the AIDS virus is the perfect metaphor for it. The malignant neglect of the last twelve years has led to a breakdown of our country's immune system, environmentally, culturally, politically, spiritually and physically.
                    —BARBRA STREISAND in *Guardian* (London), 6 November 1992

America is not old enough yet to get young again.
                        —GERTRUDE STEIN, *Everybody's Autobiography*, 1937

Together we hunted down the answers to all the seemingly insoluble riddles which a complex and callous society presented.... And yet for the sake of these answers, for the sake of American democracy, justice and brotherhood, for the sake of peace and bread and roses, and children's laughter, we shall continue to sit here [in prison] in dignity and in pride—in the deep abiding knowledge of our innocence before God and man, until the truth becomes a clarion call to all decent humanity.
                —ETHEL ROSENBERG, *Death House Letters of Ethel and Julius Rosenberg*, 1953

In the United States there is more space where nobody is than where anybody is. That is what makes America what it is.
                        —GERTRUDE STEIN, *The Geographical History of America*, 1936

The United States is just now the oldest country in the world, there always is an oldest country and she is it, it is she who is the mother of the twentieth century civilization. She began to feel herself as it just after the Civil War. And so it is a country the right age to have been born in and the wrong age to live in.
                —GERTRUDE STEIN, "Why I Do Not Live In America," *How Writing Is Written*,
                                    Robert Bartlett Haas, ed., 1974

If we get a government that reflects more of what this country is really about, we can turn the century—and the economy—around.
                        —BELLA ABZUG in *Redbook*, April 1974

In Britain the government has to come down in front of Parliament every day to explain its actions, but here the President never answers directly to Congress.
                        —BELLA ABZUG, *Bella!*, 1972

She [a woman politician] will be challenging a system that is still wedded to militarism and that saves billions of dollars a year by underpaying women and using them as a reserve cheap labor supply.

—BELLA ABZUG in *Ms.*, April 1974

"Self-government is a form of self-control, self-limitation. It goes against our whole grain. We're [Americans] supposed to go after what we want, not question whether we really need it."

—JUDITH ROSSNER, *Any Minute I Can Split*, 1969

Ours is a culture based on excess, on overproduction; the result is a steady loss of sharpness in our sensory experience. All the conditions of modern life—its material plenitude, its sheer crowdedness—conjoin to dull our sensory faculties.

—SUSAN SONTAG, *Against Interpretation*, 1966

American "energy"…is the energy of violence, of free-floating resentment and anxiety unleashed by chronic cultural dislocations which must be, for the most part, ferociously sublimated. This energy has mainly been sublimated into crude materialism and acquisitiveness. Into hectic philanthropy. Into benighted moral crusades, the most spectacular of which was Prohibition. Into an awesome talent for uglifying countryside and cities. Into the loquacity and torment of a minority of gadflies: artists, prophets, muckrakers, cranks, and nuts. And into self-punishing neuroses. But the naked violence keeps breaking through, throwing everything into question.

—SUSAN SONTAG, *Styles of Radical Will*, 1969

Bending the mind and shaking loose the body makes someone a less willing functionary of the bureaucratic machine. Rock, grass, better orgasms, freaky clothes, grooving on nature—really grooving on anything—unfits, maladapts a person for the American way of life.

—SUSAN SONTAG in *Recreation* by Mark Estrin, 1971

VIOLENCE & RAPE

(*also see* Law & Order *and* War, Weapons & the Military)

It is little wonder that rape is one of the least reported crimes. Perhaps it is the only crime in which the victim becomes the accused and, in reality, it is she who must prove her good reputation, her mental-soundness, and her impeccable propriety.

—FREDA ADLER, *Sisters in Crime*, 1975

We understand that rape is not about love or even lust, but about humiliating another human being through forced or coerced sex and sexual shame. The intended effect of rape is always the same: to utterly break the spirit of the rape victim, to drive the victim out of her (or his) body and to make her incapable of resistance and quite often out of her mind.

—PHYLLIS CHESLER, *Women and Madness*, 25th Anniversary Ed., 1997

My purpose in this book has been to give rape its history. Now we must deny it a future.

—SUSAN BROWNMILLER, *Against Our Will*, 1975

Man's discovery that his genitalia could serve as a weapon to generate fear must rank as one of the most important discoveries of prehistoric times, along with the use of fire and the first crude stone axe.

—SUSAN BROWNMILLER, *Against Our Will*, 1975

In no state of mind can a man be accused of raping his wife. How can any man steal what already belongs to him?

—SUSAN GRIFFIN in *Ramparts*, September 1971

Rape is a form of mass terrorism, for the victims of rape are chosen indiscriminately, but the propagandists for male supremacy broadcast that it is women who cause rape by being unchaste or in the wrong place at the wrong time—in essence, by behaving as though they were free.
—SUSAN GRIFFIN, "Rape: The All-American Crime," *Women: A Feminist Perspective*,
Jo Freeman, ed., 1975

Rape is no excess, no aberration, no accident, no mistake—it embodies sexuality as the culture defines it. As long as these definitions remain intact—that is, as long as men are defined as sexual aggressors and women are defined as passive receptors lacking integrity—men who are exemplars of the norm will rape women.
—ANDREA DWORKIN, *Our Blood*, 1976

As long as there is rape...there is not going to be any peace or justice or equality or freedom.
—ANDREA DWORKIN, *Letters from a War-Zone*, 1987

White men need a history that does not simply "include" peoples of color and white women, that shows the process by which the arrogance of hierarchy and the celebration of violence have reached a point of destructiveness almost out of control.
—ADRIENNE RICH, *Blood, Bread, and Poetry*, 1986

The more dubious and uncertain an instrument violence has become in international relations, the more it has gained in reputation and appeal in domestic affairs, specifically in the matter of revolution.
—HANNAH ARENDT, *Crises of the Republic*, 1972

Men who want to support women in our struggle for freedom and justice should understand that it is not terrifically important to us that they learn to cry; it is important to us that they stop the crimes of violence against us.
—ANDREA DWORKIN, *Our Blood*, 1976

Institutionalized in sports, the military, acculturated sexuality, the history and mythology of heroism, violence is taught to boys until they become its *advocates*.
—ANDREA DWORKIN, *Pornography: Men Possessing Women*, 1981

Power and violence are opposites; where the one rules absolutely, the other is absent.
—HANNAH ARENDT, *Crises of the Republic*, 1972

[The Japanese] know that it is the quickest, surest way to humiliate a community. I think that they rape almost as a religious duty, a sacrifice to the God of Victory, a symbol of their triumphant power.
—EMILY "MICKEY" HAHN, *Nobody Said* Not *to Go* by Ken Cuthbertson, 1998

The *sicario* [hired killer] did for murder in Medellín what the transistor did for the radio. Killing is easy, cheap and popular....
—TINA ROSENBERG, *Children of Cain: Violence and the Violent in Latin America*, 1991

Children learn about the world through their play. When we choose toys and games that encourage creativity, problem solving and learning, and we resolve to keep violence and racial stereotypes out of our homes, we are taking important steps towards a world without hate mongers.
—SUSAN PARTNOW in *Seattle Times*, 3 December 1988

We now understand more about what trauma is, and what it does. We understand that chronic, hidden family/domestic violence is actually more traumatic than sudden violence at the hands of a stranger, or of an enemy during war.
—PHYLLIS CHESLER, *Women and Madness*, 25th Anniversary Ed., 1997

The amount of brutality dispensed to us through both television news and "entertainment" on our home screens is staggering.
—RIANE EISLER, *Sacred Pleasure*, 1995

That even an apocalypse can be made to seem part of the ordinary horizon of expectation constitutes an unparalleled violence that is being done to our sense of reality, to our humanity.

—SUSAN SONTAG, *AIDS and Its Metaphors*, 1989

I have come to see that constitutional and human rights theories need to be expanded to include in their conceptual frameworks the most basic of human rights: the right to live free of the fear of violence.

—RIANE EISLER, *Sacred Pleasure*, 1995

The principal instances of mass violence in the world today are those committed by governments within their own legally recognized borders.

—SUSAN SONTAG, *New York Times Magazine*, 2 May 1999

We will uproot violence by facing it in ourselves;
by letting heal that which we have repressed;
by rejecting the religious, philosophical
and political beliefs that permit us to subordinate,
exclude,
isolate,
oppress,
and kill others.

—FANCHON SHUR, Dedication, *Tallit:* Prayer Shawl (a dance)

WAR, WEAPONS & THE MILITARY

(*also see* Violence & Rape)

I don't believe that the big men, the politicians and the capitalists alone are guilty of the war. Oh, no, the little man is just as keen, otherwise the people of the world would have risen in revolt long ago! There is an urge and rage in people to destroy, to kill, to murder, and until all mankind, without exception, undergoes a great change, wars will be waged, everything that has been built up, cultivated and grown, will be destroyed and disfigured, after which mankind will have to begin all over again.

—ANNE FRANK, *The Diary of a Young Girl*, 1947

Not all violence is equally reprehensible; not all wars are equally unjust.

—SUSAN SONTAG in *New York Times Magazine*, 2 May 1999

War is a culture, bellicosity is addictive, defeat for a community that imagines itself to be history's eternal victim can be as intoxicating as victory.

—SUSAN SONTAG in *New York Times Magazine*, 2 May 1999

It has been argued that, when killing is viewed as not only permissible but heroic behavior sanctioned by one's government or cause, the fine distinction between taking a human life and other forms of impermissible violence gets lost, and rape becomes an unfortunate but inevitable by-product of the necessary game called war.

—SUSAN BROWNMILLER, *Against Our Will*, 1975

We can remind the world that all the dead on both sides have not settled our differences, so now it is time for the living to renounce violence as a means of solving this conflict.

—LETTY COTTIN POGREBIN, *Deborah, Golda, and Me,* 1991

Rape is a part of war; but it may be more accurate to say that the capacity for dehumanizing another which so corrodes male sexuality is carried over from sex into war.

—ADRIENNE RICH, *On Lies, Secrets, and Silence,* 1979

Reasonable orders are easy enough to obey; it is capricious, bureaucratic or plain idiotic demands that form the habit of discipline.

—BARBARA TUCHMAN, *Stilwell and the American Experience in China,* 1970

In the empty house, alone with the maid, she no longer walked like a soldier, she no longer needed to exercise caution. But she missed the battle of the streets: the melancholy of freedom, with the horizon still so very remote.

—CLARICE LISPECTOR, *Family Ties,* 1972

The victory carried like a corpse
from town to town
begins to crawl in the casket.

—ADRIENNE RICH, "Letters: March 1969: I," *The Will to Change,* 1971

All wars are wars among thieves who are too cowardly to fight and who therefore induce the young manhood of the whole world to do the fighting for them.

—EMMA GOLDMAN in *Mother Earth,* July 1917

I am also fond of saying that a war or fighting is like a dance because it is all going forward and back, and that is what everybody likes; they like that forward

and the back movement, that is the reason that revolutions and Utopias are discouraging they are up and down and not forward and back.
—GERTRUDE STEIN, *Everybody's Autobiography*, 1937

Preparedness never caused a war and unpreparedness never prevented one.
—FLORENCE PRAG KAHN in *American Political Women* by Esther Stineman, 1980

The high state of world-industrial development in capitalistic production finds expression in the extraordinary technical development and destructiveness of the instruments of war.
—ROSA LUXEMBURG, *The Crisis in the German Social Democracy*, 1919

The war acquires comparatively little significance for children so long as it only threatens their lives, disturbs their material comfort or cuts their food ration. It becomes enormously significant the moment it breaks up family life and uproots the first emotional attachments of the child within the family group.
—ANNA FREUD, *War and Children*, with Dorothy Burlingham, 1943

Dead battles, like dead generals, hold the military mind in their dead grip.
—BARBARA TUCHMAN, *The Guns of August*, 1962

Just as war bound together the men under fire, Mary Kaye thought, it united the women left behind back home.
—JOAN MICKLIN SILVER, with Linda Gottlieb, *Limbo*, 1972

It is a secret from nobody that the famous random event is most likely to arise from those parts of the world where the old adage "There is no alternative to victory" retains a high degree of plausibility.
—HANNAH ARENDT, *Crises of the Republic*, 1972

Out of the excited fancy produced by the fears and exhaustion and panic and violence of a great battle a legend grew....

—BARBARA TUCHMAN, *The Guns of August*, 1962

Men could not sustain a war of such magnitude and pain without hope.... When every autumn people said it could not last through the winter, and when every spring there was still no end in sight, only the hope that out of it all some good would accrue to mankind kept men and nations fighting. When at last it was over, the war had many diverse results and one dominant one transcending all others: disillusion.

—BARBARA TUCHMAN, *The Guns of August*, 1962

The trouble with Eichmann was precisely that so many were like him, and that the many were neither perverted nor sadistic, that they were, and still are, terribly and terrifyingly normal.... This new type of criminal, who is in actual fact *homo generis humani*, commits his crimes under circumstances that make it well-nigh impossible for him to know or to feel that he is doing wrong.

—HANNAH ARENDT, *Eichmann in Jerusalem*, 1963

On December 7, 1941, the Japanese bombed the hell out of Pearl Harbor. Johnny got his gun. America mobilized. And social roles shifted with a speed that would have sent Wonder Woman into paroxysms of power pride.

—MARJORIE ROSEN, *Popcorn Venus*, 1973

Red Fortner felt an unaccustomed clutch in his throat. Those savages over there! We ought to bomb the hell out of them, blast them from the face of the earth! He wished some of his dove colleagues at the office could hear this girl, so young, so pretty, so brave, without even a father for her child! They'd change their tune all right.

—JOAN MICKLIN SILVER, with Linda Gottlieb, *Limbo*, 1972

The chief reason warfare is still with us is neither a secret death-wish of the human species, nor an irrepressible instinct of aggression, nor, finally and more plausibly, the serious economic and social dangers inherent in disarmament, but the simple fact that no substitute for this final arbiter in international affairs has yet appeared on the political scene.

—HANNAH ARENDT, *Crises of the Republic*, 1972

War is the unfolding of miscalculations.

—BARBARA TUCHMAN, *The Guns of August*, 1962

I can't understand it. Bella's been against the war in Vietnam so long and it's still going on.

—ESTHER SAVITSKY (mother of Bella Abzug), *Moment 1*, No. 7, February 1976

I had my disappointments in the service; I discovered that a 21-inch Admiral was only a television set.

—BELLE BARTH, Stand-up routine

The government will…go on in the highly democratic method of conscripting American manhood for European slaughter.

—EMMA GOLDMAN in *Mother Earth*, July 1917

The wars say it to us—all of Europe, all of Vietnam—and
Nuremberg: never wait to speak against these horrors.
To act against these horrors
Do not let them be abstract and distant.
They look at you with human eyes…

—MURIEL RUKEYSER, "Searching/Not Searching," *The Poetic Vision of Muriel Rukeyser* by Louise Kertesz, 1980

No promise was being accorded, the blossoms
were not doves, there was no rainbow. And when it was claimed
the war had ended, it had not ended

—DENISE LEVERTOV, "In California During the Gulf War," *Evening Train*, 1992

Because I wore a peace symbol, I had to have an extra interview to determine my suitability as a member of the military.

—SUSAN SCHNALL, "Women in the Military," *Sisterhood Is Powerful*, 1970

It wasn't a battle really, as it wasn't a war. Nor was it a game, not when you heard the poisonous shrieking of the bullets—confused, scattered, searching above your heads—there was no feeling of deep revenge or hatred. It was almost as quiet as a day's work, only moments seemed eternal and seconds endless.... Not a war, or a battle, but a fight.

—YAËL DAYAN, *Envy the Frightened*, 1960

The mother of an eighteen-year-old boy who had had to secure his mother's consent for enlisting in the Army, she now cried at the slightest provocation. "How could I tell him not to go?" she once asked Fay Clausen, the tears brimming in her eyes. "He always loved guns—from the time he was a little boy he would play with toy guns, BB guns—you know, pretended he was in the marines and things. I once got him that big illustrated history of the Second World War—it cost seventeen dollars—from American Heritage, and he read it over and over again."

—JOAN MICKLIN SILVER, with Linda Gottlieb, *Limbo*, 1972

The spirit is there. This spirit alone cannot face rifles and machine guns. Rifles and machine guns without spirit are not worth very much. But spirit without these in time can be broken with the body.

—GOLDA MEIR in *Golda by* Marie Syrkin, 1964

The will to defend the country outran the means.

—BARBARA TUCHMAN, *The Guns of August*, 1962

The only alternative to war is peace and the only road to peace is negotiations.

—GOLDA MEIR in *Twentieth-Century Women Political Leaders*
by Claire Price-Groff, 1998

The professed purpose of the United States military is to maintain the peace, but its methods towards this goal are destructive and have resulted in the promotion of suffering and death of foreign peoples, as well as of its own.
   —SUSAN SCHNALL, "Women in the Military," *Sisterhood Is Powerful*, 1970

Standing erect, like overgrown bookends on either side of Mr. MacAfee's desk, were two Air Force officers.
   —JOAN MICKLIN SILVER, with Linda Gottlieb, *Limbo*, 1972

Re the aftermath of the Los Angeles riots sparked by the Rodney King verdict in 1992:
Except for the National Guard and the fear, it wasn't really so bad.
   —EVE BABITZ, *Black Swans*, 1993

Long after the bomb falls and you and your good deeds are gone, cockroaches will still be here, prowling the streets like armored cars.
   —TAMA JANOWITZ, "Modern Saint 271," *Slaves of New York*, 1986

How can you stop those bent on genocide without making war?
   —SUSAN SONTAG in *New York Times Magazine*, 2 May 1999

War-making is one of the few activities that people are not supposed to view "realistically"; that is, with an eye to expense and practical outcome. In all-out war, expenditure is all-out, unprudent-war being defined as an emergency in which no sacrifice is excessive.
   —SUSAN SONTAG, *AIDS and Its Metaphors*, 1989

WOMEN

(*also see* Feminism & Women's Liberation *and* Men)

So, in response to my brother Sigmund Freud's infamous query, what do women want? For starters, and in no particular order: freedom, food, nature, shelter, leisure, freedom from violence, justice, music, poetry, nonpatriarchal family, community, compassionate support during chronic or life-threatening illness and at the time of death, independence, books, physical/sexual pleasure, education, solitude, the ability to defend ourselves, love, ethical friendships, the arts, health, dignified employment, and political comrades.
—PHYLLIS CHESLER, *Women and Madness,* 25th Anniversary Ed., 1997

Women's center of focus is on people rather than principles.
—RABBI SANDY EISENBERG SASSO in *Reform Judaism,* Summer 1991

The acceptance of women as authority figures or as role models is an important step in female education.... It is this process of identification, respect, and then self-respect that promotes growth.
—JUDY CHICAGO, *Through the Flower,* 1975

I'd much rather be a woman than a man. Women can cry, they can wear cute clothes, and they're the first to be rescued off sinking ships.
—GILDA RADNER in *San Francisco Chronicle,* 6 June 1979

We still live in a world in which a significant fraction of people, including women, believe that a woman belongs—and wants to belong—exclusively in the home.... The world cannot afford the loss of the talents of half its people if we are to solve the many problems which beset us.
—ROSALYN YALOW in *Les Prix Nobel Yearbook,* Tore Frängsmyr, ed., 1977

You're a noble lady and I am frightened of noble ladies. They usually land the men they know in cemeteries.

—LILLIAN HELLMAN, *Days to Come*, 1936

Women are all female impersonators to some degree.

—SUSAN BROWNMILLER, *Femininity*, 1984

Femininity, in essence, is a romantic sentiment, a nostalgic tradition of imposed limitations. Even as it hurries forward in the 1980s, putting on lipstick and high heels to appear well dressed, it trips on the ruffled petticoats and hoopskirts of an era gone by.

—SUSAN BROWNMILLER, *Femininity*, 1984

How essential it is for us to ensure that the voices of the women who century after century managed to trust *not* what they were told but their own observations, experiences, and feelings are not lost again.

—RIANE EISLER, *Sacred Pleasure*, 1995

Women have been taught that, for us, the earth is flat, and that if we venture out, we will fall off the edge. Some of us have ventured out nevertheless, and so far we have not fallen off.

—ANDREA DWORKIN, *Right-Wing Women*, 1978

No woman is really an insider in the institutions fathered by masculine consciousness. When we allow ourselves to believe we are, we lose touch with parts of ourselves defined as unacceptable by that consciousness; with the vital toughness and visionary strength of the angry grandmothers, the shamanesses, the fierce marketwomen...the millions of widows, midwives, and the women healers tortured and burned as witches for three centuries in Europe.

—ADRIENNE RICH, *Blood, Bread, and Poetry*, 1986

There is simply no dignified way for a woman to live alone. Oh, she can get along financially perhaps (though not nearly as well as a man), but emotionally she is never left in peace. Her friends, her family, her fellow workers never let her forget that her husbandlessness, her childlessness—her selfishness, in short—is a reproach to the American way of life.

—ERICA JONG, *Fear of Flying*, 1973

At this moment in history only women can (if they will) support the entry or re-entry of women into the human race.

—PHYLLIS CHESLER, *Women and Madness*, 1972

The problem that has no name—which is simply the fact that American women are kept from growing to their full human capacities—is taking a far greater toll on the physical and mental health of our countries than any known disease.

—BETTY FRIEDAN, *The Feminine Mystique*, 1963

We're being made to look like Lolitas and lion tamers.

—BARBARA TUCHMAN in *The Beautiful People* by Marilyn Bender, 1968

"What the world needs," he said, "is not a Joan of Arc, the kind of woman who allows herself to be burned on the cross. That's just a bourgeois invention meant to frighten little girls into staying home. What we require is a real female military social leader." "But that"—I smiled at him—"is just impossible. Women are tied to husband and children. Women are constructed to be penetrated; a sword or a gun in their hands is a joke or a mistake. They are open holes in which things are poured. Occasionally, it's true, a woman can become a volcano, but that's about it."

—ANNE ROIPHE, *Up the Sandbox!*, 1970

'All women hustle. Women watch faces, voices, gestures, moods. The person who has to survive through cunning."

—MARGE PIERCY, *Small Changes*, 1973

Some of us are becoming the men we wanted to marry.
—GLORIA STEINEM, Speech, Yale University, 23 September 1981

I have met brave women who are exploring the outer edge of human possibility, with no history to guide them, and with a courage to make themselves vulnerable that I find moving beyond words.
—GLORIA STEINEM, "Sisterhood," *The First Ms. Reader*, 1972

Women have come a long way. Not too long ago we were called dolls, tomatoes, chicks, babes and broads. We've graduated to being called tough cookies, foxes, bitches and witches. I guess that's progress.
—BARBRA STREISAND in *Seattle Post-Intelligencer*, 10 February 1994

She must learn again to speak
starting with I
starting with We
starting as the infant does
with her own true hunger
and pleasure
and rage.
—MARGE PIERCY, "Unlearning to Not Speak," *To Be of Use*, 1973

Implicitly adopting the male life as the norm, they have tried to fashion women out of a masculine cloth. It all goes back, of course, to Adam and Eve—a story which shows, among other things, that if you make a woman out of man, you are bound to get into trouble. In the life cycle, as in the Garden of Eden, the woman has been the deviant.
—CAROL GILLIGAN, *In a Different Voice*, 1982

A thinking woman sleeps with monsters.
—ADRIENNE RICH, "Snapshots of a Daughter-in- Law,
Snapshots of a Daughter-in-Law, 1963

Why have they been telling us women lately that we have no sense of humor—
when we are always laughing?... And when we're not laughing, we're smiling.
—NAOMI WEISSTEIN, *She Needs*, 1973

The connections between and among women are the most feared, the most
problematic, and the most potentially transforming force on the planet.
—ADRIENNE RICH, *On Lies, Secrets, and Silence*, 1979

I am not elevating women to sainthood, nor am I suggesting that all women
share the same views, or that all women are good and all men bad. Women
have screamed for war. Women, like men, have stoned black children going to
integrated schools. Women have been and are prejudiced, narrow-minded,
reactionary, even violent. *Some* women. They, of course, have a right to vote
and a right to run for office. I will defend that right, but I will not support them
or vote for them.
—BELLA ABZUG, Speech, National Women's Political Caucus, Washington,
10 July 1971

Times change. Symbols change. And so do we. We don't bury our hopes for
the future in cedar chests and mothballs anymore. We get out there and run for
our future, for our health, for our sanity. We are the women of the Eighties.
—ELAINE BERNSTEIN PARTNOW, *Hear Us Roar*, 1988

A woman can look both moral and exciting—if she also looks as if it was quite
a struggle.
—EDNA FERBER in *Reader's Digest*, December 1954

Oh Doris Lessing, my dear—your Anna is wrong about orgasms. They are no
proof of love—any more than that other Anna's fall under the wheels of that
Russian train was a proof of love. It's all female shenanigans, cultural *mishegoss*,
conditioning, brainwashing, male mythologizing. What does a woman want?
She wants what she has been told she ought to want. Anna Wulf wants orgasm,

Anna Karenina, death. Orgasm is no proof of anything. Orgasm is proof of orgasm. Someday every woman will have orgasms—like every family has color TV—and we can all get on with the real business of life.

—ERICA JONG, *How to Save Your Own Life*, 1977

But to be a female human being trying to fulfill traditional female functions in a traditional way *is* in direct conflict with the subversive function of the imagination.

—ADRIENNE RICH, *On Lies, Secrets, and Silence*, 1979

There isn't the tiniest shred of evidence that…fantasies of servitude and childish dependence have anything to do with woman's true potential.…

—NAOMI WEISSTEIN, Speech, American Studies Association, California, 26 October 1968

Each month
the blood sheets down
like good red rain.

I am the gardener.
Nothing grows without me.

—ERICA JONG, "Gardener," *Half-Lives*, 1973

A woman without a man is like a fish without a bicycle.

—Attributed to Gloria Steinem

I love, cherish, and respect women in my mind, in my heart, and in my soul. This love of women is the soil in which my life is rooted. It is the soil of our common life together. My life grows out of this soil. In any other soil, I would die. In whatever ways I am strong, I am strong because of the power and passion of this nurturant love.

—ANDREA DWORKIN, *Our Blood*, 1976

Wherever you go, you will hear all around:
The wisdom of woman to the distaff is bound.

—RAHEL MORPURGO, *The Harp of Rachel*, 1890

They say a woman's place
is to wait and serve
under the veil
submissive and dear
but I think my place is in a ship from space
to carry me
the hell out of here

—LAURA NYRO, "The Right to Vote," *Mother's Spiritual*, 1984

The glorification of the "woman's role," then, seems to be in proportion to society's reluctance to treat women as complete human beings; for the less real function that role has, the more it is decorated with meaningless details to conceal its emptiness.

—BETTY FRIEDAN, *The Feminine Mystique*, 1963

Today the problem that has no name, is how to juggle work, love, home and children.

—BETTY FRIEDAN, *The Second Stage*, 1981

In the forties emulating an ideal woman meant bobbing your hair like Betty Grable's. In the eighties, because of Jessica Lange, women have to get a Pulitzer Prize–winning actor-playwright to fall in love with them, have a child by one of the world's great dancers, be nominated for two Academy Awards, and enjoy doing the laundry alone on a farm.

—WENDY WASSERSTEIN, *Bachelor Girls*, 1990

If you were to survey celebrated women, with every step toward real success there came a baby.

—MIRIAM SCHAPIRO in *Exposures*, Brown, 1989

Oh we bathed and perfumed and depilated white ladies, in whose wombs the sanctity of the white race is entombed! What concoction of musk and boiled petals can disguise the dirt done in the name of that sanctity?

—NADINE GORDIMER, *The Late Bourgeois World*, 1966

The cumulative effect of being forced to lead circumscribed lives is toxic.... It is therefore not surprising that many women still behave as if they've been colonized.

—PHYLLIS CHESLER, *Women and Madness*, 25th Anniversary Ed., 1997

Re a "Total Woman" course: A revolutionary new idea whereby women give up their entire lives and can stay home and devote themselves to their husbands, whether they like them or not.

—EMILY LEVINE, Stand-up routine

"Woe to America where women are let free like men."

—ANZIA YEZIERSKA, *The Bread Givers*, 1925

"A woman alone, not a wife and not a mother, has no existence. No joy on earth, no hope of heaven.... You're not human!"

—ANZIA YEZIERSKA, *Red Ribbon on a White Horse*, 1950

My sisters and I had always felt that while a woman's interests ought to begin at home and ought to end there, they need not necessarily confine themselves to it alone.

—REBEKAH BETTELHEIM KOHUT, *My Portion: An Autobiography*, 1927

Women had been kept behind bars, their hands manacled, their feet tied by the ball and chain of conventionality.

—MAUD NATHAN, *Once Upon a Time and Today*, 1974

It is an undeniable fact there is no way for a smart woman to be public without being seen as a treacherous Lady Macbeth figure or bitch goddess.
—ERICA JONG in *Nation*, 25 November 1996

A free girlhood, a free choice in marriage, and brimful womanhood are the
precious rights of an American woman.

If men ever discovered how tough women actually are, they would be scared to death.
—EDNA FERBER, *A Kind of Magic*, 1963

A long girlhood, a free choice in marriage, and brimful womanhood are the precious rights of an American woman.
—MARY ANTIN, *The Promised Land*, 1912

Women, because they are not generally the principal breadwinners, can be perhaps most useful as the trail blazers, working along the bypaths, doing the unusual job that men cannot afford to gamble on.
—BETTY FRIEDAN, *The Feminine Mystique*, 1963

Woman is the ozone of the metaphysical atmosphere.
—MINNIE D. LOUIS in *American Hebrew*, 28 June 1895

I've always thought that the wombs of women form a secret, silent network of communication all over the world.
—PENINA V. ADELMAN, *Miriam's Well*, 1986

For pearls are formed in the womb of grace
Where the fertile and the barren learn to embrace.
—PENINA V. ADELMAN, "Ballad of Hannah," *Miriam's Well*, 1986

Woman after woman comes into this house [in England]…and tells me women oughtn't to have equal pay because their place is in the home, and a man has commitments and women aren't really any good at their jobs in any case, and if you give equal pay it will only do a lot of them out of jobs because people will only hire men. Every…female says the same things in the same order. Every now and then a man says it as well, but it is usually some flat-faced English nag.

—EMILY "MICKEY" HAHN, *Nobody Said* Not *to Go* by Ken Cuthbertson, 1998

…for what protections has she traded her wildness and the lives of others?…how does she stop dreaming the dream of protection?

—ADRIENNE RICH, "Virginia 1906"

She was married to Alfred Hendershot, the political adviser, and was an almost perfect person. She gave elaborate dinner parties and belonged to the Royal Guild of Needleworkers—she did fine embroidery in her two minutes of spare time.

—LAURIE COLWIN, "A Big Storm Knocked It Over," *Shaking Eve's Tree*, 1990

Down through the generations in history my ancestors prayed, "I thank thee, Lord, I was not created a woman," and from this day forward I trust that women all over the world will be able to say, "I thank Thee, Lord, I *was* created a woman."

—BETTY FRIEDAN, "Marching in Front," *Hadassah* magazine, November 1993

The feminine mystique has succeeded in burying millions of American women alive.

—BETTY FRIEDAN, *The Feminine Mystique*, 1963

American women no longer know who they are.

—BETTY FRIEDAN, *The Feminine Mystique*, 1963

A woman's fancies lightly roam, and weave
Themselves into a fairy web.

—RAHEL MORPURGO, Sonnet, *The Harp of Rachel*, 1890

The Rubicons which women must cross, the sex barriers which they must breach, are ultimately those that exist in their own minds.

—FREDA ADLER, *Sisters in Crime*, 1975

—

Today, at least in principle, the ownership of one person's body by another, the appropriation of a person's services, and the negation of a person's right to make fundamental life choices is almost universally condemned. But there is one area where, even in principle, all this has been particularly resistant to change. When it comes to women's bodies, women's services, and women's choices, the traditional notion that men should hold power, men should make choices, and men should control women's bodies is still ideologically, legally, and economically in place throughout much of our world today.

—RIANE EISLER, *Sacred Pleasure*, 1995

—

Learning is not wisdom. Innovation is not progress, and to be identical with man is not the ideal of womanhood. Some things and privileges belong to him by nature; to these, true woman does not aspire; but every woman should aspire to make of her home a temple, of herself a high priestess, of her children disciples, then will she best occupy the pulpit, and her work run parallel with man's. She may be ordained rabbi or be the president of a congregation—she is entirely able to fill both offices—but her noblest work will be at home, her highest ideal, a home.

—RAY FRANK, Papers of the Jewish Women's Congress, 1984

—

Being a woman is of special interest only to aspiring male transsexuals. To actual women it is merely a good excuse not to play football.

—FRAN LEBOWITZ, *Metropolitan Life*, 1978

—

But then again this monthly assault
the undertow, the tide that pulls
mercilessly dashing me against the rocks
this pounding of rage, overwhelming

—MERLE FELD, "Meditation on Menstruation," *Four Centuries*, 1992

When I first got my period...there should have been a blessing—*sh'asani eisha*, *she'hechianu* (Thank you, God, for having made me a woman)—because holiness was present at that moment.
—RABBI LAURA GELLER, "Encountering the Divine Presence," *Four Centuries*, 1992

WORK & WORKING

(*also see* Money, Business & Economics)

Real apprenticeship is ultimately always to the self.
—CYNTHIA OZICK, "Old Hand as Novice," *Fame and Folly: Essays*, 1996

I don't believe in careers. I believe in work.
—DEBRA WINGER in *Parade* magazine, 6 March 1994

Women globally contribute two-thirds of the world's work hours, for which—given the imbalanced, unjust, and truly peculiar nature of the accounting characteristic of dominator economics—they globally earn only one-tenth of what men do and own a mere one-hundredth of the world's property.
—RIANE EISLER, *Sacred Pleasure*, 1995

For an interest to be rewarding, one must pay in discipline and dedication, especially through the difficult or boring stages which are inevitably encountered.
—MIRRA KOMAROVSKY, *Women in the Modern World*, 1953

Reflecting the values of the larger capitalistic society, there is no prestige whatsoever attached to actual working. Workers are invisible.
—MARGE PIERCY, "The Grand Coolie Damn," *Sisterhood Is Powerful*, 1970

All the secretaries hunch at their IBM's, snickering at keys. What they know could bring down the government.

—Robin Morgan, "On the Watergate Women," *Monster*, 1972

We are human beings first, with minor differences from men that apply largely to the act of reproduction. We share the dreams, capabilities, and weaknesses of all human beings, but our occasional pregnancies and other visible differences have been used—even more pervasively, if less brutally, than radical differences have been used—to mark us for an elaborate division of labor that may once have been practical but has since become cruel and false. The division is continued for clear reason, consciously or not: the economic and social profit of men as a group.

—Gloria Steinem, "Sisterhood," *The First Ms. Reader*, 1972

There is a law of life in her hands milking,
For quiet seamen hold a rope like her.

—Lea Goldberg, "Of Bloom," *Poems from the Hebrew*, 1973

To reach those shining pebbles,
that soil where uncommon men
have labored in their virtue
and left a store
of seeds for planting!

—Denise Levertov, "A Common Ground," *The Jacob's Ladder*, 1961

Those women who stitch their lives to their machines
and daughters at the symmetry of looms.

—Muriel Rukeyser, "Ann Burlak," *Waterlily Fire*, 1962

Managers, right up to the very top of the company, will be getting their personal rewards not from giving commands and eliciting obedience but from educating and nurturing the people under them.

—Shoshana Zuboff in *Omni*, April 1991

Production on a small scale is now practically prohibitive.
—HELENA RUBINSTEIN in *Hope in a Jar: The Making of America's Beauty Culture*
by Kathy Peiss, 1998

KITTY (a social climber): I was reading a book the other day. It's all about civilization or something. A nutty kind of a book. Do you know that the guy said that machinery is going to take the place of every profession?

CARLOTTA (a former stage star): Oh my dear. That's something you need never worry about.
—EDNA FERBER, *Dinner at Eight*, with George S. Kaufman, 1932

One trouble: to be a professional anything in the United States is to think of oneself as an expert and one's ideas as semi-sacred, and to treat others in a certain way—professionally.
—MARGE PIERCY, "The Grand Coolie Damn," *Sisterhood Is Powerful*, 1970

A woman is handicapped by her sex, and handicaps society, either by slavishly copying the pattern of man's advance in the professions, or by refusing to compete with man at all.
—BETTY FRIEDAN, *The Feminine Mystique*, 1963

The degree to which a pimp, if he's clever, can confuse and delude a prostitute is very nearly unlimited.
—POLLY ADLER, *A House Is Not a Home*, 1953

Behold, let thine handmaid be a servant to wash the feet of the servants of my lord.
—ABIGAIL, Book of 1 Samuel, c. 550 B.C.E., Bible

Over five million women are at work in the United States according to the 1900 census. Despite such figures, as a nation we superstitiously hug the belief that our women are at home and our children at school.

—LILLIAN D. WALD, "Organization amongst Working Women," *Annals of the American Academy of Political Science*, Vol. 27, May 1906

A job interview is like an uncontrolled chemical reaction. Into the beaker go the characteristics (sex, age, race, physical fitness/attractiveness, previous educational and work experiences, etc.) of a particular applicant and those of a particular interviewer. Then in go the beliefs, goals, values, competencies, expectations, and prejudices of both the applicant and the interviewer, which when stirred together create both verbal and nonverbal behaviors of the applicant, to which the interviewer reacts; and of the interviewer, to which the applicant reacts. Add to the beaker the various accurate and inaccurate impressions and/or the impression that the interviewer has of other applicants and the impression the applicant has of other jobs; the degree to which the interviewer wants the applicant and the degree to which the applicant wants the job. Don't forget to include in the beaker the day, time, and place of the interview, and what might be going on in the personal and professional lives of both the applicant and the interviewers. The resulting potent chemical brew somehow transforms itself into a decision....

—SUSAN HERMAN, *Hiring Right*, 1994

A vocation is man's one true wealth and salvation.

—NATALIA GINZBURG, *Little Virtues*, 1985

"People don't look for kinds of work anymore, ma'am," he answered impassively. "They just look for work."

—AYN RAND, *Atlas Shrugged*, 1957

We reject the notion that the work that brings in more money is not more valuable. The ability to earn money, or the fact that one already has it, should carry more weight in a relationship.

—ROSALYN DREXLER, *The Cosmopolitan Girl*, 1975

Laziness may appear attractive, but work gives satisfaction.

—ANNE FRANK, *The Diary of a Young Girl*, 1947

We were wedded together on the basis of mutual work and goals.

—JUDY CHICAGO, *Through the Flower*, 1975

You can have the best service, the best service delivery plan, the sexiest product, the most efficient production system, the wisest financial plan. But without the best people, your organization simply can't function at its optimum.

—SUSAN HERMAN, *Hiring Right*, 1994

Informating [word coined by Zuboff to describe what the computer is doing— taking three-dimensional objects and events and then translating and displaying them as data] creates enormous transparency in the workplace. If you use that transparency for surveillance, to police people, they react with a whole range of dysfunctional behaviors. They sabotage the data by becoming passive. They withdraw effort and caring from their work.

—SHOSHANA ZUBOFF, *Omni*, April 1991

Everything I do is basically connected with my work. Everything.

—MURIEL SPARK, *Reality and Dreams*, 1997

YOUTH & ADOLESCENCE

(*also see* Age & Aging; Children; *and* The Human Body ... & Its Parts)

When they reach the age of fifteen and their beauty arrives, it's very exciting— like coming into an inheritance.

—EVE BABITZ, *Eve's Hollywood*, 1974

These [teenage] girls had dropped childhood, with its bond of physical dependency on parents, behind them. They had forgotten what they had been, and they did not know that they would become what their parents were. For the brief hiatus they occupied themselves with preparations for a state of being very different—a world that would never exist.

—NADINE GORDIMER, "Vital Statistics," *Not for Publication and Other Stories*, 1965

I think what is happening to me is so wonderful, and not only what can be seen on my body, but all that is taking place inside. I never discuss myself or any of these things with anybody; that is why I have to talk to myself about them.

—ANNE FRANK, *The Diary of a Young Girl*, 1947

It is normal for an adolescent to behave for a considerable length of time in an inconsistent and unpredictable manner; to fight his impulses and to accept them; to ward them off successfully and to be overrun by them; to love his parents and to hate them; to revolt against them and to be dependent on them; to be deeply ashamed to acknowledge his mother before others and, unexpectedly, to desire heart-to-heart talks with her; to thrive on imitation of and identification with others while searching unceasingly for his own identity; to be more idealistic, artistic, generous, and unselfish than he will ever be again, but also the opposite: self-centered, egoistic, calculating. Such fluctuation between extreme opposites would be deemed highly abnormal at any other time of life. At this time they may signify no more than that an adult structure of personality takes a long time to emerge.

—ANNA FREUD, *The Psychoanalytic Study of the Child*, Vol. 13, 1958

You never really lose your youth. How can you? The experiences and lessons of youth belong to you. Youth is as much a state of mind as it is a time and place in life. Just as we can be very young in some things in our later years, so, during our so-called "youth," we may be very old in others. Yes, youth is something you always have at your command.

—ELAINE BERNSTEIN PARTNOW, *Breaking the Age Barrier*, 1981

I think school is much harder than real life. People are so much more accepting when they are adults.

—NATALIE PORTMAN, *Premiere* (UK), July 1995

———

You haven't lived until you've seen a line of prepubescent Hebrew school students doing "The Time Warp" [a dance number from the cult classic *The Rocky Horror Show*] at a bat mitzvah. Now that's glamour.

—RAVEN SNOOK, *How I Became a Drag Queen Trapped in a Woman's Body*, 1997

BIOGRAPHICAL INDEX

ABBOT, PATSY A New York comedian who flourished in the 1930s and 1940s, she owned her own nightclub, Patsy's Place, and had a reputation for raunchiness.

ABEL OF BETH-MAACAH, WOMAN OF A peacemaker from this fortified city in North Palestine, in the Bible she declares her faithfulness to David. It was this "wise woman," as she is described, who was responsible for the death of Sheba, in return for which Joab called off his troops. She lived in the 1040s–970s B.C.E.

ABIGAIL She thrived in Judea in the 990s B.C.E. The wife of Nabal (or Navah), who had foolishly refused to supply David with food and supplies, she sneaked off in the night to aid David. Upon hearing of this, Nabal died of a heart attack. David then married Abigail, with whom he had a child, Chileah.

ABZUG, BELLA One of the most influential American women of the twentieth century and the second Jewish woman (after Florence Prag Kahn, see below) elected to the U.S. Congress, Abzug had deep ties to Judaism, which emanated from her extended family of Russian immigrants. Never afraid to take controversial positions, she was a fierce advocate for peace and women's rights, and became a prominent national crusader against poverty, racism, and violence in America. In 1970, she was elected to Congress on a woman's rights/peace platform. Her first vote was for the Equal Rights Amendment; she served two terms. She was a cofounder of the National Women's Political Caucus, the Women's Strike for Peace, and the Coalition for a Democratic Alternative. Born Bella Savitsky on July 24, 1920, she died in 1998.

ADELMAN, PENINA V. A writer, social worker, and folklorist, she was born in 1953. Her writings, detailing the new traditions she created among contemporary Jewish women, can be found in several anthologies. She has been working on an imaginative interpretation of a poem from Proverbs 31 called "A Woman of Strength," which gives voice to many of the nameless, faceless, spare depictions of women in the Bible.

ADLER, FREDA Born in 1934, Dr. Adler received her B.A., M.A., and Ph.D. in criminology and sociology from the University of Pennsylvania. Her research and writing has focused on areas such as criminological theory, narcotic and alcohol abuse, cross-cultural female criminality, judicial education, and maritime crime. Adviser to various governments from Australia to Kuwait to Brazil, she has been the recipient of numerous professional and scholastic awards. Adler is currently on the faculty at Rutgers University.

ADLER, POLLY Born in Poland on April 16, 1900, Adler became one of New York's most successful bordello madams of the '20s. Her autobiographical book about "the life," *A House Is Not a Home*, was made into a Hollywood film starring Shelley Winters.

ADLER, RENATA Italian-born in 1938, she was educated mainly in the United States, earning an LL.D. *(honoris causa)* at Georgetown University Law School. During thirty-five years at the *New Yorker*, Professor Adler published essays, short stories, journalistic pieces, book reviews, and film criticism. For two years, she was chief film critic of the *New York Times*. Author of two novels and five books of essays and reporting, she has received Guggenheim and Fulbright Awards, as well as the O. Henry and the Hemingway Prizes. Adler is a member of the American Academy of Arts and Letters.

AGUILAR, GRACE A popular novelist who became a prominent theologian, but was ignored as a poet, she lived from 1816–1847. An Englishwoman, Aguilar was a Sephardic writer whose themes focused on exile and assimilation just at the moment when British Jews were seeking full civil rights. She was the first Anglo-Jew to write midrashic poems about Hebrew characters and was among the first to jump the boundaries of Victorian women's "domestic sphere" to write explicitly political poetry. Some of her most powerful work is clearly proto-Zionist.

ALLRED, GLORIA [Rachel Bloom Bray] An attorney and a partner in a law firm, Allred was born in 1941 and has been practicing law for over twenty years. The recipient of countless honors for her pioneering legal work on behalf of women's rights and rights for minorities, she founded and is currently serving as president of the Women's Equal Rights Legal Defense and Education Fund. She hosts her own radio show on KABC TalkRadio in Los Angeles, and is a columnist for the *National Law Journal*. Allred has been nominated for an Emmy three times for her television commentaries on KABC-TV.

ALONI, SHULAMIT Born in Tel Aviv in 1929, Aloni was taken captive by Jordanian forces during the War of Independence. Her writings focus on political and legal subjects; she produced radio programs dealing with legislation and legal procedures. Aloni, a Labour Member of Knesset between 1965 and 1969, founded the Israel Consumers Council. In 1973 she formed the Civil Rights Movement, serving again in the Knesset (1974–1996) where, from 1992, she was Minister of Communications and the Arts, Science and Technology.

AMIR, ANDA Poet and writer Anda Pinkerfeld was born in Rzezsow, Poland, in 1902, where her father was a successful architect. With her brother, in 1920, she made *aliya* with the first pioneering group. Her family was not pleased, and it wasn't until 1932, their Polish patriotism having diminished—and the Holocaust on the horizon—that they, too, made *aliya*. Amir was known in Israel for her books for children. She died around 1980.

ANTIN, MARY One of many thousands of Eastern Europeans who emigrated to the United States in the 1890s, she was born in 1881 in Polotzk in the Russian "Pale of

Settlement" and came to America at the age of thirteen, settling in Boston with her parents and three siblings. Her emigration felt like a "second birth" to her and she left a moving and eloquent record of her experience, *The Promised Land*. Scholar Werner Sollors said, "Her book really established the genre of the immigrant autobiography." She died in 1949.

ANTLER, JOYCE Born in Brooklyn in 1942, she is a professor of American Jewish history and culture at Brandeis University in Waltham, Massachusetts. Particularly interested in Jewish women's history, she is the author or editor of eight books. Professor Antler is a founder of the Brandeis Women's Studies Program and the Graduate Consortium of Women Studies at Radcliffe College, and has served as the chair of the Massachusetts Foundation for the Humanities.

ARBUS, DIANE Born Diane Nemerov in New York City in 1923, Arbus was the sister of Howard Nemerov, U.S. poet laureate of 1988. She started out as a fashion photographer, but from about 1954 on she focused on offbeat subjects—nudists, dwarfs, drug addicts, and ugly or poor people she met on the street. Her photographs were published and exhibited to great acclaim. For a considerable time, she was married to actor-photographer Allan Arbus. In 1971, she took her own life.

ARENDT, HANNAH Born in Hannover, East Prussia, in 1906, Arendt fled the Nazis in 1941, came to the United States, and taught at leading universities. *The Origins of Totalitarianism* (1951) established her as a major political thinker. She famously had a love affair with noted philosopher Martin Heidegger, who later joined the Nazi Party. In 1950 Arendt became a U.S. citizen. In 1959 she became the first woman professor at Princeton University. She finally settled at the New School for Social Research in New York, where she taught from 1967 until her death on December 4, 1975.

ASCARELLI, DEVORAH An Italian poet and translator who lived in the 1600s, she was the first woman to write prayers that were included in an official prayer book.

BABITZ, EVE Born in 1943, Babitz has written seven books filled with wry humor and dealing with quintessential arcana, shenanigans, and happenings of Los Angeles and Hollywood.

BACALL, LAUREN Betty Joan Perske was born in New York City on September 16, 1924. After doing some modeling, she made her first film, *To Have and Have Not* (1944), at age nineteen, with Humphrey Bogart, whom she married and with whom she had two children. Bacall and Bogart costarred in three more films; he died in 1957. Famous for her husky voice and sultry good looks, Bacall won a Tony for her Broadway performance in *Applause*, a musical, in 1970. She was married to second husband Jason Robards, Jr., from 1961 to 1969.

BARA, THEDA One of the top three silent film stars in 1918, behind Mary Pickford and Charlie Chaplin, she was the first sex symbol for the masses. Almost thirty when her film career began, Bara shaved five years off her age and billed herself as the daughter of an Eastern prince, born in the shadow of the sphinx, whose name was an anagram for "death." In fact, she was born Theodosia Goodman in Ohio on July 20, 1885, to wealthy Jewish immigrant parents. She died in 1955.

BARCLAY, AVIEL Born in Nanaimo, British Columbia, in 1969, Barclay is the world's first female *sofer stam* (Jewish ritual scribe), yet she was not born a Jew. Awed by Torah from the time she was three, she was reading the Bible at age ten and taught herself Hebrew calligraphy from the *New Book of Knowledge* encyclopedia. She converted to Judaism in Vancouver and embarked on a struggle against tradition to fulfill her calling. A passage appears in the Talmud listing the individuals considered not kosher to write Torah scrolls, tefillin, and mezuzahs. Women appear on this list. Her travails included four months of study in Israel, where her mentor had her swear his identity to secrecy and where yeshiva after yeshiva refused her space. At thirty-three she converted again, this time to Orthodoxy, and embarked on the final stage of her quest to pen a Torah. She received her first commission from Kadima, a progressive congregation in Seattle, led by Rabbi Fern Feldman. The new *sofer* plans to complete the Torah for Kadima in time for Simchat Torah in 2004.

BARR, ROSEANNE An American actor and comedian, born in Salt Lake City in 1953, she did local stand-up comedy for years before things started popping: TV, film, and then, in 1989, her own series, *Roseanne*, which ran for eight seasons. During that time she divorced her husband of nearly twenty years, then married and divorced her costar Tom Arnold, and followed that with a third unsuccessful marriage. She won a Golden Globe in 1996, did a Broadway stint as the Wicked Witch of the West in *The Wizard of Oz*, and is launching a new TV series.

BARTH, BELLE Born Annabelle Salzman in New York in 1911, Barth was often referred to as the female Lenny Bruce. Her scatological style was tough and sassy, and her bawdiness attracted crowds from New York to Miami. She died in 1971.

BAT-MIRIAM, YOCHEVED Born in Keplits, Belorussia, in 1901, Yocheved Zhelezniak attended the Universities of Odessa and Moscow but settled in Eretz Yisrael where she wrote the bulk of her poems. Produced between the two world wars, they are set against a backdrop of Jewish tragedy—her childhood experiences in Russia and as a settler in Israel. After her son was killed in the 1948 War of Independence, she never wrote again. Bat-Miriam was awarded the 1964 Bialik Prize and the 1972 Israel Prize. She died in 1980.

BAUM, VICKI A native of Vienna, where she was born Hedwig Baum in 1888, Baum wrote a novel, *Menschen im Hotel* (*People in a Hotel*, 1929), which made her one of the most widely read authors of her time. She adapted a stage play from her novel, then a screenplay, *Grand Hotel*, which became an Academy Award–winning film in 1932. Her first stories appeared in print when she was fourteen. She played the harp in an orchestra in Germany, then, in 1916, married conductor Richard Lert, who had been her best friend since childhood. She gave up music as a profession in 1926 and went to work as an editor for a publishing company in Berlin. She died in 1960.

BAYES, NORA An accomplished comedian and actor who flourished in vaudeville, she was born Leonora Goldberg in Joliet, Illinois, in 1880. In the *Ziegfeld Follies* of 1908 she introduced the song "Shine On, Harvest Moon," cowritten with her second husband, Jack Norworth. She was married five times, managed her own career, was a successful songwriter, and even established her own theater in New York City. In 1944, Warner Brothers produced *Shine On, Harvest Moon*, a fictionalized version of Bayes's life. She died in 1928.

BECK, EVELYN TORTON Born in Vienna in 1933, Dr. Beck is professor emerita at the University of Maryland. Founder of the interdisciplinary fields of women's studies, Jewish women's studies, and lesbian studies, her books broke new ground in several areas. Her critique of the "Jewish American Princess" stereotype has been widely anthologized; she was among the first to insist on the inclusion of Jewish themes in women's studies and the multicultural curriculum. She lectures widely on such issues as anti-Semitism, racism, and homophobia.

BERG, GERTRUDE One of the most successful women in the history of American entertainment, she was born October 3, 1899, in the Jewish Harlem section of New York City, to immigrant parents. Her creation and portrayal of Molly Goldberg became the personification of the "Jewish mother." Brooks Atkinson, of the *New York Times*, said she "...brought out the humanity, love and respect that people should have toward each other. Her contributions to American radio, television, films and stage will always be remembered, especially by those who experienced hearing and seeing her perform." She won an Emmy in 1950 and a Tony in 1959. She died September 14, 1966.

BERNHARD, SANDRA Before becoming a manicurist in Beverly Hills, she graduated from high school in Scottsdale, Arizona. Born in 1955, she is an "original performer whose in-your-face approach to comedy is off-putting but frequently rewarding" (Leonard Maltin). She has been featured in several motion pictures and had a recurring role as an openly gay character on TV's *Roseanne*. She has written two books featuring her distinctive brand of humor. Her baby's name is Cicely Yasmin, a Moroccan name, and her Hebrew name is Rachel.

BERNHARDT, SARAH Also known as the "Divine Sarah," she was born in Paris in 1844. After a successful acting career in France, she went to London in 1876, where she quickly established herself as the leading actor of the day. In 1892 she asked Oscar Wilde to write her a play. The result was *Salome*, but while it was in rehearsal Lord Chamberlain had the play banned. In 1899 she founded the Theatre Sarah Bernhardt in Paris. Despite having had a leg amputated in 1915, Bernhardt continued to tour and appear on stage until her death in 1923. She was noted for her portrayal of Hamlet, the first woman known to have done so.

BERURIAH A renowned biblical scholar from what is now Israel, she was born in the 1210s and died in 1280, reportedly by her own hand but at her husband's provocation. Her husband, Rebbe Meir, was considered a great scholar, as was her father, Rabbi Hananya ben Teradyon. She is mentioned in the Talmud and many of her midrashim are quoted to this day.

BLUME, JUDY The daughter of Esther and Rudolph Sussman, a dentist, Blume was born in Elizabeth, New Jersey, on February 12, 1938. Her novels for children, adolescents, and adults have sold more than 75 million copies, and her work has been translated into twenty-something languages. Her book for young girls, *Are You There God? It's Me, Margaret*, published in 1970, became something of a classic. She is married to writer George Cooper; they have three grown children and one grandchild. In 1981 Blume established the KIDS Fund, which supports communication between young people and parents. Blume has received many prestigious awards and honors, and is today considered the foremost writer of children's novels.

BOOSLER, ELAYNE One of the busiest comedians touring the country today, Boosler was born in Brooklyn in 1952, and has seven brothers, all veterinarians. In between coveted waitress gigs, she studied acting, musical comedy, ballet, and voice. Her life's work is animal rescue and advocacy. To that end she has formed a very successful non-profit organization: http://www.tailsofjoy.net. Boosler is also extremely pro-active in politics and issues of the day.

BORYSENKO, JOAN [Z.] A cancer cell biologist, psychologist, and a yoga and meditation instructor, she is the cofounder and former director of the Mind/Body Clinic at New England Deaconess Hospital. She has also taught at Harvard Medical School. Dr. Borysenko is a pioneer in the emerging field of psychoneuroimmunology. Author of the best-seller *Minding the Body, Mending the Mind* (1989), she is also a lecturer and workshop leader who brings body and soul together with unprecedented clarity and sophistication. She was born in Boston in 1945 and lives in Colorado.

BOXER, BARBARA Elected to the House of Representatives in 1982, she served for ten years and was then elected to the Senate. Although she represents the state of California, she was born in Brooklyn on November 11, 1940. She met and married Stewart Boxer when she was a senior at Brooklyn College; they have two children. She famously corrected House Speaker Thomas (Tip) O'Neill's reference to "the men in Congress." Her many battles in Congress have been recognized with awards from, among others, the Anti-Defamation League, the National Council of Jewish Women, Planned Parenthood, and the American Police Hall of Fame.

BRICE, FANNY Born Fanny Borach on October 29, 1891, in New York City, she launched her career in vaudeville after winning $5 in an amateur talent contest at age thirteen. Her appearance in the 1910 *Ziegfeld Follies* propelled her to stardom, which included film appearances and her own radio program as Baby Snooks. Noted for her comic routines as well as her torch songs, she married gambler and confidence man Jules "Nick" Arnstein, with whom she had two children. Divorced in 1927, she married impresario/songwriter Billy Rose the next year, but they, too, divorced. She died of a cerebral hemorrhage on May 29, 1951. Her daughter Frances was married to movie producer Ray Stark, who produced the movie, *Funny Girl*, based on Fanny Brice's life.

BRONER, E. M. Born Esther Masserman in Detroit on July 8, 1930, the novelist got her B.A. and M.F.A. degrees from Wayne State University and her Ph.D. from Union

Graduate School in New York. She started using the name E. M. Broner to avoid rejection by publishers because she was a woman, and the name stuck. A pioneering Jewish feminist, her works reexamine the biblical matriarchs and their place in traditional texts, and create new religious ceremonies to highlight women's experiences in Jewish ritual. Broner is married to the artist Robert Broner; they have four children.

BROWNMILLER, SUSAN She was born in Brooklyn on February 15, 1935—Susan B. Anthony's birthday—a fortuitous date for this controversial feminist writer from a middle-class family who "was lucky to go to Cornell University for a couple of years on scholarships." Starting off as a Broadway actor, she soon found her calling in writing. In 1960, she joined CORE and became a political activist. She worked at *Newsweek*, then at ABC. Her activism landed her in the midst of the women's liberation movement, upon which her works have had a notable impact, in particular the watershed publication *Against O ur Will: Men, Women, and Rape*.

CARROLL, JEAN Though she is scarcely remembered, Jean Carroll was perhaps the first female stand-up comic in America. Born around 1915, she enjoyed a comeback in the late 1950s–early 1960s, when she made several appearances on the *Ed Sullivan Show*.

CHERNIN, KIM Born May 7, 1940, in the Bronx, she was exposed early on to leftist teachings and impassioned political rhetoric, yet she became a poet, a mystic, and an interpreter of women's psychological experiences. Early influences came from her shtetl-born grandmother who created Yiddish tales for women; her father, Paul Kusnitz, who recited Pushkin and regaled his daughter with "homespun tales"; and her mother, Rose Chernin, a gifted teller of tales "about madness, revolution, the struggle to survive."

CHESLER, PHYLLIS Born in 1940, Dr. Chesler is an emerita professor of psychology and women's studies, a psychotherapist, an author, and an expert courtroom witness. She has lectured and organized political, legal, religious, and human rights campaigns in the United States and in Canada, Europe, the Middle East, and Asia. A popular guest on national television and radio programs, and on college campuses, she is considered an expert commentator on the major events of our time. She is a cofounder of the Association for Women in Psychology (1969) and the National Women's Health Network (1974).

CHICAGO, JUDY This pioneering American installation artist and painter, born in 1939, took the name of her city of birth in place of her birth name, Cohen. She is married to photographer Donald Woodman. Cofounder of the Woman's Building, Feminist Studio Workshop/College, Los Angeles (1973), and the Through the Flower Foundation (1978), Chicago has created and stewarded collective works such as Womanhouse, the Dinner Party (permanently housed in the Brooklyn Museum of Art), and Birth Project. Her work and feminist philosophy have had a worldwide impact on both the art community and the larger culture.

COHEN, AMY Born in 1942, Cohen entered Madison, Wisconsin, in utero and left at age eighteen months. After that she lived in many states, none for longer than the six years she spent earning a Ph.D. in mathematics at the University of California at Berkeley. She has spent the last half of her life teaching math at Rutgers, the State University of New Jersey. Her husband, Larry Corwin, died in 1992. Her son is at grad school in Eugene, Oregon.

COHEN, LEAH HAGER She is a writer and journalist who was raised at the Lexington School for the Deaf in New York, where her father was director of child care and her mother taught the nursery school. The family lived on the premises, yet Cohen was—and is—a hearing person. She lives outside of Boston with her husband and two children.

COHEN, SASHA [Alexandra Pauline] Named after her mother's favorite ballerina, the champion ice skater was born on October 26, 1984. Cohen's mother, a former ballerina, is of Ukrainian descent, so Cohen speaks Russian. She even translated competitor Viktoria Volchkova's interview responses from Russian to English at the 2001 Trophée Lalique competition. She began skating at around the age of seven. After her breakthrough performance at the 2000 U.S. Nationals, where she won her first silver medal, she has been recognized as a skater with a very exciting future. Sasha would like to win both Olympic and World medals. She enjoys fashion design and would like to be a fashion designer later in life. For now, she sticks to designing her own dresses.

COLWIN, LAURIE Born in 1944, she was primarily a writer of fiction, but also wrote about cooking and food. Her works include *Happy All the Time* and *The Lone Pilgrim*. A native of Manhattan, Colwin was well educated and knowledgeable about just about everything (except baseball). She worked as an editor in book publishing and as a translator, from the Yiddish, for Isaac Bashevis Singer. She died in her sleep, of heart failure, in 1992; she was forty-eight.

COMDEN, BETTY Born Elizabeth Cohen somewhere between 1915 and 1919, Comden, along with her lifetime friend and partner Adolph Green, created some of America's best-loved stage and film musicals, from *On the Town* and *Singin' in the Rain* to *The Will Rogers Follies*. She has been a powerful force in American theater since the 1940s. Among the partners' awards are five Tonys, a Grammy, and an Obie. Comden has been inducted into both the Songwriters Hall of Fame and the Theater Hall of Fame.

CONNELLY, JENNIFER The Academy Award– and Golden Globe–winning best supporting actress (2001, *A Beautiful Mind*), Connelly was born in 1970 and grew up in Brooklyn Heights. She began modeling when she was ten, moved on to TV commercials, and was soon introduced to Sergio Leone, who was seeking a young girl to dance in his gangster epic *Once Upon a Time in America* (1984). Connelly is married to British actor Paul Bettany, with whom she has a son; her first son was fathered by photographer David Dugan. She has been featured in a number of films, including *House of Sand and Fog* (2003), *Waking the Dead* (2001), *Pollock* (2000), and *Requiem for a Dream*

(2000). An admirer of the Dalai Lama, she attended Yale and Stanford and speaks Italian, French, and some Japanese.

COOK, BLANCHE WEISEN Born in 1941, this American poet, journalist, and professor of history has authored many groundbreaking works, including a two-volume biography of Eleanor Roosevelt. She has taught at institutions of higher education, such as Hunter College, John Jay College, and City University of New York. Her fields of scholarship encompass women's history and U.S. international relations, war, peace, and imperialism.

CORI, GERTY THERESA The first American woman to receive the Nobel Prize for medicine and physiology (1947), which she shared with her husband, Dr. Carl F. Cori, and Dr. B. A. Houssay of Argentina, for their discovery of the course of the catalytic conversion of glycogen; she was the third female and the first Jewish American woman Noblest. Born Cori Radnitz on August 15, 1896, in Prague, she and her husband emigrated to the United States in 1922 and in 1928 became U.S. citizens. At the Washington University School of Medicine in St. Louis, Carl became chairman of the Department of Pharmacology while Cori was granted a token research position; she did not become a full professor until the year she received the Nobel. For ten years, while continuing her laboratory activities, she suffered with myelofibrosis, until she succumbed to the disease on October 26, 1957.

CROSS, AMANDA See Heilbrun, Carolyn G.

DANZIGER, RAQUY Born in Michigan in 1970, she grew up in a family of classical musicians and was trained as a pianist. In her travels to India, she discovered hand drumming. Today, Danziger's performances on the dumbek, the Egyptian goblet drum, and ancient Middle Eastern bowed instruments have made her one of the most sought-after musicians in the genre. She is also one of today's leading educators of Middle Eastern drumming, teaching hundreds of students in New York, lecturing and giving master classes and workshops all over the world, and inspiring a wave of what she calls "dumbek fever."

DAYAN, YAËL Daughter of Ruth and the late General Moshe Dayan, she was born in Israel in 1939. Elected as a Labor Party Member of Knesset in June of 1992, she continues to serve as a leading member of the Meretz party, part of the left-wing opposition to the Sharon government. She founded the Committee for the Advancement of the Status of Women and is deeply involved in the peace movement in the Middle East. The recipient of many honors, Dayan has written political commentary for both the Hebrew and foreign press, as well as eight books, throughout her career as a journalist.

DEBORAH The daughter of Abinoam, sister of Barak, wife of Lapidoth, and grandmother of Tobit, she was the Joan of Arc and savior of Israel, having led her people against the Canaanites in the 1070s B.C.E. A great prophetess and a wise judge, who notably adjudicated under a palm tree on Mount Ephraim, unlike most city judges, she is said to have possessed a moral authority inspired by God.

DECTER, MIDGE Born Midge Rosenthal on July 25, 1927, in St. Paul, Minnesota, Decter attended university there, and then in New York, where she studied at the Jewish Theological Seminary of America and New York University. Her first job was secretary to the editor of *Commentary*, published by the American Jewish Committee, where she eventually became managing editor. She is the author of several books, serves on the board of directors of the Heritage Foundation, and is a senior fellow at the Institute of Religion and Public Life. Her second husband, Norman Podhoretz, is editor of *Commentary*. Decter has four children.

DIAMANT, ANITA She started off as a freelance journalist in the Boston area, where she still resides with her husband and teenaged daughter. In 1985, she began to write about contemporary Jewish life. Her first work of fiction, *The Red Tent*, based on chapter 34 in Genesis, became a word-of-mouth best seller in 1997. Born in 1951 in Newark, New Jersey, she spent her teens in Denver. She earned a master's degree in English from the State University of New York at Binghamton.

DIAMOND, SELMA Best remembered as the feisty, whiskey-voiced bailiff Selma Hacker in the popular television sitcom *Night Court*, the actor/comedy writer was born in Montreal on August 5, 1920. She started out selling ideas for cartoons and humorous stories to magazines, then became a comedy writer for such radio and television personalities as Milton Berle, Tallulah Bankhead, Sid Caesar, and Groucho Marx, and received nominations for an Emmy and a Golden Globe. Diamond also appeared in several films. She died of lung cancer in 1985.

DILLER, PHYLLIS Born in 1917, Diller has headlined in virtually every major supper club in the United States and scores around the world. In addition to her film, television, and stage appearances, the comedian has authored four books; recorded comedy albums; launched food, beauty, and jewelry lines; appeared as a piano soloist with one hundred symphony orchestras; and is a philanthropist and humanitarian of unstinting generosity. She did all this after rearing five children. She was thirty-seven when she began her career, and has been acknowledged and honored by many organizations for her patriotic, philanthropic, and humanitarian endeavors.

DORESS-WORTERS, PAULA Born in Boston in 1948 to Polish immigrants, Doress-Worters graduated from Suffolk University, and then married in 1963 and had two children. Active in the peace and civil rights movements in the early 1960s, and later the women's movement, she cofounded the Boston Women's Health Book Collective, cowriting the first edition of *Our Bodies, Ourselves*. She continued working with BWHBC through 1998. She is currently at Brandeis University, exploring the life of Ernestine Rose (see below), an important yet little-known nineteenth-century crusader for women's rights.

DRESCHER, FRAN The Flushing, Queens, New York, actor, born September 30, 1957, was told she had to get rid of her thick accent. At twenty-one, she moved to Hollywood, then married her high school sweetheart. In 1985, the couple was robbed and Drescher was raped. The trauma eventually led to their divorce. She wrote and starred in her own TV show, *The Nanny*. Diagnosed with cancer in 2000, she wrote a book about her experience, *Cancer, Schmancer*. She doesn't have any children but says her dog Chester is the best $500 she ever spent.

DREXLER, ROSALYN Born in 1926 in the Bronx, Drexler had a childhood filled with Marx Brothers movies and vaudeville, which influenced her writing. She married Sherman Drexler, a painter and professor at City University of New York. She's written more than thirty-five plays and novels. Her first play, *Home Movies*, won the 1964 Obie; she won another in 1979. A cofounder of the Women's Theater Council in 1972, Drexler continually addresses women's issues in her work. She won an Emmy for 1974's TV special *The Lily Show*; has novelized several motion pictures under the pseudonym Julia Sorel; paints; sculpts; and is a jazz singer. Drexler's life was the subject of the 1975 documentary *Who Does She Think She Is?*

DWORKIN, ANDREA Born Andrea Spiegel in Camden, New Jersey, in 1946, Dworkin says it was growing up on the heels of the Holocaust, A-bomb warnings, and her mother's struggle with heart disease that caused her to think about survival very early. In 1972 she had an epiphany, and vowed to dedicate her life to women's liberation. Domestic violence, which led to "decades of dislocation, poverty, and hard struggle," and her rescue from it by a feminist, served as a springboard to her revolutionary writing.

EISLER, RIANE [Tennenhaus] Well-known for her international best seller *The Chalice and The Blade* (which anthropologist Ashley Montague hailed as "the most important book since Darwin's *Origin of Species*"), Eisler was born in Austria in 1931. Her family fled the Nazis. She was raised in Havana, Cuba, then emigrated to the United States. Founder and president of the Center for Partnership Studies, macrohistorian Eisler is a charismatic speaker whose pioneering work in human rights has made her an important consultant to business and government. Dr. Eisler is increasingly recognized as one of the most original thinkers of our time. She is married to philosopher and author David Loye.

ELION, GERTRUDE B. The first woman elected to the National Inventor's Hall of Fame (1991), Elion was a pioneer in drug research who shared a Nobel Prize in physiology or medicine with her research partner George Hitchings in 1988. Born in 1918, she had to battle long-standing prejudices against women in science, and initially had trouble even getting a job. Yet her work revolutionized the way drugs were developed: she reached this height without earning a Ph.D. A warm, animated woman with a great love of life, she was also an avid photographer, an eager traveler, and an opera devotee. She died in 1999.

EPHRON, DELIA Born circa 1944 to a writing family, she is the sister of Nora and daughter of screenwriters Henry & Phoebe Ephron. A humorist and screenwriter, Delia has written many books for children and adults. Her film work as a screenwriter and producer includes *You've Got Mail*, *Sleepless in Seattle*, both of which she cowrote with her sister Nora (see below), and *Michael*. She lives in New York City.

EPHRON, NORA Delia's sister (see above) was born in 1941. Married thrice (Dan Greenberg, novelist, 1; Carl Bernstein, investigative reporter, 2; Nicholas Pileggi, crime journalist/screenwriter, 3); she first made her mark as a humorist and satirist in book form and in magazine articles. Educated at Wellesley, her first movie assignment was the Oscar-nominated screenplay for *Silkwood* (1983). Then came *Heartburn*, her roman à clef about her marriage to Carl Bernstein. Ephron turned romantic with *When Harry Met Sally* and has remained so, often cowriting with Delia.

ESTHER Hadassah was given the Persian name Esther when she was married off to Ahasuerus (a.k.a. Xerxes I, 519?–465 B.C.E.), who was unaware of the maiden's Jewish roots, and so she became queen of Persia. When, at risk of her own life, she unmasked the true motives of the wicked Haman, chief counselor to Ahasuerus, in seeking to slaughter the Jews, her people were saved.

EVE The historic concept "the Mother of All Living" predates the Bible, finding roots in India and Assyria. Although we cannot consider her to be Jewish, certainly Eve, who is said to have lived c. pre-4000 B.C.E., should be considered the mother of Jews.

FALK, MARCIA [Lee] Born and raised in New York, she graduated magna cum laude from Brandeis University with a B.A. in philosophy, and from Stanford, where she earned a Ph.D. She was also a Fulbright scholar in Bible and Hebrew literature at the Hebrew University in Jerusalem. In addition to writing her own poetry, Falk has devoted herself to translating the work of other women poets, especially those writing in Hebrew and Yiddish. She is noted for her liturgical creations and her verse translation of the Song of Songs.

FEINSTEIN, DIANNE The first woman to represent California in the U.S. Senate (1992–), Feinstein was born into the Goldman family on June 23, 1933, in San Francisco. Educated at Stanford University, she won her first election as vice-president of the student body there. In 1969, she was elected to the San Francisco Board of Supervisors, from which she was considering retirement when Mayor George Moscone was fatally shot on November 27, 1978; Feinstein immediately became acting mayor. It was during this year that her second husband, neurosurgeon Bertram Feinstein, died. She served as mayor until 1988; then, with the support of her third husband, Richard C. Blum, made her successful bid for the Senate.

FELD, MERLE Co-initiator of *havurot*, celebrated throughout the United States, Feld was born in Crown Heights, Brooklyn, in 1947. Always curious about Jewish life, she became involved in peace activism during a sabbatical in Israel with her family in 1989, facilitating an all-women Israeli-Palestinian dialogue group and demonstrating regularly with Women in Black, a group protesting the Occupation. These experiences led to her play, *Across the Jordan*. Married, with two children, Feld has also written essays, poems, and a spiritual memoir.

FERBER, EDNA A novelist, playwright, and scenarist, Ferber found solace in literature throughout a nomadic midwestern childhood during which she suffered the slings of anti-Semitism. Born on August 15, 1885, in Kalamazoo, Michigan, she worked on a number of newspapers in her twenties. It was during her convalescence from a serious illness that she started to write, and was soon publishing a book a year! She began a collaboration with playwright George S. Kaufman in the mid-1920s that produced 1932's *Dinner at Eight*, followed by *Stage Door* (1936), and others. Ferber's novels are classics: *Giant* (1952), *Show Boat* (1926), and *So Big* (1925), which won her the Pulitzer Prize. Eight of her novels and two collections of short stories were made into films; Ferber wrote many of those screenplays. She lost her battle with cancer and died on April 16, 1968.

FIELDS, DOROTHY Born in 1905 into a theatrical family, this daughter of the famed vaudevillian Lew Fields fortunately did not listen to his warnings against a life in show business. With composer Jimmy McHugh, she created such hits as "I Can't Give You Anything but Love," "Sunny Side of the Street," and "I'm in the Mood for Love." She and her brother Herbert created the libretto for the musical *Annie Get Your Gun*. Her stories of persevering young women produced shows like *Redhead*, *A Tree Grows in Brooklyn*, and *Sweet Charity*. Fields was the first female lyricist to receive an Academy Award (1936), a Tony Award (1959), and membership in the Songwriters Hall of Fame (1971).

FIELDS, TOTIE Born Sophie Feldman in 1931, Totie was a New York–accented *yenta* who did self-deflating fat jokes amid extroverted *kvetching*. She began performing in the Catskills in 1963, and became a regular on *The Ed Sullivan Show* in the '70s. Diabetic, her health began to fail at that time. In 1976, her leg had to be amputated. After being fitted with an artificial leg, she returned to work saying, "I don't want anyone feeling sorry for me." Two years later, in 1978, she died, inspirational, outrageous, and funny to the end.

FIRESTONE, SHULAMITH A Canadian-American writer and editor, born in 1945, Firestone was one of the first radical feminists. She claimed that the inequality between the sexes was a result of politics and culture. Love, specifically, evolved as a type of plot designed to "keep women in their place."

FISHER, CARRIE Daughter of singer Eddie Fisher and actor Debbie Reynolds, Fisher was born in 1956. She was once married to singer-songwriter Paul Simon. Her role as Princess Leia in *Star Wars* made her a cultural icon. On the literary front, she won the Los Angeles Pen Award for best first novel, *Postcards from the Edge*, which was followed by two more best sellers. She continues to write, and is developing a TV series and two new films. Fisher is also a much sought-after "script doctor."

FRAIBERG, SELMA Born Selma Horwitz in Detroit in 1918, Fraiberg gained success in three careers: as a psychoanalyst specializing in the treatment of children, she wrote the classic *The Magic Years* (1959); in her work with blindness in infants, which led to her *Insights from the Blind* (1977); and in her work dealing with maternal bonding with infants. She founded the Child Development Project at the University of Michigan in the late 1970s, which served troubled families and trained clinicians.

FRANK, ANNE Her world-famous diary charts the years 1942 to 1944, when her family was hiding from Nazis in a sealed-off office flat in Amsterdam. Born in 1929, Anne recorded her hopes, frustrations, and observations. The diary has been translated into some sixty languages, and adapted into a stage play and several motion pictures. Anne Frank received her diary in 1942 for her thirteenth birthday. Her last entry was August 1, 1944; on August 4, the family was arrested.

FRANK, RAY The first woman accepted at Hebrew Union College (Cincinnati), Frank was in all likelihood the first woman to preach from a Jewish pulpit. Based in Oakland, California, she was born April 10, 1861. Her first sermon was on the eve of Rosh Hashanah in Spokane, Washington. Well received, she was asked back for Yom Kippur. Dubbed "the Maiden in the Temple" and "the Jewess in the Pulpit," Frank, a journalist, found herself in the midst of a new career. At times erroneously referred to as the "lady rabbi," she relinquished the pulpit when she married Simon Litman, who wrote a posthumous memoir about his wife. She died on October 10, 1948.

FRANKLIN, ROSALIND [Elsie] Born in London on July 25, 1920, she was a scientist whose life and work generated much controversy. Responsible for much of the research and discovery work that led to the understanding of the structure of deoxyribonucleic acid (DNA), she was not among those awarded the Nobel Prize for the double-helix model of DNA in 1962. Even though her father was decidedly against higher education for women, she earned a doctorate in chemistry from Cambridge University in 1945. Franklin died on April 16, 1958, at age thirty-seven from ovarian cancer. She was a true pioneer in molecular biology and a scientist of the first rank.

FREED, LYNN Born and raised in Durban, South Africa, she came to New York as a graduate student in English literature, receiving her M.A. and Ph.D. from Columbia University. She has written several novels, and her short fiction and essays have appeared in the *New Yorker, Harper's,* and *Atlantic Monthly,* among other publications; her work is included in a number of anthologies, and is in translation abroad. Freed is the recipient of several awards and fellowships. She lives in northern California.

FREUD, ANNA The founder of child psychoanalysis, she began her career under the wing of her famous father (Sigmund Freud). Born in Austria in 1895, Freud dedicated most of her life to her father and his work. Where he left off, she picked up—and made it her own. She is most noted for her work with children and the concept of children undergoing analysis. In addition, she taught at and maintained the Hampstead Child Therapy Clinic in London, where she had emigrated. Until her death in 1982, Freud never stopped refining child psychoanalysis.

FRIEDAN, BETTY [Naomi] Born Betty Goldstein on February 14, 1921, she saw for herself, as a young reporter for the *Workers' Press* in New York in the 1940s, that women were paid a fraction of what men were paid; she saw that when the men returned from the war, the women were fired. Then, when Betty Friedan asked for maternity leave, she was fired. Her book, *The Feminine Mystique,* launched the women's liberation movement. Its basis was that women's unhappiness was caused by society, which "does not permit women to accept or gratify their basic need to grow and fulfill their potentialities as human beings." She helped found NOW (the National Organization for Women) and became its first president. She worked to pass Title VII as well as the Equal Rights Amendment. She has been a visiting scholar at many universities and think tanks around the country, and has won myriad honors and awards.

FRIEDMAN, BONNIE Born in Manhattan in 1958, Friedman grew up in the Bronx. Her earlier works were written when she lived in New England. However, she and her husband now live at the top of a brownstone in Brooklyn with their two cats. An educator who currently teaches at Drew University in Madison, New Jersey, she is the author of *Writing Past Dark: Envy, Fear, Distraction and Other Dilemmas in the Writer's Life*, which is itself anthologized in seven writing textbooks, among other works.

FRISCHMANN, JUSTINE [ELINOR] The guitarist-vocalist-songwriter began performing professionally in the early '90s, forming the group Suede with her boyfriend Brett Anderson. After her relationship with Anderson ended, she formed Elastica, recruiting guitarist Donna Matthews, drummer Justin Welch, and bassist Annie Holland. In 1993, Elastica released its first single, the two-minute punk rocker "Stutter," in a limited edition that quickly sold out. The group's first album debuted in March 1995. She was born in Twickenham, England, on September 16, 1969, and studied architecture, her father's field, at University College, London.

FURNESS, BETTY Born in 1916 to a pioneering radio executive, she appeared in a string of forgettable ingenue roles in Hollywood films. She was the spokeswoman for Westinghouse for years. During Lyndon Johnson's administration, Furness was appointed to several important executive positions in the field of consumer protection. While working as consumer affairs director at New York's NBC-TV affiliate in 1974, she began a long association with the *Today Show* as the show's consumer reporter/advocate. She died in 1994.

GELLER, LAURA Her articles on Jewish feminism have appeared in *Tikkun, Sh'ma,* and *Reform Judaism.* Born in 1950, she is the first woman rabbi to lead a major metropolitan synagogue—Temple Emanuel in Beverly Hills, California. Previously, she served as executive director of the American Jewish Congress, as the University of Southern California Hillel Director, and on the faculty at the University of Judaism. She has received many honors, including the Woman of the Year Award from the California State Legislature.

GERBER, MERRILL JOAN Born in the early 1940s, this prize-winning novelist and short story writer garnered the Ribalow Award from *Hadassah* magazine for *King of the World,* "the best English-language book of fiction on a Jewish theme." Her story, "I Don't Believe This," won an O. Henry Prize Award in 1986. Prolific and well-published, she currently teaches fiction writing at the California Institute of Technology in Pasadena.

GILLIGAN, CAROL An internationally acclaimed psychologist, she was born Carol Friedman on November 28, 1936, in New York City. The social psychologist came to be known as the founder of "difference feminism"; her conclusions were published in the 1982 watershed book, *In a Different Voice: Psychological Theory and Women's Development.* After over thirty-five years on the faculty of Harvard, where she earned her doctorate, she joined the faculty of New York University in 2003. Among her many awards are the Grawemeyer Award in Education and the Heinz Award. In 1996, she was named one of *Time* magazine's twenty-five most influential people of the year.

GINSBURG, RUTH BADER An intelligent, ambitious woman, Brooklyn-born Ruth Ginsburg faced enormous discrimination as a woman in the world of law. Yet this was overcome completely when she became the second woman nominated to the Supreme Court of the United States (after Sandra Day O'Connor); President Clinton nominated her to the High Court in 1993. Born in 1933 and educated at Cornell and Columbia Universities, Ginsburg also became the first tenured female professor at Columbia. For eight years, Ginsburg did counseling for the Women's Rights Project (1972–1980), which she founded, for the American Civil Liberties Union. She has exhibited a sensitivity to women's issues and has taken moderate positions on cases before the High Court.

GINZBURG, EUGENIA [Semyonovna] Born around 1907, this Russian historian was a loyal Communist Party member when, in 1937, she was arrested and falsely charged as a Trotskyist terrorist counterrevolutionary. Her memoir, *Within the Whirlwind,* recounts the eighteen years she spent in one of Stalin's concentration camps during the Great Purges, one of nearly six million people who were arrested on trumped-up charges, millions of whom were executed or perished in prisons and camps. She survived her internment, and died a free woman in 1967. *Into the Whirlwind,* a play based on her memoir, was first produced in Russia.

GINZBURG, NATALIA [Levi] Writer, playwright, and translator, Ginzburg wrote about her unconventional family and its opposition to fascist oppression. Born in Palermo in 1916, she was Jewish on her father's side and Catholic on her mother's; she was raised an atheist. The Levi household was a meeting place for intellectuals. In 1938 she married editor and political activist Leone Ginzburg; they had three children. A hero of the Resistance, he was arrested, and died after being tortured in 1944. In hiding, Natalia returned to Rome after the Allied liberation. Her first novella, *La Strada Che Va in Città* (The Road to the City), appeared in 1942 under the pseudonym Alessandra Tornimparti. In 1964, she won the Premio Strega, the equivalent of America's Pulitzer Prize. Ginzburg was elected to the Italian Parliament in 1983 as an independent left-wing deputy. She died of cancer on October 7, 1991.

GLÜCKEL OF HAMELN (a.s.a. Glueckel) Born in Hamburg in 1645 into a prominent patrician family, she was married off to Chayim (a.s.a. Chaim) of Hameln at fourteen. She became Chayim's adviser in all practical matters, even while bearing and raising their twelve children. After his death in 1689, she carried on his business and financial enterprises, but became depressed. In an attempt to overcome her loss, she wrote a diary, a memoir of her life, begun when she was forty-six. Glückel's writings became incredibly important to historians because they are one of just a few surviving Jewish documents about that period written by a woman.

GOLDBERG, LEA Born in Kovno, Lithuania, in 1911, she immigrated to Palestine in 1935 after receiving her Ph.D. in Semitic languages at the University of Bonn. A member of the Shlonsky group of modern poets, her work became widely published. She was also a children's author, theater critic, translator (Tolstoy's *War and Peace*), editor at the *Al Hamishmar* newspaper, and a children's book editor. In 1952 she established the Hebrew University's Department of Comparative Literature, which she chaired until her death in 1970. She was awarded the Israel Prize posthumously.

GOLDMAN, EMMA An early advocate of free speech, women's rights, and labor unions, Goldman was born in Russia in 1869. She emigrated to the United States in 1886. With the anarchist Alexander Berkman, she published the paper *Mother Earth*. Between 1893 and 1917, she was imprisoned several times on such charges as inciting to riot, publicly advocating birth control, and opposition to military conscription. In 1919, she and Berkman were deported to Russia; disillusioned with the Soviet government, she left there in 1921. She died in 1940. Goldman stands as a major figure in the history of American radicalism and feminism.

GOODMAN, ELLEN Writer of a column syndicated in over four hundred newspapers, she was born Ellen Holtz in Newton, Massachusetts, on April 11, 1941. She started writing for the *Boston Globe* in 1967, working the women's pages right through her pregnancy. She was married from 1963 to 1971, when she was divorced. The five published collections of her columns all deal with social change and the family, politics, generation gaps, ethics, abortion, and the ever-changing status of women. Her second marriage, in 1982, was to Bob Levey, a fellow journalist on the *Globe*. In 1980 her columns earned Goodman the Pulitzer Prize.

GORDIMER, NADINE A South African novelist and short story writer who received the Booker Prize in 1974 and the Nobel Prize for literature in 1991, her works deal with the moral and psychological tensions of her racially divided country. A founding member of the Congress of South African Writers, she never considered going into exile, even at the height of the apartheid regime. Born in 1923 into a well-off family in Springs, Transvaal, an East Rand mining town outside Johannesburg, she is the daughter of a Jewish Latvian father and British mother. She was educated in a convent school. Her first published story appeared in the Johannesburg magazine *Forum* when she was fourteen. In addition to her literary works are books of nonfiction and television documentaries.

GORNICK, VIVIAN Born around 1935–1938, Gornick is a New York–born, –bred, and –educated writer. She began writing for the *Village Voice* in 1973, concentrating on the burgeoning feminist movement of which she was an early member. In the years since, her pieces have appeared in many major publications. She has written eight books, including *In Search of Ali-Mahmoud*, *Woman in Sexist Society: Studies in Power and Powerlessness*, and *Approaching Eye Level*. She has also taught nonfiction writing at universities; founded THEA, a not-for-profit senior residence in Manhattan for women and men in the arts; and is researching a book on Elizabeth Cady Stanton.

GOTTLIEB, DAPHNE Born in Philadelphia in 1978, this San Francisco–based performance poet's collection *Why Things Burn* (2001) has won much acclaim. She has been widely published in journals and anthologies, including http://nerve.com, *Exquisite Corpse*, and *Short Fuse*. Besides anchoring two national poetry performance tours, Gottlieb has also appeared across the country with the Slam America bus tour and with the notorious all-girl wordsters Sister Spit. She is the poetry editor of the online queer literary magazine *Lodestar Quarterly*, as well as *Other* magazine and was a co-organizer of ForWord Girls, the first spoken word festival for anyone who is, has been, or will be a girl, held in September 2002. She received her M.F.A. from Mills College.

GOTTLIEB, LINDA Golden Globe Award winner (*Dirty Dancing*, 1987), producer Gottlieb was born around 1941 in the United States. In addition to her award-winning film, the writer-producer created *Women in Limbo* and *Soldier's Girl*. She has also been an innovative executive producer for TV's daytime drama, *One Life to Live*.

GOTTLIEB, LYNN Born April 12, 1949, in Bethlehem, Pennsylvania, Gottlieb has theatrical roots: her mother was a puppeteer and director of a theater. A high school visit to Israel kindled Lynn's desire to become a rabbi—a tough row to hoe in 1964. She earned a B.S. at Hebrew University in Jerusalem, then studied at Hebrew Union College and the Jewish Theological Seminary. Gottlieb's theatrical background enabled her to use pantomime for religious services and storytelling and she became the spiritual leader of a deaf congregation in Hollis, New York. Her involvement with the New Jewish Agenda, a movement in alternative Judaism, eventually helped her become ordained in 1981. Rabbi Gottlieb travels across the nation as a storyteller.

GRANT, LEE Primarily a stage actor, she was born Lyova Haskell Rosenthal in New York City in 1929. Trained at Juilliard and the Neighborhood Playhouse, she won the New York Critics Circle Award at twenty for Broadway's *Detective Story*, garnering awards for her reprisal of the role on film. Her film career was derailed when she and her playwright husband, Arnold Manoff, were blacklisted by Hollywood. She returned to film and television in the mid-'60s, garnering two Emmy awards for outstanding performance by an actress in a supporting role in a drama for *Peyton Place* (1964) and in a leading role for *The Neon Ceiling* (1971); and an Academy Award for best supporting actress for *Shampoo* (1976). Grant became a film director in 1980 with the moving *Tell Me a Riddle*.

GRATZ, REBECCA She founded the Female Hebrew Benevolent Society and the Hebrew Sunday School Society in Philadelphia, the model for all Jewish education in America, both of which continued to do their work for 150 years. Born in 1781, she died on August 27, 1869, outliving all but her youngest sibling, most of her friends, and many of her nieces and nephews. To the end, she remained actively involved on the boards of the many organizations she'd help to found. By devoting her adult life to providing relief for the underprivileged and securing religious, moral, and material sustenance for all of Philadelphia's Jews, Gratz helped define a new identity for American women.

GREEN, HANNAH See Joanne Greenberg.

GREENBERG, BLU Born in 1936, Greenberg is an author and lecturer who cofounded and served as the first president of the Jewish Orthodox Feminist Alliance; she has served on the boards of many organizations. She was a participant in Bill Moyers's *Genesis* special on PBS and serves on the Board of Religious Advisors to PBS's *Religion and Ethics Newsweekly*. She is married to Rabbi Irving Greenberg. They have five children and twelve grandchildren.

GREENBERG, JOANNE Born in Brooklyn in 1932, Greenberg is an internationally renowned, award-winning author of twelve novels and four collections of short stories. Much of her work has been published under the pseudonym Hannah Green. Her best-selling novel, *I Never Promised You a Rose Garden*, is a semi-autobiographical account of a teenage girl's three-year struggle with madness. Greenberg was educated at the American University of Colorado, where she became interested in Native American culture. Among other honors, she received the Jewish Book Council of America Award in 1963.

GRIFFIN, SUSAN A well-known writer, poet, educator, and social thinker, she was born in 1943. Her works have been influential in several movements, shaping both ecological and feminist thought. She has been the recipient of several awards and grants, including a MacArthur grant for peace and international cooperation, and an Emmy for her play *Voices*. She lectures widely throughout the United States and Europe, and lives and teaches writing and the creative process privately in Berkeley, California.

GROSSMAN, SUSAN C. Born in 1955 in New York City, Rabbi Grossman is the spiritual leader of Beth Shalom Congregation in Washington, D.C. Before entering the rabbinate, Rabbi Grossman directed Holocaust programming for the National Jewish Resource Center (now CLAL) under Rabbi Yitz Greenberg and worked for many years as a journalist and editor. Perhaps best known for the anthology she co-edited with Orthodox activist Rivka Haut, *Daughters of the King: Women and the Synagogue* (1994), she was identified by the *Jewish Week* (New York) as one of the forty-five Jewish leaders to watch in the next century. A noted scholar, accomplished lecturer, storyteller, and author, she serves on the prestigious Committee for Jewish Law and Standards of the Conservative Movement and is currently working on the Conservative Movement's new Torah commentary. Rabbi Grossman is married to David Boder. They have one son.

GRUBER, RUTH Born in 1911 in Brooklyn, a child of Russian immigrants, she was a brilliant scholar and, at age twenty, became the youngest person in the world to obtain a Ph.D. A journalist for the *New York Times* and the *New York Herald Tribune*, she covered many dangerous stories, publishing several books about her adventures. Most famous, perhaps, was the story of the one thousand Jewish refugees she escorted from Naples, Italy, to the United States. At the age of forty, Gruber decided to "settle down": she married and was twice widowed, and has two children and four grandchildren. At age seventy-four, she visited isolated Jewish villages in Ethiopia; at age ninety she went on a twenty-city book tour. Among her many honors are a National Jewish Book Award and the Na'amat Golda Meir Human Rights Award. She is often referred to as "Mother Ruth."

GUTMANS, SAREL Some of the letters written by Gutmans, a householder from Bohemia who lived in the 1620s, have survived and are used as primary sources by scholars today.

HAHN, EMILY "MICKEY" A staff writer at the New Yorker for seventy years, she was one of the first women to receive a bachelor of science degree in engineering from the University of Wisconsin–Madison (1926). With a thirst to see the world, Hahn went on to document her international experiences in fifty-two books as well as 181 pieces for the New Yorker. The loving owner of several pet monkeys, she devoted much of her time in her later years to writing about wildlife preservation and monkeys. Born in 1905, Hahn was married to British army officer Charles Boxer. She died in New York in 1997.

HANNAH Wife of Elkanah, she was a pious woman who was, nonetheless, unhappy because of her childlessness. She prayed fervently, in private and in silence, a practice unheard of in her day. Her prayers were answered when Samuel, who was to become the great prophet and leader of Israel, was born to her. She later bore five more children.

HAWN, GOLDIE [Jean] Actor-comedian Hawn was born in Washington, D.C., on November 21, 1945, to a family who, on her father's side, descended from one of the signers of the Declaration of Independence. She has been with her partner, actor Kurt Russell, since 1983, with whom she has a son. She has another son and daughter from her first marriage, and she became a first-time grandmother in early 2004. Famed for her kooky persona on TV's Laugh-In in the early '60s, Hawn has since won a Golden Globe and an Academy Award for best actress in a supporting role for Cactus Flower (1969).

HEILBRUN, CAROLYN G. An only child, Carolyn Gold was born in East Orange, New Jersey, in 1926, but spent her childhood in Manhattan. An important feminist scholar, she was also beloved by mystery buffs under her pseudonym Amanda Cross. A Wellesley graduate, she met her husband, James Heilbrun, while he was a student at Harvard. She began teaching English literature in 1960 at Columbia, where she remained until 1993. Among her many nonfiction works were the watershed books Toward a Recognition of Androgyny (1973) and Reinventing Womanhood (1979). It was in 1964, with three children in tow, that she first created the beautiful English professor and sleuth Kate Fansler: Heilbrun did not reveal that she was Amanda Cross until after she was granted tenure at Columbia—the first woman in the English Department to earn that position. Believing in the freedom of the elderly "to choose one's death," Heilbrun took her life in July 2003.

HELLMAN, LILLIAN Hellman's childhood was spent alternately with her father's family in New Orleans' Garden District, where she was born on June 20, 1905, and her mother's family, the upper-middle-class Newhouses of New York. In 1925 she was a reader of film scenarios in Hollywood, where she met Dashiell Hammett, with whom she remained attached romantically and professionally until his death in 1960. In 1952, subpoenaed to appear before the House Un-American Activities Committee, her famous response was: "I cannot and will not cut my conscience to fit this year's fashions." She won two New York Drama Critics Circle Awards and, for her first memoir, *An Unfinished Woman* (1969), a National Book Award. A screenwriter as well, she also wrote the book for the 1957 musical *Candide*, for which Leonard Bernstein composed the music. Hellman was one of the first internationally known women playwrights. She died of cardiac arrest on June 30, 1984, at her summer home in Martha's Vineyard.

HERMAN, JUDITH LEWIS Dr. Herman, born in New York City (1942), received her degree from Harvard Medical School and her training in general and community psychiatry at Boston University Medical Center. The author of two award-winning books (*Father-Daughter Incest*, 1981; and *Trauma and Recovery*, 1992), she has lectured widely on the subject of sexual and domestic violence.

HERMAN, SUSAN Born in 1942, Dr. Herman was cofounder and director of the Interlocken Center for Experiential Education in New Hampshire through 1986. She has taught organizational behavior and human resource management at several colleges and is currently director of undergraduate studies at the School of Management, University of Fairbanks, Alaska. The author of a book and numerous scholarly articles, Dr. Herman is especially interested in Holocaust studies, cooking, mountaineering (she recently climbed the major peaks in the Grand Teton range), reading, and knitting.

HILLESUM, ETTY Born January 15, 1914, in Middelburg, Holland, she then moved to Amsterdam. Her diary, begun nine months after Hitler invaded the Netherlands, follows the two years she spent at Westerbork, a detention camp in the north of Holland, where Jews were held before transport to the death camps of Poland. Survivors have reported that she was a "shining personality" for them. Her eight handwritten notebooks, and several letters she wrote to family and friends, were first published in English as *An Interrupted Life*, (1982; originally, *Das gestoerte Leben*). In September of 1943 she was transported to Auschwitz and died there at the end of November; her entire family was also killed.

HIMMELFARB, GERTRUDE Born in 1922, she is professor emeritus of history at the Graduate School of the City University of New York, where, previously, she was chairman of the doctoral program in history. Professor Himmelfarb received her doctorate from the University of Chicago in 1950. She also studied at the Jewish Theological Seminary and at Girton College, Cambridge. The recipient of many honorary degrees and fellowships, she sits on several prestigious councils and editorial boards. The writer and editor of several books, her work focuses on Victorian England and on contemporary society and culture.

HOFFMAN, EVA (a.s.a. Ewa) Born in Poland in 1945, she is the author of several notable books, among them *Exit Into History: A Journey through the New Eastern Europe*. She received a Ph.D. in English and American Literature from Harvard. She has been a professor of literature and of creative writing at several institutions, including Columbia, the University of Minnesota, and Tufts; she was an editor and writer at the *New York Times* from 1979 to 1990, serving as senior editor of its *Book Review* from 1987 to 1990.

HOLLIDAY, JUDY Born Judith Tuvim in New York City on June 21, 1921, she got a job, after graduating from high school, in Orson Welles's Mercury Theater—as a switchboard operator. She toured the nightclub circuit with a comedy group, The Revuers, with Betty Comden (see above) and Adolph Green. They went to Hollywood and Holliday got her break with the film *Adam's Rib*, starring Spencer Tracy and Katharine Hepburn. She was signed to play Billie Dawn in *Born Yesterday*, a role she had played on stage; she won an Academy Award for her performance. Her film career was damaged by the infamous House Un-American Activities Committee, though she continued to work on stage. Only thirty-nine when she became ill with cancer, she died three weeks before her forty-fourth birthday in New York City on June 7, 1965.

HOLTZMAN, FANNY ELLEN American born in 1903, Holtzman was a highly successful entertainment lawyer during Hollywood's heyday. Jet-setting between Hollywood, New York, and Europe, she rubbed elbows with celebrities, royalty, presidents, and Supreme Court Justices. At the height of the Depression, Holtzman was a millionaire. She died in 1980.

HOWELL, CAROL K. Born in 1954 in Johnstown, Pennsylvania, her birth name was Kuperstock. Howell graduated from the Iowa Writers Workshop in 1985, taught college writing courses for twenty-six years, and now lives in Minnesota where her husband teaches at MSU and they home school their teenage son and daughter. She is finishing up her first novel (about Jewish witches in New Orleans) and beginning work on a second. Her short stories have appeared in many journals and magazines.

HOWLAND, BETTE An American writer, born in 1937, Howland was educated at the University of Chicago. In the '70s she was the recipient of a MacArthur "genius" grant as well as a Guggenheim.

HULDAH A prophetess who lived in Jerusalem and was possibly a librarian, Huldah was married to Shallum, keeper of the temple vestments. When she revealed the evil that was to befall the people of Judah because of God's anger at those who burned incense to foreign gods, she accurately prophesied that the tender-hearted King Josiah would be spared the agony of seeing his nation desolated.

HURST, FANNIE Her career spanned over fifty years, during which she wrote seventeen novels, nine volumes of short stories, and three plays; collaborated on a number of films; and hosted a television talk show. Born on October 18, 1889, in Hamilton, Ohio, to Bavarian immigrants, she was raised in St. Louis. In 1909, she went to Columbia University for graduate courses—and stayed in New York. She worked odd jobs, studied people on the street—and wrote. By 1925, she was one of the highest-paid writers in the United States. A staunch friend of Eleanor Roosevelt, Hurst supported the New Deal and labor, chaired government commissions, raised funds for refugees, and was a resolute supporter of Israel. When she died on February 23, 1968, she left $1 million to Brandeis and Washington Universities to establish professorships in creative writing. In 1915, she had secretly married pianist Jacques Danielson, and they each had their own residence; they remained happily married until his death in 1952.

HYMAN, JUDITH PARTNOW She works as a psychoanalyst, a clinical social worker, and a marriage family counselor. Born in Brooklyn, in 1938, she practices in her home office in Encino, California, where her patients can delight in viewing her garden, which she lovingly cultivates. She teaches and supervises students of psychology and psychoanalysis, creates seminars for the professional community, and has published research on fathers and their babies. She has three married children, seven grandchildren, and is the sister of Elaine Bernstein Partnow and Susan Partnow (see below).

JACOBY, SUSAN A newspaper columnist who began her career as a reporter for the *Washington Post,* Jacoby, born in 1946, is the author of numerous articles and books, among them, *Half-Jew: A Daughter's Search for Her Family's Buried Past* (2000). In it, she writes about how she was raised as a Catholic and attended parochial schools, only to discover in 1990 that she was Jewish on her father's side of the family. She lives in New York City.

JANOWITZ, TAMA In 1986, she went from relative obscurity to celebrity with her collection of offbeat, satirical short stories on Manhattan's denizens and social mores, *Slaves of New York.* Despite her star status, the writer, born in 1957, has continued to be productive, recently publishing her eighth novel.

JERUSALEM, PROSTITUTE OF [mother of the dead child] A central figure in the famous story of Solomon's wisdom, she lived c. 950 B.C.E.

JERUSALEM, PROSTITUTE OF [mother of the living child] A central figure in the famous story of Solomon's wisdom, she lived c. 950 B.C.E.

JOB, WIFE OF The Edomite from Mt. Seir who tempted her forbearing husband, she lived in the eighth century B.C.E.

JONG, ERICA The author of eight novels, she is best known for *Fear of Flying:* in print in twenty-seven languages, it has sold approximately twelve million copies worldwide. Also a poet, Jong has taught literature and writing at several universities and has received many honors. Born Emily Mann in 1942 and raised on Manhattan's Upper West Side, she attended New York's prestigious High School of Music and Art, Barnard College, and Columbia University, where she earned her M.A. in eighteenth-century English literature. Jong lives in New York City and Weston, Connecticut.

JUDITH The great heroine, she killed Holofernes, commander of Assyrian forces, when his army attacked the Jewish city of Bethulia. By so doing, the beautiful widow saved the city and brought peace to Israel. She died around 495 B.C.E.

KAHLO [DE RIVERA], FRIDA The famed Mexican painter was born on July 6, 1907.

Her father, a Jewish photographer, had emigrated from Germany to Mexico, where he met and married Frida's Mexican mother. In her late teens, Frida was in a streetcar collision that resulted in lifelong ill health and pain (she underwent thirty-two surgeries). She married the internationally famous muralist Diego Rivera, and their on-again, off-again love affair lasted until her death, on July 13, 1954. The damage to her pelvis from the accident prevented her from having children, possibly her only great regret. Kahlo was a singular personality and painter who was passionate and proud of her country and her roots.

KAHN, FLORENCE PRAG The first Jewish woman to sit in the U.S. Congress as a Representative, she served from 1925 to 1937. Born on November 9, 1866, in Salt Lake City, Utah, to Polish immigrants, her mother wrote a book titled My Life among the Mormons. They moved to San Francisco and Florence went to the University of California. In 1899, she married Julius Kahn, the newly elected Republican congressman from California. When he died, after twenty-six years of service, she was elected to replace him and served until she lost her bid for reelection in the 1936 Roosevelt landslide. She was active with Hadassah and the National Council of Jewish Women. She died on November 16, 1948, of heart disease.

KAHN, MADELINE Born on September 29, 1942, in Boston, she began acting in high school, eventually earning a doctorate in her chosen field. Featured in many Broadway productions and motion pictures, her finest years came in 1973's Paper Moon, followed the next year by Blazing Saddles as Lili Von Shtupp, a saloon singer: she was nominated for an Academy Award as best supporting actress in both films. On December 3, 1999, at age fifty-seven, Kahn died of ovarian cancer in New York.

KANIN, FAY Born in New York City in 1918, Fay Mitchell met her husband, Michael Kanin, in 1940 at RKO Studios in California, making her a sister-in-law of writer Garson Kanin and his wife, actor Ruth Gordon. Michael and Fay became a professional team devoted to screenwriting. A mover and shaker, Fay was the second female president of the Academy for Motion Picture Arts and Sciences (1983–1988) and president of the Screen Branch of the Writers Guild of America. She has produced several Broadway plays and television movies, and, during World War II, produced a radio series that promoted women's participation in the war effort. Among her awards are three Emmys and an Oscar.

KARAN, DONNA Obsessed with fashion from an early age, Karan is now one of the biggest names in fashion design. Born Donna Faske in 1948 in Queens, New York, she began experimenting with fashion while still in high school by working for Liz Claiborne as an intern. She later attended the Parsons School of Design in New York, working part time for Anne Klein. After graduating, Karan worked full time with Klein as an associate designer from 1971 until Klein's death in 1974, after which Karan branched out on her own.

KAUFMAN, BEL Born in 1911 in Germany, Belle Spiegalman emigrated to America with her family. A magna cum laude graduate of Hunter College, Kaufman went on to

win numerous awards for short stories, fiction, and nonfiction, and for a moving trib-
ute to her famous grandfather, Sholom Aleichem, titled *Memories of My Grandfather*.
The book that made her reputation was *Up the Down Staircase* (1964), which *Time* magazine called "easily the most popular novel about U.S. public schools in history."

KAUFMAN, SHIRLEY An American poet and translator, she was born in 1923 and
has lived in Israel for thirty years. Her poetry deals with daily life in Jerusalem.
Kaufman has published thirteen books of poetry and translation, winning the U.S.
Award of the International Poetry Forum in 1969 for her first book, *The Floor Keeps
Turning*.

KAUFMAN, SUE An American writer and editor, she was born in 1926 and died in
1977. Kaufamn wrote two best sellers: *Diary of a Mad Housewife* (1967) and *Falling
Bodies* (1974). Her married name was Barondess.

KAYE, JUDY American singer-actor Kaye, born around 1949, has won a slew of
awards for her stage work, including a Tony, a Theatre World Award, and an L.A.
Drama Critics' Circle Award. She has starred in Broadway shows, national tours, and
regional productions; appeared with several opera companies; and has recorded several show albums as well as her own solo album. Kaye's critically acclaimed nightclub act
has played New York and Los Angeles. She is married to actor David Green.

KELLERMAN, FAYE Born in 1952, Kellerman first introduced L.A. cop Peter Decker
and his Orthodox Jewish wife Rina Lazarus to the mystery world in 1986. Since then,
she has written ten Decker/Lazarus novels. She lives in Los Angeles with her husband,
author Jonathan Kellerman. There are close to three million copies of her books in
print.

KING, CAROLE Born on February 9, 1942, in Brooklyn, her family name was Klein.
A proficient pianist from the age of four, she was a prolific songwriter by her early teens.
When friend and neighbor Neil Sedaka embarked on his recording career, she followed
him to the New York scene, where, as a student at Queens College, she met future partner and husband, lyricist Gerry Goffin. Working as a team, they scored such pop classics as the Shirelles' "Will You Still Love Me Tomorrow," Bobby Vee's "Take Good Care
of My Baby," the Drifters' "Up on the Roof," and Little Eva's "The Locomotion." In
1967 they dissolved their partnership. She moved to Los Angeles and began a solo
career, singing as well as songwriting. Her second album, *Tapestry*, sold in excess of ten
million copies and established King as a major player in her field.

KIRCHHEIMER, GLORIA DEVIDAS She is a writer, editor, and translator whose work
has been published in a number of magazines and anthologies. Under the name Gloria
Levy, she made one of the earliest recordings of Sephardic folk songs in the United
States. She is coauthor (with Manfred Kirchheimer) of *We Were So Beloved:
Autobiography of a German Jewish Community*.

KLAGSBRUN, FRANCINE An author, columnist, and lecturer, she has written and
edited more than a dozen books. Her column, Thinking Aloud, appears monthly in the
Jewish Week. She also serves on the editorial board of *Hadassah* magazine and the

National Jewish Book Council, among others, and is an active member of the Jewish community. Klagsbrun holds an honorary Doctor of Hebrew Letters degree from the Jewish Theological Seminary. Born around 1939, she is married to Dr. Samuel C. Klagsbrun. They have a married daughter, who is a physician, and two grandchildren.

KLEINBAUM, SHARON Born around 1960, Rabbi Kleinbaum is the spiritual leader of Congregation Beth Simchat Torah in New York, the world's largest lesbian and gay synagogue. A pioneer in pastoral care for people with AIDS and their families, she was named by the *Forward*, the national Jewish weekly, as one of the country's fifty top Jewish leaders. Educated at Barnard College, Hebrew University in Jerusalem, and Oxford in England, she was ordained by the Reconstructionist Rabbinical College in Philadelphia. Rabbi Kleinbaum has lectured and published widely. She lives in Brooklyn with her partner and two daughters.

KLEPFISZ, IRENA Political activist, poet, and essayist, born in 1941, Klepfisz was fourteen when she and her mother escaped from Poland to America during World War II, the only members of their family to survive the Holocaust. In all her works, Klepfisz draws on her history of artistic and political commitment, which has long informed her precise and well-loved poetry.

KNOPF, BLANCHE WOLF She was president of Alfred A. Knopf Inc., one of the most prestigious publishing houses in the country. Born to privilege on July 30, 1894, in New York City, she married Alfred Knopf Jr. in 1916, not long after he had launched his publishing company, where she worked as all-around assistant. By 1921, she had become vice-president. Because of her knowledge of French and German, she was able to recruit many authors for the publishing house on her European trips: Guy de Maupassant, André Gide, Thomas Mann, Sigmund Freud, and others. She became president of the publishing house when her husband became chairman. Plagued by illness in her later years, she died in her sleep on June 4, 1966. A true pacesetter, Knopf paved the way for other women to break the "hardcover" ceiling in the world of publishing.

KOHUT, REBEKAH BETTELHEIM An educator and welfare worker, born in Kaschau, Hungary, in 1864, this daughter of a rabbi came to America at age three. In 1887 she married Rabbi Alexander Kohut, leader of the Conservative movement and a widower with eight children. After he died in 1894, she supported her inherited family with lectures and founded the Kohut School for Girls (1899–1904). She served as an adviser on employment to the state of New York during and after World War I, when she devoted herself to relief work for Jews in Europe. In 1923 she became president of the World Congress of Jewish Women. She died in 1951.

KOMAROVSKY, MIRRA Born in Russia in 1906, she emigrated to the United States as a teenager. A sociologist, college professor, editor, and author, Komarovsky was educated at Columbia University and taught at Barnard College (1938–1974). Her pioneering research on leisure time and unemployment, and the techniques of repeated interviews and the use of selected case histories she developed are documented in her many books and articles. She was married to Marcus A. Heyman. She died in 1999.

LANDERS, ANN Born Esther Pauline Friedman on July 4, 1918, advice columnist Landers earned a devoted following for her no-nonsense, witty style. Her parents were Russian immigrants from Vladivostok who raised their four girls in Sioux City, Iowa. In 1939, she married Jules Lederer, a hat salesman. Landers's column with the *Chicago Sun-Times*, which she stumbled into, was an immediate success in 1955 and soon went into national syndication. Landers used her position to voice her opposition to the Vietnam War, and her support for abortion rights and gun control. Her feud with her twin sister, Pauline—better known as Abigail Van Buren (see below)—fueled her popularity. At the time of her death in 2002, Landers's column was carried in over 1,200 newspapers.

LANDOWSKA, WANDA The founder of *l'Ecole de Musique Ancienne*, this Warsaw-born (1879) musician was inducted into the Recording Academy Hall of Fame. After studying at the Warsaw Conservatory, she was a prominent concert pianist before devoting herself to the harpsichord. She taught in Berlin and then in Paris, and made her first concert tour in the United States in 1923. In 1940, she emigrated to America. Teaching, playing, recording, writing, and proselytizing her beloved ancient music, she is regarded as a leader in the twentieth century's revival of the harpsichord. Married to writer Henry Lew, she died in 1959.

LAUDER, ESTÉE Born Josephine Esther Mentzer in Corona, Queens, New York, around 1904, she started her billion-dollar-a-year business with a jar of skin cream developed by her chemist uncle, initially selling it in hair salons, where she gave makeovers to bored women sitting under hair dryers. Early on, she dreamed up the hugely successful gift-with-purchase concept. She was married twice (1930–1939, 1942–1983) to Joseph Lauder, her business partner; they have been noted as generous philanthropists. At one point in her adult life, she left Judaism and converted to Roman Catholicism.

LAZARUS, EMMA Born in 1849 in New York City, she is best known for her sonnet about America, "The New Colossus," engraved on the pedestal of the Statue of Liberty. Her interest in Jewish problems was awakened by George Eliot's novel, *Daniel Deronda*, and was reinforced by the Russian pogroms of 1881–1882. Inspired, she began publishing translations of the great medieval Spanish-Jewish poets. Her essays in *Century* magazine, in reply to anti-Semitic attacks, praised her fellow Jews as pioneers of progress and expressed her joy in belonging to a people who were the victims rather than the perpetrators of massacres. She died in 1887.

LEACHMAN, CLORIS Born in Des Moines, Iowa, on April 26, 1926, Leachman is probably best known as Phyllis Lindstrom on *The Mary Tyler Moore Show*, and its spin-off *Phyllis*, yet she has had major success as a film actor, with an Academy Award–winning performance for *The Last Picture Show*; she's also won three Emmy Awards. She has had memorable turns in a number of Mel Brooks films. After twenty-six years of marriage, Leachman divorced film producer George Englund in 1979; they have five children.

LEAH One of the Four Matriarchs and the plainer daughter of Laban, who lived around 1800 B.C.E., she was innocently the cause of perhaps the first love triangle story when her father slyly sent her, under cover of darkness and veils, in place of his lovelier daughter to marry Jacob, to whom he had promised Rachel (see below). Considered one of the builders of Israel, Leah mothered Reuben, Simeon, Levi, Judah, Zebulun, and Issachar—six of the founders of the twelve tribes of Israel—and Dinah.

LEBOWITZ, FRAN Born in 1951, the humorist and journalist first hit the New York literary scene in the early '70s when Andy Warhol hired her to write a column for *Interview*. She soon became a name associated with irreverent humor and urban wit. Her books of essays, including *Metropolitan Life* and *Social Studies*, have been *New York Times* best sellers. She is also the author of a best-selling children's book, *Mr. Chas & Lisa Sue Meet Panda* (1994).

LEE, GYPSY ROSE Born Rose Louise Hovick on January 9, 1914, in Seattle, Lee made her stage debut in vaudeville at age four, starring with her sister, actor June Havoc. Her career as a burlesque artist began when she was fifteen. Dubbed the "Literary Stripper," she played higher-class venues and, in 1936, appeared in the *Ziegfeld Follies*. She wrote a couple of mystery novels, appeared in Broadway shows and in several films, and starred on her own television talk show. Her autobiography inspired the hit Broadway musical *Gypsy*, later made into a motion picture. Married three times, she had a son by director Otto Preminger. She died of cancer on April 26, 1970, in Los Angeles.

LEIFER, CAROL Born July 27, 1956, on Long Island, New York, the L.A.-based Leifer is an internationally acclaimed comic, comedy writer, and television producer. She spent three years writing for *Seinfeld*, and was the real-life inspiration for the Elaine character, played by Julia Louis-Dreyfus. Carol began her career in the late 1970s as a stand-up comic. Her big break came when David Letterman unexpectedly saw her perform, which led to twenty-five appearances on his show. One of her career dreams came true when she appeared with Johnny Carson on the *Tonight Show* two months prior to his retirement.

LERNER, GERDA Born in 1920 in Vienna into the well-to-do Kronstein family, she witnessed the Nazis' rise to power as a teenager and became involved in the underground Resistance movement. Imprisoned, then forced into exile, she found refuge in America in 1938. Here she became a naturalized citizen and married Carl Lerner; they had two children. In 1958 she returned to college and in 1966 graduated with a Ph.D. from New York's Columbia University. Dr. Lerner has since become acknowledged as one of the foremost pioneers in the field of women's history. In 1981 Dr. Lerner became the first woman in fifty years to be elected president of the Organization of American Historians.

LERNER, HARRIET GOLDHOR An internationally acclaimed expert on the psychology of women and family relationships, she was a clinical psychologist and psychotherapist at the Menninger Clinic in Topeka, Kansas, and a faculty member of the

Karl Menninger School of Psychiatry for more than two decades. She was born in Brooklyn, on November 30, 1944, to first-generation Americans, both of whom were born to Russian immigrants. Her husband, Steve Lerner, is also a clinical psychologist; they have two sons. Dr. Lerner's books, including *The Dance of Intimacy*, have been published in over thirty foreign editions with book sales of over three million. At one time, she wrote a monthly column in the now defunct *New Woman* magazine. She currently has a private practice in Lawrence, Kansas, and writes.

LEVERTOV, DENISE Poet, translator, and educator Levertov was born in Ilford, Essex, England, on October 24, 1923. Her father, raised a Hasidic Jew, had converted to Christianity; her mother was Welsh. Educated at home, Levertov decided to become a writer at age five; at seventeen her first poem was published; at twenty-three her first book came out. She married American writer Mitchell Goodman, and they moved to America, settling in New York City. She became a naturalized U.S. citizen in 1956, the same year her first American book was published, *Here and Now*. Poetry editor of the *Nation* in the '60s and of *Mother Jones* in the '70s, she went on to publish more than twenty volumes of poetry and four books of prose. In December 1997, Levertov died from complications of lymphoma.

LEVINE, EMILY Born in Nashville around 1948, raised in Connecticut and Brooklyn, and educated at Harvard, she became a television writer in L.A. after headlining in comedy clubs. When asked to speak at a think tank coconvened by Betty Friedan (see above) and the Institute for the Study of Women and Men at the University of Southern California, she welcomed the challenge of bringing her wit and intellect to a serious subject. This led to subsequent invitations, culminating in her one-woman show, "eLevine.universe," in which she synthesizes comedy and philosophy, high culture and low culture, the sublime and the ridiculous.

LEVY, NAOMI Rabbi Levy attended Cornell University where she graduated Phi Beta Kappa and summa cum laude. In 1989, she became the first female Conservative rabbi to head a pulpit on the West Coast. Her book *To Begin Again* became a national best seller and led to appearances on NBC's *Today Show* and on *Oprah*. Currently teaching at the Wexner Heritage Foundation and the Academy of Jewish Religion, Rabbi Levy lectures widely. Born in 1963, she lives in Venice, California, with her husband, Robert Eshman, editor in chief of the *Los Angeles Jewish Journal*, and their two children.

LEWINSKY, MONICA Born July 23, 1973 in San Francisco, Lewinsky was at the heart of the White House sex scandal involving President Bill Clinton. While a twenty-one-year-old unpaid intern at the White House in 1995, Lewinsky began a sexual relationship with Clinton; she was betrayed by her friend Linda Tripp, who secretly recorded telephone conversations in which Lewinsky described her relationship with the president. The rest is history. Andrew Morton's book, *Monica's Story*, recounts these events from Lewinsky's point of view. She has since launched a signature line of handbags and hosted the Fox reality series *Mr. Personality*.

LICHTENSTEIN, TEHILLA Born Tehilla Hirschensohn in Jerusalem, Palestine, in 1893, she came to America and cofounded the Society of Jewish Science in 1922. She received a B.A. from Hunter College and an M.A. from Columbia University, and was one of the first women to occupy a Jewish pulpit in the United States. She was the author of a number of books, including *What it Means to Be a Jew* (1943) and *Choosing Your Way to Happiness* (1954). Married to Rabbi Morris Lichtenstein, she died in 1973.

LIEBMAN, WENDY Voted Best Female Stand-up by the American Comedy Awards in 1997, Liebman is originally from Roslyn, Long Island, New York, and was born in 1961. She worked at a local woman's college as an administrative assistant for six years while pursuing stand-up comedy at nightclubs all over New England. In 1990 she made her television debut on the *Tonight Show Starring Johnny Carson*. Since then, she has been a regular on *Late Show with David Letterman*, has done two television specials, and has made many other television appearances. She continues to work major clubs around the country.

LISPECTOR, CLARICE Universally recognized as the most original and influential Brazilian woman writer of her time, she was born on December 10, 1920, in Tchechelnik, a small village in the Ukraine. She and her family emigrated to northeastern Brazil when she was two months old. That region's ritualistic storytelling and traditional folklore deeply influenced her writing. Her mother died when she was not yet nine years old; eleven years later, her father died. After graduating from college in 1943, she married diplomat Maury Gurgel Valente, with whom she had two sons and from whom she separated in 1956. During their marriage they were forced to leave Brazil at times. The couple shuttled back and forth from there to European countries for about sixteen years, settling for a few years in Washington, D.C. Throughout her life Lispector worked as a journalist as well as a novelist. On December 9, 1977, she died of cancer, in Rio.

LOT'S DAUGHTER (the elder) Her mother allegedly turned into a pillar of salt when, upon fleeing Sodom, she looked back. She bore a child incestuously by her father, Lot, nephew of Abraham, as did her sister. Their sons, Moab (seed of father) and Ben-ammi (son of kinsman), were ancestors of the Moabites and the Ammonites.

LOUIS, MINNIE D. A cofounder of the National Council of Jewish Women in 1893 and, earlier, the Downtown Sabbath School (later the Hebrew Technical School for Girls) in New York in 1880, she was American-born in 1841. She and her staff at the school dispensed "religion and cookies in equal measure." She died in 1922.

LUXEMBURG, ROSA Revolutionary leader, journalist, and socialist theorist, Luxemburg was murdered in Berlin on the night of January 15, 1919, while being transported to prison during the German revolution. She was an advocate of mass action, spontaneity, and workers democracy. Born in 1870 in Zamosc, in Russian Poland, into a Jewish middle-class family, she moved to Switzerland in 1889 and entered the University of Zürich, first studying natural sciences and political economy, later switching to law. During her career as a journalist she became one of the leaders of the Social

Democratic Party of the Kingdom of Poland and Lithuania and produced almost seven hundred articles, pamphlets, speeches, and books. During the 1905 Russian Revolution she developed the idea that socialism is a revolutionary process which transforms political and economic relations toward ever greater democratic control by the workers themselves. In 1912 appeared her major theoretical work, *The Accumulation of Capital*, in which she tried to prove that capitalism was doomed and would inevitably collapse on economic grounds.

MARGOLIS, SUE She was born into a "typically dysfunctional Jewish family" in Ilford, Essex, England, in the 1960s. Married to the biographer and journalist Jonathan Margolis, she has three children. She has worked for many years as a radio broadcaster and journalist and has published several humorous novels.

MARY, THE VIRGIN The mother of Jesus and the wife of Joseph, she is represented in the Talmud as a professional braider of women's hair (not a high calling in those days). She had other children whom defenders of the virgin birth claim were by Joseph from a previous marriage. Her cousin Elizabeth achieved sainthood. The only known dates of her life were from around 7 B.C.E. to 25 C.E.

MATHEWS, JESSICA TUCHMAN President of the Carnegie Endowment for International Peace, Mathews's career includes esteemed posts in the executive and legislative branches of government, in management and research in the nonprofit arena, and in journalism. She wrote a weekly column for the *Washington Post* and has written for many news, scientific, and foreign policy journals. Dr. Mathews came to Washington in 1973, the year she received her Ph.D. in molecular biology from the California Institute of Technology. She appears regularly on radio and television. Born in New York City in 1946, she is the daughter of the Pulitzer Prize–winning historian Barbara Tuchman (see below). Mathews has two children.

MATTHEWS, JILL The Junior Flyweight Champion of the World in 1998, she was born in 1964 in Manhattan and trains at Gleason's Gym in Brooklyn. A punk rock singer/guitarist, she holds a bachelor's degree in nutrition from Hunter College. In 1995 she was the first woman to win a Golden Gloves competition in New York City. She is married to David Turetsky, a Park Avenue labor attorney who doubles as her boxing manager and as the drummer in their band, Times Square. Her father-in-law, Arnold Turetsky, is a well-known Conservative rabbi. Matthews fights under the name "the Zion Lion."

MAY, ELAINE The daughter of Jack Berlin, a writer-director-actor for the Yiddish theater, was born in 1932. An improvisational comedian, she found stardom when she teamed with Mike Nichols in the 1960s; together they rose from Chicago's *Second City* to headline in nightclubs, do television, make recordings, and write their own Broadway show. After a less than amicable split, she turned to film acting, directing, and writing. She and Nichols made up years later and wrote the movie *The Birdcage* (1996). May was married as a teenager; her daughter, actor Jeannie Berlin, was born before Elaine turned eighteen.

MEIR, GOLDA A legend in her own time, Meir was one of the few women in the world to have led a nation. Her compassion for the needy, her sense of equity, and her penchant for peacemaking were characteristics apparent even when she was a youngster growing up in Milwaukee. Born to Moshe and Bluma Mabovitch in Kiev, Ukraine, on May 3, 1898, the family emigrated to the United States in 1906. After a teaching career in the United States, she and her husband, Morris Meyerson, settled in Palestine (1921), first on a kibbutz, then in Tel Aviv, where she devoted herself to the Histadrut, the national labor confederation. She was appointed to many important posts, was one of the signatories of the Declaration of the Establishment of Israel on May 14, 1948, and, in 1969, became Israel's fourth prime minister, a position she held until 1974, when she stepped down. Particularly remembered for her eloquent appeals for peace at the United Nations and her country-saving fund-raising efforts in the United States, Meir has acquired folk-hero status, and is ingrained in the public's imagination as a *bubbe* figure who rose to greatness in her nation's hour of need. Meir died in Jerusalem on December 8, 1978.

MERMAN, ETHEL Dubbed the "Queen of Broadway," Merman got her first billing as five-year-old Little Ethel Zimmerman at the local Republican Club. Born on January 16, 1909, in Astoria, New York, she learned from her father how to read music and play the piano. Her Broadway debut was in 1930's *Girl Crazy*. Her fame built on her leading roles in five Cole Porter musicals, then Irving Berlin's *Annie Get Your Gun* and *Call Me Madam*. In 1959, she starred as Mama Rose in *Gypsy*. Merman also appeared in fourteen musical films, including *Anything Goes* (1936) and *There's No Business Like Show Business* (1954). Married and divorced four times, she had two children. Her last marriage, to actor Ernest Borgnine, lasted only 38 days. Throughout her six-decade career, Merman amassed over six thousand Broadway performances, prompting Lloyds of London to deem her the healthiest and most dependable actor in the American theater. Ten months after undergoing brain surgery, Merman died of a heart attack in 1984.

MESSING, DEBRA Best known as the costar of the hit television series *Will and Grace*, Messing was born on August 15, 1968, in Brooklyn, but she grew up in Providence, Rhode Island. A graduate of Brandeis University, she majored in theater arts there, then earned an M.F.A. from New York University. She is married to actor Daniel Zelman. She won an Emmy (2003) as best actress in a comedy series—her first win after four previous nominations. During her free time, she supports charities such as the Gay Men's Health Crisis, AmFAR, and Best Friend's Pet Sanctuary.

MEYER, ANNIE NATHAN Among her illustrious forebears and relatives was an American revolutionary hero; her cousin was Benjamin Nathan Cardozo, the second Jewish Justice of the U.S. Supreme Court; and her sister was Maud Nathan, the outspoken suffragist (see below). Most noted for cofounding Barnard College with her cousin, Emma Lazarus (see above), in 1889, Meyer was a prolific writer: twenty-six plays, numerous articles, three novels, an autobiography, and two books of nonfiction.

Most of her themes centered on the conflicts that women experienced in having a career and marriage. She married her cousin, Alfred Meyer, a prominent physician. She was born in New York City on February 19, 1867, and died there on September 23, 1951. She was an early critic of Nazi Germany and an ardent Zionist.

MICHAL She became queen of Israel, and was a bit of an upstart. She pleaded with her father, Saul, king of Israel, to allow her to marry David, his successor. In those days, it was unheard of to avow romantic love openly. Doting Dad acquiesced to his youngest child, which was fortunate for David, because Michal later saved David's life.

MIDLER, BETTE The Divine Miss M was born in Honolulu in 1945. She made her stage debut in New York City in 1966, where she developed a popular nightclub act. Her first album won her the first of two Grammy Awards; she won a special Tony Award for her record-breaking Broadway show *Bette at the Palace* (1974). Among myriad other awards are three Emmys (*Bette Midler in Concert: Diva Las Vegas*, 1997; the *Tonight Show Starring Johnny Carson* episode, 1992; and *Bette Midler: Ol' Red Hair Is Back*, 1978) and three Golden Globes (*Gypsy*, 1993; *For the Boys*, 1991; and *The Rose*, 1979). She has been in a string of successful films. She also penned a children's book, *The Saga of Baby Divine*. Married to Martin von Haselberg, Midler has one child, Sophie.

MILGROM, SHIRA Born in 1951, Milgrom is a prominent Reform rabbi and educator in Westchester, New York. She is married to David Elcott, currently U.S. director of interreligious affairs for the American Jewish Committee.

MIRIAM The older sister of Moses, she was truly his savior. It was she who guarded the basket in which he floated as a babe, and she who cajoled pharaoh's daughter into hiring her own mother as a wet nurse for her brother. When Miriam and her brother Aaron challenged Moses, who was taking all the credit for saving their people, Miriam was stricken with leprosy, from which she recovered. It is said that a well followed the prophetess during her people's forty-year journey through the desert, quenching the thirst of all. When she died, around 30 B.C.E., near Kadesh, the well is said to have dried up.

MOÏSE, PENINA One of the most prolific and creative writers of poetry on Jewish themes in America, she was the first Jew to publish a book of poetry in the United States. Her father had emigrated to the West Indies from Alsace, France, before moving to South Carolina. The sixth of nine children, Penina was born in Charleston on April 23, 1797. When she was twelve years old, her father died; her mother was very ill, and Penina was left to manage the household. Her poems started to be published that same year. She became superintendent of the first Jewish religious school in Charleston. She experienced problems with her eyesight and recurring headaches the last fifteen years of her life, and died on September 13, 1880.

MOLODOWSKY, KADYA Born in Russia in 1894, this American émigré was among the most accomplished and prolific of modern Yiddish poets, having published six major books of poetry, as well as fiction, plays, essays, and children's tales. She was the recipient of the Itzik Manger Prize, the most prestigious award in the world of Yiddish letters. Molodowsky explored a variety of issues in her work, ranging from social protest to women and religion, from national identity to political responsibility. She died in 1975.

MONROE, MARILYN Born Norma Jean Baker, on June 1, 1926, in Los Angeles, she spent most of her childhood and teen years in foster homes. She went to Hollywood to become an actor in 1946. It wasn't until 1950, after small roles in *The Asphalt Jungle* and *All About Eve*, that her career took off. Determined to shed her image as a sex symbol, she began to study at Lee Strasberg's Actors Studio in New York City. She was briefly married to baseball star Joe DiMaggio in 1954. During her marriage to playwright Arthur Miller (1956–1961), she converted to Judaism. On August 5, 1962, Monroe was found dead of an overdose of barbiturates in her home in Los Angeles.

MONTAGU, LILY Founder and spiritual leader of the Liberal Jewish Synagogue in London and of the World Union for Progressive Judaism, she was the key figure in the foundation of Youth Clubs UK. Her sympathies were based on an empathetic understanding of the tensions in women's lives between private responsibilities and public expectations; as a jurist, she was alert to gender inequality and injustice. Born in 1873 to a wealthy Orthodox Anglo-Jewish family, she was initially influenced by a visionary dream; she dedicated herself to a single life of service to her community. She died in 1963.

MONTEFIORE, JUDITH In 1812 Judith Cohen, whose uncle was Nathan Mayer Rothschild, married Moses Montefiore. Born in 1784, she and her husband first traveled to Eretz Yisrael in 1827, during which time Judith kept a diary. Later, her husband gained some renown: he was Sheriff of London (1837–1838), and was knighted by Queen Victoria. He received a baronetcy in 1846 in recognition of his humanitarian efforts on behalf of the Jews. Lady Judith died in 1862.

MORGAN, ROBIN American poet, writer, anthologist, and feminist, Morgan, born in 1941, cofounded the New York Radical Feminists (1967) and WITCH (Women's International Terrorist Conspiracy from Hell). As a young child in the '40s, she had her own radio program, then later played Dagmar in the '50s television series *I Remember Mama*. She worked in the civil rights, antiwar, and feminist movements from the 1950s through the 1970s, came out as a lesbian in the '60s, and helped revive Ms. in 1990. Her anthologies, *Sisterhood Is Powerful* (1970) and *Sisterhood Is Global* (1984) are classic syntheses of the women's movement.

MORPURGO, RAHEL (a.s.a. Rachel) Little is known about this gifted poet who worked as a seamstress and signed herself, "*nefel eshet yaacov murpurgo,* Wife of Jacob Morpurgo, Stillborn." She was born in 1790 into the Italian Sephardic Luzzatto family; her cousin, it seems, was Samuel David Luzzatto, a philologist, poet, and biblical scholar who studied Hebrew with his father, who, though a turner by trade, was an eminent Talmudist. Rahel died in 1871.

MOSKOWITZ, FAYE Chair of the English Department at George Washington

University in Washington, D.C., Moskowitz was born in Detroit in 1930. A late bloomer, she received her B.A. at forty and published her first book at fifty-five. Her newest work is *Peace in the House: Tales From a Yiddish Kitchen* (2003). She is also the editor of *Her Face in the Mirror: Jewish Women on Mothers and Daughters*.

MYERHOFF, BARBARA Even as a child, entranced by the tales her grandmother shared in their Cleveland kitchen, anthropologist Myerhoff knew that stories "could transform the world." Born in 1935, she studied the ways in which men and women from diverse cultures used their stories and sacred rituals to imbue their lives with meaning. She was a renowned scholar, heading the University of Southern California's Anthropology Department in Los Angeles, where she lived and raised her family. Her influence reached far beyond academia, and she touched a broad audience with her books and films. She died in 1985.

MYERSON, BESS Born in 1924, Myerson was the first (and, so far, only) Jewish Miss America. She went on to become a popular television personality, a public servant, and a generous philanthropist. Her encounters with anti-Semitism strengthened her resolve to fight racial bigotry; she spoke vociferously on behalf of the Anti-Defamation League of B'nai B'rith. As Commissioner of Consumer Affairs of New York City (1969–1973), Myerson was architect of the most far-reaching consumer protection legislation in the country at that time. Her many achievements include being a cofounder of the Museum of Jewish Heritage in New York. She has served in posts under Presidents Lyndon Johnson, Gerald Ford, and Jimmy Carter.

NAOMI The wife of Elimelech, who was widowed young and whose children died during a severe famine, she was the mother-in-law of the devoted Ruth, who followed Naomi back to her people. She was the great-great grandmother of King David.

NATHAN, MAUD An outspoken advocate for better working conditions for women and for the right of women to vote, she is best known for her twenty-one-year leadership of the Consumers' League of New York, becoming president in 1897. Born on October 20, 1862, in New York City, she was the great-granddaughter of American Revolutionary War hero and rabbi Gershom Mendes Seixas; a first cousin of Emma Lazarus (see above) and Supreme Court Justice Benjamin Nathan Cardozo; and sister of Annie Nathan Meyer (see above). Nathan married her first cousin, Frederick Nathan, founder of the International Men's Suffrage League; they had a daughter who died when she was eight years old. Nathan died on December 15, 1946.

NATTEL, LILIAN Born in Montreal in 1956, she now lives in Toronto with her husband and daughter. A full-time writer, she is the author of *The River Midnight* and *The Singing Fire*.

NEVELSON, LOUISE A pioneer in environmental sculpture, she used pieces of wood, found objects, cast metal, and other materials to construct huge walls or enclosed boxes of complex rhythmic abstract shapes. Born on September 23, 1899, in Kiev, Russia, her family immigrated to the United States in 1904, settling in Rockland, Maine, where there were only thirty Jewish families. Louise knew at an early age that she wanted to be an artist. Her nine-year marriage produced her only child, Myron, who later became a famous sculptor. The year 1967 was the turning point of her life: the Whitney Museum exhibited her work. She continued to create and exhibit her works throughout her life. She died on April 17, 1988.

NIEDERMAN, SHARON Born March 3, 1948, Niederman grew up in New Jersey and has lived in Colorado and New Mexico for her "adult life." She is an award-winning author and journalist who specializes in features, profiles, and essays relating to history, cuisine, architecture, travel, and traditions of New Mexico and the Southwest. She has written and edited seven books and has also written museum exhibit catalogs, including "Jewish Pioneers of New Mexico." She currently resides in Albuquerque.

NYRO, LAURA Born on October 18, 1947, in the Bronx, songwriter-singer Nyro was the daughter of an accomplished jazz trumpeter. She reputedly completed her first composition when she was eight years old. Her main influences ranged from Bob Dylan to John Coltrane, though her talents seem more akin to songwriters Carole King and Ellie Greenwich. Nyro's empathy for soul and R&B enhanced her individuality. She retired from music briefly, but reemerged in 1975 upon the disintegration of her marriage. Nyro remains a singularly impressive performer whose influence is widespread. She died on April 8, 1997.

OCHS, VANESSA L. Born in 1953 in Rochester, New York, Dr. Ochs is a senior associate at CLAL—the National Jewish Center for Learning and Leadership in New York, director of Jewish Studies at the University of Virginia, and associate professor of religious studies at UVA. The author of *Words on Fire, Safe and Sound*, and *The Jewish Dream Book*, she lives with her husband in Charlottesville, Virginia, and takes pleasure in gardening and modern dance. She and her husband have two grown daughters.

OLSEN, TILLIE Her parents, Samuel and Ida Lerner, who were never formally married, participated in the abortive 1905 Russian Revolution, after which they fled to America, settling in the Midwest, where Tillie was born in 1912. Raised on a farm in poverty, Olsen, the second of six children, cared for her younger siblings. Her father eventually rose to become state secretary of the Nebraska Socialist Party. Her background convinced Olsen that capitalism blights human development. One of the few children in her working-class neighborhood to attend an academic high school, she was introduced by an exceptional teacher to the works of Shakespeare, De Quincey, Coleridge, and Edna St. Vincent Millay. She is the author of *Tell Me a Riddle; Silences; When Writer's Don't Write;* and *Mother to Daughter, Daughter to Mother,* among others.

ORLOVA, RAISA DAVYDOVNA Born in Moscow in 1918, Orlova grew up indoctrinated into the Soviet system only to become a disenchanted and active dissident. A literary critic, author, and diplomat, she wrote of her experiences in *Memoirs: the Testament of a Conscience of a Russian Writer—A Searching Portrayal of the Troubled Inner Life of a Great Culture*. She was married to Lev Kopelev, also a dissident and a distinguished philologist and renowned expert on German literature. Orlova died in Cologne, Germany, in 1989.

OSTRIKER, ALICIA SUSKIN A poet and critic, born in 1937, Ostriker has received several honors and awards; her poetry collection *The Crack in Everything* (1996) was a National Book Award finalist. Her poetry and essays have appeared in many journals, and she has written several other books, including *A Woman Under the Surface* and *Green Age*.

OZICK, CYNTHIA The highly accomplished writer was born in New York City on April 17, 1928. Her parents, both pharmacists, were Russian immigrants who embraced the Litvak tradition of skepticism, rationalism, and antimysticism—as opposed to the exuberant emotionalism of the Hasidic community. At the age of five, Ozick entered *heder* for religious instruction, where the rabbi told her *bobe*, "Take her home; a girl doesn't have to study." Ozick is especially grateful to her grandmother for bringing her back to school the very next day, insisting that she be accepted, and dates her feminism to that time. Some of her works have included *The Pagan Rabbi and Other Stories*, *The Puttermesser Papers* and *Fame and Folly: Essays*. Ozick has won half a dozen coveted awards and grants, including both a Guggenheim and a National Endowment for the Arts fellowship. She has received several honorary doctorates and was invited to deliver the Phi Beta Kappa oration at Harvard University in 1974.

PALEY, GRACE [Goodside] Born in New York City in 1922, she studied at Hunter College and New York University. She taught at Columbia and Syracuse Universities during the 1960s, then joined the faculty at Sarah Lawrence College. Early in her career she was a poet, but she is most noted for her mastery of the short story form, for which she has received many honors. A feminist and peace activist, she lives in New York City and Thetford, Vermont. Her works have included *Enormous Changes at the Last Minute*, *Later the Same Day*, and *Just As I Thought*. She was the first recipient of the Edith Wharton Citation of Merit. She has also received a Guggenheim fellowship (1961), a grant from the National Endowment for the Arts (1966), an award from the National Institute of Arts and Letters (1970), and a senior fellowship from the National Endowment for the Arts in recognition of her lifetime contribution to literature (1987).

PALTROW, GWYNETH Born September 28, 1972, and raised in Los Angeles, Paltrow won the best actress Oscar for *Shakespeare in Love* in 1998. Other starring roles include *Proof* (2004), *Sylvia* (2003), *The Royal Tenenbaums* (2001), *The Talented Mr. Ripley* (1999), *A Perfect Murder* (1998), *Great Expectations* (1998), and *Emma* (1996). Her late father was director Bruce Paltrow, who died of cancer in 2002; her mother is actor Blythe Danner. On her father's side, Paltrow is descended from a long line of rabbis. The original Paltrow family name is Paltrowich and there are distinguished members in several countries. A cousin was Lord Taylor, the late Lord Chief Justice of the United Kingdom. She describes her philosophy as "universal," but her cultural background as Jewish. She has said that her father would probably prefer that she marry a Jewish guy. Paltrow is a genuine superstar with tremendous range, in drama as well as comedy (witness her appearances on *Saturday Night Live*)—and she can sing.

PAPPENHEIM, BERTHA She was the cofounder and leader of Jüdischer Frauenbund, the Jewish feminist movement in Germany (1904). A famous patient of Sigmund Freud's, known as Anna O, Pappenheim was the director of an orphanage and a reformer who crusaded against the sexual exploitation of women and children. She was also a dramatist, essayist, and poet, who was born in Vienna in 1859 and died in Iselberg in 1936.

PARENT, GAIL Author of *Sheila Levine Is Dead and Living in New York*, Parent, born in 1940, is a writer and scenarist whose humorous bent has come through in novels, teleplays, and screenplays; she sometimes writes in partnership with Kevin Parent. In 1998 she coauthored a nonfiction book with Dr. Connell Cowan—*The Art of War for Lovers*.

PARKER, DOROTHY She was born in 1893 to a Jewish father (Rothschild) and a Scottish mother who died when Parker was five years old; her father remarried a strict Roman Catholic, whom Dorothy bitterly disliked. Parker always maintained an image of herself as an outsider and often said of herself that she was "just a little Jewish girl trying to be cute." Her first volume of poetry, *Enough Rope* (1926), became an instant best seller. She became a core member of the celebrated Algonquin Round Table. Her acerbic and irreverent brand of humor distinguished Parker's work and made it memorable. She died in 1967.

PARTNOW, ELAINE BERNSTEIN Born in Los Angeles on October 28, 1941, she started off as an actor, then, in her thirties, began writing: her first published work, *The Quotable Woman*, has become a classic and is in its fifth edition. In the 1980s she created a series of living history portrayals of notable women, which she has presented to hundreds of educational, civic, and professional institutions. She has lived in Los Angeles, New York, Seattle, and New Orleans, and now resides on a small island in northern Florida with her husband, dogs, and cat. Partnow is the editor of this volume and sister of Susan Partnow (see below) and Judith Partnow Hyman (see above). Her other books include *The Female Dramatist* (with her niece, Lesley A. Hyatt), *Photographic Artists and Innovators* (with her husband, former photographer and author Turner Browne), and *Breaking the Age Barrier*.

PARTNOW, SUSAN Born in Los Angeles on February 20, 1947, she is active in Seattle as an organizational development and training consultant, mediator, and facilitator, dedicated to creating a world that works for all. She helps large, diverse groups face complex issues. Partnow is a lifelong activist, community builder, and peacemaker, board member of the Compassionate Listening Project, and cocreator of Conversation Cafes. She *kvells* over her grown children, who bring precious wisdom to her world.

PETCHESKY, ROSALIND Writer, health activist, and researcher, Petchesky was born in 1942. She is the cofounder and coordinator of the International Reproductive Rights Research Action Group (IRRRAG) and a professor of political science and women's studies at Hunter. She wrote *Abortion and Woman's Choice* and edited IRRRAG's comparative study, *Negotiating Reproductive Rights*.

PICON, MOLLY For over seventy years, Picon, star of Yiddish theater and film, delighted audiences with her comic song and dance performances. Born in a tenement building on New York's Lower East Side in 1898, Molly began performing at the Yiddish Theater, where her mother was a seamstress, when she was just a child. Her work on stage and in Yiddish and Hollywood films helped keep Yiddish culture alive. Picon continued to perform well into her eighties. She died on April 6, 1992, from Alzheimer's disease at the age of 94.

PIERCY, MARGE Magazine editor, poet, feminist, novelist, and founder of Movement for a Democratic Society (MDS), Piercy was born March 31, 1936, in Detroit. Although her father was not a Jew, she was raised a Jew by her grandmother and her mother. She has been married twice: She lived in France with her first husband, a French Jew who was a particle physicist and antiwar activist; her second husband was a computer scientist with whom she moved to Cape Cod, where she remains, though they divorced. She continues to write, and travels a great deal, giving readings, workshops, and lectures.

PLAIN, BELVA A New Jersey resident, she was born in New York City in 1919. Plain says she started writing when she learned the alphabet; she was twenty-five when her first short story was published. Upon her graduation from Barnard as a history major, the novelist married Dr. Irving Plain, a union that thrived for over forty years until his death in 1988. They had three children. She was a Cub Scout mother and president of the P.T.A., and now has six grandchildren. Among her twenty-one novels are *Promises*, *Harvest*, *Legacy of Silence*, and *Evergreen*.

POGREBIN, LETTY COTTIN One of America's outstanding feminist journalists, she cofounded *Ms.* and is the author of a number of nonfiction books relating to women's issues, including *Deborah, Golda, and Me: Being Female and Jewish in America* and *Getting Over Getting Older*. She's written nonsexist books for and about children, such as *Stories for Free Children*, as well as a novel, *Three Daughters*. Born on June 9, 1939, in Queens, New York, she graduated cum laude from Brandeis University, then went to work for a book publisher, Bernard Geis Associates; ten years later, she was vice president. Pogrebin was one of the founders of the National Women's Political Caucus in 1971. She worked with actor Marlo Thomas on the *Free to Be You and Me* books, records, and television show. She has been fighting anti-Semitism all her life and was outspoken when she encountered it in the feminist movement.

POLIER, JUSTINE WISE The first woman judge in New York, she used her position on the Family Court bench to fight for the rights of the poor and disempowered for thirty-eight years. She strove to implement juvenile justice law as treatment, not punishment. Born into privilege in New York in 1903, nonetheless she had a deep understanding of how poverty and racism brought most children to her court, and always offered respect and individual attention to the children and families who appeared before her. Her father, the prominent rabbi Stephen Wise (1874–1979), established the Free Synagogue (1907) to ensure he could speak with absolute freedom in the pulpit. She died in 1987.

PORTER, SYLVIA One of the most successful financial columnists in America, her syndicated column had over forty million readers at its peak. Born Sylvia Feldman to Russian immigrants in Patchogue, Long Island, New York, on June 18, 1913, she was only twelve when her father died. A freshman in college at the time of the stock market crash in 1929, Porter switched her major to economics. A year before she graduated cum laude, she married Reed R. Porter. In 1935, she went to work for the *New York Post*; three years later, she became the paper's financial editor. It wasn't until 1942 that readers discovered that S. F. Porter, the byline she used, was a woman. Author of a number of books, most notably *Sylvia Porter's Money Book*, she was a pioneer in a field that had been dominated by men. She died in 1991.

PORTMAN, NATALIE Discovered in a pizza parlor by a Revlon agent, Natalie Hershlag didn't find modeling very interesting and instead pursued a career in acting. Her big break was in 1994's award-winning film *The Professional* (a.k.a. *Léon*), in which she costarred with Jean Reno and Gary Oldman as the protégée of a hit man. The next year she starred in *Heat* with Al Pacino and Robert DeNiro. In 1997, Portman hit Broadway as the lead actor in *The Diary of Anne Frank*. Two years later she was starring as the young Queen Amidala in *Star Wars: The Phantom Menace*. In the spring of 1999 she graduated from high school with honors. Born June 9, 1981, in Jerusalem, the Boston resident continues to keep busy acting and pursuing her psychology studies at Harvard University.

PRIESAND, SALLY The first woman rabbi in the Reform movement, ordained in 1972, Priesand was born in Cleveland in 1947. She earned a B.A. from the University of Cincinnati and an M.A. from Hebrew Union College–Jewish Institute of Religion in Cincinnati. She was first named rabbi of Temple Beth El in Elizabeth, New Jersey, then went to the Monmouth Reform Temple in Tinton Falls, New Jersey, in 1981. Active in many civic and religious organizations, she wrote *Judaism and the New Woman* (1975).

RACHEL (1) She bore two sons, Joseph and Benjamin, who were the progenitors of two of the twelve tribes of Israel. It was to win Rachel that Joseph labored fourteen years for Laban, her father. When she and Jacob decided to leave Laban and return to Jacob's land of Canaan, she craftily took her father's teraphim. Laban caught up with them and there was a dramatic confrontation. She died bearing Benjamin around 1732 B.C.E., and is the only one of the Four Matriarchs not buried in the Hebron cave.

RACHEL (2) Born Blaustein or Bluewstein in Vyatka, Russia, in 1890, Rachel emigrated to Israel in 1909 but shuttled back and forth between France, Russia, and an Israeli kibbutz, finally settling in 1919 in a lonely one-room apartment in Tel Aviv, where she lived the final five years of her life. During those years she wrote most of her poetry. She died at the age of forty. Rachel's life has taken on mythic proportions for her admirers. Some of her best-known verse expresses love for Eretz Yisrael and a nostalgia for the Sea of Galilee, near which she was buried.

RADNER, GILDA [Susan] Born June 28, 1946, in Detroit, Gilda joined John Belushi and Dan Aykroyd on the *National Lampoon Radio Hour* (1974) after performing in

Toronto's Second City comedy club. Then came television's *Saturday Night Live* (1975–1980), where she developed memorable characters such as Roseanne Rosannadanna and Babwa Wawa; she won an Emmy in 1978. She teamed up with actor-comedian Gene Wilder on film in *Hanky Panky* (1982), and the pair fell in love; they married two years later. She went on to star on Broadway in her own one-woman show. In 1986, Radner began a long, arduous battle against ovarian cancer. After her death on May 20, 1989, Wilder established the Gilda Radner Ovarian Detection Center at Cedars-Sinai Medical Center in Los Angeles.

RAND, AYN The eldest of three sisters, Alissa Rosenbaum was born on February 2, 1905, in St. Petersburg, Russia. She declared herself an atheist in her early teens, opposing religion or any other form of "mysticism," and avowing that selfishness was a virtue and altruism a vice. She emigrated to the United States at age twenty-one. *The Fountainhead* was published, sold to the film studios, and Rand was hired to write the screenplay for the 1949 movie version. The Nathaniel Branden Institute, based on Rand's theory of objectivism, was organized by her eponymous consort (born Blumenthal). She was working on a miniseries based on her novel, *Atlas Shrugged*, at the time of her death, on March 6, 1982.

REBEKAH One of the Four Matriarchs, and a sister of Laban, she was the mother of Esau and Jacob. Praying in the wilderness during her pregnancy, she had a vision that Jacob, the younger, should inherit rather than the older. When she overheard Isaac preparing Esau for this blessing, she helped her favorite son deceive his blind father.

REINHARZ, SHULAMIT Dutch born in 1946, the professor of sociology directs the Women's Studies Program at Brandeis University in Massachusetts. Married to Brandeis President Jehuda Reinharz, an Israeli born émigré with whom she has two daughters, Dr. Reinharz is also the founding director of the Hadassah International Research Institute on Jewish Women.

RESNIK, JUDITH She was a member of the *Challenger* spacecraft team that exploded on January 28, 1986, killing everyone on board. A mission specialist on the maiden voyage of the space shuttle *Discovery* in 1984, she became the second American woman to travel in space (after Sally Ride). She was born on April 5, 1949, in Akron, Ohio, received a B.S. from Carnegie-Mellon University in Pittsburgh in 1970, and a doctorate in electrical engineering from the University of Maryland, College Park, in 1977. She was a classical pianist, a gourmet cook, a jogger, and a bicyclist. And she was working on obtaining her pilot's license.

RICH, ADRIENNE [Cecile] Born in Baltimore in 1929, she is the author of nearly twenty volumes of poetry, including *Snapshots of a Daughter-in-Law* and *The Fact of a Doorframe*, as well as several books of nonfiction prose, among them *Of Woman Born: Motherhood as Experience and Institution* and *On Lies, Secrets, and Silence*. An ardent feminist and champion of lesbian rights, Rich has received innumerable honors, prizes, and fellowships for her work, including the Bollingen Prize, the National Book Award, and a MacArthur fellowship. She lives in northern California.

RICHMAN, JULIA The first female district superintendent of schools in the city of New York, and a founder of the Young Women's Hebrew Association, she had to battle her family to become a teacher (in those days, middle-class Jewish girls didn't go to work). Her innovations, leadership, and curriculum brought an entire new dimension to public school education at the beginning of the twentieth century. Born on October 12, 1855, in New York City, she died while on vacation in Cherbourg, France, on June 24, 1912.

RIVERS, JOAN Born Joan Molinsky in Brooklyn in 1933, the talk show host, actor, and comedian gained notoriety while working as the regular stand-in for Johnny Carson (1983–1986) and honing her act in comedy clubs. She won an Emmy for the *Joan Rivers Show* (1989–1993) and has also appeared on other television programs and in feature films. Following the suicide of her husband, producer Edgar Rosenberg, Rivers and her daughter, Melissa, starred together in *Tears and Laughter* (1994). In 1998 she and Melissa began cohosting fashion specials on the E! cable network.

ROIPHE, ANNE [Richardson] The best-selling author of fourteen books, both fiction and nonfiction, Roiphe was born in 1935. *Up the Sandbox!* is perhaps her best-known book; others include *Fruitful: A Real Mother in the Modern World* and *Married: A Fine Predicament*. More recently she published a memoir, *1185 Park Avenue: A Memoir*. Her articles and reviews have appeared in many major magazines and she writes a regular column for the *New York Observer*. She lives with her husband, Dr. Herman Roiphe, in New York City. One of her children, Katie, is also an author whose work includes *The Morning After: Fear, Sex and Feminism*.

ROSE, ERNESTINE LOUISE [Potowski] Rose helped organize the first National Woman's Rights Convention in 1850, in Massachusetts. Born January 13, 1810, in Piotrkow, Poland, the daughter of an Orthodox rabbi, she left home in 1827, after her mother's death. She became a disciple of social reformer Robert Owen, and married fellow Owenite, William Rose, a jeweler and silversmith, and a gentile. They emigrated to New York City in 1836. There, for thirty years, she took an active role in the National Women's Suffrage Association. When her health started to fail, she and her husband returned to England, where she died in Brighton in 1892.

ROSEN, MARJORIE Born in 1942, American writer and film historian Rosen is the author of *Popcorn Venus: Women, Movies and the American Dream* (1973), a pioneering examination of how women's thoughts and dreams have been mirrored and molded by film. Rosen is an editor of the *New York Times Magazine* and a frequent contributor to several major publications.

ROSENBERG, ETHEL She and her husband Julius Rosenberg are the only U.S. citizens to have been executed for treason. Born in New York City in 1915, she was part of a transatlantic spy ring. Julius was an engineer with the U.S. Army Signal Corps, and Ethel's brother, David Greenglass, who saved his own life by turning state's evidence, worked at the nuclear research station at Los Alamos. There was great controversy over the case; many people felt that the Rosenbergs were the victims of the witch-hunt atmosphere and anti-Semitism in the United States in the early 1950s. They were executed in 1953.

ROSENBERG, TINA Born in 1960, this American political writer was the first freelance journalist to receive a five-year MacArthur fellowship "genius" award. Her writings have appeared in the *New Republic*, the *Washington Post*, the *New Yorker*, *Harper's*, and the *New York Times Magazine*. Formerly a visiting fellow at the National Security Archive and a senior fellow at the World Policy Institute, she won a Pulitzer Prize in 1996 and the National Book Award in 1995 for *The Haunted Land*.

ROSENFELD, BOBBIE Canadian born in 1904, Rosenfeld's career ground to a halt just one year after winning an Olympic gold medal for a Track and Field event. Struck with severe arthritis, she recovered sufficiently in 1931 to star on championship softball and ice hockey teams again, but a second attack in 1933 forced her to retire permanently from athletics. Rosenfeld then moved to coaching track and softball and into the field of sports writing. Her column, Sports Reel, began its twenty-year run in the *Toronto Globe and Mail* in 1937. First as an athlete, then as a writer, Rosenfeld helped topple traditional barriers against women's participation in sports. She died in 1969.

ROSENSTEIN, HARRIET Born around 1932, Rosenstein is an American journalist who was very active in the '70s, writing feminist articles.

ROSENTHAL, IDA Although she and her husband William came to America penniless, they became wealthy, successful, and generous philanthropists. She was born Ida Kaganovich on January 9, 1886, near Minsk, Russia. A dressmaker, at nineteen she joined her fiancé in New York; they wed and started their own business. The Rosenthals designed a bra with two pockets, instead of the towel-like brassiere worn up to that point, and Maidenform Brassieres was born. In 1949 they came up with the slogan, "I dreamed that I went shopping in my Maidenform bra." William died in 1958, but Ida continued going to her office every day until her death on March 29, 1973, at the age of eighty-seven.

ROSSNER, JUDITH The New York novelist, born in 1935, gained fame for her bestselling 1975 novel *Looking for Mr. Goodbar*, the first in a long series of works that capture shifting social climates and explore women's changing roles across generations. *Goodbar* was made into a film in 1977, and her novel *Emmeline* was the basis of an opera that received its world premiere in 1996. Rossner has two grown children.

RUBINSTEIN, HELENA Born in Cracow, Poland, on December 25, 1870, the eldest of fifteen children, she began her beauty empire in Melbourne, Australia, in 1902, then moved to London, where she met and married an American journalist, and then brought her cosmetics business to the United States, where her products became a mainstay. She divorced her first husband in 1937 to marry Russian Prince Artchil Gourielli-Tchkonia, twenty-five years her junior. He died in 1955; her son Horace died in 1958. Committed to the welfare of Israel, she founded the Helena Rubinstein Pavilion of Contemporary Art in Tel Aviv and a foundation to fund Israeli health organizations. She died in New York City on April 1, 1965.

RUDNER, RITA She won the 1990 American Comedy Award as best female stand-up, had her own comedy variety series in England, and did a special for HBO, *Born to Be Mild*. Rudner has made numerous appearances on the *Tonight Show* and *Late Night with David Letterman*. A native of Miami, she left home at age fifteen to seek fame and fortune on the Broadway stage. Married to English comedy producer Martin Bagmen, she now makes her home on the West Coast and, when not performing, she devotes her time to writing screenplays and books. Rudner keeps her age a mystery, but was probably born around 1960 in South Florida.

RUKEYSER, MURIEL Biographer, writer, civil rights activist, poet, translator, and film editor, Rukeyser was born in New York City in 1913, and educated at Vassar College and Columbia University. Certain events had a serious impact on her life and poetry, including the Scottsboro trial in Alabama and the civil war in Spain. The violence and injustice she saw led her to document in her poetry her own emotional responses within the context of a greater political or social event, in such works as *Beast in View*, *Breaking Open*, *The Life of Poetry*, and *The Speed of Darkness*. She died in New York City in 1980.

RUTH She was born a Moabite but changed her faith and residence when she married Boaz of Bethlehem, thus becoming the great-grandmother of David and, consequently, an ancestor of Jesus. Upon the death of her husband, she stayed with her mother-in-law, Naomi, insisting that Naomi's people, the Israelites, become Ruth's people, and Naomi's God, Ruth's God. Loyal and true, her very name connotes "friendship" or "refreshment." She lived in the 1100s B.C.E.

RYDER, WINONA Born Winona Laura Horowitz on October 29, 1971, Ryder was named after the Minnesota town (Winona) where she was born. She mostly grew up in Petulama, California, a town north of San Francisco, on a commune. Her parents were close friends with such famous "counterculture" figures as Allen Ginsberg and Timothy Leary, who was her godfather. She starting acting when still a teenager. Her 2002 arrest and conviction for shoplifting created such a stir that it almost superseded what has been a stellar career, starring in such fine films as *Mr. Deeds* (2002), *Autumn in New York* (2000), *Girl, Interrupted* (1999), *Alien: Resurrection* (1997), *The Crucible* (1996), *Little Women* (1994), *The House of the Spirits* (1993), *The Age of Innocence* (1993), *Dracula* (1992), *Mermaids* (1990), *Edward Scissorhands* (1990), and *Beetlejuice* (1988).

SACHS, [LEONIE] NELLY Nobel Prize–winning poet, playwright, and translator, born in Berlin in 1891, Sachs fled from Nazi Germany in 1940, settled in Stockholm, and took Swedish citizenship. Once she mastered the language, she translated some of the great Swedish poets. Her career as a poet did not start until she was nearly fifty years old; her body of work focuses on the cycle of suffering, persecution, exile, and death that characterizes the life of the Jewish people and includes *O the Chimneys* and *The Seeker and Other Poems*. Her best-known play, *Eli* (1951), has been widely acclaimed. She shared the Nobel Prize for literature in 1966. She died in 1970.

SAMPTER, JESSIE (Ethel) A poet and writer, Sampter, born in 1883 or 1893, grew up in a highly assimilated home. Her father was one of the pioneers of the Ethical Culture Movement. Influenced by Henrietta Szold and others, she became a Zionist and emigrated to Palestine in 1919. First in Jerusalem, then in Rehovot, she established evening classes for Yemenite working girls. She settled in Kibbutz Givat Brenner, where she devoted herself to the Rest Home and continued with her writing and teaching until her death in March 1938. Her writings and sketches of kibbutz life had a significant influence on U.S. Zionist circles.

SARAH (a.s.a. Sarai) One of the Four Matriarchs, who lived from about 1987 to 1860 B.C.E., she was the wife of Abraham, with whom she bore Isaac. It is said she lived to 127 years of age, and that Abraham purchased the Cave of Machpelah in Hebron to bury her.

SASSO, SANDY EISENBERG The first woman ordained by the Reconstructionist movement, she has been the rabbi of Congregation Beth-El Zedeck in Indianapolis since 1977 and received her doctor of divinity degree after twenty-five years in the rabbinate. The recipient of many honors, she is the author of nationally acclaimed children's books, including *Adam & Eve's First Sunset*, *In God's Name*, and *But God Remembered: Stories of Women from Creation to the Promised Land*. She writes a monthly column in the *Indianapolis Star* on issues relating to religion and spirituality. She and her husband, Rabbi Dennis C. Sasso, are the first practicing rabbinical couple in world Jewish history. They have two children.

SAVITSKY, ESTHER She was the very supportive mother of Bella Abzug. Her husband, Emmanuel, who died in 1933, was a butcher who called his Lower East Side New York store the "Live and Let Live Butcher Shop." A Russian émigré, born Esther Tanklefsky in the 1880s, she died sometime in the 1970s.

SCHAEFFER, SUSAN FROMBERG She is the author of twelve novels, including *Falling* and *The Snow Fox*; five volumes of poetry; one book of short stories; and two novels for children, most notably *The Witch and the Weather Report*. Born in Brooklyn in 1941, Schaeffer taught at Brooklyn College for twenty-eight years but finally decided to return to her alma mater, where she earned all three of her degrees and feels most at home; she is now a professor of English at the University of Chicago and divides her time between Chicago and Vermont.

SCHAPIRO, MIRIAM Canadian-born in 1923, American collage artist and feminist Schapiro developed "femmage," a form of collage using such media as lace and fabric. Married to artist Paul Brach, she worked with Judy Chicago (see above) in executing *Womanhouse* (1972), a project highlighting the traditional crafts and folk art of American women.

SCHNALL, SUSAN Born Susan Levine in 1943, she is a military rights activist who has written articles advocating for those rights. A Navy nurse, Lt. Schnall once rented a plane and dropped antiwar leaflets on her base.

SCHNEIR, MIRIAM The feminist historian, writer, and editor was born in 1933 in New York City. The pioneering collection of writings she edited in 1972, *Feminism:*

The Essential Historical Writings, was a watershed book that helped to define the women's movement and reveal how radically transformative a force it is throughout the world; it was reissued in 1994 with a companion volume, *Feminism in Our Time*. Her husband, Walter Schneir, is a writer with whom she has frequently collaborated; they have three children. In 1965, they coauthored *Invitation to an Inquest*, an influential study of the espionage case of Julius and Ethel Rosenberg (see above). She lives in Westchester County, New York, and San Miguel de Allende, Mexico.

SENESH, HANNAH One of Zionism's and modern Judaism's heroes, Senesh (or Szenes) was born in Budapest, Hungary, in 1921. Her father was a playwright and journalist who died when she was six. At the time of *Kristallnacht*, Senesh volunteered for the *Haganah* (the underground Jewish self-defense army). In June 1944, she parachuted into Yugoslavia near the Hungarian border, was captured, imprisoned under brutal conditions, then murdered by a firing squad at the age of twenty-three. Her poems, made famous in part because of her tragic death, reveal a woman imbued with hope even in the face of adverse circumstances.

SHALOM, IMMA Several stories are told in the Talmud of Shalom, who was the wife of Eliezer ben Hyrcanus and the sister of Gamaliel II, both famous first-century C.E. rabbis. Shalom, who was born in 50 C.E. and whose name translates from the Hebrew as Mother of Peace, once attempted to intercede in an inheritance dispute. She also tried but was unable to prevent the death of her husband in a controversy with her brother.

SHORE, DINAH Born Frances Rose Shore in Winchester, Tennessee, in 1920, Shore was the first woman to have her own television variety show and won Emmys every year from 1954 to 1959. She began singing on the radio in New York City and by 1943 had her own radio show. During World War II, Shore became the first woman to visit GIs on the front lines. Her long marriage to actor George Montgomery ended in divorce. In 1972 she founded the Dinah Shore Classic, one of the first important big-purse tournaments for women golfers.

SHUR, FANCHON Born in 1935, Shur was the creator of the Fanchon Shur Ceremonial Dance Theater (1974); she also founded Growth in Motion in 1978. Fanchon has choreographed and created pieces for film, concert, stage, and communal celebrations. Her work merges psychology, multicultural sacred ceremonies, theater, dance, chanting, and Jewish traditions with ancient and contemporary women's spirituality. She is married to Israeli musician and composer Bonia Shur.

SIBYL, THE JEWISH Also known as the Hebrew Sibyl, or Sabbe of Palestine, she lived in the 190s B.C.E. and probably died in 165 B.C.E. A skilled prophetess, she was represented as a woman of prodigious old age, uttering prophecies in ecstatic frenzy in Greek hexameters, handed down in writing. Some histories allege that she was the wife of one of Noah's sons, said to have been saved in the ark; others that she was a descendant of Noah's. She was held to be the daughter of the ancient Chaldean historian Berosus.

SIGNORET, SIMONE Born Simone Kaminker in Wiesbaden, Germany, in 1921, she was raised in Paris by her actor mother. Simone left her job as a typist to become a film extra in *Le Prince Charmant* (1942) and soon graduated to leading roles. She won British and American Academy Awards for *Room at the Top* (1959), and gained further recognition for *Ship of Fools* (1965). Married to actor Yves Montand in 1951, she matured into one of France's most distinguished character actors and died in 1985.

SILLS, BEVERLY Coloratura soprano Sills, who won the Presidential Medal of Freedom in 1980, was born Belle Miriam Silverman on May 25, 1929, in Brooklyn. Her mother provided her with lessons in dance, voice, and elocution. When her father died in 1949, her singing in private clubs eked out a living for her and her mother. She debuted at the New York City Opera in 1955. Her marriage to newspaper publisher Peter Buckley Greenough came with two small children—Meredith, who is practically deaf, and Peter Jr., who is mentally retarded. In 1975, she made her debut at the Metropolitan Opera and received an eighteen-minute ovation. She continued to sing there until her retirement from singing to become the codirector of the New York City Opera.

SILVER, JOAN MICKLIN Born in 1935, she began writing scripts for educational film companies before cowriting the screenplay for the Vietnam wives movie *Limbo* (1972) and making her directing debut with *Hester Street* (1975), a story about Jewish immigrants in turn-of-the century New York, which earned critical acclaim. She has since directed several motion pictures, including *Crossing Delancey* (1988), her most popular film to date.

SILVERMAN, SARAH Perhaps best known as one of Kramer's girlfriends on *Seinfeld*, the actor-comedian was in the cast of *Saturday Night Live* for one season (1993–1994) and had a big role on *The Larry Sanders Show*. She has appeared in such films as *Bullworth, There's Something About Mary*, and *Evolution*. New England-born (1971) and -bred, she is one of four daughters: sister Susan is a rabbi who, with her husband Yosef Abaramowitz, wrote *Jewish Family & Life: Traditions, Holidays, and Values for Today's Parents and Children*; sister Laura plays the receptionist on Comedy Central's *Dr. Katz*; and sister Jody is an aspiring screenwriter.

SIMON, RACHEL She was a British diarist and community activist whose husband, Oswald Simon, was the founder of the "Sunday movement," which aimed to establish a universalistic Church of Israel as a religious fellowship of Christian theists and liberal Jews. She was born in 1824 and died c. 1900.

SNOOK, RAVEN A performer and writer, she was born in New York City in 1971. She is best known for her solo show *How I Became a Drag Queen Trapped in a Woman's Body*, which she has performed in New York City, San Francisco, Philadelphia, and Berlin. She was typecast as a vampire on ABC's sitcom *Talk to Me*, passed as a "female drag queen" on *The Maury Povich Show*, played a dominatrix/self-help guru in *Slo-Mo* on Cinemax, and was part of the original downtown cast of *Urinetown*. Snook has also told stories at the Moth and the *Heeb* Magazine Storytelling Series, and published articles in *Time Out NY*, the *Village Voice*, the *New York Post* and *Heeb*.

SNOW, PHOEBE Born Phoebe Laub on July 17, 1952, in New York City, the singer-songwriter borrowed her stage name from the Lackawanna Railroad's passenger train, called Phoebe Snow, which ran from Hoboken, New Jersey, to Buffalo, New York. She took piano lessons as a child and as a teenager began writing poetry. In the early 1970s, she played the local clubs in New York's Greenwich Village, singing blues, folk, and pop songs. In 1974, her eponymous debut album reached number five on the album charts and won her a Grammy nomination for best new artist. In May of 1998, Phoebe received the Cultural Achievement Award, presented by New York City Mayor Rudolph Giuliani. She sings jazz, pop, rock, soul, gospel—she can do it all. She credits Aretha Franklin as an early influence.

SOKOLOW, ANNA Born in 1920, Sokolow was a dancer and choreographer of uncompromising integrity. Her upbringing amidst the left-wing movements of New York's Jewish immigrant communities shaped her approach to her creative endeavors. In her dance, she explored pressing issues like the Great Depression, the Holocaust, Jewish rituals and themes, and the alienated youth of the 1960s, challenging audiences to think deeply about themselves and their society. Sokolow worked in numerous countries in a variety of theater forms and, in 1998, was inducted into the National Museum of Dance's Hall of Fame. She died in 2000.

SOLOMON, HANNAH GREENEBAUM Solomon established the National Council of Jewish Women (1893), the first national association of Jewish women. Born in 1858, she was a superb organizer who emphasized unity and orchestrated agreements among Jewish, gentile, and government groups on local, national, and international levels. As a reformer she believed that "woman's sphere is the whole wide world," but at the same time she felt a woman's primary responsibility was to her family. Her commitment and energy were legendary. In an era when Jewish women's voices were rarely heard, her example of powerful speech and organization paved the way for new, more radical possibilities. She died in 1942.

SONTAG, SUSAN Critic and writer Sontag was born in New York City in 1933 but grew up in Arizona and Los Angeles. She was educated at the University of Chicago, Harvard, and Oxford before settling in New York City to teach and write. Best known for her critical essays and cultural analyses, she also wrote and directed her own movie, *Duet for Cannibals* (1969). Her concerns and writings have gained her a reputation as America's answer to "Continental intellectuals." Her son by an early marriage, David Rieff, is also an author.

SPARK, MURIEL [Sarah] Her Jewish father lived in Edinburgh, Scotland, where Muriel Camberg was born in 1918. There she became editor of *Poetry Review* (1947–1949), and published poetry, short stories, and critical biographies, including works on Wordsworth, Mary Shelley, and Emily Brontë. She is best known for her novels, especially *The Prime of Miss Jean Brodie* (1961; filmed 1969). An autobiography, *Curriculum Vitae*, appeared in 1992. She lives in Italy, and was made a Dame of the British Empire in 1993.

SPEWACK, BELLA Born in 1899, the Cohen family emigrated from Bucharest to New York City when Bella was an infant. She met husband Sam Spewack when they were both working as reporters. Soon after they wed, the couple began collaborating; together they generated some of the world's best-loved comedies and musical comedies, including *Kiss Me, Kate* (1948), their adaptation of Shakespeare's *Taming of the Shrew*, which won a Tony Award. In addition to their stage work, the Spewacks wrote twenty screenplays. As an interesting aside, it was during Bella's press agent years that she initiated the now-entrenched Girl Scout cookie sales. She died in 1990.

SPOLIN, VIOLA Recognized internationally for her "Theater Games" system of actor training, she was born November 7, 1906, in Chicago, and was initially trained to be a settlement worker. It was while she worked for the Works Progress Administration's Recreational Project (1939–1941) that she developed techniques that were later formalized in her classic text, *Improvisations for the Theatre* (1963). She established and conducted several theater companies in Chicago and Hollywood, sometimes with her son, producer-director Paul Sills. Two subsequent books on her techniques have bolstered the use of Spolin's systems throughout the country. She died November 22, 1994.

STEIN, GERTRUDE Stein's groundbreaking writing experiments reflect her genius for toying with language and its meanings. She hailed from Allegheny, Pennsylvania, where she was born in 1874, the seventh child of German immigrants. By the time she was seventeen years old, both her parents had died. She earned a B.A. magna cum laude at the Harvard Annex (later Radcliffe College), then studied briefly at Johns Hopkins Medical School. In 1903 she and her brother, Leo, left for Paris and the art world. Their close relationship ended when Leo became aware of his sister's lesbianism. Alice B. Toklas became Gertrude's lifelong companion, and their home became a hub for some of the greatest artists and writers of the modern era. In addition to her many books, including *The Making of Americans*, *The Autobiography of Alice B. Toklas*, and *Everybody's Autobiography*, she wrote over seventy-six operas and plays, winning an Obie in 1964 for *Four Saints in Three Acts*. She died in 1946.

STEINEM, GLORIA Born March 25, 1934, in Toledo, Ohio, the young Steinem was left to care for both herself and her mother after her parents' divorce. Upon graduating Phi Beta Kappa and magna cum laude from Smith College in 1956, she spent two years in India, where she became involved with the nonviolent protest movement. She returned to the States with a new awareness of social and political issues. Starting out as a freelance journalist, in 1968 she joined the founding staff of *New York* magazine, writing the column City Politic. In the late '60s she became one of feminism's most articulate and outspoken leaders. She helped form the National Women's Political Caucus in 1971 and, the following year, launched *Ms.* magazine, serving as its editor for the next fifteen years. She's written several books, notably *Outrageous Acts and Everyday Rebellions* and *Revolution from Within*, and has lectured worldwide. In September 2000, Steinem was married for the first time, at the age of 66, to David Bale, a South African–born entrepreneur.

STERN, EDITH MENDEL Born in 1901, Stern was an American social critic, writer, and early feminist who wrote many books addressing such societal concerns as the role of the housewife, mental illness, and aging. She died in 1975.

STILLER, NIKKI Author of *Mothers and Daughters in Medieval English Literature* (1980) and *The Figure of Cressida in British and American Literature: Transformation of a Literary Type* (1990). She is currently on the faculty at the New Jersey Institute of Technology in Newark.

STOKES, ROSE PASTOR Born in poverty in Russia in 1879, her family moved to the East End of London when she was a child. She emigrated to Cleveland, where she worked in a factory and wrote for the *Jewish Daily News*, then moved to New York, joined the Socialist Party, and met and married millionaire socialist James Phelps Stokes, whom she later divorced. In 1917 Rose was arrested, charged, and sentenced to ten years in prison under the Espionage Act for writing, in a letter to the *Kansas City Star*, that "no government which is for the profiteers can also be for the people...." She died of breast cancer in Frankfurt, Germany, on June 20, 1933.

STREISAND, BARBRA At the age of twenty, Streisand was a Broadway star. At twenty-four, she won an Academy Award and a Golden Globe. She's also won seven Grammys, an Emmy, and a second Oscar—to name a few of her honors. She has enjoyed success as a concert star, actor, writer, film director, and producer. Born on April 24, 1942, in Brooklyn, and raised by her widowed mother, she began her career singing in Greenwich Village bars and clubs right out of high school. Her first break, playing Miss Marmelstein in *I Can Get It for You Wholesale*, led to her starring role as Fanny Brice in *Funny Girl*. Streisand was married to actor Elliott Gould, with whom she had a son. Currently she is married to actor James Brolin. Outspoken on women's rights, abortion, AIDS research, sexism, and women's abuse, Streisand has received many awards and much recognition for her philanthropic contributions to society.

STRUG, KERRI [Allison] She made all the headlines at the 1996 Olympics in Atlanta when she vaulted with an ankle injury, helping her gymnastics team win the gold! Born in Tucson on November 19, 1977, this Los Angeles resident began gymnastics in 1982. She is also a 1992 Olympic bronze medalist and three-time World Championship medalist. Kerri's older brother and sister also compete in gymnastics; her father is a heart surgeon in Tucson. She studied communications at UCLA, and has taught gymnastics to young people.

SULLAM, SARAH COPIA Born in 1592, Sullam was a highly accomplished noble-woman living in Venice. She devoted herself to poetry and the sciences, for which she enjoyed a fine reputation. She wrote a small work on the "Immortality of the Soul." Several of her poems and sonnets were published in the seventeenth century. She died in 1641.

SUSANNA The daughter of Hilkiah and the wife of Joakim is a biblical figure said to have befriended Jesus; some scholars, however, place her death at 538 B.C.E.

SUZMAN, HELEN Born Helen Gravonsky in Germiston, Transvaal, in 1917, this South African politician studied at Witwatersrand University, then became a lecturer there (1944–1952). Deeply concerned about the apartheid system erected by the National Party, she joined the Opposition, and was elected to Parliament in 1953, where she remained until 1989. She gradually gained the respect of the black community and, for years the sole MP of the Progressive Party, proved to be a fierce opponent of apartheid. In 1978 she received the UN Human Rights Award.

SZOLD, HENRIETTA One of the first Americans to work actively for a return of the Jewish homeland in Palestine, Szold, who was born in Baltimore on December 21, 1860, defined a new identity for American Jewish women as communal leaders and as providers of health care and social services in the land of Israel. Among her many contributions were the founding of Hadassah: the National Women's Zionist Organization of America (1912), and the directing of Youth Aliya, whose goal was to bring young Jews to Eretz Yisrael. Through her accomplishments, Szold achieved international prominence as an educator, social reformer, and Zionist. She moved to Jerusalem in 1920. Although childless herself, she was "mother" to the thousands of young refugees from Nazi Germany saved from the Holocaust. She died on February 14, 1945.

TAGER, MARCIA An American author, teacher, storyteller, artist, and therapist who is a graduate of the Reconstructionist Rabbinical College, she serves as rabbi-*haver* of the Philadelphia P'nai Or Religious Fellowship, and is the founding rabbi of P'nai Or of Princeton, New Jersey. She teaches in many different Jewish and interfaith settings, and with her husband, Jack Kessler, a traditionally trained cantor, often leads workshops and retreats.

TAYLOR, ELIZABETH Born February 27, 1932, in London, Taylor moved with her family to Los Angeles in 1939 to escape the havoc of World War II. She made her screen debut at the age of ten and became a child star with *National Velvet* (1944). Generally considered one of the most beautiful women alive, Taylor won Oscars for *Butterfield 8* (1960) and *Who's Afraid of Virginia Woolf?* (1966). Her personal life captured the public's fascination in 1950, when, at age eighteen, she embarked on the first of eight marriages, all but the last to men of great renown (Nicholas Conrad Hilton Jr., Michael Wilding, Mike Todd, Eddie Fisher [during which time, 1959–1964, she converted to Judaism], Richard Burton [twice], John Warner, and Larry Fortensky). In recent years she has devoted herself to humanitarian causes. One of the first major celebrities to publicly support AIDS research, she was honored with the Jean Hersholt Humanitarian Award (1992). In 1999, Taylor was made a Dame of the British Empire. She has nine grandchildren and a great-grandson.

TAYLOR, RENEE An accomplished actor, writer, comedian, and director, Renee Taylor was nominated for an Emmy for her work in television's *The Nanny*. Born on March 19, 1933, in New York, she married actor-writer-director Joseph Bologna in 1965, and the couple was nominated for an Academy Award for their first screenplay, *Lovers and Other Strangers*, and won an Emmy Award for their television special *Acts of Love and Other Comedies*, just two of their many collaborations. Taylor also wrote the best-selling satire, *My Life on a Diet*. The couple's son, Gabriel, is a writer and actor.

TEKOA, WOMAN OF The wise woman employed by Joab to persuade David to bring home his banished son, Ab-salom.

TEUBAL, SAVINA J. Born in England in 1926, the writer spent many years in Argentina before settling in Southern California, where she founded Sarah's Tent: Sheltering Creative Jewish Spirituality. A biblical scholar, in 1986 she created the first *Simchat Hochmah* ceremony with the help of Rabbi Drorah Setel and Debbie Friedman, the well-known Jewish musician.

TUCHMAN, BARBARA The first woman president of the American Academy of Arts and Letters (1979), Tuchman was awarded two Pulitzer Prizes for nonfiction for her historical books on men of war: *The Guns of August* (1962) and *Stillwell and the American Experience in China, 1911–1945* (1971). She was born on January 30, 1912, in New York City. Her father, Maurice Wertheim, was a banker, publisher, philanthropist, and president of the American Jewish Committee (1941–1943). Her maternal grandfather was ambassador to Turkey, and her uncle, Henry Morgenthau, Jr., was secretary of the treasury under President Franklin D. Roosevelt. After receiving a B.A. from Radcliffe College, she went to work for the *Nation*, a magazine owned by her father. In 1939, she married Dr. Lester Reginald Tuchman, a New York internist; they had three daughters, one of whom is Jessica Tuchman Mathews, the environmental scientist (see above). Tuchman died on February 6, 1989.

TUCKER, SOPHIE A singer and entertainer, born Sophie Abuza in Russia in 1884 and brought to the United States as a child, she first performed in vaudeville in blackface, singing ragtime melodies. She almost stole the show in the *Ziegfeld Follies of 1909*. She helped popularize songs by black composers, such as Eubie Blake, and was also known for racy lyrics. She appeared in several stage and movie musicals, but was especially well known as a nightclub torch singer. A union activist, she served as president of the American Federation of Actors in 1938. "The Last of the Red-Hot Mamas," as she billed herself in later years, died in 1966.

TUSSMAN, MALKA HEIFETZ Born in the Ukraine in 1893, Tussman was the last Yiddish-language recipient of the prestigious Itzik Manger Prize for Yiddish Letters. She completed six books of verse; *With Teeth in the Earth* has been translated into English. When she died in 1987, she left a last unpublished manuscript. Her poetry reveals the richness and complexity of a woman's life. Having lived many years in Tel Aviv, she spent her final years in Berkeley, where her son was a professor of philosophy.

TYLER, ROBIN Born about 1949, she started out impersonating Judy Garland in gay bars in pre-Stonewall New York City. With little support for women in stand-up comedy in the 1960s, Tyler created a rather defensive and hostile persona. In 1978, she became the first out lesbian to appear on national television, when she performed in a Showtime comedy special hosted by comedy pioneer Phyllis Diller (see above). Tyler has subsequently left the stand-up stage and now devotes her energy to organizing women's music festivals and other events, including the Millennium March on Washington, D.C., in May 2000.

ULINOVER, MIRIAM Born in Poland sometime between 1888 and 1894, Ulinover's Yiddish poems in her two collections, *Maïn bobes oïtzer* (The Grandmother's Treasures) and *Shabès*, were inspired by *tkhines* (see Glossary). She died in 1944.

VAN BUREN, ABIGAIL One of America's most widely read advice columnists, she was in the unique position of having a twin sister, Ann Landers (see above), who was also one of America's most widely read advice columnists. She was born Pauline Esther Friedman in 1918 in Sioux City, Iowa. The rivalry of the twins was almost as sharp as their wit. Abigail launched her "Dear Abby" column in 1956 which, like her sister's, became internationally syndicated. She too gained a dedicated following as well as many public service awards, particularly for publicizing public health issues.

VIORST, JUDITH Born Judith Stahl in Newark, New Jersey, in 1931, Viorst is the author of several works of fiction and nonfiction, for children as well as adults. Particularly noted for her humor and satirical verse, she is also a journalist and has been the recipient of various awards, including an Emmy Award in 1970 for poetic monologues written for a CBS television special, "Anne, the Woman in the Life of a Man." She is also noted for her psychological writings and is a graduate of the Washington Psychoanalytic Institute. She lives in Washington, D.C., with her husband, political writer Milton Viorst.

VOLK, PATRICIA A novelist, memoirist, and short story writer, Volk has had her work published in dozens of magazines, including *Atlantic Monthly*, the *New York Times Magazine*, the *New York Times Book Review*, the *New Yorker*, *Playboy*, and *Redbook*. She was a weekly columnist for *New York Newsday*. Her most recent book is a memoir, titled *Stuffed*. She lives in New York City.

WALD, LILLIAN D. Cofounder of the NAACP, the Federal Children's Bureau, and the Women's League for Peace and Freedom, among others, Wald, born in 1867, was a practical nurse who started off by establishing the Henry Street Settlement and the Visiting Nurse Service on New York's Lower East Side. Championing the causes of public health nursing, housing reform, suffrage, world peace, and the rights of women, children, immigrants, and working people, Wald became an influential leader in city, state, and national politics. Although she achieved international recognition, her efforts were always grounded in the belief that the world was simply an expanded version of the culturally diverse neighborhood. She died in 1940.

WALTERS, BARBARA She was born on September 25, 1931, in Boston. Her father was the owner of New York City's famous nightclub, the Latin Quarter. Raised in Miami and New York, she was educated at Sarah Lawrence College. After graduation, she moved to New York City, where she broke through the "man's world of television journalism" by landing interviews with members of the Kennedy family, the widow of Dr. Martin Luther King Jr., and other VIPs. In 1976, ABC hired her away from NBC at a record-breaking $1 million a year. Married and divorced, with an adopted daughter, Walters has a unique ability to draw out her subject; the clarity of her interviews underlie her continuing success.

WASSERSTEIN, WENDY The voice of American feminism for many mainstream audiences, Wasserstein is somewhat controversial among feminists. She is, perhaps, America's most produced female playwright, and the first to have won the Antoinette Perry (Tony) Award for best play; she has also received the New York Drama Critics Circle Award, and the Pulitzer Prize for drama, along with several other honors. Born in Brooklyn in 1950, she earned her B.A. at Mount Holyoke, the setting for *Uncommon Women and Others*, written for her Yale M.A. thesis. The play that won her the Pulitzer Prize was 1989's *The Heidi Chronicles*. Hers has been called "a wry, self-deprecating humor which helps her avoid righteousness without losing her sting."

WEINSTOCK, LOTUS The performance artist-comedian described her humor as a mix between her California cosmic right brain and her Philadelphia Jewish left brain. Born Marlena Weinstock in Philadelphia in 1943, she started performing under the name Maurey Haydn in Greenwich Village in the mid-sixties. After the 1966 death of her boyfriend, famed comic Lenny Bruce, she reclaimed the name Weinstock, but traded in "Marlena" for "Lotus." Her heyday was at Los Angeles' Comedy Store in the mid-'70s. She died of a malignant brain tumor in August 1997 at the age of fifty-four. Her daughter, Lili Hayden, is a classically trained pop violinist.

WEISBERG, RUTH An artist who works in painting, drawing, printmaking, and large-scale installations, Weisberg is the dean of the School of Fine Arts at the University of Southern California in Los Angeles. Born in Chicago in 1942, she began taking art classes at age five. She was educated at the University of Michigan and the Accademia di Belle Arti in Perugia, Italy. In addition to numerous solo and group exhibitions, Weisberg has been the recipient of many honors. In 1990 she became the first woman to serve as president of the College Art Association.

WEISMAN, LESLIE KANES Born in 1945, she is a founding faculty member of the School of Architecture at the New Jersey Institute of Technology (1975). She has taught at several institutions and is a public speaker who addresses issues of gender, race, and class discrimination. A pioneer in design education, she is a cofounder of the Women's School of Planning and Architecture and of Sheltering Ourselves: A Women's Learning Exchange, an international educational forum on housing and economic development for women, ongoing since 1987.

WEISSTEIN, NAOMI A lifelong feminist, born in Chicago in 1939, Weisstein developed a heightened sense of militancy in the male-dominated world of science at Harvard, where she earned her Ph.D. She has belonged to numerous civil rights organizations and became known for her powerful oratory. A comedian and keyboardist in the Chicago Women's Liberation Rock Band (1970–1973), she routinely brought down the house with her comic monologues. Neuroscientist Weisstein cofounded American Women in Psychology (1970), among other professional organizations. She is currently a professor of psychology at the State University of New York, Buffalo. Her pioneering essay, "*Kinder, Kirche, Kuche* as Scientific Law" (*Sisterhood Is Powerful*,

1971), is probably the best known of the dozens of articles she has written for major publications.

WESTHEIMER, RUTH Known to millions simply as Dr. Ruth, Westheimer reached the turning point in her career when she gave a lecture to New York broadcasters about the need for sex education programming. She was born Karola Ruth Siegel on June 4, 1928, in Frankfurt, Germany. Her privileged childhood was shattered when the SS abducted her father and she was sent to a Swiss school: she never saw her family again. After an injury while in the Jewish underground in Israel, then five years and a marriage in Paris, she emigrated to New York with her husband. Dr. Ruth got a scholarship to the New School for Social Research, gave birth to a baby girl, and divorced the Frenchman. She worked as a housemaid to support her daughter while earning her master's degree. She met her great love, Manfred Westheimer, also a Jewish refugee, on a ski trip in the Catskills. They married in 1961 and had a son. Dr. Ruth currently lives in the Washington Heights area of New York. She has published several books, among them *The Encyclopedia of Sex* and *Conquering the Rapids of Life: Making the Most of Midlife Opportunities*.

WILLIAMS, PEARL She was a New York comedian who flourished throughout the 1930s and 1940s with a reputation for "being dirty," upon which she prided herself.

WINGER, DEBRA A film actor born in Cleveland in 1955, Winger saw her career take off with *Urban Cowboy* in 1980. She's twice been nominated for Oscars—for *An Officer and a Gentleman* (1982) and *Terms of Endearment* (1985). She was once married to actor Timothy Hutton.

WINTERS, SHELLEY Daughter of a tailor's cutter, Shirley Shrift was born on August 18, 1922. A star of stage and screen, Winters has garnered two Academy Awards (1959, 1965) and an Emmy (1964). Married and divorced three times, she had a daughter with Italian actor Vittorio Gassman. Her third marriage was to actor Anthony Franciosa. Winters's early acting training was under the tutelage of actor Charles Laughton. She roomed with Marilyn Monroe when they were both starting out in Hollywood. Her first Oscar was for her role as Mrs. Van Daan in *The Diary of Anne Frank* (1959).

WITKOVSKY, SUSAN Born in 1942, she grew up in Los Angeles, where she currently lives. A longtime educator, she devoted her early years to establishing quality child-care programs and wrote the model city program (San Francisco) for Head Start. She currently works with young adults in literacy, math, and GED training through the Los Angeles school district, where she has been recognized for her successful and innovative curriculum materials and methods. Witkovsky is a lifelong participant in the movement for peace and justice. She is the single mother of a teenage boy.

WOLF, NAOMI American feminist and Rhodes scholar, Wolf was born in 1962. She graduated from Yale in 1984. Among her books is *The Beauty Myth*, which the *New York Times* called one of the seventy most significant books of the century. Her essays appear regularly in the *New Republic*, the *New York Times*, the *Wall Street Journal*, the *Washington Post*, *Glamour*, *Ms.*, and other publications.

YALOW, ROSALYN Born in 1921, she was raised and lives in New York City. By seventh grade, Rosalyn Sussman was committed to mathematics. She graduated from Hunter College with honors and degrees in chemistry and physics. Yalow overcame great odds and discrimination as the only woman among four hundred men at the University of Illinois College of Engineering Physics Department. She received her Ph.D. in nuclear physics. Beginning in 1950, she worked at the Bronx Veterans Hospital laboratory with Dr. Sol Bernson. They discovered how to measure small amounts of hormones in the human body by using radioisotopes. The method is called RIA and it revolutionized the vital need to determine the amount of foreign material in the blood. Yalow was the first woman to receive the Albert Lasker Award (1976) and the second woman to receive the Nobel Prize for Medicine (1977).

YANKOWITZ, SUSAN A New Jersey native, born in 1941, she is a playwright whose work addresses a wide array of sociological problems. She grew up in a working-class neighborhood and was educated at Sarah Lawrence College and the Yale School of Drama. She married Herbert Leibowitz, a writer and editor, with whom she had a son. Her plays, including *Night Sky*, have been staged in such diverse locations as London, Paris, Algeria, Israel, and Iran. Also a screenwriter, she has penned several PBS teleplays. Yankowitz has taught at many institutions and is the recipient of several grants and awards.

YEZIERSKA, ANZIA The author, who sometimes used the pseudonym Hattie Mayer, was born in a mud hut in the village of Pinsk c. 1880–1885. At fifteen, she and her family emigrated to New York City, where she worked in a sweatshop while studying English at night school. She was granted a scholarship to attend Columbia University to train as a domestic-science teacher. She divorced twice, had one daughter, and had a romantic relationship with philosopher John Dewey. In the 1930s, Yezierska worked for the Works Progress Administration's Writers Project in Manhattan. Her books include *The Bread Givers*, *Hungry Hearts and Other Stories*, and her autobiography, *Red Ribbon on a White Horse*. In the last decades of her life, she documented the plight of Puerto Rican immigrants in New York. She died in 1970.

ZUBOFF, SHOSHANA A professor at the Harvard Business School since 1981, where she earned her Ph.D. in social psychology, Zuboff has authored dozens of articles on the subject of information technology in the workplace: her book *In the Age of the Smart Machine* (1988) is regarded as a definitive work. She now concludes that today's managerial capitalism has become an obstacle to wealth creation. She summarizes a new approach, "distributed capitalism," in a more recent book, *The Support Economy* (2002), coauthored with her husband, Jim Maxmin, a former CEO and a philosophy Ph.D. They have two children. Zuboff, who was born in 1951, lived a good part of her life in Argentina and other parts of South America and once tended a small herd of llamas.

ZYGMUNTOWICZ, ITKA FRAJMAN Born in Poland in 1926 during Passover, she and her family were forced from their home first to the Nowe-Miasto Ghetto in 1941, then to Auschwitz. Itka was shunted to Ravensbruck, then Malchow, where she remained until the liberation. She was the only member of her family to survive. She met her husband, Rachil, also a survivor, the following year. They had two sons in Sweden, where Itka earned a degree in fashion design. In 1953 she and her family emigrated to the United States, settling in Philadelphia, where they had two more sons; they also have two grandsons.

GLOSSARY

adonai elohaynu, adonai ekad (Hebrew) see *sh'ma Yisrael,* below

aliyah or *aliya* (Hebrew) literally, "go up"; the ones honored to bless or read the Torah "make *aliyah,*" go up to the bimah (the platform from which services are conducted in a synagogue). Also said of Jews who move to Israel; i.e., they make *aliyah.*

Baal Shem Tov (Hebrew) The early life of Rabbi Yisrael Baal Shem Tov is shrouded in mystery. He was the founder of one of the most important religious movements in Jewish history, Hasidism, in the early eighteenth century. When Rabbi Yisrael was thirty-six years old, in 1734, he became known as the Baal Shem Tov—the Master of the Good Name.

bobe (Yiddish) grandmother

Bobe-mayse (**a.s.a.** *bubbe mayseh* **and** *bubbe meises*) (Yiddish) tall tales; old wives', tales

bubkes (Yiddish) something trivial, worthless, insultingly disproportionate to expectations; absurd, foolish, nonsensical

cabrones (Spanish) bastards

Catskills (English) Mountain resort area in upstate New York frequented by Jews; often referred to as the "Borscht Belt"

daven (Yiddish) pray

dayenu (Hebrew) Enough!

farblondjet (Yiddish) all mixed up

ferklempt (Yiddish) miserable; bad mood

golem (Yiddish folklore) a creature made out of a lump of clay; a kind of servant magically brought to life, using kabbalah (Jewish mysticism); colloquially, a clumsy, awkward character

goy (plural: goyim) (Yiddish) non-Jewish people

gringo (Mexican slang) white person; American white person

Haggadah (Hebrew) literally, the "telling" of the Passover story; refers to the book of home liturgy used at the Passover ritual meal

havurot (**a.s.a.** *chavurot,* **plural for** *chavurah*) (Hebrew) one's community or fellow congregants; religious fellowship

heder (**a.s.a.** *cheder*) (Hebrew) an elementary religious school

hochmah (Hebrew) Jewish wisdom (or law)

homo generis humani (Latin) human being

kimosabe (**a.s.a.** *kemosahbee*) (Native American, probably Black Foot) faithful friend

Kinder, Kirche, Kuche (German) children, church (or churchgoing), kitchen (connoting "woman's place")

Kishineffing (Russian) from Kishinev, the capital of Moldavia, near the Russia-Poland border; the site of massive and terrible pogroms around 1938

Kristallnacht (German) translates as "night of broken glass"; refers to the organized anti-Jewish riots in Germany and Austria on November 9 and 10, 1938. These riots marked a major transition in Nazi policy, and were, in many ways, a harbinger of the "Final Solution."

kvell (Yiddish) glow with pride

kvetching (Yiddish) complaining

lain (Yiddish) leading prayer; read or chant from the Torah

mama-loshen (**a.s.a.** *mameloshn*) (Yiddish) mother tongue

maven (Yiddish) expert

mensh (**a.s.a.** *mensch, mentsh*) (Yiddish) good person, someone who's solid and down to earth; someone to admire

meschumedim (**a.s.a.** *meshumeides*) (Yiddish) a willing convert from Judaism; an apostate; a pariah

midrash (Hebrew) teaching story or interpretation of sacred text

mishegoss (Yiddish) literally, insanity, madness; common use: craziness, trouble, nonsense, absurdity

naches (Yiddish) great joy

oy (Yiddish) oh no; alas; depending on context and delivery, many meanings

plotz (Yiddish) to burst or explode; also, to be infuriated

seder (Hebrew) order, or order of the service (used on Passover)

schnuckle (German) a kind of small sheep; *schnuckelchen* means darling or pet

shabès (Hebrew) sabbath; in Yiddish, *shabbat*

Shechinah (**a.s.a.** *Techninnah* or *Schekhinah*) (Hebrew) literally, indwelling; connotes the feminine presence of God

sh'ma Yisrael adonai elohaynu, adonai ekad (Hebrew) Hear, O Israel! The Lord our God, the Lord is One

schmuck (Yiddish) jerk; idiot; no-goodnik; a detestable person. (Literally "jewel"; metaphor for penis!)

shtetl (Yiddish) small village, especially the little Jewish communities of Eastern Europe

shul (Yiddish) synagogue

sicario (Italian) hired killer

simcha (Hebrew) a happy occasion; a celebration. *Simchat Hochmah,* or Joy of Wisdom, is a ceremony celebrating the transition of women from their midlife to their eldering years; *Simchat Torah* is a holiday that rejoices over the Torah.

sofer stam (Hebrew) Jewish ritual scribe

tallit (Hebrew) prayer shawl

tefillin (a.k.a. phylacteries) (Hebrew) icons placed on upper left arm and on forehead during prayer to help focus on the mind and heart

teraphim (Hebrew) a small image or idol representing an ancient Semitic household god

tikkun olam (Hebrew) healing or repairing the world

tkhines (Yiddish) from the Hebrew *tehinnah*, which means supplication, it can refer either to an individual prayer or to a collection of such prayers

Walpurgisnacht (German) an episode or a situation having the quality of nightmarish wildness; also the eve of Beltane, a witches' Sabbath

yenta (Yiddish) gossip or busy-body

yeshivot (Hebrew) in the United States, a school where secular and religious subjects are studied. Also, a rabbinical college; an academy for Talmudic study.

Yom Hashoah (Hebrew) Holocaust Remembrance Day

LIST OF FULL &
ABBREVIATED TITLES

ANTHOLOGIES & HISTORIES

Antler, Joyce (ed.), *America and I: Short Stories by American Jewish Women Writers*, 1990 [*America and I*, 1990]

Barclay, Aviel, cited in "Black Fire on White Paper" by Leah Eichler, *Moment: A Conversation on Jewish Culture, Politics, and Religion*, http://www.momentmag.com/olam/olam1.html, 2003 [*Moment*, 2003]

Beck, Evelyn Torton (ed.), *Nice Jewish Girls: A Lesbian Anthology*, 1989 [*Nice Jewish Girls*, 1989]

Bernays, Doris Fleischman (ed.), *An Outline of Careers for Women*, 1928 [*Careers for Women*, 1928]

Berry, Dawn Bradley, *The 50 Most Influential Women in American Law*, 1996 [*Women in American Law*, Berry, 1996]

Betsko, Kathleen, and Rachel Koenig, *Interviews with Contemporary Women Playwrights*, 1987 [*Contemporary Women Playwrights*, Betsko, 1987]

Brown, Ann, and Arlene Raven, *Exposures, Women & Their Art*, 1989 [*Exposures*, Brown, 1989]

Cowley, Malcolm (ed.), *Writers at Work* (First Series), 1958 [*Writers at Work* (1st), 1958]

Duncan, Philip D. (ed.), *Politics in America 1998*, 1999 [*Politics in America*, 1998]

Epstein, Lawrence J., *The Haunted Smile: The Story of Jewish Comedians in America*, 2001 [*Haunted Smile*, Epstein, 2001]

Forman, Frieda, Ethel Raicus, Sarah Silberstein Swartz, and Margie Wolf (eds.), *Found Treasures: Stories by Yiddish Women Writers*, 1994 [*Found Treasures*, 1994]

James, Edward T. (ed.), *Notable American Women, 1607–1950: A Biographical Dictionary*, 1971 [*Notable American Women*, 1971]

Klagsbrun, Francine (ed.), *The First Ms. Reader*, 1972 [*First Ms. Reader*, 1972]

Kobler, Franz (ed.), *A Treasury of Jewish Letters: Letters from the Famous and the Humble*, 1953 [*Treasury of Jewish Letters*, 1953]

Kunitz, Stanley J., and Howard Haycraft, *Twentieth Century Authors*, 1942 [*20th Century Authors*, Kunitz, 1942]

Martin, Linda, and Kerry Segrave, *Women in Comedy*, 1986 [*Women in Comedy*, Martin, 1986]

Mezey, Robert (ed.), *Poems from the Hebrew*, 1973 [*Poems from the Hebrew*, 1973]

Morgan, Robin (ed.), *Sisterhood Is Powerful*, 1970 [*Sisterhood Is Powerful*, 1970]

Nash, Bruce, and Allan Zullo (eds.); Kathryn Zullo (compiler), *Lawyer's Wit and Wisdom*, 1995 [*Lawyer's Wit and Wisdom*, 1995]

National Women's Political Caucus Conference [NWPC Conference]

Niederman, Sharon (ed.), *Shaking Eve's Tree: Short Stories of Jewish Women*, 1990 [*Shaking Eve's Tree*, 1990]

Plimpton, George (ed.), *Writers at Work*, Eighth Series, 1988 [*Writers at Work* (8th), 1988]

Proceedings of the First Convention of the National Council of Jewish Women (Philadelphia), 1896 [NCJW Proceedings, 1896]

Sargeant, Winthrop, *Divas: Impressions of Six Opera Superstars*, 1959 [*Divas*, Sargeant, 1959]

Shafer, Yvonne, *American Women Playwrights, 1900–1950*, 1995 [*American Women Playwrights*, Shafer, 1995]

Shapiro, Jerrold Lee, Michael J. Diamond, and Martin Greenberg (eds.), *Becoming a Father*, 1995; cited, "Shifting Patterns of Fathering in the First Year of Life" by Judith Partnow Hyman [*Becoming a Father*, 1995]

Trevelyan, Raleigh (ed.), *Italian Writing Today*, 1967 [*Italian Writing Today*, 1967]

Umansky, Ellen M., and Dianne Ashton (eds.), *Four Centuries of Jewish Women's Spirituality*, 1992 [*Four Centuries*, 1992]

Unterbrink, Mary, *Funny Women: American Comediennes, 1860–1985*, 1987 [*Funny Women*, Unterbrink, 1987]

Wolfe, Don (ed.), *American Scene: New Voices*, 1963 [*American Scene*, 1963]

INDIVIDUAL WORKS

Abzug, Bella; Mel Ziegler (ed.), *Bella!*, 1972 [*Bella!*, 1972]

Adelman, Penina V., *Miriam's Well: Rituals for Jewish Women around the Year*, 1986 [*Miriam's Well*, 1986]

Amir, Anda; Sue Ann Wasserman (tr.), *Land of Israel*, 1987 [*Land of Israel*, 1987]

Brownmiller, Susan, *Against Our Will: Men, Women, and Rape*, 1975 [*Against Our Will*, 1975]

Decter, Midge, *The New Chastity and Other Arguments Against Women's Liberation*, 1972 [*The New Chastity*, 1972]

Drexler, Rosalyn; Richard Gilman (ed.), *The Line of Least Existence and Other Plays*, 1967 [*The Line of Least Existence*, 1967]

Eisler, Riane, *The Chalice and the Blade: Our History, Our Future*, 1987 [*The Chalice and the Blade*, 1987]

————. *Sacred Pleasure: Sex, Myth, and the Politics of the Body*, 1995 [*Sacred Pleasure*, 1995]

————. *Tomorrow's Children: A Blueprint for Partnership Education in the 21st Century*, 2000 [*Tomorrow's Children*, 2000]

Falk, Marcia, *The Book of Blessings: New Jewish Prayers for Daily Life, the Sabbath, and the New Moon Festival*, 1996 [*The Book of Blessings*, 1996]

Ginzburg, Natalia; Dick Davis (tr.), *The Little Virtues*, 1985 [*Little Virtues*, 1985]

Ginzburg, Eugenia, *Within the Whirlwind* (1979), Ian Boland, tr., 1981 [*Within the Whirlwind*, 1979]

Glückel of Hameln; Marvin Lowenthal (tr.), *The Memoirs of Glückel of Hameln*, 1692, 1977 [*Memoirs*, 1692]

Gruber, Ruth, *Haven: The Unknown Story of 1,000 World War II Refugees*, 1983 [*Haven*, 1983]

Herrera, Hayden, *Frida: A Biography of Frida Kahlo*, 1983 [*Frida*, Herrera, 1983]

Hillesum, Etty; Arthur Pomerans (tr.), *An Interrupted Life: The Diaries of Etty Hillesum 1941–1943 (Das gestoerte Leben)*, 1983 [*An Interrupted Life*, 1983]

Hubbard, Ruth, Mary Sue Henifin, and Barbara Fried, (eds.), *Women Look at Biology Looking at Women*, 1979 [*Women Look at Biology Looking at Women*, 1979]

Klein, Melanie; Juliet Mitchell (ed.), *The Selected Melanie Klein*, 1987 [*Melanie Klein*, 1987]

Kolmar, Gertrud; Henry A. Smith (tr. & intro.), *Dark Soliloquy*, 1975 [*Dark Soliloquy*, 1975]

Landowska, Wanda; Denise Resout (ed.), *Landowska on Music*, 1964 [*Landowska on Music*, 1964]

Lazarus, Emma; Morris U. Schappes (ed. & intro.), *Emma Lazarus: Selections from Her Poetry and Prose*, 1982 [*Emma Lazarus*, 1982]

Lispector, Clarice; Giovanni Pontiero (tr.), "Preciousness" (1960), *Family Ties*, 1972 [*Family Ties*, 1972]

Lowenthal, Marvin, *Henrietta Szold: Her Life and Letters*, 1942 [*Henrietta Szold*, Lowenthal, 1942]

Meir, Golda; Israel Shenker and Mary Shenker (eds.), *As Good as Golda*, 1970 [*As Good as Golda*, 1970]

Molodowsky, Kadya; Kathryn Hellerstein (ed. & tr.), *Paper Bridges*, 1999 [*Paper Bridges*, 1999]

Morpurgo, Rahel; I. Castiglione (ed.), *Ugab Rachel* ["The Harp of Rachel"], 1890 [*The Harp of Rachel*, 1890]

Ochs, Vanessa L., *Words on Fire: One Woman's Journey into the Sacred*, 1999 [*Words on Fire*, 1999]

Olsen, Tillie, *Silences: When Writer's Don't Write*, 1965 [*Silences*, 1965]

Orlova, Raisa Davydovna; Samuel Cioran (tr.), *Memoirs*, 1983 [*Memoirs*, 1983]

Partnow, Elaine, *Hear Us Roar: A Woman's Connection* (play), 1988 [*Hear Us Roar*, 1988]

Partnow, Susan, and Elaine Partnow, *Everyday Speaking for All Occasions: How to Express Yourself with Confidence and Ease*, 1998 [*Everyday Speaking*, 1988]

Picon, Molly, with Jean Bergantini Grillo, *Molly! An Autobiography*, 1980 [*Molly!*, 1980]

Pogrebin, Letty Cottin, *Deborah, Golda, and Me: Being Female and Jewish in America*, 1991 [*Deborah, Golda, and Me*, 1991]

Rich, Adrienne, *Poems: Selected and New (1950–1974)*, 1974 [*Poems*, 1974]

Roiphe, Anne, *Fruitful: A Real Mother in the Modern World*, 1996 [*Fruitful*, 1996]

Senesh, Hannah, *Hannah Senesh: Her Life and Diary*, 1966 [*Hannah Senesh*, 1966]

Shargel, Baila Round, *Lost Love: The Untold Story of Henrietta Szold*, 1997 [*Lost Love*, Shargel, 1997]

Shulman, Alix Kates (ed.), *Red Emma Speaks*, 1972 [*Red Emma Speaks*, 1972]

Shur, Fanchon, *The Book of Blessings: A Feminist-Jewish Reconstruction of Prayer*, 1992 [*The Book of Blessings*, 1992]

Sigerman, Harriet Marla, "Daughters of the Book: A Study of Gender and Ethics in the Lives of Three American Women" (Ph.D. diss., Univ. of Massachusetts), 1992 ["Daughters of the Book," Sigerman, 1992]

Stokes, Rose Pastor, Herbert Shapiro, and David L. Sterling, (eds.), *I Belong to the Working Class: The Unfinished Autobiography of Rose Pastor Stokes*, 1992 [*I Belong to the Working Class*, 1992]

Syrkin, Marie, *Golda Meir: Woman with a Cause*, 1984 [*Golda Meir*, Syrkin, 1984]

Tussman, Malka Heifetz; Marcia Falk (tr.), *With Teeth in the Earth: Selected Poems of Malka Heifetz Tussman*, 1992 [*With Teeth in the Earth*, 1992]

Umansky, Ellen M. (ed.), Sermon to the Reform Synagogue, Berlin (August 1928), *Lily Montagu: Sermons, Addresses, Letters and Prayers*, 1985 [*Lily Montagu*, 1985]

Viorst, Judith, *It's Hard to Be Hip Over Thirty and Other Tragedies of Married Life*, 1968 [*It's Hard to Be Hip Over Thirty...*, 1968]

Zipser, Arthur, and Pearl Zipser, *Fire and Grace: The Life of Rose Pastor Stokes*, 1989 [*Fire and Grace*, Zipser, 1989]

Index of Women Quoted

Notes

Notes

Notes

Notes

Notes

Notes

Notes

Notes

AVAILABLE FROM BETTER BOOKSTORES.
TRY YOUR BOOKSTORE FIRST.

Bar/Bat Mitzvah

The Bar/Bat Mitzvah Memory Book
An Album for Treasuring the Spiritual Celebration
By Rabbi Jeffrey K. Salkin and Nina Salkin
A unique album for preserving the spiritual memories of the day, and for recording plans for the Jewish future ahead. Contents include space for creating or
recording family history; teachings received from rabbi, cantor, and others;
mitzvot and *tzedakot* chosen and carried out, etc.
8 x 10, 48 pp, Deluxe Hardcover, 2-color text, ribbon marker, ISBN 1-58023-111-X **$19.95**

Bar/Bat Mitzvah Basics: A Practical Family Guide to Coming of Age Together
Edited by Helen Leneman. Foreword by Rabbi Jeffrey K. Salkin.
6 x 9, 240 pp, Quality PB, ISBN 1-58023-151-9 **$18.95**

For Kids—Putting God on Your Guest List: How to Claim the Spiritual Meaning
of Your Bar or Bat Mitzvah *By Rabbi Jeffrey K. Salkin*
6 x 9, 144 pp, Quality PB, ISBN 1-58023-015-6 **$14.95** *For ages 11–12*

Putting God on the Guest List: How to Reclaim the Spiritual Meaning of Your
Child's Bar or Bat Mitzvah *By Rabbi Jeffrey K. Salkin*
6 x 9, 224 pp, Quality PB, ISBN 1-879045-59-1 **$16.95**

Tough Questions Jews Ask: A Young Adult's Guide to Building a Jewish Life
By Rabbi Edward Feinstein 6 x 9, 160 pp, Quality PB, ISBN 1-58023-139-X **$14.95** *For ages 13 & up*
Also Available: **Tough Questions Jews Ask Teacher's Guide**
8½ x 11, 72 pp, PB, ISBN 1-58023-187-X **$8.95**

Bible Study/Midrash

Hineini in Our Lives: Learning How to Respond to Others through 14 Biblical Texts,
and Personal Stories *By Norman J. Cohen*
6 x 9, 240 pp, Hardcover, ISBN 1-58023-131-4 **$23.95**

Ancient Secrets: Using the Stories of the Bible to Improve Our Everyday Lives
By Rabbi Levi Meier, Ph.D. 5½ x 8½, 288 pp, Quality PB, ISBN 1-58023-064-4 **$16.95**

Moses—The Prince, the Prophet: His Life, Legend & Message for Our Lives
By Rabbi Levi Meier, Ph.D.
6 x 9, 224 pp, Quality PB, ISBN 1-58023-069-5 **$16.95**; Hardcover, ISBN 1-58023-013-X **$23.95**

Self, Struggle & Change: Family Conflict Stories in Genesis and Their Healing Insights
for Our Lives *By Norman J. Cohen* 6 x 9, 224 pp, Quality PB, ISBN 1-879045-66-4 **$16.95**

Voices from Genesis: Guiding Us through the Stages of Life *By Norman J. Cohen*
6 x 9, 192 pp, Quality PB, ISBN 1-58023-118-7 **$16.95**

Congregation Resources

Becoming a Congregation of Learners: Learning as a Key to Revitalizing
Congregational Life *By Isa Aron, Ph.D. Foreword by Rabbi Lawrence A. Hoffman.*
6 x 9, 304 pp, Quality PB, ISBN 1-58023-089-X **$19.95**

Finding a Spiritual Home: How a New Generation of Jews Can Transform the
American Synagogue *By Rabbi Sidney Schwarz*
6 x 9, 352 pp, Quality PB, ISBN 1-58023-185-3 **$19.95**

Jewish Pastoral Care: A Practical Handbook from Traditional & Contemporary Sources
Edited by Rabbi Dayle A. Friedman 6 x 9, 464 pp, Hardcover, ISBN 1-58023-078-4 **$35.00**

The Self-Renewing Congregation: Organizational Strategies for Revitalizing
Congregational Life *By Isa Aron, Ph.D. Foreword by Dr. Ron Wolfson.*
6 x 9, 304 pp, Quality PB, ISBN 1-58023-166-7 **$19.95**

Or phone, fax, mail or e-mail to: **JEWISH LIGHTS Publishing**
Sunset Farm Offices, Route 4 • P.O. Box 237 • Woodstock, Vermont 05091
Tel: (802) 457-4000 • Fax: (802) 457-4004 • www.jewishlights.com
Credit card orders: (800) 962-4544 (8:30AM–5:30PM ET Monday–Friday)
Generous discounts on quantity orders. SATISFACTION GUARANTEED. Prices subject to change.

Children's Books

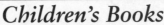

Because Nothing Looks Like God
By Lawrence and Karen Kushner
What is God like? The first collaborative work by husband-and-wife team Lawrence and Karen Kushner introduces children to the possibilities of spiritual life. Real-life examples of happiness and sadness invite us to explore, together with our children, the questions we all have about God, no matter what our age.

11 x 8½, 32 pp, Full-color illus., Hardcover, ISBN 1-58023-092-X **$16.95** *For ages 4 & up*

Also Available: **Because Nothing Looks Like God Teacher's Guide**
8½ x 11, 22 pp, PB, ISBN 1-58023-140-3 **$6.95** *For ages 5–8*

Board Book Companions to Because Nothing Looks Like God
5 x 5, 24 pp, Full-color illus., SkyLight Paths Board Books, **$7.95** each *For ages 0–4*

What Does God Look Like? ISBN 1-893361-23-3

How Does God Make Things Happen? ISBN 1-893361-24-1

Where Is God? ISBN 1-893361-17-9

The 11th Commandment: Wisdom from Our Children
by The Children of America
"If there were an Eleventh Commandment, what would it be?" Children of many religious denominations across America answer this question—in their own drawings and words.

8 x 10, 48 pp, Full-color illus., Hardcover, ISBN 1-879045-46-X **$16.95** *For all ages*

Jerusalem of Gold: Jewish Stories of the Enchanted City
Retold by Howard Schwartz. Full-color illus. by Neil Waldman.
A beautiful and engaging collection of historical and legendary stories for children. Each celebrates the magical city that has served as a beacon for the Jewish imagination for three thousand years. Draws on Talmud, midrash, Jewish folklore, and mystical and Hasidic sources.

8 x 10, 64 pp, Full-color illus., Hardcover, ISBN 1-58023-149-7 **$18.95** *For ages 7 & up*

The Book of Miracles: A Young Person's Guide to Jewish Spiritual Awareness
By Lawrence Kushner. All-new illustrations by the author.
6 x 9, 96 pp, 2-color illus., Hardcover, ISBN 1-879045-78-8 **$16.95** *For ages 9–13*

In Our Image: God's First Creatures
By Nancy Sohn Swartz
9 x 12, 32 pp, Full-color illus., Hardcover, ISBN 1-879045-99-0 **$16.95** *For ages 4 & up*

From SKYLIGHT PATHS PUBLISHING

Becoming Me: A Story of Creation
By Martin Boroson. Full-color illus. by Christopher Gilvan-Cartwright.
Told in the personal "voice" of the Creator, a story about creation and relationship that is about each one of us. In simple words and with radiant illustrations, the Creator tells an intimate story about love, about friendship and playing, about our world—and about ourselves.

8 x 10, 32 pp, Full-color illus., Hardcover, ISBN 1-893361-11-X **$16.95** *For ages 4 & up*

Ten Amazing People: And How They Changed the World
By Maura D. Shaw. Foreword by Dr. Robert Coles. Full-color illus. by Stephen Marchesi.
Black Elk • Dorothy Day • Malcolm X • Mahatma Gandhi • Martin Luther King, Jr. • Mother Teresa • Janusz Korczak • Desmond Tutu • Thich Nhat Hanh • Albert Schweitzer • This vivid, inspirational, and authoritative book will open new possibilities for children by telling the stories of how ten of the past century's greatest leaders changed the world in important ways.

8½ x 11, 48 pp, Full-color illus., Hardcover, ISBN 1-893361-47-0 **$17.95** *For ages 7 & up*

Where Does God Live? *By August Gold and Matthew J. Perlman*
Using simple, everyday examples that children can relate to, this colorful book helps young readers develop a personal understanding of God.

10 x 8½, 32 pp, Full-color photo illus., Quality PB, ISBN 1-893361-39-X **$8.99** *For ages 3–6*

Children's Books
by Sandy Eisenberg Sasso

Adam & Eve's First Sunset: God's New Day
Engaging new story explores fear and hope, faith and gratitude in ways that will
delight kids and adults—inspiring us to bless each of God's days and nights.
9 x 12, 32 pp, Full-color illus., Hardcover, ISBN 1-58023-177-2 **$17.95** *For ages 4 & up*

But God Remembered
Stories of Women from Creation to the Promised Land
Four different stories of women—Lillith, Serach, Bityah, and the Daughters of
Z—teach us important values through their faith and actions.
9 x 12, 32 pp, Full-color illus., Hardcover, ISBN 1-879045-43-5 **$16.95** *For ages 8 & up*

Cain & Abel: Finding the Fruits of Peace
Shows children that we have the power to deal with anger in positive ways.
Provides questions for kids and adults to explore together.
9 x 12, 32 pp, Full-color illus., Hardcover, ISBN 1-58023-123-3 **$16.95** *For ages 5 & up*

God in Between
If you wanted to find God, where would you look? This magical, mythical tale
teaches that God can be found where we are: within all of us and the relationships between us.
9 x 12, 32 pp, Full-color illus., Hardcover, ISBN 1-879045-86-9 **$16.95** *For ages 4 & up*

God's Paintbrush: Special 10th Anniversary Edition
Wonderfully interactive, invites children of all faiths and backgrounds to
encounter God through moments in their own lives. Provides questions adult and
child can explore together.
11 x 8½, 32 pp, Full-color illus., Hardcover, ISBN 1-58023-195-0 **$17.95** *For ages 4 & up*

Also Available: **God's Paintbrush, 1st Edition** ISBN 1-879045-22-2 **$17.95**

Also Available: **God's Paintbrush Teacher's Guide**
8½ x 11, 32 pp, PB, ISBN 1-879045-57-5 **$8.95**

God's Paintbrush Celebration Kit
A Spiritual Activity Kit for Teachers and Students of All Faiths, All Backgrounds
  Additional activity sheets available:
  8-Student Activity Sheet Pack (40 sheets/5 sessions), ISBN 1-58023-058-X **$19.95**
  Single-Student Activity Sheet Pack (5 sessions), ISBN 1-58023-059-8 **$3.95**

In God's Name
Like an ancient myth in its poetic text and vibrant illustrations, this
award-winning modern fable about the search for God's name celebrates the
diversity and, at the same time, the unity of all people.
9 x 12, 32 pp, Full-color illus., Hardcover, ISBN 1-879045-26-5 **$16.95** *For ages 4 & up*

Also Available as a Board Book: **What Is God's Name?**
5 x 5, 24 pp, Board, Full-color illus., ISBN 1-893361-10-1 **$7.99** *For ages 0–4 (A SkyLight Paths book)*

Also Available: **In God's Name video and study guide**
Computer animation, original music, and children's voices. 18 min. **$29.99**

Also Available in Spanish: **El nombre de Dios**
9 x 12, 32 pp, Full-color illus., Hardcover, ISBN 1-893361-63-2 **$16.95** *(A SkyLight Paths book)*

Noah's Wife: The Story of Naamah
When God tells Noah to bring the animals of the world onto the ark, God also calls
on Naamah, Noah's wife, to save each plant on Earth. Based on an ancient text.
9 x 12, 32 pp, Full-color illus., Hardcover, ISBN 1-58023-134-9 **$16.95** *For ages 4 & up*

Also Available as a Board Book: **Naamah, Noah's Wife**
5 x 5, 24 pp, Full-color illus., Board, ISBN 1-893361-56-X **$7.95** *For ages 0–4 (A SkyLight Paths book)*

For Heaven's Sake: Finding God in Unexpected Places
9 x 12, 32 pp, Full-color illus., Hardcover, ISBN 1-58023-054-7 **$16.95** *For ages 4 & up*

God Said Amen: Finding the Answers to Our Prayers
9 x 12, 32 pp, Full-color illus., Hardcover, ISBN 1-58023-080-6 **$16.95** *For ages 4 & up*

Current Events/History

The Story of the Jews: A 4,000-Year Adventure—A Graphic History Book
Written & illustrated by Stan Mack
Through witty, illustrated narrative, we visit all the major happenings from biblical times to the twenty-first century. Celebrates the major characters and events that have shaped the Jewish people and culture.
6 x 9, 288 pp, illus., Quality PB, ISBN 1-58023-155-1 **$16.95**

The Jewish Prophet: Visionary Words from Moses and Miriam to Henrietta Szold and A. J. Heschel *By Rabbi Michael J. Shire* 6½ x 8½, 128 pp, 123 full-color illus., Hardcover, ISBN 1-58023-168-3 **$25.00**

Shared Dreams: Martin Luther King, Jr. & the Jewish Community
By Rabbi Marc Schneier. Preface by Martin Luther King III.
6 x 9, 240 pp, Hardcover, ISBN 1-58023-062-8 **$24.95**

"Who Is a Jew?": Conversations, Not Conclusions *By Meryl Hyman*
6 x 9, 272 pp, Quality PB, ISBN 1-58023-052-0 **$16.95**

Ecology

Ecology & the Jewish Spirit: Where Nature & the Sacred Meet
Edited by Ellen Bernstein 6 x 9, 288 pp, Quality PB, ISBN 1-58023-082-2 **$16.95**

Torah of the Earth: Exploring 4,000 Years of Ecology in Jewish Thought
Vol. 1: Biblical Israel: One Land, One People; Rabbinic Judaism: One People, Many Lands
Vol. 2: Zionism: One Land, Two Peoples; Eco-Judaism: One Earth, Many Peoples
Edited by Rabbi Arthur Waskow
Vol. 1: 6 x 9, 272 pp, Quality PB, ISBN 1-58023-086-5 **$19.95**
Vol. 2: 6 x 9, 336 pp, Quality PB, ISBN 1-58023-087-3 **$19.95**

Grief/Healing

Against the Dying of the Light: A Parent's Story of Love, Loss and Hope
By Leonard Fein
In this unusual exploration of heartbreak and healing, Leonard Fein chronicles the sudden death of his 30-year-old daughter and shares the hard-earned wisdom that emerges in the face of loss and grief.
5½ x 8½, 176 pp, Hardcover, ISBN 1-58023-110-1 **$19.95**

Grief in Our Seasons: A Mourner's Kaddish Companion *By Rabbi Kerry M. Olitzky*
4½ x 6½, 448 pp, Quality PB, ISBN 1-879045-55-9 **$15.95**

Healing of Soul, Healing of Body: Spiritual Leaders Unfold the Strength & Solace in Psalms *Edited by Rabbi Simkha Y. Weintraub, C.S.W.*
6 x 9, 128 pp, 2-color illus. text, Quality PB, ISBN 1-879045-31-1 **$14.95**

Jewish Paths toward Healing and Wholeness: A Personal Guide to Dealing with Suffering *By Rabbi Kerry M. Olitzky. Foreword by Debbie Friedman.*
6 x 9, 192 pp, Quality PB, ISBN 1-58023-068-7 **$15.95**

Mourning & Mitzvah, 2nd Edition: A Guided Journal for Walking the Mourner's Path through Grief to Healing *By Anne Brener, L.C.S.W.*
7½ x 9, 304 pp, Quality PB, ISBN 1-58023-113-6 **$19.95**

The Perfect Stranger's Guide to Funerals and Grieving Practices
A Guide to Etiquette in Other People's Religious Ceremonies *Edited by Stuart M. Matlins*
6 x 9, 240 pp, Quality PB, ISBN 1-893361-20-9 **$16.95** *(A SkyLight Paths book)*

Tears of Sorrow, Seeds of Hope: A Jewish Spiritual Companion for Infertility and Pregnancy Loss *By Rabbi Nina Beth Cardin*
6 x 9, 192 pp, Hardcover, ISBN 1-58023-017-2 **$19.95**

A Time to Mourn, A Time to Comfort: A Guide to Jewish Bereavement and Comfort *By Dr. Ron Wolfson* 7 x 9, 336 pp, Quality PB, ISBN 1-879045-96-6 **$18.95**

When a Grandparent Dies: A Kid's Own Remembering Workbook for Dealing with Shiva and the Year Beyond *By Nechama Liss-Levinson, Ph.D.*
8 x 10, 48 pp, 2-color text, Hardcover, ISBN 1-879045-44-3 **$15.95** *For ages 7–13*

Abraham Joshua Heschel

The Earth Is the Lord's: The Inner World of the Jew in Eastern Europe
5½ x 8, 128 pp, Quality PB, ISBN 1-879045-42-7 **$14.95**

Israel: An Echo of Eternity *New Introduction by Susannah Heschel*
5½ x 8, 272 pp, Quality PB, ISBN 1-879045-70-2 **$19.95**

A Passion for Truth: Despair and Hope in Hasidism
5½ x 8, 352 pp, Quality PB, ISBN 1-879045-41-9 **$18.99**

Holidays/Holy Days

7th Heaven: Celebrating Shabbat with Rebbe Nachman of Breslov
By Moshe Mykoff with the Breslov Research Institute
Based on the teachings of Rebbe Nachman of Breslov. Explores the art of consciously observing Shabbat and understanding in-depth many of the day's traditional spiritual practices.
5⅛ x 8¼, 224 pp, Deluxe PB w/flaps, ISBN 1-58023-175-6 **$18.95**

The Women's Passover Companion
Women's Reflections on the Festival of Freedom
Edited by Rabbi Sharon Cohen Anisfeld, Tara Mohr, and Catherine Spector
A groundbreaking collection that captures the voices of Jewish women who engage in a provocative conversation about women's relationships to Passover as well as the roots and meanings of women's seders.
6 x 9, 352 pp, Hardcover, ISBN 1-58023-128-4 **$24.95**

The Women's Seder Sourcebook
Rituals & Readings for Use at the Passover Seder
Edited by Rabbi Sharon Cohen Anisfeld, Tara Mohr, and Catherine Spector
This practical guide gathers the voices of more than one hundred women in readings, personal and creative reflections, commentaries, blessings, and ritual suggestions that can be incorporated into your Passover celebration as supplements to or substitutes for traditional passages of the haggadah.
6 x 9, 384 pp, Hardcover, ISBN 1-58023-136-5 **$24.95**

Creating Lively Passover Seders: A Sourcebook of Engaging Tales, Texts & Activities
By David Arnow, Ph.D.
7 x 9, 416 pp, Quality PB, ISBN 1-58023-184-5 **$24.99**

Hanukkah, 2nd Edition: The Family Guide to Spiritual Celebration
By Dr. Ron Wolfson. Edited by Joel Lurie Grishaver.
7 x 9, 240 pp, illus., Quality PB, ISBN 1-58023-122-5 **$18.95**

The Jewish Family Fun Book: Holiday Projects, Everyday Activities, and Travel Ideas
with Jewish Themes *By Danielle Dardashti and Roni Sarig. Illus. by Avi Katz.*
6 x 9, 288 pp, 70+ b/w illus. & diagrams, Quality PB, ISBN 1-58023-171-3 **$18.95**

The Jewish Gardening Cookbook: Growing Plants & Cooking for
Holidays & Festivals *By Michael Brown*
6 x 9, 224 pp, 30+ illus., Quality PB, ISBN 1-58023-116-0 **$16.95**;
Hardcover, ISBN 1-58023-004-0 **$21.95**

Passover, 2nd Edition: The Family Guide to Spiritual Celebration
By Dr. Ron Wolfson with Joel Lurie Grishaver.
7 x 9, 352 pp, Quality PB, ISBN 1-58023-174-8 **$19.95**

Shabbat, 2nd Edition: The Family Guide to Preparing for and Celebrating the Sabbath
By Dr. Ron Wolfson 7 x 9, 320 pp, illus., Quality PB, ISBN 1-58023-164-0 **$19.95**

Sharing Blessings: Children's Stories for Exploring the Spirit of the Jewish Holidays
By Rahel Musleah and Michael Klayman
8½ x 11, 64 pp, Full-color illus., Hardcover, ISBN 1-879045-71-0 **$18.95**   *For ages 6 & up*

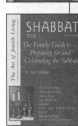

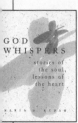

Inspiration

God in All Moments
Mystical & Practical Spiritual Wisdom from Hasidic Masters
Edited and translated by Or N. Rose with Ebn D. Leader
Hasidic teachings on how to be mindful in religious practice and how to cultivate everyday ethical behavior—*hanhagot*. 5½ x 8½, 192 pp, Quality PB, ISBN 1-58023-186-1 **$16.95**

Our Dance with God: Finding Prayer, Perspective and Meaning in the Stories of Our Lives *By Karyn D. Kedar* 6 x 9, 176 pp, Quality PB, ISBN 1-58023-202-7 **$16.99**

Also Available: **The Dance of the Dolphin** (Hardcover edition of *Our Dance with God*)
6 x 9, 176 pp, Hardcover, ISBN 1-58023-154-3 **$19.95**

The Empty Chair: Finding Hope and Joy—Timeless Wisdom from a Hasidic Master, Rebbe Nachman of Breslov *Adapted by Moshe Mykoff and the Breslov Research Institute*
4 x 6, 128 pp, 2-color text, Deluxe PB w/flaps, ISBN 1-879045-67-2 **$9.95**

The Gentle Weapon: Prayers for Everyday and Not-So-Everyday Moments—
Timeless Wisdom from the Teachings of the Hasidic Master, Rebbe Nachman of Breslov *Adapted by Moshe Mykoff and S. C. Mizrahi, together with the Breslov Research Institute*
4 x 6, 144 pp, 2-color text, Deluxe PB w/flaps, ISBN 1-58023-022-9 **$9.95**

God Whispers: Stories of the Soul, Lessons of the Heart *By Karyn D. Kedar*
6 x 9, 176 pp, Quality PB, ISBN 1-58023-088-1 **$15.95**

An Orphan in History: One Man's Triumphant Search for His Jewish Roots
By Paul Cowan. Afterword by Rachel Cowan. 6 x 9, 288 pp, Quality PB, ISBN 1-58023-135-7 **$16.95**

Restful Reflections: Nighttime Inspiration to Calm the Soul, Based on Jewish Wisdom
By Rabbi Kerry M. Olitzky & Rabbi Lori Forman
4½ x 6½, 448 pp, Quality PB, ISBN 1-58023-091-1 **$15.95**

Sacred Intentions: Daily Inspiration to Strengthen the Spirit, Based on Jewish Wisdom
By Rabbi Kerry M. Olitzky and Rabbi Lori Forman
4½ x 6½, 448 pp, Quality PB, ISBN 1-58023-061-X **$15.95**

Kabbalah/Mysticism/Enneagram

Seek My Face: A Jewish Mystical Theology
By Dr. Arthur Green
This classic work of contemporary Jewish theology, revised and updated, is a profound, deeply personal statement of the lasting truths of Jewish mysticism and the basic faith claims of Judaism. A tool for anyone seeking the elusive presence of God in the world. 6 x 9, 304 pp, Quality PB, ISBN 1-58023-130-6 **$19.95**

Zohar: Annotated & Explained
Translation and annotation by Dr. Daniel C. Matt. Foreword by Andrew Harvey, SkyLight Illuminations series editor.
Offers insightful yet unobtrusive commentary to the masterpiece of Jewish mysticism that explains references and mystical symbols, shares wisdom of spiritual masters, and clarifies the *Zohar*'s bold claim: We have always been taught that we need God, but in order to manifest in the world, God needs us.
5½ x 8½, 160 pp, Quality PB, ISBN 1-893361-51-9 **$15.99** *(A SkyLight Paths book)*

Cast in God's Image: Discover Your Personality Type Using the Enneagram and Kabbalah
By Rabbi Howard A. Addison
7 x 9, 176 pp, Quality PB, Layflat binding, 20+ journaling exercises, ISBN 1-58023-124-1 **$16.95**

Ehyeh: A Kabbalah for Tomorrow *By Dr. Arthur Green*
6 x 9, 224 pp, Hardcover, ISBN 1-58023-125-X **$21.99**

The Enneagram and Kabbalah: Reading Your Soul *By Rabbi Howard A. Addison*
6 x 9, 176 pp, Quality PB, ISBN 1-58023-001-6 **$15.95**

Finding Joy: A Practical Spiritual Guide to Happiness *By Dannel I. Schwartz with Mark Hass*
6 x 9, 192 pp, Quality PB, ISBN 1-58023-009-1 **$14.95**; Hardcover, ISBN 1-879045-53-2 **$19.95**

The Gift of Kabbalah: Discovering the Secrets of Heaven, Renewing Your Life on Earth
By Tamar Frankiel, Ph.D.
6 x 9, 256 pp, Quality PB, ISBN 1-58023-141-1 **$16.95**; Hardcover, ISBN 1-58023-108-X **$21.95**

The Way Into Jewish Mystical Tradition *By Lawrence Kushner*
6 x 9, 224 pp, Quality PB, ISBN 1-58023-200-0 **$18.99**; Hardcover, ISBN 1-58023-029-6 **$21.95**

Life Cycle
Parenting

The New Jewish Baby Album: Creating and Celebrating the Beginning of a Spiritual Life—A Jewish Lights Companion
By the Editors at Jewish Lights. Foreword by Anita Diamant. Preface by Sandy Eisenberg Sasso.
A spiritual keepsake that will be treasured for generations. More than just a memory book, *shows you how—and why it's important—*to create a Jewish home and a Jewish life. Includes sections to describe naming ceremony, space to write encouragements, and pages for writing original blessings, prayers, and meaningful quotes throughout.
8 x 10, 64 pp, Deluxe Padded Hardcover, Full-color illus., ISBN 1-58023-138-1 **$19.95**

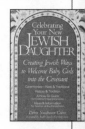

The Jewish Pregnancy Book: A Resource for the Soul, Body & Mind during Pregnancy, Birth & the First Three Months
By Sandy Falk, M.D., and Rabbi Daniel Judson, with Steven A. Rapp
Includes medical information on fetal development, pre-natal testing and more, from a liberal Jewish perspective; prenatal *Aleph-Bet* yoga; and ancient and modern prayers and rituals for each stage of pregnancy.
7 x 10, 208 pp, Quality PB, b/w illus., ISBN 1-58023-178-0 **$16.95**

Celebrating Your New Jewish Daughter: Creating Jewish Ways to Welcome Baby Girls into the Covenant—New and Traditional Ceremonies
By Debra Nussbaum Cohen 6 x 9, 272 pp, Quality PB, ISBN 1-58023-090-3 **$18.95**

The New Jewish Baby Book: Names, Ceremonies & Customs—A Guide for Today's Families *By Anita Diamant* 6 x 9, 336 pp, Quality PB, ISBN 1-879045-28-1 **$18.95**

Parenting As a Spiritual Journey: Deepening Ordinary and Extraordinary Events into Sacred Occasions *By Rabbi Nancy Fuchs-Kreimer*
6 x 9, 224 pp, Quality PB, ISBN 1-58023-016-4 **$16.95**

Embracing the Covenant: Converts to Judaism Talk About Why & How
Edited and with introductions by Rabbi Allan Berkowitz and Patti Moskovitz
6 x 9, 192 pp, Quality PB, ISBN 1-879045-50-8 **$16.95**

The Guide to Jewish Interfaith Family Life: An InterfaithFamily.com Handbook
Edited by Ronnie Friedland and Edmund Case 6 x 9, 384 pp, Quality PB, ISBN 1-58023-153-5 **$18.95**

Making a Successful Jewish Interfaith Marriage: The Jewish Outreach Institute Guide to Opportunities, Challenges and Resources
By Rabbi Kerry Olitzky with Joan Peterson Littman 6 x 9, 176 pp, Quality PB, ISBN 1-58023-170-5 **$16.95**

The Perfect Stranger's Guide to Wedding Ceremonies
A Guide to Etiquette in Other People's Religious Ceremonies *Edited by Stuart M. Matlins*
6 x 9, 208 pp, Quality PB, ISBN 1-893361-19-5 **$16.95** *(A SkyLight Paths book)*

How to Be a Perfect Stranger, 3rd Edition
The Essential Religious Etiquette Handbook
Edited by Stuart M. Matlins and Arthur J. Magida
The indispensable guidebook to help the well-meaning guest when visiting other people's religious ceremonies.

A straightforward guide to the rituals and celebrations of the major religions and denominations in the United States and Canada from the perspective of an interested guest of any other faith, based on information obtained from authorities of each religion. Belongs in every living room, library, and office.
6 x 9, 432 pp, Quality PB, ISBN 1-893361-67-5 **$19.95** *(A SkyLight Paths book)*

Divorce Is a Mitzvah: A Practical Guide to Finding Wholeness and Holiness When Your Marriage Dies *By Rabbi Perry Netter. Afterword by Rabbi Laura Geller.*
6 x 9, 224 pp, Quality PB, ISBN 1-58023-172-1 **$16.95**

A Heart of Wisdom: Making the Jewish Journey from Midlife through the Elder Years
Edited by Susan Berrin. Foreword by Harold Kushner. 6 x 9, 384 pp, Quality PB, ISBN 1-58023-051-2 **$18.95**

So That Your Values Live On: Ethical Wills and How to Prepare Them
Edited by Jack Riemer and Nathaniel Stampfer 6 x 9, 272 pp, Quality PB, ISBN 1-879045-34-6 **$18.95**

Meditation

The Handbook of Jewish Meditation Practices
A Guide for Enriching the Sabbath and Other Days of Your Life
By Rabbi David A. Cooper
Easy-to-learn meditation techniques for use on the Sabbath and every day, to help us return to the roots of traditional Jewish spirituality where Shabbat is a state of mind and soul. 6 x 9, 208 pp, Quality PB, ISBN 1-58023-102-0 **$16.95**

Discovering Jewish Meditation: Instruction & Guidance for Learning an Ancient Spiritual Practice *By Nan Fink Gefen, Ph.D.* 6 x 9, 208 pp, Quality PB, ISBN 1-58023-067-9 **$16.95**

A Heart of Stillness: A Complete Guide to Learning the Art of Meditation
By Rabbi David A. Cooper
5½ x 8½, 272 pp, Quality PB, ISBN 1-893361-03-9 **$16.95** *(A SkyLight Paths book)*

Meditation from the Heart of Judaism: Today's Teachers Share Their Practices, Techniques, and Faith *Edited by Avram Davis*
6 x 9, 256 pp, Quality PB, ISBN 1-58023-049-0 **$16.95**

Silence, Simplicity & Solitude: A Complete Guide to Spiritual Retreat at Home
By Rabbi David A. Cooper
5½ x 8½, 336 pp, Quality PB, ISBN 1-893361-04-7 **$16.95** *(A SkyLight Paths book)*

Three Gates to Meditation Practice: A Personal Journey into Sufism, Buddhism, and Judaism *By Rabbi David A. Cooper*
5½ x 8½, 240 pp, Quality PB, ISBN 1-893361-22-5 **$16.95** *(A SkyLight Paths book)*

The Way of Flame: A Guide to the Forgotten Mystical Tradition of Jewish Meditation
By Avram Davis 4½ x 8, 176 pp, Quality PB, ISBN 1-58023-060-1 **$15.95**

Ritual/Sacred Practice

The Jewish Dream Book
The Key to Opening the Inner Meaning of Your Dreams
By Vanessa L. Ochs with Elizabeth Ochs; Full-color Illus. by Kristina Swarner
Vibrant illustrations, instructions for how modern people can perform ancient Jewish dream practices, and dream interpretations drawn from the Jewish wisdom tradition help make this guide the ideal bedside companion for anyone who wants to further their understanding of their dreams—and themselves.
8 x 8, 120 pp, Full-color illus., Deluxe PB w/flaps, ISBN 1-58023-132-2 **$16.95**

The Rituals & Practices of a Jewish Life: A Handbook for Personal Spiritual Renewal *Edited by Rabbi Kerry M. Olitzky and Rabbi Daniel Judson*
6 x 9, 272 pp, illus., Quality PB, ISBN 1-58023-169-1 **$18.95**

The Book of Jewish Sacred Practices: CLAL's Guide to Everyday & Holiday Rituals & Blessings *Edited by Rabbi Irwin Kula and Vanessa L. Ochs, Ph.D.*
6 x 9, 368 pp, Quality PB, ISBN 1-58023-152-7 **$18.95**

Science Fiction/
Mystery & Detective Fiction

Mystery Midrash: An Anthology of Jewish Mystery & Detective Fiction
Edited by Lawrence W. Raphael. Preface by Joel Siegel.
6 x 9, 304 pp, Quality PB, ISBN 1-58023-055-5 **$16.95**

Criminal Kabbalah: An Intriguing Anthology of Jewish Mystery & Detective Fiction
Edited by Lawrence W. Raphael. Foreword by Laurie R. King.
6 x 9, 256 pp, Quality PB, ISBN 1-58023-109-8 **$16.95**

More Wandering Stars: An Anthology of Outstanding Stories of Jewish Fantasy and Science Fiction *Edited by Jack Dann. Introduction by Isaac Asimov.*
6 x 9, 192 pp, Quality PB, ISBN 1-58023-063-6 **$16.95**

Wandering Stars: An Anthology of Jewish Fantasy & Science Fiction
Edited by Jack Dann. Introduction by Isaac Asimov.
6 x 9, 272 pp, Quality PB, ISBN 1-58023-005-9 **$16.95**

Spirituality

The Alphabet of Paradise: An A–Z of Spirituality for Everyday Life
By Rabbi Howard Cooper
In twenty-six engaging chapters, Cooper spiritually illuminates the subjects of our daily lives—A to Z—examining these sources by using an ancient Jewish mystical method of interpretation that reveals both the literal and more allusive meanings of each. 5 x 7¾, 224 pp, Quality PB, ISBN 1-893361-80-2 **$16.95** *(A SkyLight Paths book)*

Does the Soul Survive?: A Jewish Journey to Belief in Afterlife, Past Lives & Living with Purpose *By Rabbi Elie Kaplan Spitz. Foreword by Brian L. Weiss, M.D.*
Spitz relates his own experiences and those shared with him by people he has worked with as a rabbi, and shows us that belief in afterlife and past lives, so often approached with reluctance, is in fact true to Jewish tradition.
6 x 9, 288 pp, Quality PB, ISBN 1-58023-165-9 **$16.99**; Hardcover, ISBN 1-58023-094-6 **$21.95**

First Steps to a New Jewish Spirit: Reb Zalman's Guide to Recapturing the Intimacy & Ecstasy in Your Relationship with God
By Rabbi Zalman M. Schachter-Shalomi with Donald Gropman
An extraordinary spiritual handbook that restores psychic and physical vigor by introducing us to new models and alternative ways of practicing Judaism. Offers meditation and contemplation exercises for enriching the most important aspects of everyday life. 6 x 9, 144 pp, Quality PB, ISBN 1-58023-182-9 **$16.95**

God in Our Relationships: Spirituality between People from the Teachings of Martin Buber *By Rabbi Dennis S. Ross*
On the eightieth anniversary of Buber's classic work, we can discover new answers to critical issues in our lives. Inspiring examples from Ross's own life—as congregational rabbi, father, hospital chaplain, social worker, and husband—illustrate Buber's difficult-to-understand ideas about how we encounter God and each other. 5⅛ x 8¼, 160 pp, Quality PB, ISBN 1-58023-147-0 **$16.95**

The Jewish Lights Spirituality Handbook: A Guide to Understanding, Exploring & Living a Spiritual Life *Edited by Stuart M. Matlins*
What exactly is "Jewish" about spirituality? How do I make it a part of my life? Fifty of today's foremost spiritual leaders share their ideas and experience with us.
6 x 9, 456 pp, Quality PB, ISBN 1-58023-093-8 **$19.99**; Hardcover, ISBN 1-58023-100-4 **$24.95**

Bringing the Psalms to Life: How to Understand and Use the Book of Psalms
By Dr. Daniel F. Polish
6 x 9, 208 pp, Quality PB, ISBN 1-58023-157-8 **$16.95**; Hardcover, ISBN 1-58023-077-6 **$21.95**

God & the Big Bang: Discovering Harmony between Science & Spirituality
By Dr. Daniel C. Matt 6 x 9, 216 pp, Quality PB, ISBN 1-879045-89-3 **$16.95**

Godwrestling—Round 2: Ancient Wisdom, Future Paths
By Rabbi Arthur Waskow 6 x 9, 352 pp, Quality PB, ISBN 1-879045-72-9 **$18.95**

One God Clapping: The Spiritual Path of a Zen Rabbi *By Rabbi Alan Lew with Sherril Jaffe*
5½ x 8½, 336 pp, Quality PB, ISBN 1-58023-115-2 **$16.95**

The Path of Blessing: Experiencing the Energy and Abundance of the Divine
By Rabbi Marcia Prager 5½ x 8½, 240 pp., Quality PB, ISBN 1-58023-148-9 **$16.95**

Six Jewish Spiritual Paths: A Rationalist Looks at Spirituality *By Rabbi Rifat Sonsino*
6 x 9, 208 pp, Quality PB, ISBN 1-58023-167-5 **$16.95**; Hardcover, ISBN 1-58023-095-4 **$21.95**

Soul Judaism: Dancing with God into a New Era
By Rabbi Wayne Dosick 5½ x 8½, 304 pp, Quality PB, ISBN 1-58023-053-9 **$16.95**

Stepping Stones to Jewish Spiritual Living: Walking the Path Morning, Noon, and Night *By Rabbi James L. Mirel and Karen Bonnell Werth*
6 x 9, 240 pp, Quality PB, ISBN 1-58023-074-1 **$16.95**; Hardcover, ISBN 1-58023-003-2 **$21.95**

There Is No Messiah... and You're It: The Stunning Transformation of Judaism's Most Provocative Idea *By Rabbi Robert N. Levine, D.D.*
6 x 9, 192 pp, Hardcover, ISBN 1-58023-173-X **$21.95**

These Are the Words: A Vocabulary of Jewish Spiritual Life *By Dr. Arthur Green*
6 x 9, 304 pp, Quality PB, ISBN 1-58023-107-1 **$18.95**

Spirituality/Lawrence Kushner

The Book of Letters: A Mystical Hebrew Alphabet
Popular Hardcover Edition, 6 x 9, 80 pp, 2-color text, ISBN 1-879045-00-1 **$24.95**
Deluxe Gift Edition with slipcase, 9 x 12, 80 pp, 4-color text, Hardcover, ISBN 1-879045-01-X **$79.95**
Collector's Limited Edition, 9 x 12, 80 pp, gold foil embossed pages, w/limited edition silkscreened print, ISBN 1-879045-04-4 **$349.00**

The Book of Miracles: A Young Person's Guide to Jewish Spiritual Awareness
All-new illustrations by the author
6 x 9, 96 pp, 2-color illus., Hardcover, ISBN 1-879045-78-8 **$16.95** *For ages 9–13*

The Book of Words: Talking Spiritual Life, Living Spiritual Talk
6 x 9, 160 pp, Quality PB, ISBN 1-58023-020-2 **$16.95**

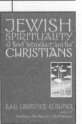

Eyes Remade for Wonder: A Lawrence Kushner Reader
Introduction by Thomas Moore
6 x 9, 240 pp, Quality PB, ISBN 1-58023-042-3 **$18.95**; Hardcover, ISBN 1-58023-014-8 **$23.95**

God Was in This Place & I, i Did Not Know
Finding Self, Spirituality and Ultimate Meaning
6 x 9, 192 pp, Quality PB, ISBN 1-879045-33-8 **$16.95**

Honey from the Rock: An Introduction to Jewish Mysticism
6 x 9, 176 pp, Quality PB, ISBN 1-58023-073-3 **$16.95**

Invisible Lines of Connection: Sacred Stories of the Ordinary
5½ x 8½, 160 pp, Quality PB, ISBN 1-879045-98-2 **$15.95**

Jewish Spirituality—A Brief Introduction for Christians
5½ x 8½, 112 pp, Quality PB Original, ISBN 1-58023-150-0 **$12.95**

The River of Light: Jewish Mystical Awareness
6 x 9, 192 pp, Quality PB, ISBN 1-58023-096-2 **$16.95**

The Way Into Jewish Mystical Tradition
6 x 9, 224 pp, Quality PB, ISBN 1-58023-200-0 **$18.99**; Hardcover, ISBN 1-58023-029-6 **$21.95**

Spirituality/Prayer

Pray Tell: A Hadassah Guide to Jewish Prayer
By Rabbi Jules Harlow, with contributions from Tamara Cohen, Rochelle Furstenberg, Rabbi Daniel Gordis, Leora Tanenbaum, and many others
A guide to traditional Jewish prayer enriched with insight and wisdom from a broad variety of viewpoints—from Orthodox, Conservative, Reform, and Reconstructionist Judaism to New Age and feminist. Offers fresh and modern slants on what it means to pray as a Jew, and how women and men might actually pray. 8½ x 11, 400 pp, Quality PB, ISBN 1-58023-163-2 **$29.95**

My People's Prayer Book Series
Traditional Prayers, Modern Commentaries
Edited by Rabbi Lawrence A. Hoffman
Provides diverse and exciting commentary to the traditional liturgy, helping modern men and women find new wisdom in Jewish prayer, and bring liturgy into their lives.

Each book includes Hebrew text, modern translation, and commentaries from all perspectives of the Jewish world.
Vol. 1—The *Sh'ma* and Its Blessings
7 x 10, 168 pp, Hardcover, ISBN 1-879045-79-6 **$23.95**
Vol. 2—The *Amidah*
7 x 10, 240 pp, Hardcover, ISBN 1-879045-80-X **$24.95**
Vol. 3—*P'sukei D'zimrah* (Morning Psalms)
7 x 10, 240 pp, Hardcover, ISBN 1-879045-81-8 **$24.95**
Vol. 4—*Seder K'riat Hatorah* (The Torah Service)
7 x 10, 264 pp, Hardcover, ISBN 1-879045-82-6 **$23.95**
Vol. 5—*Birkhot Hashachar* (Morning Blessings)
7 x 10, 240 pp, Hardcover, ISBN 1-879045-83-4 **$24.95**
Vol. 6—*Tachanun* and Concluding Prayers
7 x 10, 240 pp, Hardcover, ISBN 1-879045-84-2 **$24.95**
Vol. 7—Shabbat at Home
7 x 10, 240 pp, Hardcover, ISBN 1-879045-85-0 **$24.95**

Spirituality/The Way Into... Series

The Way Into... Series offers an accessible and highly usable "guided tour" of the Jewish faith, people, history and beliefs—in total, an introduction to Judaism that will enable you to understand and interact with the sacred texts of the Jewish tradition. Each volume is written by a leading contemporary scholar and teacher, and explores one key aspect of Judaism. The Way Into... enables all readers to achieve a real sense of Jewish cultural literacy through guided study.

The Way Into Encountering God in Judaism By Neil Gillman
6 x 9, 240 pp, Quality PB, ISBN 1-58023-199-3 **$18.99**; Hardcover, ISBN 1-58023-025-3 **$21.95**
Also Available: **The Jewish Approach to God: A Brief Introduction for Christians**
By Neil Gillman 5½ x 8½, 192 pp, Quality PB, ISBN 1-58023-190-X **$16.95**

The Way Into Jewish Mystical Tradition By Lawrence Kushner
6 x 9, 224 pp, Quality PB, ISBN 1-58023-200-0 **$18.99**; Hardcover, ISBN 1-58023-029-6 **$21.95**
The Way Into Jewish Prayer By Lawrence A. Hoffman
6 x 9, 224 pp, Quality PB, ISBN 1-58023-201-9 **$18.99**; Hardcover, ISBN 1-58023-027-X **$21.95**
The Way Into Torah By Norman J. Cohen
6 x 9, 176 pp, Quality PB, ISBN 1-58023-198-5 **$16.99**; Hardcover, ISBN 1-58023-028-8 **$21.95**

Spirituality in the Workplace

Being God's Partner
How to Find the Hidden Link Between Spirituality and Your Work
By Rabbi Jeffrey K. Salkin. Introduction by Norman Lear.
6 x 9, 192 pp, Quality PB, ISBN 1-879045-65-6 **$17.95**

The Business Bible: 10 New Commandments for Bringing Spirituality & Ethical
Values into the Workplace By Rabbi Wayne Dosick
5½ x 8½, 208 pp, Quality PB, ISBN 1-58023-101-2 **$14.95**

Spirituality and Wellness

Aleph-Bet Yoga
Embodying the Hebrew Letters for Physical and Spiritual Well-Being
By Steven A. Rapp. Foreword by Tamar Frankiel, Ph.D., and Judy Greenfeld. Preface by Hart Lazer
7 x 10, 128 pp, b/w photos, Quality PB, Layflat binding, ISBN 1-58023-162-4 **$16.95**

Entering the Temple of Dreams
Jewish Prayers, Movements, and Meditations for the End of the Day
By Tamar Frankiel, Ph.D., and Judy Greenfeld
7 x 10, 192 pp, illus., Quality PB, ISBN 1-58023-079-2 **$16.95**

Minding the Temple of the Soul
Balancing Body, Mind, and Spirit through Traditional Jewish Prayer, Movement, and
Meditation By Tamar Frankiel, Ph.D., and Judy Greenfeld
7 x 10, 184 pp, illus., Quality PB, ISBN 1-879045-64-8 **$16.95**
Audiotape of the Blessings and Meditations: 60 min. **$9.95**
Videotape of the Movements and Meditations: 46 min. **$20.00**

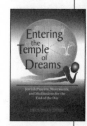

Spirituality/Women's Interest

Lifecycles, Vol. 1: Jewish Women on Life Passages & Personal Milestones
Edited and with introductions by Rabbi Debra Orenstein
6 x 9, 480 pp, Quality PB, ISBN 1-58023-018-0 **$19.95**

Lifecycles, Vol. 2: Jewish Women on Biblical Themes in Contemporary Life
Edited and with introductions by Rabbi Debra Orenstein and Rabbi Jane Rachel Litman
6 x 9, 464 pp, Quality PB, ISBN 1-58023-019-9 **$19.95**

Moonbeams: A Hadassah Rosh Hodesh Guide *Edited by Carol Diament, Ph.D.*
8½ x 11, 240 pp, Quality PB, ISBN 1-58023-099-7 **$20.00**

ReVisions: Seeing Torah through a Feminist Lens *By Rabbi Elyse Goldstein*
5½ x 8½, 224 pp, Quality PB, ISBN 1-58023-117-9 **$16.95**

White Fire: A Portrait of Women Spiritual Leaders in America
By Rabbi Malka Drucker. Photographs by Gay Block.
7 x 10, 320 pp, 30+ b/w photos, Hardcover, ISBN 1-893361-64-0 **$24.95** *(A SkyLight Paths book)*

Women of the Wall: Claiming Sacred Ground at Judaism's Holy Site
Edited by Phyllis Chesler and Rivka Haut
6 x 9, 496 pp, b/w photos, Hardcover, ISBN 1-58023-161-6 **$34.95**

The Women's Haftarah Commentary: New Insights from Women Rabbis on
the 54 Weekly Haftarah Portions, the 5 Megillot & Special Shabbatot
Edited by Rabbi Elyse Goldstein 6 x 9, 560 pp, Hardcover, ISBN 1-58023-133-0 **$39.99**

The Women's Torah Commentary: New Insights from Women Rabbis on the 54
Weekly Torah Portions *Edited by Rabbi Elyse Goldstein*
6 x 9, 496 pp, Hardcover, ISBN 1-58023-076-8 **$34.95**

The Year Mom Got Religion: One Woman's Midlife Journey into Judaism
By Lee Meyerhoff Hendler
6 x 9, 208 pp, Quality PB, ISBN 1-58023-070-9 **$15.95**; Hardcover, ISBN 1-58023-000-8 **$19.95**

See Holidays for *The Women's Passover Companion: Women's Reflections on
the Festival of Freedom* and *The Women's Seder Sourcebook: Rituals &
Readings for Use at the Passover Seder.*

Travel

Israel—A Spiritual Travel Guide: A Companion for the Modern Jewish Pilgrim
By Rabbi Lawrence A. Hoffman 4¾ x 10, 256 pp, Quality PB, illus., ISBN 1-879045-56-7 **$18.95**
Also Available: **The Israel Mission Leader's Guide** ISBN 1-58023-085-7 **$4.95**

12 Steps

100 Blessings Every Day
Daily Twelve Step Recovery Affirmations, Exercises for Personal Growth &
Renewal Reflecting Seasons of the Jewish Year
By Rabbi Kerry M. Olitzky. Foreword by Rabbi Neil Gillman.
Using a one-day-at-a-time monthly format, this guide reflects on the rhythm of
the Jewish calendar to help bring insight to recovery from addictions and com-
pulsive behaviors of all kinds. Its exercises help us move from *thinking* to *doing.*
4½ x 6½, 432 pp, Quality PB, ISBN 1-879045-30-3 **$15.99**

Recovery from Codependence: A Jewish Twelve Steps Guide to Healing Your Soul
By Rabbi Kerry M. Olitzky 6 x 9, 160 pp, Quality PB, ISBN 1-879045-32-X **$13.95**

Renewed Each Day: Daily Twelve Step Recovery Meditations Based on the Bible
By Rabbi Kerry M. Olitzky and Aaron Z.
Vol. 1—Genesis & Exodus:
6 x 9, 224 pp, Quality PB, ISBN 1-879045-12-5 **$14.95**
Vol. 2—Leviticus, Numbers & Deuteronomy:
6 x 9, 280 pp, Quality PB, ISBN 1-879045-13-3 **$14.95**

Twelve Jewish Steps to Recovery
A Personal Guide to Turning from Alcoholism & Other Addictions—Drugs, Food,
Gambling, Sex...
By Rabbi Kerry M. Olitzky and Stuart A. Copans, M.D. Preface by Abraham J. Twerski, M.D.
6 x 9, 144 pp, Quality PB, ISBN 1-879045-09-5 **$14.95**

Theology/Philosophy

Aspects of Rabbinic Theology
By Solomon Schechter. New Introduction by Dr. Neil Gillman.
6 x 9, 448 pp, Quality PB, ISBN 1-879045-24-9 **$19.95**

Broken Tablets: Restoring the Ten Commandments and Ourselves
Edited by Rachel S. Mikva. Introduction by Lawrence Kushner. Afterword by Arnold Jacob Wolf.
6 x 9, 192 pp, Quality PB, ISBN 1-58023-158-6 **$16.95**; Hardcover, ISBN 1-58023-066-0 **$21.95**

Creating an Ethical Jewish Life
A Practical Introduction to Classic Teachings on How to Be a Jew
By Dr. Byron L. Sherwin and Seymour J. Cohen
6 x 9, 336 pp, Quality PB, ISBN 1-58023-114-4 **$19.95**

The Death of Death: Resurrection and Immortality in Jewish Thought
By Dr. Neil Gillman 6 x 9, 336 pp, Quality PB, ISBN 1-58023-081-4 **$18.95**

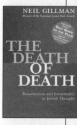

Evolving Halakhah: A Progressive Approach to Traditional Jewish Law
By Rabbi Dr. Moshe Zemer
6 x 9, 480 pp, Quality PB, ISBN 1-58023-127-6 **$29.95**; Hardcover, ISBN 1-58023-002-4 **$40.00**

Hasidic Tales: Annotated & Explained
By Rabbi Rami Shapiro. Foreword by Andrew Harvey, SkyLight Illuminations series editor.
5½ x 8½, 240 pp, Quality PB, ISBN 1-893361-86-1 **$16.95** *(A SkyLight Paths Book)*

A Heart of Many Rooms: Celebrating the Many Voices within Judaism
By Dr. David Hartman
6 x 9, 352 pp, Quality PB, ISBN 1-58023-156-X **$19.95**; Hardcover, ISBN 1-58023-048-2 **$24.95**

Judaism and Modern Man: An Interpretation of Jewish Religion
By Will Herberg. New Introduction by Dr. Neil Gillman.
5½ x 8½, 336 pp, Quality PB, ISBN 1-879045-87-7 **$18.95**

Keeping Faith with the Psalms: Deepen Your Relationship with God Using the
Book of Psalms *By Daniel F. Polish*
6 x 9, 272 pp, Hardcover, ISBN 1-58023-179-9 **$24.95**

The Last Trial
On the Legends and Lore of the Command to Abraham to Offer Isaac as a Sacrifice
By Shalom Spiegel. New Introduction by Judah Goldin.
6 x 9, 208 pp, Quality PB, ISBN 1-879045-29-X **$18.95**

A Living Covenant: The Innovative Spirit in Traditional Judaism
By Dr. David Hartman 6 x 9, 368 pp, Quality PB, ISBN 1-58023-011-3 **$18.95**

Love and Terror in the God Encounter
The Theological Legacy of Rabbi Joseph B. Soloveitchik
By Dr. David Hartman
6 x 9, 240 pp, Quality PB, ISBN 1-58023-176-4 **$19.95**; Hardcover, ISBN 1-58023-112-8 **$25.00**

Seeking the Path to Life
Theological Meditations on God and the Nature of People, Love, Life and Death
By Rabbi Ira F. Stone 6 x 9, 160 pp, Quality PB, ISBN 1-879045-47-8 **$14.95**

The Spirit of Renewal: Finding Faith after the Holocaust
By Rabbi Edward Feld 6 x 9, 224 pp, Quality PB, ISBN 1-879045-40-0 **$16.95**

Tormented Master: The Life and Spiritual Quest of Rabbi Nahman of Bratslav
By Dr. Arthur Green 6 x 9, 416 pp, Quality PB, ISBN 1-879045-11-7 **$19.99**

Your Word Is Fire: The Hasidic Masters on Contemplative Prayer
Edited and translated by Dr. Arthur Green and Barry W. Holtz
6 x 9, 160 pp, Quality PB, ISBN 1-879045-25-7 **$15.95**

I Am Jewish
Personal Reflections Inspired by the Last Words of Daniel Pearl

Almost 150 Jews—both famous and not—from all walks of life, from all around the world, write about Identity, Heritage, Covenant/Chosenness and Faith, Humanity and Ethnicity, and *Tikkun Olam* and Justice.
Edited by Judea and Ruth Pearl
6 x 9, 304 pp, Hardcover, ISBN 1-58023-183-7 **$24.99**

JEWISH LIGHTS BOOKS ARE AVAILABLE FROM BETTER BOOKSTORES. TRY YOUR BOOKSTORE FIRST.

About Jewish Lights

People of all faiths and backgrounds yearn for books that attract, engage, educate, and spiritually inspire.

Our principal goal is to stimulate thought and help all people learn about who the Jewish People are, where they come from, and what the future can be made to hold. While people of our diverse Jewish heritage are the primary audience, our books speak to people in the Christian world as well and will broaden their understanding of Judaism and the roots of their own faith.

We bring to you authors who are at the forefront of spiritual thought and experience. While each has something different to say, they all say it in a voice that you can hear.

Our books are designed to welcome you and then to engage, stimulate, and inspire. We judge our success not only by whether or not our books are beautiful and commercially successful, but by whether or not they make a difference in your life.

For your information and convenience, at the back of this book we have provided a list of other Jewish Lights books you might find interesting and useful. They cover all the categories of your life:

Bar/Bat Mitzvah	Life Cycle
Bible Study / Midrash	Meditation
Children's Books	Parenting
Congregation Resources	Prayer
Current Events / History	Ritual / Sacred Practice
Ecology	Spirituality
Fiction: Mystery, Science Fiction	Theology / Philosophy
Grief / Healing	Travel
Holidays / Holy Days	Twelve Steps
Inspiration	Women's Interest
Kabbalah / Mysticism / Enneagram	

Stuart M. Matlins

Stuart M. Matlins, Publisher

Or phone, fax, mail or e-mail to: **JEWISH LIGHTS Publishing**
Sunset Farm Offices, Route 4 • P.O. Box 237 • Woodstock, Vermont 05091
Tel: (802) 457-4000 • Fax: (802) 457-4004 • www.jewishlights.com
Credit card orders: **(800) 962-4544** (8:30AM–5:30PM ET Monday–Friday)
Generous discounts on quantity orders. SATISFACTION GUARANTEED. Prices subject to change.

For more information about each book, visit our website at www.jewishlights.com